Enterprise Information Systems

Rainer Weber
Technische Hochschule Nürnberg Georg Simon Ohm
Nürnberg, Germany

ISBN 978-3-662-71717-2   ISBN 978-3-662-71718-9   (eBook)
https://doi.org/10.1007/978-3-662-71718-9

Translation from the German language edition: "Betriebliche Anwendungssysteme" by Rainer Weber,
© Der/die Herausgeber bzw. der/die Autor(en), exklusiv lizenziert an Springer-Verlag GmbH, DE, ein
Teil von Springer Nature 2025. Published by Springer Berlin Heidelberg. All Rights Reserved.

Preface

Topic

This book is about enterprise information systems, both transactional and analytical, their integration in a system landscape, and their operation. A particular concern is to establish a closer connection with computer science topics than is usual in many textbooks on information systems. Thus, computer science methods are used, for example, for the modeling of business objects and business data or for the integration of enterprise information systems. The book gives an overview of the functionality of enterprise information systems and deepens that in examples. However, it does not extensively list the functions of the various types of enterprise information systems. The interested reader will find references in the corresponding chapters.

The book is based on Weber (2025), which is in German. So mainly it is a translation but adapted for the international readership. This applies in particular to the references to further reading, with which readers can delve deeper into individual topics if they wish.

To illustrate concepts, realizations in selected enterprise information systems are described. A certain balance was sought: commercial and open-source software, software for small, medium-sized, and large companies. Also, the availability of literature for further reading played a role in the selection. In the book, in addition to examples of software from the market leader SAP, there are also some on the ERP system Microsoft Dynamics 365 Business Central, the system Vtiger CRM, the business intelligence system Pentaho, and the Big Data software Hadoop and Spark.

Contents

Abbreviations

ABAP	Advanced Business Application Programming
ACID	Atomicity, Consistency, Isolation, Durability
ANSI	American National Standards Institute
API	Application Programming Interface
ASP	Application Service Providing
BI	Business Intelligence
BPEL	Business Process Execution Language
BPM	Business Process Management
BPMN	Business Process Model and Notation (formerly Business Process Modelling Notation)
BW	Business Warehouse
CAD	Computer Aided Design
CDR	Common Data Representation
CICS	Customer Information Control System
CO	Controlling
CORBA	Common Object Request Broker Architecture
CPU	Central Processing Unit
CRM	Customer Relationship Management
CRUD	Create, read, update, delete
CSV	Comma (or Character) separated Value
DB	Database
DCE	Distributed Computing Environment
DLL	Dynamic Link Library
DSS	Decision Support System
DWHS	Data Warehouse System
EAI	Enterprise Application Integration
EDI	Electronic Data Interchange
EDIFACT	Electronic Data Interchange for Administration, Commerce and Transport
EIS	Executive Information System
EJB	Enterprise Java Bean
EPC	Event-driven Process Chain
ERP	Enterprise Resource Planning
ETL	Extraction, Transformation, Loading

FI	Financials
GB	Gigabyte (2^{30} Byte)
GUI	Graphical User Interface
HR	Human Resources (Personnel)
HTML	Hypertext Markup Language
HTTP	Hypertext Transfer Protocol
ID	Identification, Identifier
IDL	Interface Definition Language
IEEE	Institute of Electrical and Electronics Engineers
IOT	Internet of Things
ISO	International Organization for Standardization
IT	Information Technology
JAAS	Java Authentication and Authorization Services
Java EE	Java Enterprise Edition
JAXP	Java API for XML Processing
JCA	Java Connector Architecture
JDBC	Java Database Connectivity
JEE	Java Enterprise Edition
JMS	Java Messaging Service
JNDI	Java Naming and Directory Interface
JSON	JavaScript Object Notation
JSP	Java Server Page
JTA	Java Transaction API
KB	Kilobyte
MB	Megabyte (2^{20} Byte)
MIS	Management Information System
MM	Materials Management
MOLAP	Multidimensional OLAP
MOM	Message-oriented Middleware
MTE	Monitoring Tree Element
OASIS	Organization for the Advancement of Structured Information Standards
ODS	Operational Data Store
OLAP	Online Analytical Processing
OLTP	Online Transaction Processing
OMG	Object Management Group
OSI	Open Systems Interconnection
PB	Petabyte (2^{50} Byte)
PC	Personal Computer
PDF	Portable Document Format
PLM	Product Lifecycle Management
POP3	Post Office Protocol 3
PP	Production Planning
R/2	Real-time System Version 2 (actually not an abbreviation)
R/3	Real-time System Version 3 (actually not an abbreviation)

RAM	Random Access Memory
REST	Representational State Transfer
RFID	Radio-frequency Identification
RMI	Remote Method Invocation
ROLAP	Relational OLAP
RPC	Remote Procedure Call
RTF	Rich Text Format
SaaS	Software as a Service
SAX	Simple API for XML
SCM	Supply Chain Management
SD	Sales and Distribution
SMTP	Simple Mail Transfer Protocol
SOA	Service-oriented Architecture
SOAP	Formerly an abbreviation for "Simple Object Access **Protocol**"
SPOF	Single Point of Failure
SQL	Structured Query Language
SSD	Solid-state Drive
SSO	Single Sign-on
TB	Terabyte (2^{40} Byte)
TCO	Total Cost of Ownership
TCP/IP	Transmission Control Protocol and Internet Protocol
TP-Monitor	Transaction Processing Monitor
UDDI	Universal Description, Discovery and Integration
UML	Unified Modeling Language
URI	Universal Resource Identifier
URL	Universal Resource Locator
W3C	World Wide Web Consortium
WORM	Write Once, Read Multiple
WS	Web service
WSDL	Web Service Description Language
WS-I	Web Service Interoperability Organization
XDR	eXternal Data Representation
XML	eXtended Markup Language
XSL	Extensible Stylesheet Language
XSLT	XSL Transformations

Introduction

1

"Exactly right," said the hedgehog, jumped onto the tree and flew away.
(The original source is unknown to me.)

Summary
This chapter provides an overview of the book and introduces its three parts on System Models, Integration, and Operation.

Learning Objective

• Overview!

Many people will associate the term *Enterprise information system* with an *ERP system*. An ERP system implements the standard processes of companies: purchasing, inventory management, sales, accounting, and often also human resources and production. "Standard" is used here in the sense of "usual" or "best practices." So, the "standard" is not defined by a standardization organization like ISO or ANSI. Accordingly, most companies, from large ones to small ones, will use a standard software for the standard processes, not custom software. Only micro-enterprises like craftsmen, lawyers, or doctors – thus numerically even the majority of all companies – often let service providers such as tax consultants handle the legally necessary standard processes (accounting, annual financial statements and tax return, payroll accounting, which is only a part of what an ERP system offers).

For many companies, especially smaller and medium-sized ones, an ERP system is already sufficient. They do not need an additional enterprise information system. However, the situation is different for large companies. They often have requirements that go beyond the functionality of ERP systems offered on the market: customer relationship management systems with specialized functions for marketing, sales, and service, supply chain management systems for planning the supply chain, or data warehouse systems for advanced data analysis. They may even have several systems of the same type, e.g., ERP systems, for example, in different parts of the group. The number can amount to hundreds of larger and smaller systems and beyond. We use the term *system landscape* for this set of interconnected systems. The systems do not work separately from each other but exchange data with each other, or one system calls a function of another one. More generally speaking, various techniques are used to integrate the systems.

An enterprise system can either be installed in the company ("on-premises") or it can be operated by another organization, often the vendor of the standard software. So the company just rents the software ("cloud"). Access to cloud software is web-based. A mix of on-premises and cloud systems is possible.

We can distinguish systems, as done above, based on their purpose or application content, for example, an ERP system or an SCM system. Another way to classify systems—and this is what we will use in this book—is according to the way data is processed: The functionality may be *transactional* or *analytical*. In transactional functionality, a single data record is processed, which is usual in day-to-day business. For example, a clerk creates an invoice or updates a supplier master record. In analytical functionality, a large number of data records are processed (usually the records are just read) at the same time. Examples are:

- A monthly sales analysis.
- The calculation of the optimal production plan for a period using linear optimization.
- The suggestion of maintenance work on a machine, determined using machine learning methods, based on data provided via the Internet of Things.

We see that there is a wide spectrum of analytical functionality. In fact, in today's typical enterprise information systems, both forms of functionality—transactional and analytical—are usually found in different proportions. Thus, an ERP system is primarily intended for day-to-day business, but it usually also contains standard analysis ("reports").

Standard software must be adapted to the needs of the company. This adaption can range from configuration (e.g., customizing settings) to programming (e.g., enterprise-specific extensions). And finally, when using the systems, care must be taken, among other things, to ensure that employees have just the necessary permissions to perform their tasks and that the software is efficient and runs as error-free as possible.

This outlines the content of the book: Analytical and transactional systems are connected, adapted, and operated in a system landscape using various integration techniques. The details are presented in three parts (see Fig. 1.1).

Part I: System Models

Part I deals with the two types of enterprise information systems, transactional and analytical systems.

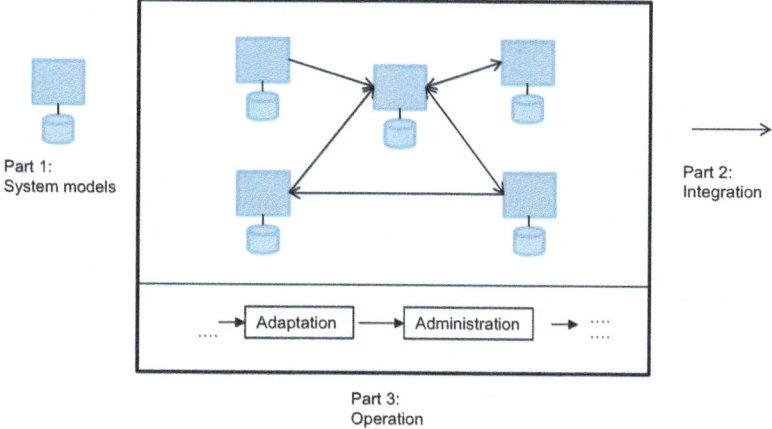

Fig. 1.1 Overview

Chapter 2 provides an overview of Part I and introduces a layer model to describe systems: business data, business objects, business processes, and business interfaces. Chapter 3 applies the model to transactional systems. Chapter 4 deals with analytical systems. It introduces various forms of analytics: from the "classic" data warehouse system to machine learning and Big Data techniques.

The following two chapters are orthogonal to the previous ones. Chapter 5 deals with the platform on which an enterprise system runs: Both the "classic" three-tier client-server architecture is addressed, as well as the newer aspect of in-memory computing with its implications for application design. Chapter 6 discusses deployment options for business application software: It is divided into the pairs on-premises and cloud on the one hand and monolithic systems and microservices on the other hand.

Part II: Integration
The topic of Part II is integration, i.e., the connection of enterprise information systems into a system landscape. We get to know various techniques that are used in system landscapes, often in combination with each other. Although configuration also plays a role in integration techniques, software development is often required. Thus, the topics in this part are more technical, closer to computer science.

Chapter 7 provides an overview of Part II. Chapter 8 introduces the concept of the system landscape, the combination of several enterprise information systems. Chapter 9 presents the first integration technique: the integration via the user interface, illustrated with portal systems. Chapter 10 deals with integration through data exchange. XML is chosen as a representative of techniques for exchanging structured business data. In addition, JSON is briefly discussed. Furthermore, the role of message brokers is highlighted, along with associated methods such as publish and subscribe. Chapter 11 deals with integration via function call, illustrated by Web services. In Chap. 12, the integration via process management systems is explained, including cross-system business processes.

Part III: Operation
Part III is not about system structures but about methods used in the implementation and operation of enterprise information systems in a company.

Chapter 13 provides an overview of the part and shows a phase model for the life cycle of an enterprise information system. In the following chapters, four aspects are deepened: Chap. 14 deals with the selection and implementation of business standard software in a company. The topic of Chap. 15 is the adaptation and extension of standard software with different means: configuration and programming. Chapter 16 presents the organizational issue of access control in enterprise information systems. Chapter 17 mentions some tasks of system administration.

Chapter 18 provides a summary and provokes thinking about how enterprise information systems are today and how we wish they should be. Moreover, the chapter includes an overview of abstract concepts that were addressed in the various chapters using examples. It tries to make the "thinking in structures" explicit, a frequently mentioned benefit of abstract sciences like computer science and mathematics.

The book contains exercises and suggested solutions. Many tasks are conceptual in nature and can be tackled with "paper and pencil." But it is often more helpful to use word processing and graphics programs, especially when modeling business processes, business objects, and business data. A few tasks require access to an ERP system. We chose the prevalent system SAP S/4HANA.

In addition, questions in the manner of (Kemper and Eickler 2015) are inserted throughout the text, intended to stimulate reflection on what has just been read. At the end of the chapters, there are also questions for self-assessment of learning objectives.

1.1   Self-Assessment

1. What does "standard" mean in the term "standard software"? And why is such a standard possible in Enterprise Information Systems?
2. What is the difference between operational and analytical functionality, both from a functional and technical perspective?
3. What role does analytical functionality play in an ERP system?

Reference

Kemper, A., Eickler, A.: Datenbanksysteme, 10th edn. De Gruyter Oldenbourg, Berlin (2015)

Part I
System Models

Overview of Part I

2

Any particular sections you fancy? Or merely the whole thing?
Samuel Beckett (Endspiel Fin de partie Endgame,
Suhrkamp Paperback 171, first edition,
Frankfurt a. M., 1974, p. 102)

Summary
This chapter serves as a framework for the following chapters, which all deal with the different types of enterprise information systems, the underlying platforms, and deployment forms. A layer model for enterprise information systems is introduced for classification.

Learning Objective

- Get to know a layer model for enterprise information systems as a framework for the following chapters.

Simply put, an enterprise system is a software system that contains business application programs and has its own data storage in the form of a database. We will refine this in the course of the book.

We use the following layer model to describe enterprise information systems (Fig. 2.1). Layer models of this kind are often found in slightly different forms in the literature (see Lankhorst et al. 2017, p. 260). The lowest layer of our model is the *hardware platform*, i.e., computers including all peripheral devices and communication networks that connect the computers. A layer above is the *system software platform*. It includes the operating system, the communication software (usually TCP/IP-based) for using computer networks, and the database system, which is almost always used in an enterprise information system.

© The Author(s), under exclusive license to Springer-Verlag GmbH, DE, part of Springer Nature 2025
R. Weber, *Enterprise Information Systems*,
https://doi.org/10.1007/978-3-662-71718-9_2

Fig. 2.1 Layer model of
enterprise systems

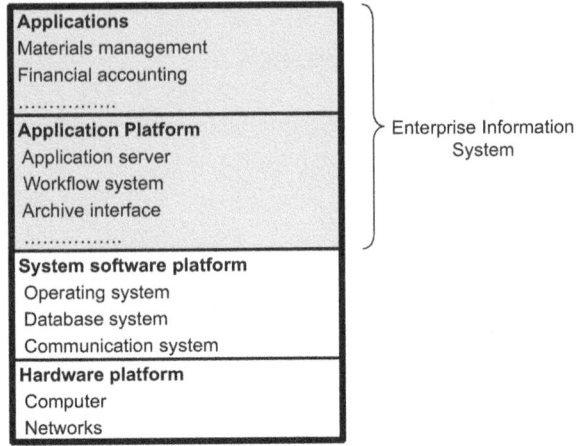

In principle, it would be possible to develop an enterprise information system based on the system software platform. However, it turns out that typical basic functionality for enterprise information systems can be identified, which can be used by any business application. Providing this in a layer simplifies application development considerably. This is why there is a software acting as a bridge between applications and the system software platform, which we call *application platform* or, briefly, *platform* in this book. It can include a variety of application-independent functions, such as a runtime system, programming interfaces for transaction management, for communication via HTTP or for archiving old data, and a workflow system for controlling business processes. (The terminology may be a little bit inconsistent here: The hardware and system software platform *contain* what the name stands for, whereas the application platform denotes *what* it offers.)

If you add the "business content" to the application platform, i.e., the *applications*, you get an *enterprise information system*. However, the enterprise information system cannot be used immediately after installation. The company-specific settings must be configured beforehand (customizing).

The term "applications" may seem a bit vague here. As a first approximation, one could see them as the application programs and everything related to them, such as database tables. We will define it more precisely below (keywords—business processes, objects, and data).

In this book, we hardly deal with those layers that are already extensively covered in computer science (hardware, system software). Instead, we focus more on the applications, and we will also delve into the application platform in one chapter.

In currently available enterprise information systems, there are often M:N usage relationships between different implementations of the lower layers. This is called *platform independence*: (Why is the name not quite accurate?)

- A system software platform can run on different hardware platforms, e.g., the Linux operating system runs on different computers. Conversely, different system software platforms can be used for a hardware platform.

- The same applies to the relationship between the application platform and the system software platform.

Only the application platform and the enterprise information system are not always decoupled in this way. The standard Java Enterprise Edition achieves this at least for Java application programs (see Chap. 5). However, proprietary, non-standardized application platforms are also in use, even widely.

A layer can internally consist of several similarly structured components but appear largely homogeneous to the higher-level layer.

- Thus, the application platform can contain multiple identically structured application servers. From a functional perspective, it doesn't matter to the applications whether there is one or more application servers. (What other reasons could there be for multiple application servers?)
- In the system software platform, a database system can be designed as a multi-processor system for performance enhancement and fail safety, with mirrored hard drives; for the application platform, however, it is only *one* database.
- In the hardware platform, computers with multiple cores are used, primarily for performance enhancement.

In this respect, we are dealing with *distributed systems* (Tanenbaum and van Steen 2014). As is known with distributed systems, however, there are situations where it becomes apparent that multiple components are in use, such as in certain error cases.

Only on the application layer is the structure of multiple identical components transparent to the user, difficult, and not widespread. The idea would be to make a system landscape appear like a large enterprise information system. The layer then internally regulates how data and functionality are distributed. One approach in this direction is microservices (see Chap. 6).

In our model, the application layer is further subdivided into the (sub-)layers (Fig. 2.2):

- *Business data*: They are stored persistently, i.e., permanently, in the database system.
- *Business objects*: In the sense of object-oriented modeling, they include business functions in addition to the business data.
- *Business processes*: This is where the chaining of business functions takes place.

  In addition, there are *business interfaces*, which are possible on all sub-layers. These terms are discussed in detail in Chap. 3.

Fig. 2.2 Layers of applications

	P – Business processes
I – Business interfaces	O – Business objects
	D – Business data

Fig. 2.3 Integration of
two systems

Many companies not only use one enterprise system but several, which work together and are functionally specialized: In addition to transactional systems for daily business, there are analytical systems, among others for data analysis, discussed in Chap. 4. They are integrated into a *system landscape* (Fig. 2.3). For simplicity, only two systems are shown, only the "applications" layer because it is primarily important for this consideration. Each enterprise information system has its own business data, business objects, and business processes.

In addition, there are cross-system business processes, whose steps use functionality from different systems. There might be a central cross-system business process control. This can be realized by a superordinate system, which is responsible for controlling the subsystems. A cross-system business process can also arise, at least virtually, by internal business processes of systems 1 and 2 communicating with each other, usually through message exchange. Both, cross-system business process control and message exchange, are forms of integration technology that connects systems via their business interfaces. Overall, the entirety of the business processes results in a *process landscape*, complementing the system landscape.

Often, there are not only integration relationships between systems of a system landscape on the layer of business processes but also on the layers of business objects and business data. Thus, business data can be sent from one system to another, or business objects of one system can call methods of a business object of another system. Of course, such interactions can also be seen as part of a cross-system business process.

Integration technology is the topic of the second part of the book.

In the first part of the book, we look at the two basic types of enterprise information systems, transactional and analytical systems. Separately from that, we will discuss the application platform, particularly the client/server architecture, which underlies all system types. And we will look at how systems can be deployed. This concerns the location and organization of operation: purchasing software licenses (alternatively, using open-source software) and installation at the company ("on-premises") or as rental software, operated by another organization and accessed via a Web browser (cloud computing). It also concerns the structure of the application software: a monolithic system or a loosely coupled set of microservices.

2.1   Self-Assessment

1. On which layers in Fig. 2.1 would you locate the following things: Web browser, supplier master record, document scanner, document management system, customer interaction center?

2. Why is the version change easier for system software than for standard business software?
3. What layers does our model for application functionality consist of?
4. Name several use cases where business data is sent to another system!
5. Can you imagine an example where you notice that an enterprise information system is a distributed system?

References

Lankhorst, M., et al.: Enterprise Architecture at Work, 4th edn. Springer, Berlin (2017)
Tanenbaum, A., van Steen, M.: Distributed Systems, 2nd edn. Pearson new international edition. Pearson, Harlow (2014)

Transactional Systems

3

HAMM *gloomingly:* Then it is a day like any other day.
CLOV As long as it lasts. *Pause.* All life long the same inantities.
Samuel Beckett (Endspiel Fin de partie Endgame,
Suhrkamp Paperback 171, first edition,
Frankfurt a. M., 1974, p. 64)

Summary
Transactional systems are described according to the three-layer model of the previous chapter, consisting of business data, business object, and business process. Business interfaces serve to integrate systems.

Learning Objectives

- Learn to understand transactional systems by means of a model.
- Be able to model business object classes in UML.
- Be able to model a business process in BPMN according to the three-layer model of the chapter.

3.1   ERP Systems

(a) **Concept**

As the first type of system, we look at *transactional systems*. Economically, we can see a "transaction" as a business transaction. Usually, it is also technically represented as a "transaction" or, to be more precise, a database transaction.

© The Author(s), under exclusive license to Springer-Verlag GmbH, DE,
part of Springer Nature 2025
R. Weber, *Enterprise Information Systems*,
https://doi.org/10.1007/978-3-662-71718-9_3

The best-known transactional systems are *Enterprise Resource Planning Systems* (*ERP Systems*), and we will use these in the following for explanation. The term "Enterprise Resource Planning" might be a little bit misleading, as the word *planning* is not primarily used in the sense of planning systems (see Sect. 4.5). The functions of ERP systems are today very similar and largely standardized, in particular in software for small and medium-sized enterprises. The standardization concerns of course only the content of the functions, not the terminology or even the user interfaces or data structures of the systems. The standardization results from many regulations (accounting, labor law) and the fact that the basic business processes in companies are very similar, resulting in "best practices" processes (see also (Bradford 2015, p. 98)).

(b) **Functional Areas at a Glance**

We use the following terms: The *functionality* of a system is the set of all its *functions*. The functions can be divided into *functional areas*, which can be hierarchically organized. For example, the functional area "accounting" will contain the (sub-)functional areas "financial accounting" and "cost accounting." An example of how the ERP functionality for an industrial company can be structured is shown in Fig. 3.1.

In each functional area, the functions process and store certain data, e.g., in the functional area "purchasing" among others the data "supplier" and "purchase order." The functions include at least create, modify, display, and often also delete. (Delete is a critical function. In which cases is it easily possible, in which not? Why are data sometimes only "logically deleted," i.e., only removed from the database and archived?) Later, we will deepen both data and functions. In particular, we will discuss what the term "API" in Fig. 3.1 means.

At the overview level, you can't see the individual functions yet. For this, we need to take a deeper look into the functionality. We do this exemplarily for the area "purchasing," which we use throughout the book in examples.

(c) **One Area in Detail: Purchasing**

It contains the functions of purchasing, structured according to which data is processed (see Fig. 3.1). On the one hand, there are master data (more on this term and transaction data a little later): supplier, material, and the relation

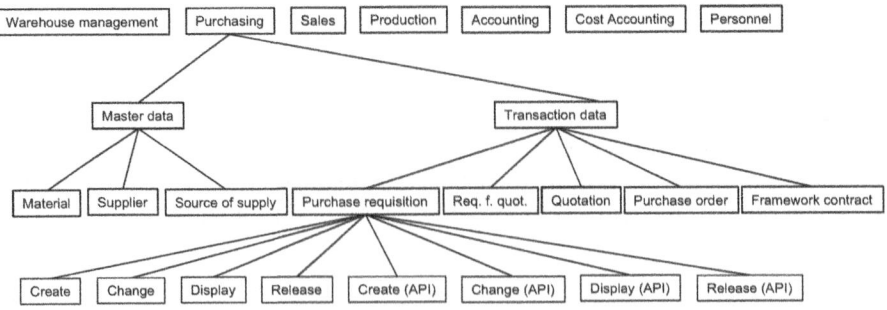

Fig. 3.1 ERP: functional areas and functions

between the two, the sources of supply. A source of supply contains the information which material can be procured from which supplier at which conditions. We introduce the material master here; but since it is also important for other functional areas, it is often located at a central point, e.g., in menus. On the other hand, there are transaction data: purchase requisition (a need is determined, either in the context of the material requirements planning or directly created by a user), request for quotation (to the supplier), quotation (from the supplier), and purchase order (to the supplier). Orders can also be organized according to outline agreements, another business data, if such were negotiated to obtain advantageous conditions with a certain commitment.

At first glance, an ERP system contains "everything a company needs." We will see in Chap. 4 why there may be additional systems.

(d) **Characteristics of ERP Systems**

Let's now move away from the functionality and take a look at the essential characteristics of ERP systems (see Fig. 3.2, where only some of the functional areas are shown):

- Above all, coverage of *internal business data* processing. "Internal," i.e., interaction with business partners (customer, supplier), is not particularly intensively supported. "Business data," i.e., functions not directly related with business data, e.g., CAD software or office software, are usually only linked via interfaces (see Sect. 3.6).
- Focus on *transactional* functions, i.e., day-to-day business. Analyses and planning are indeed present, but not as pronounced as in more specialized systems (see Chap. 4).
- *Dialog and background functions*: Clerks work with dialog programs, with screen masks serving as a graphical user interface, e.g., when placing an order. A background function, on the other hand, does not require human intervention; an example is payroll accounting.

Fig. 3.2 An ERP system

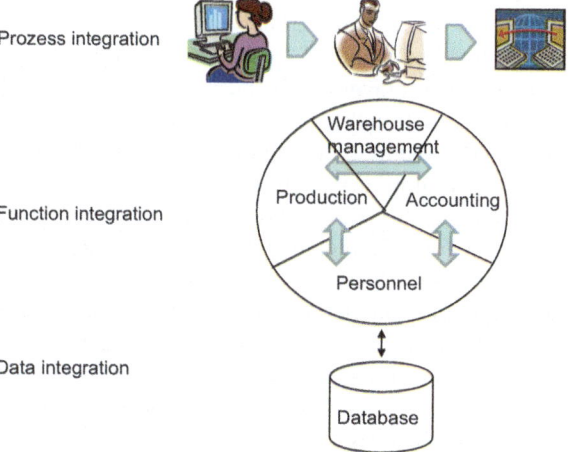

Prozess integration

Function integration

Data integration

- *Data integration*: All applications access a common database. For example, both purchasing and production planning use different parts of the material master data.
- *Function integration*: The functions are coordinated with each other so that the result of one function can be used by a subsequent function. From my point of view, the linkage between functions is also important: one function may automatically trigger a subsequent one. Some might already consider this a form of process integration—the separation is not easy in my opinion. For example, when goods are received (function of warehouse management), an accounting entry (function of financial accounting) is automatically created at the same time.
- *Process integration*: The functions are put in a particular order, resulting in a (business) process. For example, in the purchasing process, it will be specified that a purchase request is subject to a one- or multi-level approval before it can be converted into an order.
- *Standard software*: Today, standard software is generally used for transactional systems, especially ERP systems, as opposed to custom software. There are open-source ERP systems, but currently, their distribution is not high (Gronau 2021, p. 26); see also Sect. 6.4. This may be particularly due to the fact that the license costs only make up a small part of the total cost of software use (see Chap. 14).

3.2   The Three-Layer Model for Transactional Functionality

We use the model introduced in Chap. 2 to describe the functionality of transactional systems. According to system theory—we use the term "theory" here in a relaxed way—an "artificial" model represents a "real" system. An example for illustration from another area: A small airplane model can test the aerodynamic properties of a projected airplane. Different models are used for different purposes. Our purpose: We want to understand the functionality of transactional systems. (What is in our case the "system?" The source code of the enterprise information system? Or is this already a "model?" And what about the stored data?)

In the lowest layer are the business data. As already mentioned in the functionality, the transactional functions are usually grouped according to the business data. This hand-in-hand treatment of data and functions is common in computer science, today most familiar in object-oriented programming: classes with attributes (data) and methods (functions). We adopt this principle in our model. Data can then be described, for example, in UML class diagrams through the attributes of classes and the associations between the classes. The transition to objects simply consists in supplementing the methods—an object model is built on the (semantic) data model. Similarly, we could use a data modeling approach, the entity-relationship model. But why switch the modeling language without further use? If we want it to be more concrete, we can view the database tables as a logical data model. We will delve deeper into business data in Sect. 3.3.

In the middle layer, methods and events are added to the data (attributes). All three components are used in the highest layer, in business processes. It should be emphasized again: This is a model of application functionality, not object-oriented classes in a specific programming language. Even though our model is object oriented, a function in the system does not necessarily have to be implemented by a method in the system (!) but could, for example, be provided as a Web application. Or the system uses classes but at a different level of granularity. Thus, we mainly use the object-oriented view to summarize data and functions and to express relationships to other business objects via associations or attributes. An object-oriented implementation is not excluded, but not mandatory from our model perspective. We will make little use of other object-oriented concepts. For example, we do not address inheritance. We will delve deeper into business objects in Sect. 3.4.

We describe business processes using the language BPMN, linking them to business objects. We will delve deeper into business processes in Sect. 3.5.

Now let us look at a small example (see Fig. 3.3) in order to illustrate the previous rather abstract thoughts more concretely. The functions are grouped as methods in the classes "order" and "goods receipt." The methods of the classes process business data (attributes), which are persistently, i.e., permanently, stored in database tables. For simplicity, only one database table is shown in the figure for the business data, and the database tables of the line-items are omitted. The methods of the business objects are called in a logical order, which corresponds to the business process. In Fig. 3.3, the first activity uses the method `order.create`. For easier mapping, the activity was named accordingly. The same applies to the second activity.

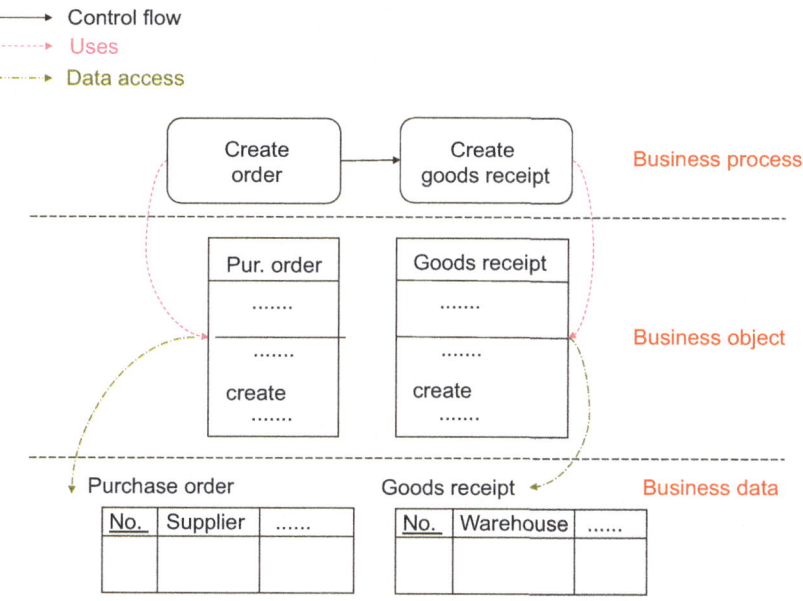

Fig. 3.3 Modeling view

Because the terms "business data," "business objects," and "business processes" are somewhat long and unwieldy, we often simply speak of data, objects, and processes when "business" is clear from the context.

We will now delve deeper into all of this by reflecting about data, objects, and processes and their interrelationships. We will also look at business interfaces, which are necessary for the integration of systems into their environment—people, other systems, and "things."

3.3   Business Data

Business data or *data* are digital representations or records of business transactions (this leads to the concept of transaction data) and the involved persons and things (this leads to the concept of master data). Some of the things are more concrete, others are artifacts (e.g., a bill of materials). (What is the system, what is the model in this context?)

Technically, business data are complex data structures that are persistently stored in a database. For storage, business data is usually broken down into parts that are stored in separate, related tables. (Why is one table not enough? Example?) An example is the business data material. It has attributes such as a unique identification (identifier), the basic unit of measure, the order unit of measure, the valuation price, and many more. In our model, we do not consider, for example, the identifier and the basic unit of measure as separate business data but merely attributes of the business data material. An attribute can be simple; elementary, e.g., the basic unit of measure; or composite, e.g., an address.

In data modeling, it is determined which data should be business data in a system and how they are mapped to tables of a database system. Data can therefore be represented at a more abstract level by entity-relationship diagrams or similar modeling techniques, at a more concrete level by database tables. We will get to know further representations in Chap. 10: the formats XML and JSON.

With transactional systems, we will often focus on the next higher level, the business objects, especially for describing functionality and for use in business processes, although of course business data also play a role. Analytical systems, on the other hand, focus on business data.

3.3.1   Manifestations

To better understand business data, we look at various classification options, often dichotomies (divisions into two areas), each focusing on one aspect of business data: first, some about the attributes of business data and then some about complete business data. In this way, we learn about the various manifestations of business data.

A. **Classifications of Attributes**

We want to start with a classification according to the data type, still largely independent of how the attribute is used in business data or a database table (see Table 3.1).

Table 3.1 Attributes: classification options

(a) Simple	ID	(b) ID/value	ID		Value	
		(c) Key	Key field		Non-key field	
		(d) Key type	Primary key		Foreign key	
		(e) Reference	Reference to business data		Fixed	
		(f) Assignment	Internal		External	
		(g) Name	ID		Description	
	(h) Storage		Stored		Calculated	
(a) Composite	(i) Width/depth		Columns		Rows	
	Reference	(j) Dimensions	Number		Unit	
		(k) Texts	Without language ID	With original language ID	With original language ID and language-ID	

(a) **Simple and Composite Attributes**

An attribute can be "simple," i.e., it does not consist of several parts, e.g., a material number. Composite (structured, "complex") attributes, on the other hand, consist of several parts, e.g., an address, consisting of zip code, city, street, and house number. First we will look at the simple attributes and then at the composite ones (see i).

(b) **Identifier or Value**

We can classify the simple attributes according to whether they are an *identifier* (identification) or represent a value. The word "identifier" is often abbreviated to *ID* and often also referred to as *number* or *code*. The identifier is often numeric, but alphanumeric IDs are also common. Usually, no distinction is made between upper- and lowercase letters for practical reasons; they are not case sensitive. (Why?) Identifiers are linked with other data, e.g., the identifier material number with dependent attributes such as the type of the material or a status identifier (status "1") with a text ("approved"; see g). The values, on the other hand, largely stand for themselves (see however j). Examples of values are the last name and date of birth of a person or the weight and a price of a material, both without quantity or currency unit. (Which category would these be?)

We will look at identifiers quite extensively (d–g), and for values we will look at texts (g, k), numbers (j) and calculated values (h). But first, there's a distinction that arises with database tables.

(c) **Key Attribute and Non-key Attribute**

Business data is identified by one or more key attributes taken together (in the latter case, it is a composite key; cf. database tables: primary key). Identifiers are used for key attributes.

(d) **Identifier: Primary or Foreign Key (Reference)**

An identifier can be used as a primary key and thus identify the data itself. Or it can refer to other data (foreign key attribute). For example, an order has a reference to a supplier. This results in relationships between the business data. We will look at this in the following.

(e) **Identifier: Reference to Business Data, Fixed or Customizing Data**

Not only business data can be referenced. Think, e.g., of a status identifier. For example, a purchase requisition may contain an attribute "state." Among others, the values 1 (for "new") and 2 (for "released") could be states. (By the way, what kind are "new" and "released?"). The values 1 and 2 can be "hard coded"—that is what is meant by "fixed" in the headline. Or they can be set in a customizing.

(f) **Identifier: Internal or External Number Assignment**

Whenever we need a new value for an identifier, it can be generated in two ways:

- *Internal number assignment*: The number (viz., the identifier, the ID) is automatically assigned by the system. Usually, the system simply increments the last assigned number.
- *External number assignment*: The user assigns an ID. Of course, the system checks whether the proposed ID is still free. A number assignment may be customizable, specifying, e.g., the number range or the structure of the numbers.

(g) **Identifier or Designation**

Users will at most remember those identifiers they frequently use. Other than that, they will prefer designations (descriptions, names), i.e., texts. So usually both are available for each attribute: the identifier for the system and the text for the user.

Sometimes, even several designations are available for an attribute, varying in length. Designations are language specific. They could be translated, which is important in multinational companies. The user will see the designation in his login language.

(h) **Stored and Calculated Attributes**

In addition to values that are entered by users in input fields of screen masks and that are subsequently stored in database tables, some attributes might be virtual, i.e., calculated from other attributes when the user displays some business data. For example, an amount could be shown in the corporate currency, even though it is only stored in the currency of a business transaction. A currency conversion occurs "on the fly," i.e., the attribute's value is calculated.

Now let's return to our classification by data types. We did not yet look at composite data types. In short, it can go in breadth or in depth—or in both directions:

(i) **Structured Attributes: Multiple Columns or Rows**

An attribute can have multiple columns. An example: An address within business data (columns town, zip code, etc.). But it can also have multiple rows. For example, a supplier could have multiple bank details. We see that we can also combine the two types.

In relational database tables, both cases are excluded for a single table field. With business data, our modeling is more flexible in the first place. But we must take provisions when we map such business data to database tables later on.

Common multi-line data in programming languages are lists and arrays. The selector is a number (first line, second line, etc.). In business data, however, more complex selectors can also occur. A typical example is organization-dependent data. For example, a material could have different accounting valuation prices in different organizations. The selector would then be the organization: For every organization we could have one value.

Another frequent case is historized data: There may be multiple rows that are valid for different periods of time. Of course, this is also possible for the business data itself, not just for an attribute. In this case not only the current value is stored but the value valid for a specified period in time (*historization*). In database tables, the key of business data is then supplemented by a validity period: The values of the dependent attributes of the business data then only apply in this validity period. (Analogously, one can deal with historized attributes.) If the data is to apply until further notice, an unrealistic largest date (12/31/9999) can be used, for example, which simplifies database selection. If the value changes at a later date, the "until" value of the previous interval is changed, and another interval with the new data value is added. In fact, there are also more difficult forms of historization, which we will not go into here.

In the following, we will look at another aspect in structured attributes, namely, when two attributes have a close relationship to each other (j and k).

(j) **Numbers and Units**

If a value is a number, it is often an amount of money or a quantity. Such numbers are not understandable on their own; they need a currency or quantity unit alongside. Therefore, in these cases, there will always be a relationship of the number to another attribute.

(k) **Texts and Languages**

A text is a string that contains words of a natural language. (Are there also borderline cases? What about a last name, for example, Winterbottom? Or external numbers in item f?) In the simplest case, a text is stored in only one language, and the language ID is not stored. This could occur in a system that is used in only one country, so the language will be clear in that context. The next stage is to still store only one text in one language, but the language ID is stored too. For example, the language ID attribute is set to EN, i.e., the text is written in English. Finally—the greatest comfort—the text can be available in many languages. It may have been created in one language, the "original language," and then translated into one or more other languages. Multi-language support and translation may be a requirement in international companies.

Texts have various uses, mainly designation or informative text, as in a comment.

B. Classifications of Complete Business Data

Let's now turn to the classifications of business data as a whole. Most of the classifications can be found, for example, in Heilig et al. (2006, p. 23). The most important distinction is between master and transactional data (Table 3.2).

(a) Master and Transactional Data

Master data represent people, organizations, and "things" of different kinds. Many of them participate repeatedly in business transactions. There are concrete and artificial things, for example, on the one hand, a material and, on the other, a bill of materials. Technically, master data are those with a long-term relevance, which are repeatedly referenced in transactional data.

An example is the material: Material 1400, for example, can be requested and ordered over many years. The material number (ID) 1400 remains, and some attributes of master data, however, may change more or less frequently. For example, the valuation price will change frequently, if it is a moving average price. A rare change might occur with the order quantity unit, when, from a certain point in time, not boxes but pallets are ordered. Even the designation (as opposed to the material number) can change. You might sometimes read "master data are data that rarely change," and I think this is a bit misleading. Other master data are:

- Customer
- Supplier
- Bill of materials
- Routing
- Personnel (master record of an employee)
- Cost center

Common and synonymous are the words "material master data," "material master," and "material master record."

Transactional data reflect the everyday business transactions. An example is the purchase requisition. An employee needs 10 pieces of material 1400 for production. So, he creates a purchase requisition. The purchase

Table 3.2 Data types: classification options

(a) Duration	Master data	Transaction data
(b) Numbers	Stock data	Flow data
(c) State transitions	State data	Event data
(d) Purpose	Business data	Change data
(e) Temporal relevance	Active data	Passive data
(f) Structure	Structured data	Unstructured data
(g) Repeat structure	Header data	Line-item data

requisition includes attributes such as the creator and the creation date. Other transactional data are:

- Order
- Invoice
- Material document
- Accounting document

Transactional data are only relevant for a limited period of time:[1] For a purchase requisition, this will be until the requested material arrives. After that, the transactional data may still be kept in the system for traceability and analysis. In fact, business data usually remain "forever," but certainly at some point, they will be archived to cheaper storage (cf. Sect. 17.4).

At a closer look, not every business transaction is represented by its own transactional data, but transactional data can sometimes bundle several closely related business transactions. For example, when a purchase requisition is changed, this could be seen as another business transaction after its creation. Nevertheless, from a pragmatic point of view, it is sensible to simply set an attribute "last change on" of the purchase requisition.

(b) **Stock and Flow Data**

Both stock and flow data relate to numbers. *Flow data* are transactional data that reflect inflows or outflows, e.g., material movements. *Stock data* accumulate such flow data. An example is the material stock. It may be looked up by displaying the material master data. These types of data will be central in Chap. 4. (Are there other transactional data than flow data?)

In the narrower sense, flow or stock data are just numbers and thus attributes of business data, not independent business data. In a broader sense, however, the entire business data that contains the number is considered a flow or stock data, e.g., the complete material movement, which includes further attributes such as storage location or time. The same applies to the following classification into state and event data.

(c) **State and Event Data**

State and event data are based on the model of state transition systems, also known as "automata" in computer science. *State data* in the narrower sense represent a state of master or transaction data. So they are actually not complete business data but only an attribute of it. For example, a purchase requisition could be in the "released" state, a material in the "blocked for orders" state. The state is then an attribute of that data. *Event data* represent state changes, e.g., "order has been changed". We will discuss events further below in Sect. 3.5. They are also related to the change data that follows.

---

[1] According to Plattner and Zeier (2011, p. 92), companies typically store data for 10 years, but only use 20% of it, namely that of the last 2 years. Thus, less than 1% of orders are modified in the year after they are generated (Plattner and Zeier 2011, p. 97).

(d) **Change Data**

Change data log changes to business data. In the simplest case, they only record that a change took place and when, which may be sufficient for unstructured data (see below). For structured data, however, the specific change can be recorded. For example, the old and the new value can be logged when updating the data record. Change data can be written for both master and transaction data. In many countries, it is legally required for financial applications to store the change history of data records (Plattner and Zeier 2011, p. 109).

(e) **Active and Passive Data**

Active data are used in ongoing business processes, *passive* data are not—they are only kept for analytical, statistical purposes (Plattner and Zeier 2011, p. 93).

(f) **Structured and Unstructured Data**

So far, we have only looked at *structured* data, i.e., those that exist as a data structure and that usually are stored in a relational database. In addition, there are *unstructured* data, mainly various types of documents such as:

- Scanned invoices
- PDF document templates for simplified data entry
- Word processing files, e.g., for documentation

Some of them are memory intensive, e.g., think of images or even videos. Because they only have a few, mostly technical attributes, they are usually not stored in databases but in *document management systems* and similar systems (content management systems, archive systems). Judging from their content, they are mostly transaction data, but some belong to master data, e.g., the picture of an employee or of a material used in a product catalog.

In the case of scanned documents, corresponding structured data is usually stored for this unstructured data, often "typewritten," so that the data is also available in a processable form. For example, an incoming invoice (letter) is scanned to make it easily available to the clerks in the company. A link exists from the structured data, so the original document can be displayed whenever needed. (Are such data independent business data or merely attributes of other business data?)

In fact, the boundary between structured and unstructured data is not sharp. For example, entries from forms of a known, fixed structure, e.g., evaluation forms, can be read by optical character recognition (OCR). Or a full-text search is possible in word processing, although the selection is more difficult than with database tables. Most difficult is text recognition in scanned handwritten documents. On the other hand, XML documents are easier to handle (see Chap. 10).

(g) **Header and Line-Item Data**

Many business data, especially transaction data, share the "header and line-item data" structure (Fig. 3.4). (Do you have an example of line-items for master data?)

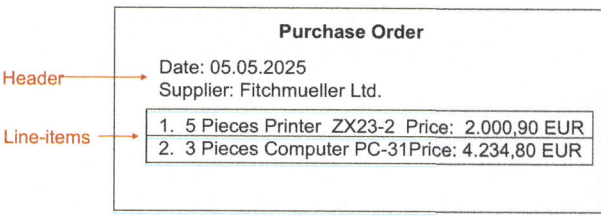

Fig. 3.4 Header and line-item data

The header contains the data that applies to all line-items. The following data are almost always present in the header:

- Creator (user)
- Creation date
- Status

The line-item data, on the other hand, vary greatly. (Do you consider line-item data independent business data or part of the (header) business data?)

3.3.2   Relationships Between Business Data

There are relationships between individual business data (hence the term "Entity Relationship Model"). In UML class diagrams, which we can also use for business data modeling, they are represented by associations. The associations are supplemented by multiplicities (see Fig. 3.5). Later, when we move from business data to business objects, which we want to implement in an object-oriented language, we have to think about how to implement these relationships. After all, object-oriented languages only use attributes and methods, no associations. (What possibilities of implementation come to mind? Could you combine them? Why?) When we map the business data to database tables, the relationships are implemented by primary keys, foreign keys, and mapping tables. At the modeling level, we leave it at the associations.

Usually, it is quite obvious if a relationship between two business data exists. What is more tricky are the multiplicities, especially the lower limits. In an M-to-N relationship (in UML, we would rather write "*" instead of "M" and "N"), for M, the values 0 or 1 are most common. Which one to choose in a specific case requires careful thought. It is important to emphasize that these limits must apply to the business data at all times. Just thinking of usual situations might result in picking the wrong value. An example (Fig. 3.5): A supplier will probably receive request for quotation at some point. But initially, when creating a new supplier, there is no order yet. And finally, you do not know if this will ever happen.

The limits actually set conditions (consistency conditions, also called integrity conditions in database systems). A database system switches from one consistent state to another consistent state. You can imagine it like a lily pond, with a frog

Fig. 3.5 Association

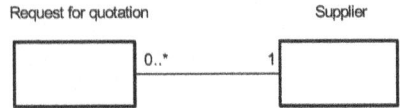

jumping back and forth between the lilies. (Here, the analogy limps a little: Compared to a database system, a lily pond has few states or lilies. How many states are there in a database system?) In between is water: no consistent state! So, when we set multiplicities, we restrict the behavior of the application software, and we do ("hard-code") this at the program level, not at the configuration level (customizing). (We could also send a request for a material to several suppliers. Why is the multiplicity at the supplier then not "1..*"?)

If we have two associations between the same business data, we should label them with a role name. With a single association, the role is usually clear from the context. With two, however, the question arises: Which is which?

So far, we have always talked about business data at the type level. At the instance level, for example, there can be materials 1400 (short for "the material with the ID or number 1400") and 1401, with different attribute values.

3.3.3 Multi-Tenancy

The previous considerations were oriented toward the content of the business data. Multi-tenancy is an orthogonal concept to this: A multi-tenant system has several data areas (*tenants*), which can be used by different enterprises or organizations. Each data area contains master, transaction, and customizing data. Users log in to a tenant, and they see and edit only the data of that tenant (data isolation). A use case of tenants is one tenant for each subsidiary in a corporation. Another use case is tenants for testing and training.

Depending on the system architecture, the same database tables or different database tables can be used for the different tenants. In the case of the same database tables, the tenant is a primary key field in all master, transaction, and customizing database tables. With different database tables, the tenant identification can appear in the identifiers of the database tables (such as "Customer_M1" or "Customer_M2").

3.4   Business Objects

We use our object-oriented modeling view to group the transactional functions as methods in classes of business objects. Let's look at an example (Fig. 3.6).

It depicts a class for an order in the notation of a UML class diagram. It shows which attributes (ID, creator, creation date) an order has and which methods (in other words, functions, operations, services) it offers. In addition, events are listed in the section below the methods; we will soon discuss them.

Fig. 3.6 Business objects

purchase order
ID creator creation date …
create change display release create_API change_API …
created changed …

At the instance level, an *object reference* points to an *object* (in other words, an *object instance*) of a class. Often, the term "business object" is also used for the type, i.e., the class (the "business object order"). From the context, however, it is usually clear what is meant.

Objects and classes with methods and attributes are familiar from object-oriented programming. However, three special features should be mentioned:

- (Reminder:) They are objects of the *modeling view*, not necessarily in terms of software implementation.
- They are *persistent* objects.
- The objects can have *events* in addition to methods and attributes.

In the following sections, we will discuss these differences.

Business objects represent business data, i.e., suppliers, orders, and invoices (see Sect. 3.3; the granularity is the same), with functions (methods) being added. Simply put, a method belongs to a specific class if it mainly changes or reads its objects, i.e., the underlying business data. In Exercise 3.3, we will practically deal with the modeling of business objects. Whereas business objects usually have coarse-grained methods, object-oriented programming development often involves classes of much finer granularity.

3.4.1 Attributes

We can keep the discussion of the attributes short, because what we said about business data applies here equally. Nevertheless, there are a few special features to point out.

Unlike the "usual," *transient* objects in object-oriented languages like C++ or Java, a persistent object does not only live during the runtime of the program that calls its methods. It lives constantly in the database (usually it sleeps), even when it is currently not used in any program. When a program terminates or even the system is shut down, the business objects remain and are still available after system restart.

A persistent object is identified by an *object reference*, which in the simplest case consists of the class name and the (persistent) ID of the object. This suffices to identify an object within a system. If you want to identify objects across systems, you can achieve this, for example, by adding the identification of the system. We assume that each class of business objects contains an ID attribute, which can be used to build the object reference. If you know the object reference, you can load the object from the database and view it, for example, with the display method in a screen mask.

We looked at data storage in database tables in Sect. 3.3. In the simplest case, this might be just one table per class, as suggested in Fig. 3.3. However, in most cases, it will be several tables. This is particularly due to normal form theory of relational databases, where, e.g., a multi-row attribute is stored in a separate database table. A tree structure is a more natural model of business data (see Chap. 10). The programming technique *object-relational mapping* bridges this structural difference between trees/objects and database tables. An example is Hibernate (2020).

When a persistent object needs to be processed, a *runtime object* (*transient object*) is created as a proxy (see Fig. 3.7). We remind ourselves again that the terms are also meaningful at the modeling level, even if the implementation is not in an object-oriented programming language. The runtime object is essentially a copy of the persistent object that can be processed at runtime. The values of the attributes are copied from the database at the time of object instantiation. During processing, the runtime object will temporarily deviate from the persistent object when data in the runtime object are changed but not yet written back to the database. In Fig. 3.7 for ease of explanation, it is assumed that the data of the object is only located in a single database table (blue line). One table row (or parts of it relevant for processing) is copied into the main memory (RAM) and processed there. Finally, it is updated in the database. When a runtime object is built in order to update the business object, a lock is set. Therefore, at any time, there will be at most one such runtime object for modification operations. Strictly speaking, this interplay between persistent and transient object only applies to magnetic disk or SSD-based databases, which are still most common in enterprise information systems. In in-memory systems, it is different (see Sect. 5.1.3.2), but here too, precautions for transaction consistency are necessary.

So far, our somewhat simplified view was: Business object = business data + methods. But should all business data attributes really be also attributes of the business object? The answer could be yes and no, in a way. Because of course all

Fig. 3.7 Persistent and transient object

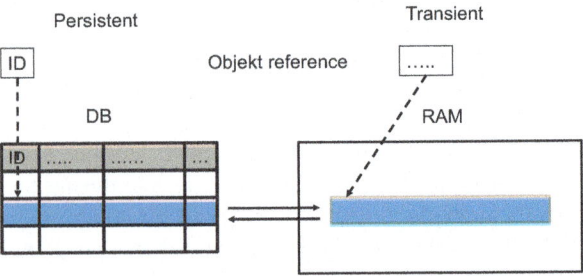

business data attributes must be loaded when they are processed in a method. But we know from object-oriented programming that differences in the visibility can be made ("public," "private," "protected"). Our purpose for business objects is their use in business processes, the top level of our model. Therefore, we will usually not make all business data attributes "public." When processing a persistent object in a program, just its ID attribute suffices to load all data that need to be processed from the corresponding database tables into memory (cf. "get methods"). Apart from the ID attribute, the other attributes that we need for our three-layer model are those referenced in business processes in conditions. For example, if a business process has a branch depending on the status of a purchase requisition, "state" should be an attribute of the purchase requisition. (When defining the business objects, you might not yet have a complete picture of all business processes available in the system. How would you then proceed with the attribute definition?) This is also useful for performance reasons, as the business data are often located in several tables. So, loading only those data "on demand" from those tables that are needed in a particular situation saves performances.

A related question is creating a copy of the business object's data, which can be transferred to another system.[2] We will cover this in detail in Chap. 10. The question here is how we deal with attributes referencing other business objects. Including a copy of the referenced object is not a viable choice. In particular, the referenced object will usually reference yet other objects. In practical cases, e.g., when an order is sent as an EDI message, a pragmatic solution will be chosen: including just those referenced data that make the transferred data meaningful.

Example: With an order, of course, the order line-items are included. In the order line-items, one would include the material number as it is known to the recipient of the EDI message (this might be different from the material number in the sender's ERP system).

Theoretically, it was also possible to include all references in the copy and only evaluate them on demand. This is called *lazy loading*; the opposite, reading the entire object network, is *eager loading* (Bauer and Gregory 2016, Chap. 12).

3.4.2 Methods

Again, we use classifications to better understand methods. From object-orientation, we already know a first one: static and non-static (instance-specific) methods.

A second distinction is between constructors, destructors, and other methods. With persistent data, the situation is a bit more nuanced: There are constructors (and destructors), but these only concern runtime objects, as in object-oriented programming. Creating a new persistent object can be better imagined as a static method that

---

[2] This task initially appears less challenging than loading objects along with classes in Java (Coulouris et al. 2005, p. 210); in the latter case, the program code can also be loaded, so that transferred methods can also be executed on the target computer.

stores new business data in the database. The destruction then corresponds to the deletion or archiving of the business data.

Another obvious classification is into reading and writing methods, with deletion being considered a writing method.

See Table 3.3 for the following classifications.

(a) **Dialog and Background Methods**

Clerks perform functions in user dialog, i.e., the methods use screen masks. In addition, there are functions that are executed in the background, i.e., without direct user interaction. Examples include:

- Printing payroll statements at the end of the month
- Automatically sending an order via Electronic Data Interchange
- The call of the function "create purchase requisition" by a remote call from another system, e.g., a Web-based procurement system (see Chap. 11)

Background functions are often scheduled for automatic execution at certain times, e.g., daily at 9:00 p.m. (batch jobs).

The dialog methods correspond to the functions that users find in their transactional system's menu. A user may see some of the background methods when scheduling them in batch jobs. Other background methods are part of the programming interface (Application Programming Interface (API)) (see Sect. 3.7, marked with "API" in Fig. 3.6).

It seems obvious to build the dialog method on the API method. This avoids duplication of program code. The dialog method would then pass the data entered in the dialog fields to the API method when the "save" button is pressed, call this method, and visualize potentially returned error messages. A drawback of that approach is that data is not checked before hitting the "save" button. Another reason why the API method differs from the corresponding dialog method is that the API method could have been implemented much later than the dialog method and a refactoring of the dialog method was waived for short-term economic considerations.

(b) **Methods with and Without Parameters**

In the last example, we see that some methods can only be called sensibly with parameters, as this is the only way to pass data. With a dialog method, we must distinguish the input parameters from the input fields of the screen mask of the

Table 3.3 Methods: classification options

(a) Processing	Dialog	Background
(b) Parameter	With	Without
(c) Scope of use	Intern	Extern
(d) Content	Standardized	Class-specific
(e) Generality	General	Specific
(f) Degree of automation	Manual ↔	Fully automated
(g) Number of data	One record	Many records

user interface. The input parameters are filled by the calling program, i.e., before the method is executed. The input fields on the other side are entered by the user during method execution. A value of an input parameter could be entered as a default value, which the user may override. If no input parameter is present or none is passed, all inputs must be made by the user. So, with a dialog method, the input will mostly be made by the user. (Do all background methods need parameters?)

(c) **Internal and External Methods**

Depending on the context, different things can be meant by this (with some overlapping): on the one hand, whether it is a published interface (API; external) or an internal function that should preferably not be used for such a purpose for stability reasons. On the other hand, whether a method can only be called internally in the company or also from outside, i.e., by business partners (in which case it should also be a published interface) (Example?).

(d) **Standard Methods and Class-Specific Methods**

For each business data, whether master or transaction data, there will be the "classic" functions (methods): create, display, modify, and possibly delete (also called CRUD functions after the corresponding database operations "create, read, update, delete"). Deleting is a delicate operation. Because master data could already have been used in transaction data, e.g., an order to a supplier, if the supplier were deleted afterward, the reference to the supplier in the order would fail. In this case, deletion is not possible, i.e., it is (hopefully) prohibited by the system. In addition to these functions, often there are class-specific methods, e.g., release an order: it just modifies the status attribute. There are also selection functions, which provide lists of business data according to selection criteria, but this already falls into the realm of analytical systems.

(e) **General and Special Methods**

In some systems, in addition to methods that process the entire business data (general methods, "Swiss Army knives"), there are also those that only allow a partial view, i.e., special methods. "Why such methods" one might ask. After all, the general ones can do everything that the special ones can do and more. The reason may be that you do not want to provide some users with the general method. Technically this could also be solved with permissions (see Chap. 16). But it is often considered safer to not assign a method to a user rather than to restrict its use. In addition to the permission aspect, ergonomics may also play a role: General methods may appear overloaded, as they are intended for a different user group.

(e) **Degree of Automation: From Manual to Fully Automated**

Here the question arises: How do the user and the system share the work that needs to be done to accomplish a task? What part does the user take on, and what part of the system? The following list shows the spectrum:

- Data entry by the user (entering data and texts, making yes/no decisions). The system's share is then just an appropriate user interface, e.g., easy-to-use screen masks, according to the habit of the user (e.g., designed according to the "look and feel" of "smartphones"), or voice input.

- Entry of data which come from other media. The approach is to provide a smart integration. This could be electronic data transmission, so that manual data entry is completely eliminated or only has to be dealt with in case of errors or OCR technology.
- Creation of business data from other business data, e.g., turn a request for quotation into a quotation or create an invoice for an order. This implies that the system copies data as far as possible.
- Methods based on explicit business rules. Business rules could be set, e.g., when customizing a system, they are thus decoupled from the application logic.
- Methods based on implicit business rules. This includes artificial intelligence techniques or more precisely machine learning (see Sect. 4.3). Although no explicit rules are set, implicit rules can be deduced from the training data (past data). Especially when applying implicit rules, it will make sense that the method results are considered suggestions that the user may override. An example is the classification of service requests: Based on the text of the request, it is classified and, based on the classification, directed to the responsible employee for processing (Seubert 2022, p. 313).
- In some cases, fully automated processing by background methods (without parameters) is possible (cf. Sect. 3.1, payroll run). Only error cases or cases recognized as critical or unsolvable are passed on to humans.

We will return to machine learning in Sect. 4.3, because it actually involves analytical functionality.

(g) **Process Single Business Data or Many**

In transactional systems, a function usually processes single business data, one at a time, e.g., update a supplier master record, create an order, or release a purchase requisition. But we have already seen an example where a large amount of business data is processed: a payroll run for all employees of a company. The same function is applied for each employee. Different from this is a calculation where dependencies exist between the processed data. We will look at these cases in Chap. 4.

3.4.3 Events

In addition to attributes and methods, *events* play a role in business processes. They represent state changes of business objects. We write events in a class diagram in a third compartment below the methods.

Examples:

- Purchase requisition created (even the creation of a new business object is considered a state change)
- Goods arrived
- Safety stock of a material exceeded

Events can be used in business processes (see Sect. 3.5) to

- Start business processes. For example, the event "purchase requisition created" could start a release process, "safety stock of material exceeded" a procurement process.
- Synchronize business processes during their run. For example, "goods arrived" can resume the purchasing process, which is waiting after the order has been placed.

Instead of automatically handling events, a critical event is often only recorded in a log so that a monitor can manually react to it (alert management).

Events in business processes are known from the notation of the Event-Driven Process Chain (EPC) (Scheer et al. 2005). There they alternate with functions. In fact, not all EPC events would be modelled as business object events: A decision would be made as to which events are intended for starting or synchronizing business processes and which only signify "function executed."

As before, we also want to look at classifications for events:

(a) **Object, Time, and Condition Events**
   In a time event, unlike the previously mentioned object events, no business object is directly involved. Examples are "every evening at 9:00 PM" or "one day later."

   Condition events cannot be tied to a single business object but to the state of the system, which is determined by all business objects together. Thus, several business objects can play a role in such an event. An example would be "when the effort in a period is significantly higher than the return," where the "significantly" would still need to be specified.

(b) **Events With or Without Parameters**
   The case is similar to the corresponding one with methods. Events can bring additional information in parameters, for example, about a state change. (Example?)

3.5   Business Processes

Whereas in the early days of enterprise information systems data was the pivot point (enterprise data model), today, processes have taken over this role. You will already have a basic understanding of business processes from other lectures. Let's briefly repeat the essential concepts, focusing on modeling: A *business process* (hereinafter simply *process*) consists of *activities*, which are linked together (*control flow*). An activity is either performed by human *agents* (employees, users), usually using transactional systems, or it is executed automatically, without human interaction, by the system—here we see again our classification into dialogue and background processing or manual and automated processing. The program executed in an activity is called the *activity implementation*. A process definition thus includes:

- Control flow
- Data flow
- Agent assignment

In the literature, definitions of the term "business process" often include phrases like "… that provides a benefit for an internal or external customer …." The goal is of course correct. But should this be part of the definition from a technical point of view? It's like adding to the definition of a car, "… that brings joy while driving …"—is it not a car if the driver does not feel joy? Furthermore, it is often indicated that a business process has an input and an output. It should be noted that inputs and outputs do not only occur at the beginning and end of the process. Inputs occur in many dialog activities during the process flow. Similarly, the outputs often result step by step, through calculations (writing to the database) or sending messages in the individual activities.

3.5.1 Control Flow

In the previous sections, we used UML class diagrams to model business data and business objects. Similarly, we need a notation for business processes, and we choose *Business Process Model and Notation (BPMN)* (Freund and Rücker 2019) for the representation of our example process (see Fig. 3.8) and in the exercises. BPMN is a graph-based language and extensive in terms of defining the control flow: There are over 50 symbols for it. We will look at the most important language constructs needed for our purposes. If you are already familiar with BPMN, it may serve as a short review and for BPMN newcomers as a quick start.

BPMN 2.0 is also suitable for executable process definitions. Since some modeling aspects are solved product specifically, e.g., execution attributes, process definitions between different process management systems (see Chap. 12) are only partially interchangeable (Freund and Rücker 2019, p. 183).

In addition to standardization, the following advantages of BPMN over other process notations are mentioned in (Freund and Rücker 2019, p. 89):

- Collaborative processes: Inter-company processes can be formulated with the language construct message flow between processes. In addition, BPMN 2.0 has *choreography diagrams* and *conversation diagrams* (as manifestations of collaboration diagrams) (Freund and Rücker 2019, p. 94 ff.). We will come back to this in Chap. 12.
- Rich event modeling, which we have already partially seen above. Events are also used for error and escalation handling.

From my point of view, BPMN can model processes more precisely than, for example, EPC or UML. But the effort to learn the notation is higher. As far as only the modeling at the business level is concerned, the notation will probably not be used in its full extent in practice, but one will limit oneself to a few important symbols (Silver 2017, p. V)—similar to what can be observed with UML in practice.

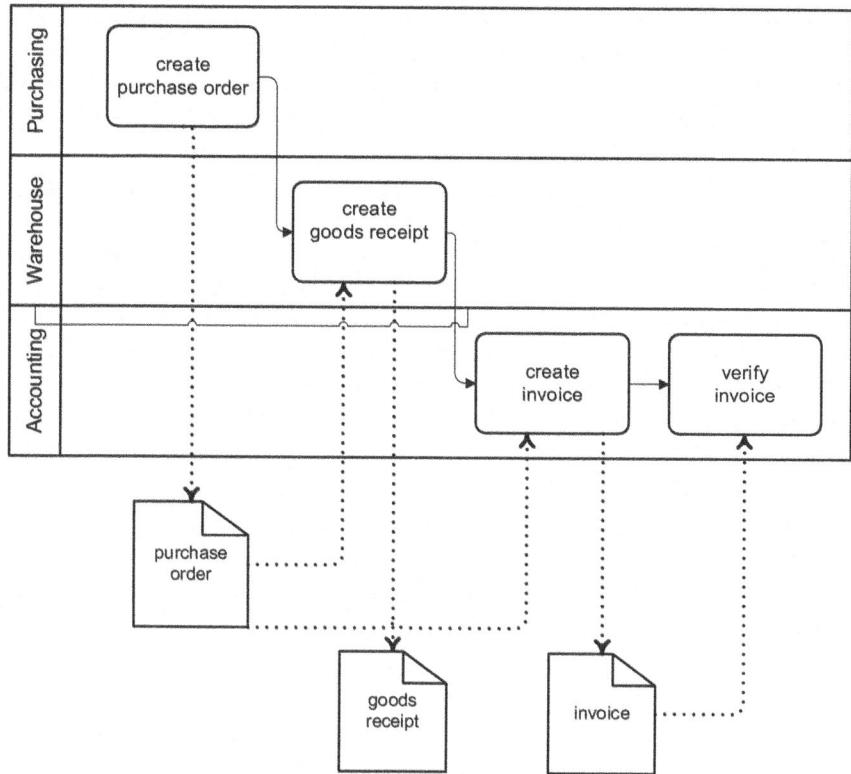

Fig. 3.8 Business process "purchasing"

In Fig. 3.8, we see the purchasing process in a simplified form in a BPMN diagram. More precisely, we see a *process definition* (type level), also called *process model*. A *process instance* (instance level) would be a concrete execution of the process definition at a certain time, e.g., the one that starts on 04/08/2025 at 10:42:33 AM with the order of five printers and three PCs. From the context, it is usually clear whether "process" refers to the process definition or instance.

The naming of the activities, such as "create order," suggests the activity implementation: the create method of the order class (see Sect. 3.4). This shows the connection between business process and business object: The activity implementation is a method of a business object. Naming activities according to this convention is not a must, but it facilitates better understanding.

We are looking at processes with the highest level of detail. In a coarser representation, an activity could stand for a (sub-)process.

Each activity mainly deals with exactly one business object, which is created (e.g., activity create order) or edited (e.g., check invoice). In addition, to the business object, sometimes, parameters are used, such as additional business objects, and elementary data like a release code in an activity "release order" or a return code. In the second activity, "create goods receipt," in addition to the main object "goods receipt," which is created, the secondary object "order" plays a role, as the goods receipt is booked with reference to the order.

In the example process, the control flow is just a sequence of activities. BPMN offers language constructs for more complex control flows and more precise specifications:

- Activity: It can be more precisely determined whether it is processed in dialog, as a background step or "manually," i.e., without IT support.
- Connectors: These represent different types of branching. Important connectors are the "exclusive or" (alternative), the "logical and" (parallel section), and an event-based control, where the branch with the next occurring event is chosen.
- Events: There is a rich spectrum for this, divided into various categories, e.g., the receipt of a message, a time event, or a condition becoming true. It is also distinguished whether the event takes place at the start of the process, at the end of the process, or during the process.

Figure 3.9 shows the node types used for this, including refinements.

A process with a large, often predominant proportion of dialog activities is called a *workflow* in jargon. In a narrower, more precise sense, a workflow is a business process that is controlled by a workflow management system (see Chap. 12). Dialog activities are common in processes for:

- *Data entry*: all create methods, such as creating orders, invoices, goods receipts, or material master data.
- *Data adjustment*: related to data collection; all change methods, such as changing a vacation request when a vacation for a certain period is not granted.

Fig. 3.9 Refinement of some BPMN nodes

- *Approval* (also called release): release of a purchase requisition, invoice verification, vacation request approval.

In some cases, fully automated business processes are possible that do not require user dialog: processing chains, for example, organized in coordinated batch jobs.

3.5.2   Data Flow

In addition to the control flow, there is the *data flow*, which determines how data is passed between activities. An activity requires as data the object reference to the business object whose method is called and possibly additional method parameters. The data flow can occur from step to step or indirectly via the process, depending on which notation is used to define the control flow. In the case of business objects, we can also call it *object flow* (shown dotted in Fig. 3.8). If a business object is created in one step, it can, for example, be checked or further processed in the next step. Therefore, the business object, or the object reference to be more precise, must "flow." In fact, in many processes, the same business object is processed over large parts, and changes, checks, and additions are made to it. The data flow must be consistent with the control flow, i.e., the required data must have flown to a step when control has reached it.

For the *data flow* within a pool, *data objects* can be used (especially in BPMN 2.0, particularly data input, data output, and data storage (Freund and Rücker 2019, p. 25)). However, the definition of data structures or business objects is not part of BPMN itself; this is done via *extension points*. The standard notation for data description is XML Schema (Freund and Rücker 2019, p. 179; see Sect. 10.3.4). Expressions can be formulated, e.g., for conditions; the default setting is the XPath Expression Language, an XML standard for defining expressions (Freund and Rücker 2019, p. 179); see also Chap. 10. A *message flow* is defined between process parts in different organizations ("pools"; see below).

In Fig. 3.8, the data flow is represented by dotted arrows. The arrowhead indicates whether an object is created by an activity or is referenced.

3.5.3   Agent Assignment

Finally, in the left column of Fig. 3.8, we have the *agent assignment*. It defines *who* has to perform the activity. We distinguish between concrete and abstract agents. The *concrete agents* are the users who could perform the activities (Mortimer Whipsnade, Mildred Peabody, etc.). Often, not exactly one user may do the job, but there is a group of possible agents to choose from. One of them will execute the activity. However, it is at least cumbersome to directly assign a set of concrete agents, i.e., users, to the activities. Moreover, such agent sets often change. Therefore, *abstract agents* are usually used for the assignment. These are agents in the form of *user groups*, *roles*, *positions*, and similar things. Thus, the agent assignment is indirect and often coarse grained. For creating a purchase order, the purchasing department is responsible. Any purchaser working there could create an order. The abstract agent (in the simplest case) would be the user group of purchasing employees. Another example of an abstract agent is the company's security officer. The concrete agent, on the other hand, is determined as the user who currently holds this position or role.

Another distinguishing feature in agent assignment is the difference between static and dynamic assignment. The agents can be *statically* defined: A static agent assignment depends only on the process definition. A dynamic agent assignment depends on the process instance, usually on the business object instance being processed or on other runtime data. This is the case, for example, if specific clerks are responsible for different supplier groups to check their invoices. A case in point is the "superior" agent assignment: The superior of an employee will, for example, check an employee's leave request. Formally, a dynamic agent assignment can be understood as an attribute or a method of a business object, which returns a set of abstract agents as a result. In Fig. 3.10, the dynamic agent assignment "invoice checker for <invoice>" returns the agent Bisbee for invoice 17, while the dynamic agent assignment "superior of <employee>" returns the agent McGargle for the employee Pepperday.

The static agent assignment can be visualized in BPMN via swim lanes (i.e., positions, roles, departments). In Fig. 3.8, all agent assignments are static. However,

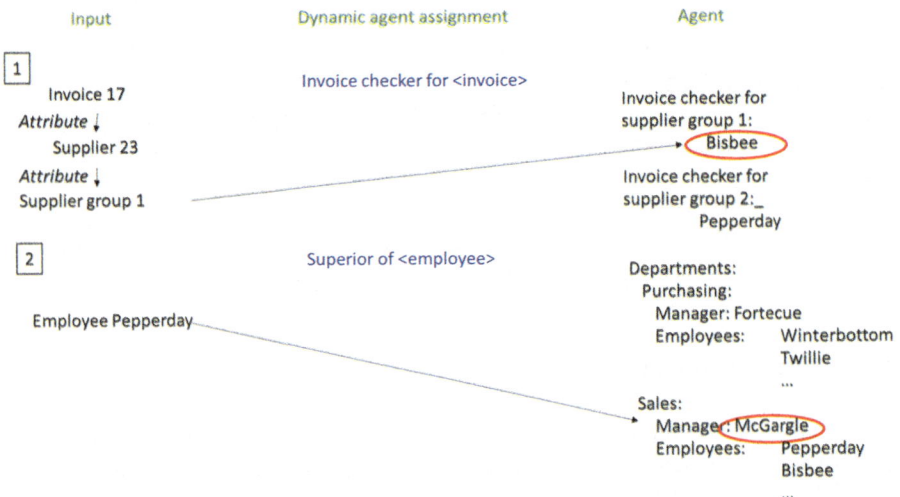

Fig. 3.10 Dynamic agent assignment

I see no means in BPMN for an explicit dynamic agent assignment. BPMN supports two types of swim lanes: *Pools* for the cooperating companies and *swim lanes* (in the narrow sense) for the agents within a company.

3.5.4 Execution of Processes

The execution of a process definition is a process instance. How does this happen in everyday business? We can distinguish two types:

(a) *Without the support of a process management system*: This is the most usual case. Here, the respective agents start the activities when it makes sense for them. Looking at the purchasing process from Fig. 3.8, a purchaser will decide when to create an order. The basis for the decision will be open purchase requisitions. When the goods arrive, a warehouse employee will book a goods receipt. When the invoice arrives, a corresponding employee in accounting will record the invoice. Another employee in accounting will recognize that the invoice is ready to be booked, check it, and finally book it. That's the control flow.

　The employees also execute the data flow. For example, the warehouse employee will enter the corresponding order number in a field when creating the goods receipt.

　The agent assignment is based on organizational rules and according to the permissions of the employees. For example, the goods receipts could be processed in a cooperative way—the next available employee records the next goods receipt. The person who checks which invoices will be regulated in accounting. Employees can see from the status of the invoices which ones need to be checked and do so if they have the appropriate permissions.

(b) *With the support of a process management system*: Here, the process management system handles the control and data flow as well as the agent assignment (see Chap. 12).

3.5.5 Characteristics

Business processes have always existed in essence, but the very term became popular with "Business Process Reengineering" (Hammer and Champy 1994). In a broader sense, "business process" is also used for applications ("the purchasing business process") and even for a company's overall economic activity ("supporting the business processes").

　As in the sections on business data and business objects, we want to better understand business processes using various classifications.

(a) **Definition of Business Processes**

Transactional systems support business processes. On the one hand, they offer the activity implementations (e.g., the method `purchaseOrder.create`). On the other hand, the control flow is at least partially already implicit in the software, which results from process integration.

Examples:

- A goods receipt for an order can of course only take place after the order has been created.
- A purchase requisition can only be released after it has been created.

Such obvious dependencies, legal regulations, and common practice restrict the set of business processes that are realizable with a transactional system (cf. Fig. 3.11).

Some restrictions, however, are less obvious and are set up in the transactional system in one of several possible ways. They further narrow the process set, also visualized in Fig. 3.11. Part of the process logic is "hardwired" in the software, which makes reorganization of processes difficult. Or some methods may only be available with user interface, making processes with automated calls at least more complex to implement. Nevertheless, transaction systems often leave room for different configurations of processes, e.g., whether a four-eyes principle should be applied in invoice verification. Sometimes, it can be set in customizing; sometimes, it is simply the way it is done in the company.

So also in the case that processes are not explicitly modeled, the set of processes that can be realized with a transactional system is predetermined. We could call them *implicit processes*. (What determines the scope of this set?)

Companies define their processes either *informally*, for example, through organizational regulations. It can happen that the process definition is only "in people's heads," and often each person only knows a part of the process well.

Or the processes are defined more or less formally—we speak of *modeled* business processes. There are two forms:

- *Reference processes*: They can be proposed as standard processes by the software vendor or by standardization committees.

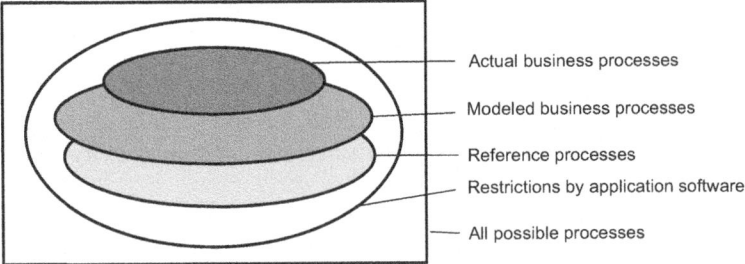

Fig. 3.11 Process sets

- *Modeled company processes*: A company may model its company-specific processes. They can be based on the reference processes but also go beyond them (see Fig. 3.11).

The modeling can be done:

- With a *modeling tool* in order to document business processes.
- With a *business process management system* or a workflow management system (see Chap. 12) in order to control business processes (process automation). As it takes quite some effort to automate business processes, but not only for this reason, today, only a small part of the business processes is automated with such tools. The automation benefit in daily operation must be compared with the costs for process development, maintenance, and administration.

  Finally, the processes as they are run in a company (the *actual* processes in Fig. 3.11) might not follow their definitions. The reasons might be that the modeled processes are no longer up to date or that people consciously or unconsciously just do not strictly adhere to the process definitions.

(b) **Without or with a Process Management System**

  As mentioned in the previous classification, processes can be automated with appropriate tools, viz., process management systems (cf. Chap. 12).

(c) **Degree of Automation**

  Continuing this thought, we distinguish between these processes:

- Fully automated
- Partially automated
- Non-automated

  "Automated" here does not mean that we use a transactional system, as opposed to doing it with "paper and pencil" or using, e.g., word processing programs. We assume that a transactional system is used anyway. We rather distinguish whether an activity is executed by a user (with a dialog function of the transactional system), automatically (by the transactional system alone), or mixed (some activities are automated, others are not).

(d) **Standardization**

  In this classification, we distinguish between, on the one hand, standard processes, which are largely predetermined due to legal requirements or "best practices," and, on the other, company-specific processes. Some cases may be mixed, for example, a predefined standard process in a transactional system with some company-specific additions (see Chap. 15).

(f) **Core and Support Processes**

  Core processes concern directly the business of a company, such as the processing of sales orders. Support processes facilitate these core processes, e.g., in human resources.

(f) **Process Patterns**

  Design patterns in software development are well-known (cf. (Gamma et al. 1994)). Patterns can also be identified in business processes—less or more formally. See workflowpatterns (2024) for a more formal approach.

(h) **Intra-company and Inter-company Processes**
Inter-company processes describe how business partners cooperate. Standardization, techniques, and tools for automation exist (cf. Electronic Data Interchange (EDI) and Chap. 10).

(h) **Intra-system and Inter-system Processes**
In an intra-system business process, all activities happen in just one transactional system. In inter-system processes, the activities happen in different transactional systems. Inter-company processes are almost always inter-system. But even within a single company, with multiple transactional systems, inter-system processes will be present (see Chap. 12).

3.6   Business Interfaces

3.6.1   Motivation

As comprehensive as the functionality of an ERP system appears at first glance, it does have its limits. Therefore, other adjacent software systems play a role in a company. Figure 3.12 shows examples.

Some explanations about the systems linked in Fig. 3.12:

- Time recording system: Employees record their working time with magnetic cards. The working time data is used in the ERP system for time evaluation.
- Content Management System: It stores unstructured data, e.g., text documents.
- email system: The ERP system may send emails to business partners or employees.
- Telephony system: A user may call a supplier just at the push of a button in the transactional system—he does not need to type in the telephone number.
- EDI subsystem: Orders to suppliers can be sent via Electronic Data Interchange (EDI) in a close integration, and correspondingly orders can be received from customers.
- Archive system: Over time, more and more data accumulate in the database, which decreases its performance. It makes sense, therefore, to move old data to

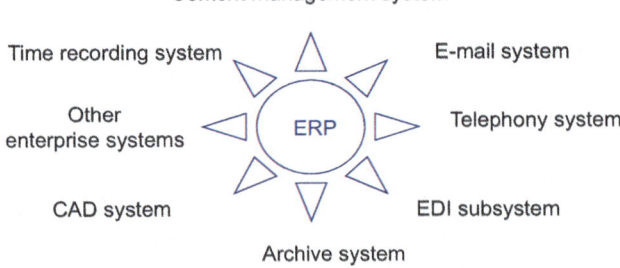

Fig. 3.12 Business interfaces of an ERP system

an archive system. Deletion is usually not an option for reasons of traceability (see Sect. 3.1).

- CAD system: Technical drawings are part of technical data processing, but they are related to business data (material master, bill of materials).
- Other enterprise information systems: Data can be transmitted to a data warehouse system for analysis. This and other forms of integration of enterprise information systems are discussed in Part II.

The systems mentioned are connected to the ERP system via business interfaces. We use the term *business interfaces* to distinguish these content-related interfaces from the technical integration possibilities (e.g., HTTP, RPC, XML). When the context is clear, the word *interface* will suffice. In our modeling view, business interfaces can be seen as connection possibilities of an enterprise information system to another system, which offers external data, objects, or processes that complement the internal ones. Accordingly, interfaces are possible at all three levels. Most common are programming interfaces (APIs) of the ERP system, which are used by the external systems. Manufacturers, e.g., of time recording systems, generally support these interfaces, if the ERP system is widely used. To give the customer more confidence that the integration works smoothly, manufacturers often have their product certified by the vendor of the enterprise information system. However, certification costs will have to be paid.

3.6.2 Characteristics

We now want to take a closer look at the rather abstract term "interface." A system needs an interface in order to interact with its *environment*. The environment can be:

- Another system: We then speak of a *system interface*. This is what we usually think of when we hear the word "interface," as in the examples in Sect. 3.6.1.
- User: A *user interface* is of course needed in any case.
- "Things": In the "Internet of Things" (IoT), "things" (e.g., machines or cars) communicate with each other or with other software via sensor data. Such software can also be an transactional system. The communication can happen directly or indirectly via other software systems. The things could technically be considered mini systems, so basically, this interface is also a system interface.

We will take a closer look at the topic of "IoT" further below. User interfaces are covered in Chap. 5. Here we concentrate on the system interface.

Fig. 3.13 System interface

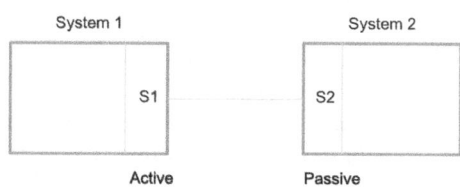

Fig. 3.14 Communication
via middleware

Table 3.4 Interfaces

Classification			Content	
Operation	Interaction	Partner type	Semantics	
		Active/passive		
		Operating principle		
	Data	Protocol	Syntax	
		Data flow		
		Format		
Provision	Built-in / in-house development			

So, let's look at system-to-system interaction (see Fig. 3.13). The two systems 1 and 2 want to interact with each other, e.g., system 1 could send data to system 2. For this to work, both systems need interfaces because system 1 must send data and system 2 must receive it.

Just as it makes sense for two people to use the same language in order to understand each other, the two systems need matching interfaces. The interfaces will not be the same but, like a plug and a socket, fit together. If the two interfaces do not directly fit together but are very similar in content, they can in many cases be bridged via middleware (adapter, gateway, converter) ("M" in Fig. 3.14). That is, a translation takes place during the interaction, similar to an interpreter between people.

Systems usually have many interfaces, sometimes even several of the same type (e.g., user interface; which could these be?).

Two things are important when describing an interface (see Table 3.4):

- *Classification*: The properties of the technical design, without specifying the content of the interface.
- *Content*: What information is transmitted (semantics), and how is it coded (syntax)?

A. **Classification**

To get an overview of the variety of how interfaces can be designed, here are some features. They mainly concern the mode of operation (items a–f) but also who provides the interface (item g). There are dependencies between some features. We look at this from the perspective of system 2, which receives a supplier master data record from system 1.

(a) **Partner Type**

What is the type of the communication partner: System, user, or "thing?" In our example, the partner type is "system."

(b) **Active/Passive Interface**

Which communication partner controls or initiates the communication (active), which one reacts to it (passive)? In our example, system 2 has a passive interface. (What would be an active interface here?) The distinction "active/passive" is found in non-symmetrical communication. But we will also get to know symmetrical ones: functions of two systems integrated with portals and process management systems, where both communication partners (functions) have the same interface (Chaps. 9 and 12).

(c) **Functional Principle**

Is the interaction calling a *dialog function*, a *background function*, or a *data transmission*? In a dialog function, a user interacts with the system via screen masks. The partner type is therefore always "user." In contrast, no user is involved in a background function call. In data transmission, a single instance of business data or a bundle of several is sent. In our example, it is a "data transmission."

(d) **Protocol**

What communication protocol do the systems use, and what is the communication channel? For example, a function call could be made based on the HTTP protocol (Chap. 11): Or data could be stored in a file directory, what we assume in our example. And there are yet other possibilities.

(e) **Data Flow**

This can be *input* (the system receives input data), *output* (the system delivers output data), or *input and output* (both as with a user interface or a method call). In our case, it is "input."

(f) **Format**

How is the data encoded, e.g., XML, CSV files (see Chap. 10), or, in the case of user interfaces, e.g., HTML? The list of encoding types or formats is in fact open. From the description of our example, it is not clear which case applies here. We assume that the data is encoded in XML.

(g) **Provision**

Is the interface part of the standard software? Or is it an in-house development of the company that uses the software (Chap. 15)? From the description of our example, it is not clear which case applies here. We assume that it is a built-in interface.

    We will look at further aspects in Sect. 11.6 when we have gained a better understanding of integration techniques.

B. **Content**

So far, we did not yet talk about the content of the interface: *Which* function is called? *Which* data is transmitted? How does this look like in detail: What parameters are there? What data fields are there? What are the data types of parameters and data fields? This could in principle be stated in one step. For methodological reasons, however, we distinguish two:

(a) **Semantics**

What kind of data is it, e.g., supplier (master data) or order (transaction data)? Which fields are used? This is the business view of the interface. In our example, this has not yet been specified in detail. The supplier data will include the supplier number, the supplier's name, its address, and many others. We need to determine which ones we need in our integration.

(b) **Syntax**

How is the content encoded, e.g., which field names are used, what data types are used for the fields, and what field lengths? This is also still open in our example. Later we will be able to specify this in the form of an XML schema document (see Chap. 10). Once the content is known, there are endless possibilities to encode it, even using one specific encoding technique (e.g., XML). (Why?) Therefore, this needs to be specified as well.

3.6.3   Excursion: Internet of Things

Not only people or other (enterprise) systems can communicate with an enterprise information system. In the "Internet of Things "(IoT), "things" (e.g., components, containers) capture data using sensors and transmit them to an enterprise information system, often in preprocessed form. Manual input is eliminated in this case, which leads to higher automation and lower error rate.

The "things" can also communicate with each other via the IoT. Through the sensor data, a virtual, digital representation of the "thing" is created, which is called a *digital twin*. This also enables the control of the things. The digital twin can be enriched with business data from an enterprise information system (usually master data) (Seubert 2022, p. 165). Some examples from (Seubert 2022) illustrate this:

- In "predictive maintenance," sensor data provide a model of a machine's condition. Maintenance work can be initiated as needed (see Sect. 4.3.2).
- Automatic inventory management: The items (materials) identify themselves automatically upon goods receipt and dispatch, without manual data entry (Seubert 2022, p. 160).

Problems with IoT are the variety of protocols—different things have different protocols—and the management of the devices (Seubert 2022, p. 161).

Enterprise information systems provide interfaces to read sensor data. It often makes sense not to transmit all data to the enterprise information system but to preprocess them (*Edge Computing*). This leads to faster reactions and reduces the amount of transmitted data (Seubert 2022, p. 162). ("Edge" because the processing takes place at the "edge" of the network.)

In terms of functionality, the methods used are mostly analytical, which we will address in the next chapter.

3.7   Examples

In the market of ERP systems, there is a division into software for larger companies and for smaller companies. For larger companies, somewhat simplified, there has been a consolidation to only a few vendors, like SAP and Oracle. SAP is a

traditional vendor of business application software. Oracle is a company that grew
with database software and later also developed application software but above all
bought out some of the other major enterprise software vendors and now has their
products in its portfolio (PeopleSoft, JD Edwards, Siebel). For smaller companies,
there is a large number of products, many of them only available in local markets.
Microsoft should also be mentioned as a global player, especially with the product
Microsoft Dynamics 365 Business Central (and earlier versions go by the names
Microsoft Dynamics NAV and "Navision").

In the following, we will discuss three examples that we will continue in further
chapters:

- SAP S/4HANA, which along with its predecessors is widely used in larger
  companies
- Microsoft Dynamics 365 Business Central, an ERP system for small and
  medium-sized businesses
- Vtiger, an open-source CRM system

3.7.1 SAP S/4HANA and Predecessors

ERP systems have a long tradition at SAP, starting from the first widespread standard business software SAP R/2 for mainframes, over the client-server product SAP
R/3, and the follow-up product SAP ERP to the latest product SAP S/4HANA
(Saueressig et al. 2023). SAP S/4HANA is the result of continuous further development and not a complete redesign, the majority of the functions of SAP ERP are
found in it.

With SAP R/3, the application functionality was divided into the functional areas
logistics, accounting, and human resources and further into subareas ("modules").
In practice, this terminology has been retained to this day. The most important modules are in logistics materials management (MM), production planning (PP), and
sales and distribution (SD). In accounting, it is financials (FI, the external accounting) and controlling (a more accurate term would be "cost accounting and controlling," CO). In human resources, there is only the human resources (HR) module.

A major innovation in SAP S/4HANA is the use of the SAP HANA database
system. It is an in-memory database (see Sect. 5.1.3.2), which allows much faster
access than disk-based database systems. Functions were added that particularly
well exploit this performance. Some others were rewritten, e.g., the material requirements planning (Saueressig et al. 2023, p. 276). Even though it is a transactional
system, there is also analytical functionality in it, for which the in-memory technology is particularly beneficial (see Chap. 4). Internally, simplified data structures
have been introduced in some places, also because the in-memory technology can
do without sum and index tables, which reduces the storage requirement.

Another innovation is Web-based user interfaces with the JavaScript-based technology SAP Fiori for new or rewritten functions ("Fiori Apps"), organized in the
role-based SAP Fiori Launchpad (Saueressig et al. 2023, p. 68). In the predecessor
products, Microsoft Windows-based user interfaces predominated (SAP GUI for

Windows), though a Java GUI was also available. In addition to the new Fiori apps, many functions from the predecessor SAP ERP have been adopted. They can be called via a Web browser and also still via the SAP GUI. For native SAP Fiori apps, the connection to the business logic is made using REST-based (see Sect. 11.8) OData services.

On the one hand, new functionality was added; on the other hand, a consolidation was made. The "principle of one" says there shall be only one approach for a requirement; see (Saueressig et al. 2023, p. 36). For example, in SAP ERP, there was the (old) general ledger in accounting and the new general ledger; in SAP S/4HANA, only the new one is available.

Companies must make appropriate adjustments when migrating from an old SAP system to SAP S/4HANA.

SAP S/4HANA can both be installed on-premises and used as public or private cloud software (see Sect. 6.1). However, these variants have different degrees of adaptation possibilities (see Chap. 15).

3.7.2   Microsoft Dynamics 365 Business Central

Microsoft, which primarily makes its revenue from Windows operating systems and Office applications, has also entered the enterprise information systems market. It purchased the Danish company Navision, which had developed ERP systems. The product, after several name changes, a few years ago to Microsoft Dynamics NAV, is currently marketed under the name Microsoft Dynamics 365 Business Central (Ebert and Hauptmann 2023) (Demiliani and Tacconi 2018a) and targets small and medium-sized businesses.

It has the following functional areas (Ebert and Hauptmann 2023, p. 4):

- Financial management (accounting)
- Sales, marketing, and service
- Supply chain management (purchasing, warehouse, sales, production, logistics, and project management)
- Business intelligence/reporting

It has interfaces to Microsoft products such as Microsoft Office and the portal (see Chap. 9) Microsoft SharePoint.

It is available on-premises and as a cloud product (see Sect. 6.1) (Ebert and Hauptmann 2023, p. 6). In contrast to Microsoft Dynamics NAV, for which there was a Windows and a Web client, only the Web client is available here. In addition, there are apps for mobile devices (smartphone, tablet) (Ebert and Hauptmann 2023, p. 10).

The system has a tenant concept (see Sect. 3.3.3), where the data of different tenants, unlike, e.g., in SAP software, are stored in separate database tables—the tenant name is part of the name of the database table (Ebert and Hauptmann 2023, p. 65). Microsoft SQL Server is used as the database system in on-premises installations (Ebert and Hauptmann 2023, p. 6).

3.7.3 Vtiger CRM

Vtiger CRM is an example of an open-source enterprise software (Rossi 2011; Piepiorra 2007). It is not an ERP system but a CRM system. We mention it in this chapter, because it includes transactional CRM functionality (see Sect. 8.3) and even some ERP functionality. Accordingly, there is functionality such as marketing, sales, support (with a trouble ticket system), but also analytics, and a customer portal. In addition to the open-source version, there is a cloud version, operated by the company Vtiger of the same name. The software runs on a platform with Apache as a Web server, a MySQL database, and PHP as the programming language.

In Vtiger CRM, there are various *modules* (in this book's terminology, they correspond more to business data), e.g., leads (in CRM technology, a lead is a first contact with an interested person or company which could later become a customer), quotations, organizations, and campaigns.

3.8 Exercises and Suggested Solutions

(a) Exercises

Exercise 3.1 (Master and Transaction Data)
Indicate for the following data whether it is master or transaction data:

- Request for quotation
- Quotation
- Business partner
- Outline agreement
- Bank details of a customer
- Payment from a customer
- Order in XML format
- Current date

Exercise 3.2 (Database Table Structure)

(a) What are the table structures for purchase orders?
(b) What is the table structure for the material description?
(c) Assume that the master data for material requirements planning for a material is plant dependent, with attributes, e.g., which requirements planning procedure should be used in the respective plant for the material. What is the table structure in the material master for requirements planning?

Exercise 3.3 (Modeling of Business Objects)
Model the purchasing system described below using a UML class diagram. In the classes, you only need to mention the attributes and methods used in purchasing:

Employees create purchase requisitions when they need materials. Several materials can be requested in a purchase requisition. Purchase requisitions need to be released if a certain amount is exceeded. The check is usually carried out by the employee's superior.

Purchasers generate orders from released purchase requisitions. Although the applicant can suggest a supplier as a source for each material, the purchasers do not have to adopt these suggestions. In addition, purchasers can convert materials from different purchase requisitions collectively into orders to get better purchasing conditions.

The orders are transmitted either in paper form or via Electronic Data Interchange, depending on the supplier.

Exercise 3.4 (API Methods)
Consider two methods that perform the same task, e.g., create a purchase order. The first method is a dialog method, and the second is the corresponding API method, i.e., a method that can be executed without direct user dialog. What parameters will the second method have?

Exercise 3.5 (Business Process)
Model the following business processes in a BPMN diagram in the form presented in Sect. 3.5 (Fig. 3.8). They are processes for purchase requisition processing:

(a) (simple) An employee creates a purchase requisition. We simplify by assuming that it only contains one line-item. Then the purchase requisition must be released by an employee who has the appropriate authorization. Subsequently, the creator will look at the purchase requisition and recognize from the status whether it was released or rejected.
(b) (more difficult) Now we draw the process boundary at another point: We focus just on the approval process. Accordingly, the process starts after the purchase requisition has been created. (How do you represent this?) In addition, the employee should not need to check the purchase requisition's state but receive an email telling him whether the purchase requisition was released or rejected. (The complicated part here is the email. Think about which class you want to use for this, what the text of the email should look like in each case, and how it interacts with the purchase requisition. What is the signature of a corresponding method?)

(b) Suggested Solutions for the Exercises

Exercise 3.1 (Master and Transaction Data)

- Request for quotation: transaction data.
- Quotation: transaction data.
- Business partner: master data.
- Framework contract: This could be seen as a borderline case between master and transaction data.
- Bank details of a customer: Neither-nor. It is not independent business data but part of the master data "customer"; it is just an attribute.
- Payment of a customer: transaction data.

- Order in XML format: transaction data.
- Current date: Neither-nor. It is not independent business data; it can appear as an attribute in many business data.

Exercise 3.2 (Database Table Structure)

(a) Header table: ID (key field), creation date, creator, supplier, etc.
Line-item table: ID (key field), line-item number (key field), material number, quantity, unit of measure, delivery date, etc.
    We limit ourselves to the most important attributes to illustrate the principle. Those interested in a "real" example should look at the database tables in an ERP system. In large systems, the tables can have 100–200 attributes.

(b) Material number (key field), language (key field), and designation. This is called a text table.

(c) Material number, plant (both key fields), MRP procedure, etc. So here we have organization-dependent data. a–c show that business data requires several database tables of different structure.

Exercise 3.3 (Modeling of Business Objects)
See Fig. 3.15.
    The separate classes for header and line-items, both for the purchase requisition and the order, are important in order to be able to accurately represent the relationships between purchase requisitions and purchase orders. Furthermore, the releases could also be based on line-items. The master data is only rudimentarily modeled, as it is used in various business processes.

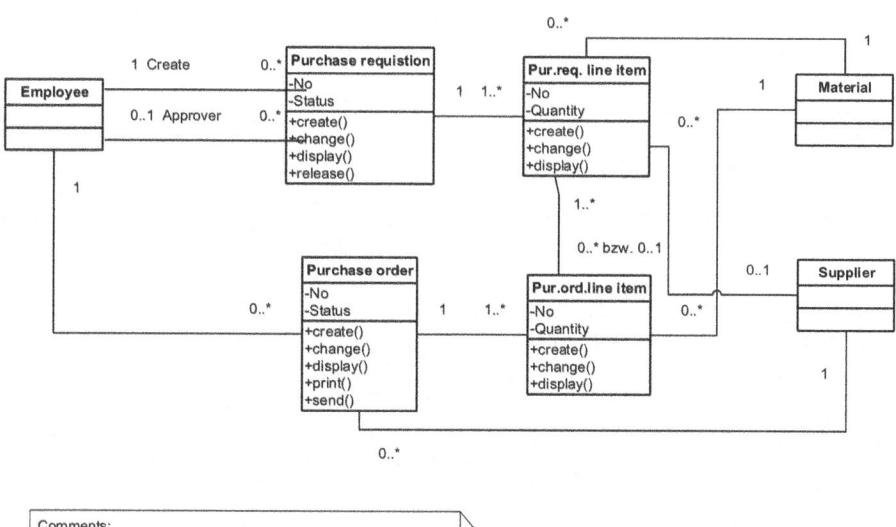

Fig. 3.15 Class diagram "purchasing"

Special attention should be paid to the multiplicities, as they define restrictions for the business processes. Some multiplicities could have been chosen differently, with effects on the business processes.

Exercise 3.4 (API Method)
It will have parameters that, taken together, correspond to all input fields of the first method. Only then is the functionality equivalent.

Exercise 3.5 (Business Process)
See Fig. 3.16 for exercise part (a) and Fig. 3.17 for exercise part (b).

For exercise part (b), the method `message.send` of an application-independent class `message` is used in the diagram. This allows notifications to be generated in many business processes.

The method `message.send` has three input parameters: `recipient` (email address), `form`, and `businessObject`. The recipient should receive the email. We use the data flow `purchaseRequestion.creator.emailAddress`. `creator` is an attribute of type class `user`, which in turn has an `emailAddress` attribute. The `form` is a text template into which application data can be integrated. It can be filled by the data flow, for example, with the ID `purchaseRequisition_approved`. The application data are attributes of the object, here `purchaseRequisition`, e.g., `purchaseRequisition.creator.name`, `purchaseRequisition.creationDate`, which can appear in the text of the form and be replaced by current values at runtime. (Why is the general term `businessObject` used, not `purchaseRequisition`? What is the class of `object`?)

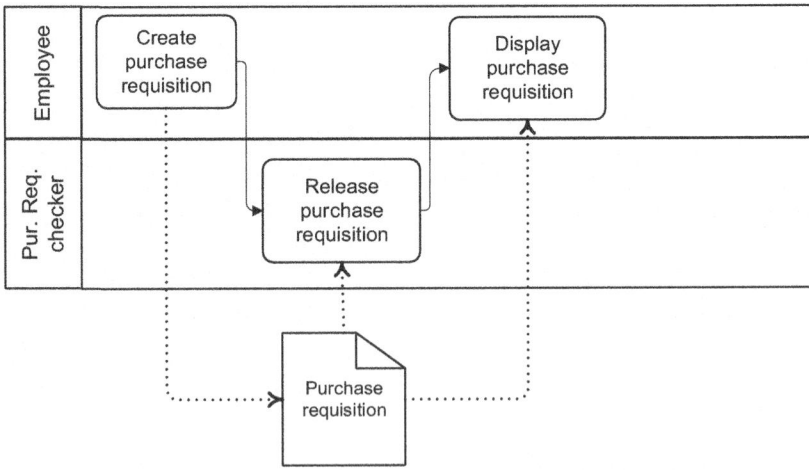

Fig. 3.16 Business process "Purchase Requisition Release," Exercise Part (a)

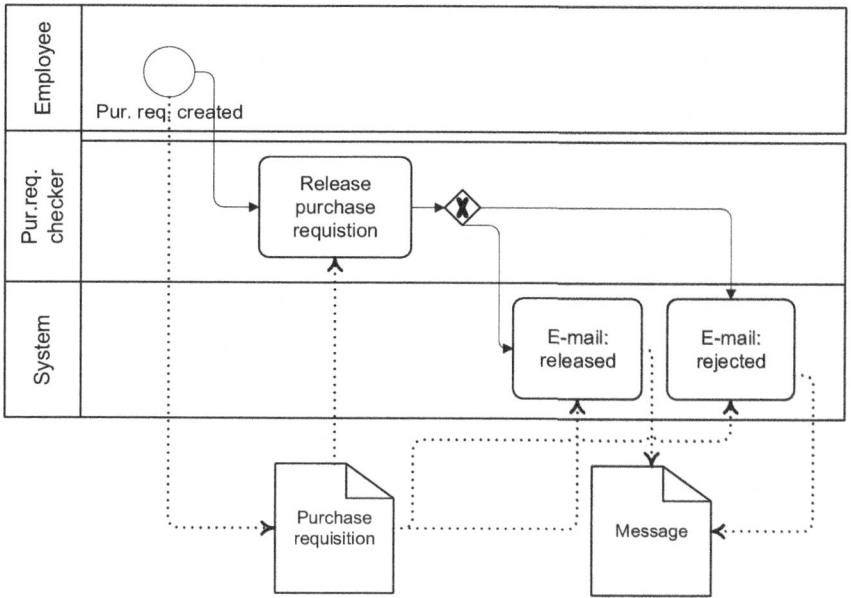

Fig. 3.17   Business process "Purchase Requisition Release," Exercise Part (b)

3.9   Self-Assessment

3.1 ERP Systems

1. Why does an ERP system usually also have analysis functionality (standard reports) built in?
2. What does "data integration" mean? What functionality would it require if the system did not have this?
3. Does functional integration require data integration?

3.2 The Three-Tier Model for Transactional Functionality

4. What is the relationship between business data and business objects?
5. What is the relationship between business objects and business processes?
6. At what level of our model is an API located?

3.3 Business Data

7. Why are master data rarely deleted?
8. In which cases could you delete master data without problems?
9. Are all transaction data flow data?
10. Is a goods receipt transaction data or change data?

11. How do you recognize whether business data is "active?"
12. Give examples of business data with header and line-item structure. Can you also think of an example of master data with this structure?
13. You are setting up a system and are considering whether to set up an external or internal number assignment for business data. What criteria do you use for your decision?
14. Why is case sensitivity not important for IDs? How would you implement this when developing an enterprise information system?

3.4 Business Objects

15. We use the model of business objects. In system theory, a model represents a system. What is the "system" in our case?
16. Transactions are used in database systems. For your review: What does the term "ACID" mean, which you surely heard in a lecture about database systems?
17. What do database transactions have to do with enterprise information systems? What about business objects?
18. Do methods of business objects have parameters? If yes, which ones (example)? If no, why not?
19. What is the difference between a persistent object and an object in a programming language like Java? Is there a relationship between them?
20. What methods are commonly used in business objects? Why?
21. What is the purpose of methods without user dialogue (GUI, screen masks)?
22. We are modeling the association between the classes "customer" and "sales order." What multiplicities do you suggest?
23. What events would you anticipate for the class "production order?"
24. Associations do not exist in classes of a programming language. What do you do with associations when you want to implement a UML class diagram in a programming language?
25. What connections (in a general sense) exist between different classes of business objects?

3.5 Business Processes

26. Explain the difference between static and dynamic agents!
27. Is it static or dynamic agents that are represented in the swim lanes of a BPMN diagram?
28. Explain the terms "implicit" and "explicit business processes!"

3.6 Business Interfaces

29. You are coupling two systems. Do both systems need an interface or just one of them?
30. Can you give an example of an interface at the business process level?

References

Further Reading

Those interested in a more comprehensive presentation of the functions of an ERP system in a vendor-neutral manner will find this, for example, in:
Bradford, M.: Modern ERP, 3rd edn. North Carolina State Univ, Raleigh, NC (2015)

The modeling of classes with UML, although not specifically for business objects, is compactly described in:
Fowler, M.: UML Distilled: A Brief Guide to the Standard Object Modeling Language. Addison-Wesley, Boston (2004)

The modeling of business processes with BPMN is shown in the following books, although not in conjunction with business objects as in our book:
Freund, J., Rücker, B.: Real-life BPMN, 4th ed. Camunda. (2019)
Silver, B.: BPMN Quick and Easy: with Method and Style. Cody-Cassidy Press, Altadena, CA (2017)

This is a concise description of BPMN and its usage, limited to the most important language constructs of BPMN. More extensive but similar is:
Silver, B.: BPMN Method and Style, 2nd edn. Cody-Cassidy Press, Aptos, CA (2011)

Further Cited Literature and Sources

Bauer, C., Gregory, G.: Java Persistence with Hibernate, 2nd edn. Manning, Greenwich (2016)
Coulouris, G., Dollimore, J., Kindberg, T.: Distributed Systems, 4th edn. Addison-Wesley, Harlow (2005)
Demiliani, S., Tacconi, D.: Microsoft Dynamics 365 Business Central Development Quick Start Guide. Packt Publishing, Birmingham (2018)
Gamma, E., Helm, R., Johnson, R.: Design Patterns. Elements of Reusable Object-Oriented Software. Pearson, London (1994)
Gronau, N.: ERP-Systeme: Architektur, Management und Funktionen des Enterprise Resource Planning, 4th edn. De Gruyter Oldenbourg, Munich (2021)
Hammer, M., Champy, J.: Reengineering the Corporation. Addison-Wesley, Reading, MH (1994)
Heilig, L., Karch, S., Böttcher, O., Hofmann, C.: SAP NetWeaver Master Data Management. Galileo Press, Bonn (2006)
Hibernate: https://hibernate.org/ (2020). Accessed 1 Nov 2024
Piepiorra, F.: vtiger CRM v5.x. bomots. Saarbrücken (2007)
Plattner, H., Zeier, A.: In-Memory Data Management. Springer, Berlin (2011)
Rossi, I.D.: vtiger CRM. Beginner's Guide. Packt Publishing, Birmingham (2011)
Saueressig, T., Stein, T., Boeder, J., Kleis, W.: SAP S/4HANA—Architecture. Rheinwerk, Boston (2023)
Scheer, A.-W., Thomas, O., Adam, O.: Process modeling using event-driven process chains. In: Dumas, M., van der Aals, W., ter Hofstede, A.H.M. (eds.) Process-Aware Information Systems. Wiley, Hoboken, NJ (2005)
Seubert, H.: SAP Business Technology Platform, 2nd updated and expanded edn. Rheinwerk, Bonn (2022)
workflowpatterns: http://www.workflowpatterns.com/ (2024). Accessed 1 Nov 2024

Analytical Systems

4

I want you to wash and shuffle the numbers.
That's why I had you come.
Just for washing, someone else would have sufficed.
*Haruki Murakami (Hard-boiled Wonderland und das Ende der Welt,
Insel, first edition, Frankfurt a. M., 1995, p. 47, translated.)*

Summary

Analytical systems are used to analyze large sets of data, as opposed to single-record processing in transactional systems. We use the term "analytical functionality" in a general way. It ranges from reports in an ERP system to machine learning and mathematical optimization methods in planning. We focus on data warehouse systems, but we look also briefly at other types of analytical functionality.

Learning Objectives

- To get to know analytical systems using the example of data warehouse systems.
- To be able to create a multidimensional data model for an scenario.
- To get an overview of other analytical methods: data science including statistical methods and machine learning, Big Data, and planning.

© The Author(s), under exclusive license to Springer-Verlag GmbH, DE,
part of Springer Nature 2025
R. Weber, *Enterprise Information Systems*,
https://doi.org/10.1007/978-3-662-71718-9_4

4.1   General

4.1.1   Analytical Functionality

In this chapter, we deal with *analytical systems* as opposed to transactional systems (Chap. 3). Transactional systems are used to handle day-to-day business, which is reflected in the creation, editing, or changing of individual master or transaction data, for example, processing a single order, not several at once. In analytical systems, many data are analyzed together, e.g., in an analysis of all purchase orders of a quarter of a year. We thus perform calculations (in a broad sense) based on many business data. The basic idea is to use extensive past and present data for decisions and planning for the future. (In transactional systems, "mass maintenance" is often carried out for master data, e.g., by changing an attribute on many master data at the same time. Is this also analytical functionality?)

This can be illustrated abstractly in Fig. 4.1. In (a), the general case is shown: The selection criterion determines which business data shall be analyzed. The attributes are specified (e.g., the values in orders), and restrictions are made, typically to referenced master data and periods (e.g., the period "last quarter," "in the purchasing organization South"). This results in a set of selected data. Data can be condensed (aggregated), e.g., not five hundred order values from five hundred orders but only a sum value, calculated from the five hundred orders. With the selected dataset, further, often more complex calculations can then be carried out, e.g., a demand list of materials can be created from inventory levels and customer orders or a production plan from the demand list.

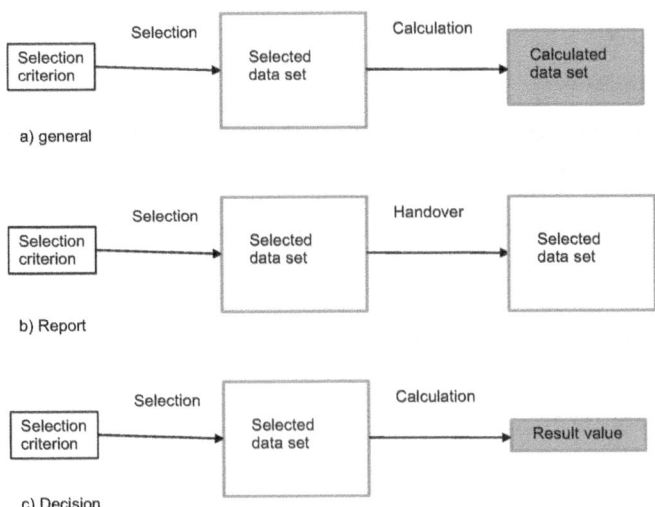

Fig. 4.1 Analytics

Let's look at various typical processing patterns and relate them to the general model:

1. Analyze data visually
   Such analyses are also called *reports*. We read a large amount of data and display them (or a subset of them) in the simplest case as a result list. However, simple calculations can also be carried out with the data (subsumed under "selection" in Fig. 4.1b): Data can be condensed, e.g., the monthly sums of all orders for a year can be calculated, broken down by purchasing organizations. After data selection, with or without aggregation, no further calculations are made, and the calculated dataset already corresponds to the selected one (see Fig. 4.1b). The data are just visualized, in tables, bar charts, etc. The goal is to display the data to the users as ergonomically as possible so that they can draw conclusions from it. In other words, the "calculation" takes place (apart from the data condensation) in the analyst's head. This is how static reports work. By way of contrast, in interactive reports (OLAP analysis; Sect. 4.2.3.5), the user can trigger further interactions (filtering, aggregating) with corresponding calculations while viewing the charts.

2. Analyze data statistically
   Data can be statistically analyzed, e.g., for correlations. The goal is to test hypotheses for dependencies or general patterns using statistical calculations. The statistical analysis corresponds to the calculation in the general model. The calculated amount of data corresponds to the statistical statement, which can have different content depending on the statistical method. In the simplest case, it is just a number, like the correlation coefficient, which in Fig. 4.1c corresponds to the "result value." Another example is a trend analysis for the sale of a product.

3. Data mining
   Data is analyzed, but there are no assumptions of dependencies between the data. The goal is to discover dependencies using data mining algorithms. These algorithms correspond to the calculation in the general model. Apart from that, the relationship with the general model is like with the statistical analysis.

4. Optimization methods
   Starting from a set of production-related data, among others, materials to be produced by certain delivery dates, an optimal production plan is calculated with a model of linear optimization. In general, methods from (numerical) mathematics or operations research are used for optimization. The goal is to determine the best possible plan, beyond a rough estimate. Ideally, all actual data (including machine utilization possibilities) are known, so the theoretically optimal plan is also practically optimal. With the optimization method, the calculation in the general model, we thus arrive at a production plan, the calculated dataset (see Sect. 4.5).

5. Forecasting methods
   From past sales figures, a sales plan for the future is calculated using a forecasting model (e.g., exponential smoothing). The goal is to extrapolate plans for the future from the past. There is uncertainty or a risk, because the actual future data,

e.g., number of sales orders, could differ greatly from the past. The calculation is the forecasting method, and the calculated dataset is the sales plan.

6. Machine learning

   In a common method of machine learning, learning models are trained from past data to determine their parameters. They are then applied to present data, and the statements derived for them are hopefully as accurate as the known ones from the training data (more on this in Sect. 4.3). The present data corresponds to the selected dataset, the learning model to the calculation, and in the simplest case, the result can simply be a decision or a decision proposal (see Fig. 4.1c).

It would be more precise to speak not of transactional and analytical *systems* but of transactional and analytical *functionality*. Because in every ERP system some analytics is integrated, e.g., some standard reports, enterprise information systems will often consist of a mixture of transactional and analytical functionality, with more emphasis on the one or the other. Therefore, it is legitimate to speak of a (predominantly) transactional or a (largely) analytical system. For the understanding of the systems, i.e., the purpose of the book, the distinction is useful in any case. There is a connection (interface) between transactional and analytical systems, because the data of the analytical systems are largely fed from the transactional systems. But we will see that there are also other data sources.

This chapter is organized as follows: In the rest of Sect. 4.1, we deal with aspects that are important for many methods of analytical functionality. The following sections describe several important analysis methods. The focus is on data warehouse systems, as they are the "classic" of analytical functionality and many considerations also apply to other methods. In recent years, other methods have come into the spotlight: machine learning, Big Data processing, and in-memory technology. We also want to gain an overview of these, in order to understand analytical functionality and its interaction with transactional functionality.

4.1.2 Differences Between Transactional and Analytical Systems

To illustrate the differences between transactional and analytical functionality more clearly and in more detail, we compare a pure transactional system with a separate, pure analytical system, here a data warehouse system.

Since the data is generated in the transactional systems, analyses could principally be carried out there. There are mainly three reasons for a separate analytical system in larger companies (We will later also look at in-memory systems, where the situation is different, see Sect. 4.2.5):

- Different system load behavior
- Analysis of data from different data sources
- Consideration of historical data

First, regarding the different system load behavior (see Fig. 4.2, similar to Egger et al. (2004, p. 26); the image is only qualitative; it was not created by

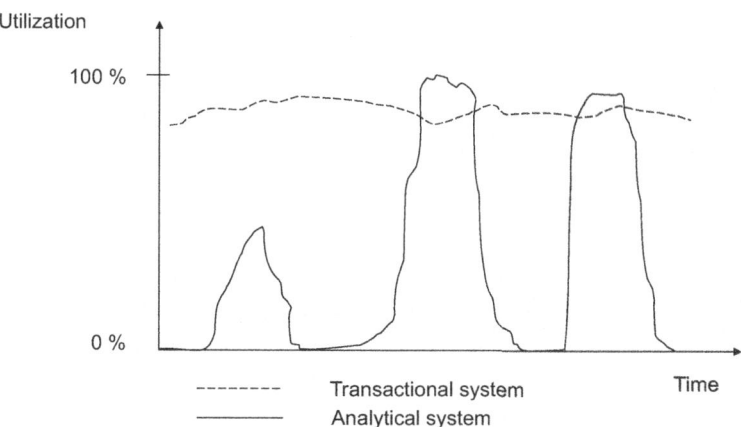

Fig. 4.2 System load: transactional vs. analytical systems (Egger et al. 2004, p. 26)

measurements). In transactional systems, the system load during core working hours is largely the same. This results from the fact that many clerks constantly handle many small business transactions with roughly equal load using dialog programs. In analytical systems, on the other hand, there is a low system load over long stretches, namely, when no analyses are being carried out and no data is being imported. When analyzing a large dataset, the system load is heavy. The system load profile is thus characterized by sporadic load peaks. If you operate both types of applications, transactional and analytical, intensively in *one* system, this could lead to performance problems: The analyses temporarily affect the daily business, i.e., poor system response times for the clerks, or the analyses would drag on. By separating into two systems, this is avoided. As a consequence, the analysis-relevant data of the transactional system is transferred to the analytical one.

As for the analysis of data from different data sources: In larger companies, often not only one transactional system is used but several, e.g., for different regions or specialized for different tasks (customer relationships, supply chain). We will look more closely at the reasons for this in Exercise 8.1. Whereas the business transactions can be handled well separately in the individual transactional systems, comparisons between the data of the different systems are also of interest. Analytical systems are used to carry out such cross-system comparisons in analyses (Fig. 4.3).

The figure shows two ERP systems (e.g., for different regions) and a CRM system (Customer Relationship Management). The CRM system manages customer relationships, e.g., customer contacts such as customer visits or phone calls. We will take a closer look at CRM systems in Chap. 8; for now, a rough idea is sufficient. In the analytical system, data from the different systems is merged. Thus not only the sales data of customers can be analyzed separately in the two ERP systems, but they can easily be compared. In addition, the number of customer contacts that were needed for sales can be related from the CRM system.

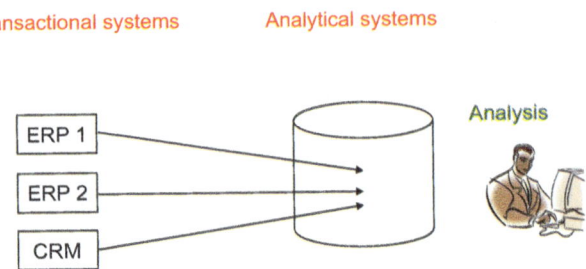

Fig. 4.3 Interaction of transactional systems and analytical system

Similar examples for the analysis across different databases arise in the case of company takeovers and during system migration (see Chap. 13; Zitzelsberger 2011). In general, there is the requirement to merge many data sources, from data stored in mainframes to typical enterprise information systems to locally stored spreadsheet data (Zitzelsberger 2011). In addition, external data sources can be added, e.g., market research data.

The third reason is the consideration of historical data: In transactional systems, often only the current data is efficiently stored. For analyses, however, one would like to compare "snapshots" at different times. Therefore, the data in the analytical system must be stored historically (see Sect. 3.3.1).

After the main reasons for the separation of the systems, we now look at the differences between transactional and analytical systems that are important for the design of analytical systems (see Table 4.1; it refers to Egger et al. 2004, p. 25).

The purpose of a transactional system is daily business; it primarily involves clerks, such as accountants, purchasers, and sellers. The analytical system, on the other hand, allows analysis for *decision support*. Analyses can be helpful for the different hierarchical levels of executives. Important areas for analysis are controlling, marketing, and supply chain management.

In transactional systems, data is often written (created, changed), e.g., sales orders or production orders. In analytical systems, once the data has entered the system, it is only read in analyses.[1] Accordingly, a system can be designed differently in terms of performance for mixed write/read behavior compared to read-only.

The transactions in transactional systems are "small" in the sense that they usually only access a small amount of data, e.g., in a purchase order in addition to the actual order data the master data material and supplier. Complex analyses in analytical systems, on the other hand, read large amounts of data, e.g., all orders in different business areas during a certain period, provided the order data is not already stored in a condensed form.

The applications in transactional systems are "stable" in the sense that, for example, the same functionality is always used to create an order. The business transaction is standardized, including the more or less frequently occurring special cases.

---

[1] There are exceptions, such as the "slowly changing dimensions"; see Sect. 4.2.3.4.

Table 4.1 Properties of transactional and analytical systems

Transactional system	Analytical system
Daily business	Analyses for decision support
Much writing access, optimized for this	After loading only reading access, optimized for this
Many small transactions	Complex queries
Stable applications	Dynamic applications for ever-changing analyses
Application-oriented (materials management, production, etc.)	Subject-oriented (supplier, customer, product, etc.)
Current state of the data	Historical data
Normalized data	Denormalized data, multidimensional

Simple forms of analysis are also provided, e.g., check for which purchase orders a goods receipt has already been posted. In analytical systems, there are certain regular standard analyses, e.g., a sales statistic for a period in a business area. The result of such an analysis is called a *report*, and the activity is called *reporting*. However, executives often want special analysis for questions not yet thought of, called "ad hoc analyses" (Vaisman and Zymányi 2022, p. 70). Analytical systems should provide means to easily fulfill such wishes.

The transactions of transactional systems are arranged in functional areas such as purchasing, production, and sales. In analytical systems, on the other hand, the structure is according to "subjects" (*subject orientation*; (Vaisman and Zymányi 2022, p. 63)), such as suppliers, customers, and products.

In many cases, the current value of data is sufficient for the application programs in transactional systems, e.g., the current stock level of a material. The level at an earlier point in time is usually not decisive for daily business and is therefore not directly stored. Instead, such values can often only be determined by recalculating goods movements, i.e., "reconstructed." On the other hand, in analytical systems, the change over time is of interest in order to uncover trends and for forecasting. An example is trends of order values over the months of a year. The data must therefore be efficiently analyzable with a time reference. Therefore, the data in analytical systems is stored *historically* (historization; see Sect. 3.3.1), e.g., the stock of material PC31 on 11/01/2025.[2]

The data of transactional systems is usually in a largely normalized form in relational database systems, i.e., free of redundancy. As we will see later, the data of analytical systems in the case of a data warehouse system is usually also in relational database systems, but the semantic data model differs: A multidimensional data model is used (see Sect. 4.2.3), which can be mapped to database tables. For storage, non-normalized representations are common to gain performance.

---

[2] In Plattner and Zeier (2011, p. 30), numbers from an analysis are mentioned: An enterprise information system for a medium-sized company contains 100 GB transactional data and 1 TB analytical data, one for a large company 35 TB transactional data and 40 TB analytical data.

Due to the separation of transactional and analytical systems, however, comprehensive analyses, which include both historical and current data, are no longer easily possible (see Sect. 4.2.5).

4.1.3 Characteristics of Analytical Functionality

In Sect. 4.1.1, we saw that analytical functionality can be multifaceted. To better understand the various facets, let's take a look at some different characteristics of analytical functionality and their systems. First, we look at some characteristics that only concern the data to be analyzed ("passive part"; items a to e) and then those that concern the design of the functionality ("active part"; items e to i); at item e, there is an overlap.

(a) **Volume**

How large is the dataset to be analyzed? It can be small (structured data in smaller companies) to medium (structured data in larger companies) to large (Big Data scenarios, usually also involving unstructured data; see Sect. 4.4).

(b) **Type of Data**

A rough division can be made into structured, semi-structured, and unstructured data (see Sect. 3.3.2). Semi-structured data has some attributes like structured data, but the main component is unstructured. An example is an email message. It has attributes in the message header such as the sender ("From") and the recipient ("To"). The main component is usually a text, often supplemented by attachments such as images. (Don't unstructured data also have attributes?)

A finer subdivision can be made according to storage forms, encodings, or media types: Database table contents, CSV data, texts, audio data, video data, and many more. (What type of data is an XML file? See Chap. 10.)

(c) **Time Reference**

While the data always comes from the past (when storing it, the present is over), the question arises, for which period statements shall be made? It can be the past, when past periods are described and compared with data from a long time ago, e.g., the sales figures of the last years. It can be the present, to describe the current state and to make statements for now or the short-term future, e.g., a production plan for the upcoming days. Or it can be the future, for example, to set up a sales plan for the coming year.

(d) **Data Sources**

Are the data from your own company or from external data sources, e.g., from market research companies?

(e) **Data Quality**

This includes aspects like consistency, availability, and uniformity, especially when data come from different data sources with different formats and different quality levels (see Sect. 4.2.2). What functions are available for data cleaning? When are these functions applied (data provision, analysis)? How much data cleaning and transformation is needed for an analysis?

(f) **Performance**

What is the performance of the analytical system (processors, memory)? Are the data stored on a magnetic disk SSD or in an in-memory database? How much parallelism do the processors allow? It influences data access time and the performance of the analyses. Different performance classes can be defined.

(g) **Integration into an Existing System or Dedicated System**

This property is related to the previous one, as with a dedicated system, a higher performance is usually sought. But there are also organizational reasons. Let's look at the situation.

We want to provide analytical functionality in addition to transactional functionality. The question arises whether we want to perform analyses directly in a transactional system or use an additional system, tailored to analyses. For smaller companies with low data volumes, the question will not arise. They also have only few data sources, perhaps only an ERP system. So, it makes sense to perform the analyses directly there. An ERP software that already contains the most important standard analyses will do.

As shown in Sect. 4.1.2, the situation for larger companies is different. Hence mainly for performance reasons (many data sources, large amounts of data, need for complex analyses), dedicated systems, especially data warehouse systems, are used. While in-memory systems promise to eliminate performance problems, the situation that a large company has many data sources remains—a large system landscape will not shrink to just one system in the medium term. In addition, of course, some analyses of transactional data can already be carried out in the transactional systems.

(h) **Purpose**

What is the purpose of the analysis? To understand a situation (retrospective), to predict, plan, or decide?

(i) **Method**

From a user's business perspective, the technical process visualized in Fig. 4.1a appears as follows: Abstractly speaking, the user is looking for an answer to a question that should result from a set of stored data using an analysis method. The analysis method determines the selection and the calculation. The calculated data and its interpretation by the user are the answers. The question can be concrete and have a clear answer, such as "Who were the top ten customers last month?" The answer is the list of customers along with their sales figures, represented, e.g., in a bar chart. Another likewise concrete question, albeit with an uncertain answer, is: "Which customers are at high risk of leaving in the coming fiscal year?" A less specific question is: "What purchasing patterns are there in our online store?"

As we have already seen in the introductory Sect. 4.1.1, there are quite different analysis methods. The following classification shows the spectrum:

1. Calculation with correct result: An example is mathematical optimization, e.g., linear optimization. Both the dataset to be analyzed and the optimization criterion are defined. Mathematically, this determines the result, i.e., the solution set. The result may be unique, or there may be multiple results or none at all, if con-

ditions cannot be met. The correctness is guaranteed by the mathematical model. But the user will have to check the validity of the model for the specific real system.

2. Heuristics with approximate result: The case is similar to 1 (the solution set is defined at the time of calculation), but no suitable calculation method is known for the question, or it is too computationally intensive. Therefore, one is satisfied with a calculation method with acceptable computational performance and an approximate, albeit not necessarily the optimal result. An example is the distribution of costs between cost centers, where a relatively fair distribution will suffice.

3. Heuristics with a "good" result: The case is similar to 2, but this time, it is not known whether there is a "correct" result (e.g., an optimal value) or it is uncertain. An example is a forecasting method that calculates a sales plan for the future from past data. The actual sales will only be seen in the future. And what the optimal sales plan would have been may not even be apparent by then. Many methods fall into this category: in addition to forecasting methods, also statistical regression analyses, machine learning methods, and data mining. The view can be directed toward the future (forecasting methods) or the present and past (e.g., in classification; see Sect. 4.3.2). In some cases, the quality will only be judged by a human, e.g., was the right person recognized in a picture?

4. Interactive analysis: While the previous methods always meant background processing, without human involvement in the "calculation," the calculation can sometimes also be performed by a human. An example is (visual) OLAP analysis (see Sects. 4.1.1 and 4.2.3.5). A user navigates through the data, and he thinks ("calculates") and arrives at a result. Some steps could be supported by methods of types 1 to 3.

The methods have the following properties:

- Quality: How certain is it that the answer is correct (confidence)? How accurate is the answer?
- Traceability: This could also be seen as an aspect of quality. With some methods, especially in machine learning, it can be difficult to understand how the solution was achieved. This issue is addressed in "explainable artificial intelligence."
- Complexity/Cost: Different methods with varying degrees of accuracy or certainty have different computational costs.

Therefore, in each case, it is necessary to check which method is appropriate for which situation.

An alternative classification is by the methods machine learning, statistics, mathematical optimization, interactive planning, etc.

4.1.4   The Basic Analytical Process

To perform an analysis, a few steps are executed—it is a small business process (What would be the classes of business objects used here?):

1. *Provide raw data*: The data may already be contained in the system where the analysis takes place, for example, an analysis of transactional data in an ERP system. However, in many cases, they come from different data sources and can be inconsistent and of varying quality. They can be provided, for example, for a data warehouse system (see Sect. 4.2) or in a "data lake" for Big Data systems (see Sect. 4.4).
2. *Clean/transform raw data*: If data are inconsistent, of poor quality, or not in uniform formats, they need to be cleaned or transformed before an analysis.
3. *Provide analysis data*: A subset of all data will be selected for a particular analysis. In some cases, some further transformation may be needed for efficient analysis. This transformation can be more or less complex. For example, some methods need data that are normalized to a certain numerical interval. If the data is needed for exactly one analysis, steps 2 and 3 can coincide.
4. *Perform analysis*: What is done here varies of course very much, depending on the analysis method.
5. *Use analysis result*: The same applies to this step. It could be a visual presentation to a user, but it could also mean an automated decision or providing a plan.

So, the general process needs to be adapted to the specific case. We will do this in the following section for data warehouse systems.

4.2 Data Warehouse Systems

4.2.1 Terms

(a) **Data Warehouse System**

In a *Data Warehouse System* (in this book, we use the abbreviation DWHS), structured data is analyzed, which was provided and merged from various data sources. There are various possibilities for the analysis:

- *Standard report*: A sales representative receives monthly sales figures or can retrieve them on the intranet. The standard report is pre-fabricated for the employees.
- *Interactive analysis*: An employee conducts interactive analyses. Some skills and training will be needed to do this job.
- *Special analysis*: Specialists search, for example, with data mining, for new insights.

DWHS are widely used analytical systems in companies. The term was coined by Bill Inmon (1993). The idea is a "warehouse of data" where the shelves are organized by subject areas. Specific technologies and techniques have been established for such systems. A DWHS includes in particular the data provision from the transactional systems, the data storage, and the subsequent analysis of the data (Bauer and Günzel 2013, p. 8). The term Enterprise Data Warehouse is related. It is used in several ways:

1. As a more specific term than data warehouse: In a company, different business areas may have smaller data warehouses. However, there will only be one global Enterprise Data Warehouse with all the company data.
2. Synonymous with data warehouse.
3. Synonymous with Core Data Warehouse (see Sect. 4.2.2).

Historical predecessors of data warehouse systems are *Management Information Systems (MIS)*, *Decision Support Systems (DSS)*, and *Executive Information Systems (EIS)*. All did not meet the expectations, partly for technical reasons but more because the functionality and system philosophy did not match the working methods and needs of the potential users (Egger et al. 2004, p. 27 ff.).

(b) **Online Analytical Processing (OLAP)**

This is the primary analysis method in the DWHS. OLAP is contrasted with *OLTP: Online Transaction Processing*, which is a transaction-oriented work in a transactional system (Chap. 3). A transactional system offers only simpler analysis on the transactional data of its database. With OLAP, a user performs interactive operations on a data cube (see Sect. 4.2.4).

(c) **Business Intelligence (BI)**

For many, this is synonymous with data warehouse systems. For others, it is an area that includes parts such as knowledge management in addition to the DWHS.

4.2.2 The ETL Process

ETL stands for *Extraction, Transformation, and Loading*. It describes the three phases of how data from data sources, mainly transactional systems, enter the DWHS. It is the adaption of the process described in Sect. 4.1.4 for data warehouse systems. In Fig. 4.4, in addition to the phases, the various components of data storage in a DWHS are shown.

The *extraction* takes place in each transactional system. Data is selected and made available for the further phases. The data are written into a workspace of the

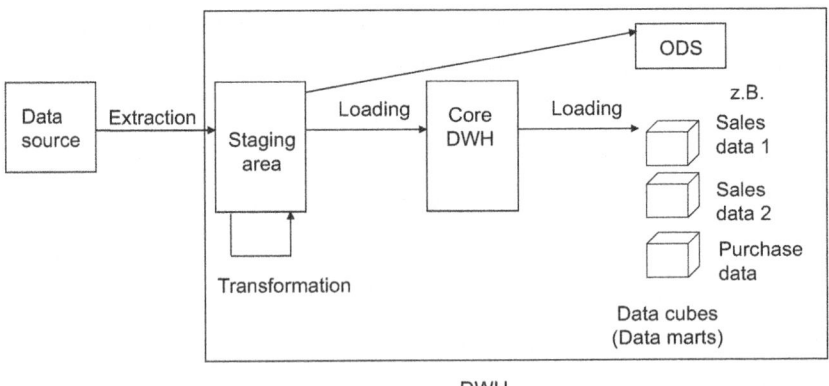

Fig. 4.4 Components of a DWHS and ETL

DWHS, called *staging area* (Vaisman and Zymányi 2022, p. 67). In fact, in Fig. 4.4, it says more generally *data source*. Because although the data mainly come from transactional systems, for example, market research data or planning data can also be used for comparisons.

In the *transformation*, the data from the various data sources are unified or cleaned.

The *loading* is the transfer of the cleaned data into the DWHS. In fact, the data is often stored in up to three different forms.

- *Enterprise Data Warehouse* (Vaisman and Zymányi 2022, p. 68): Here the data is stored in a fine-grained form, not intended for analyses. It is an integrated dataset for long-term storage. The terms *Core Data Warehouse* and simply *Data Warehouse* are also commonly used. The idea is to store more data than is currently needed for the analysis. At a later point in time, new requirements for the analysis may arise, e.g., that data should be analyzed in a more fine-grained way than they are currently stored in the data cubes (see below). If the required data is already in the Enterprise Data Warehouse, only the data cubes must to be adjusted and refilled from the Enterprise Data Warehouse. There is no need for a new ETL process, which might be difficult anyway with some historical data. The data are usually stored in largely normalized form, similar to transaction systems, thus avoiding redundancy.
- *Data cubes*: A data cube contains a subset of the enterprise data warehouse tailored to an analysis scenario. The data are stored in a form optimized for efficient analysis. The term *data mart* is sometimes used synonymously with data cube. It may also have the meaning of an excerpt of a data cube or of a data warehouse, for example, for a business area.[3] In the example, there are two data marts for two individual sales areas. In addition, there is a data mart for purchasing data. Data marts offer two advantages: faster data access due to the storage form and the smaller amounts of data. On the other hand, there are advantages with respect to access control. Disadvantages lie in the redundancy and higher administrative effort.
- *Operational Data Store* (*ODS*): In a common form of the ODS, these are fine-grained, non-condensed data, which only need to be available for a short time for analysis and are then deleted. A typical ODS example is supermarket point of sale data. Such ODS data is not historized, usually only stored for several days and regularly refreshed. Differences to the enterprise data warehouse are on the one hand that it is not the complete, integrated, and long-term view of the business data and, on the other hand, that the data is intended for analysis.[4]

So far, we have assumed that the data from the various transactional systems are copied into a consolidated Enterprise Data Warehouse and from there into data cubes, which integrate data from different systems. However, a form of *virtualization* can also be used: In the DWHS, initially, organizationally separate data cubes

---

[3] In Bauer and Günzel (2013, p. 62), the concept is called analysis database (for *Data Mart*). Mehrwald (2010, p. 313) generally calls the level of data cubes *Data Mart Layer*.

[4] For the exact relationship between ODS and Enterprise Data Warehouse as well as various classes of ODS data, see Bauer and Günzel (2013, p. 60 f.).

are set up, e.g., according to the regionally used transactional systems. Then the individual physical data cubes are integrated via a *virtual data cube* (Wolf and Yamada 2010, p. 174 ff.). This is a form of partitioning (see Sect. 4.2.4); in Mehrwald (2010, p. 161), it is called *model partitioning*. The ETL logic can thus run separately into the individual data cubes. This also achieves a certain fault tolerance: If one of the source systems is not available, the ETL process can still take place in the others. In addition, a decentralized analysis referring only to one of the organizational units can be carried out separately, leading to better performance.

(a) *Extraction*

We distinguish the following kinds of extraction:

- *Initial data import*: This is carried out once when the DWHS or a new data source is introduced. This initializes the DWHS. To do this efficiently, database systems provide so-called *bulk loader* programs (Bauer and Günzel 2013, p. 65).
- *Incremental data import*: This takes place regularly, transferring new and changed data, so-called deltas.

How are data changes recognized in the transactional system, in order to use them for incremental data import? There are several mechanisms for this, which vary in complexity. The most comfortable way is if the transactional system already provides the extraction logic (*extractors*, i.e., extraction programs). This is usually the case when the transactional system and the DWHS come from the same software vendor. The user then only needs to configure which data (e.g., sales data, possibly filtered by certain sales organizations) are transferred at what time intervals and with what granularity. In other words, the extraction logic is already part of the standard software of the transactional system. Only customizing is necessary.

The situation is more difficult if extractors in the transactional system must be developed. A good starting point is the change data mentioned in Sect. 3.3.1. If they are available, they can be evaluated for determining the deltas. Some other techniques for detecting changes (according to Egger et al. 2004, p. 40, and Bauer and Günzel 2013, p. 56):

- *SQL triggers*: This is an event-driven mechanism (see Sect. 10.5.3) in a database system. With an SQL trigger, you can define that a custom-written program is called each time a change operation takes place in a certain database table. The program can record the data changes in a modification table or in a file and regularly transfer these to the DWHS.
- *Log files*: In the transactional system, data changes are recorded in log files. The log files are evaluated, the data manipulation operations determined, and the data is then transferred to the DWHS accordingly.
- *Snapshot comparison*: The table content at two points in time is compared, and the differences are calculated: There exist some algorithms for doing this.

It is important to distinguish whether the changes are determined with database system support (this is possible with the three methods mentioned) or whether the application programs are modified or extended. The latter can be complex, especially if the program code is difficult to access. With database system support, for example, a snapshot can be defined like a view. Changes are logged in the snapshot log, which is then evaluated. The direct comparison of snapshots by application programs can be inefficient (Bauer and Günzel 2013, p. 93).

When should an extraction take place? There are various possibilities (Bauer and Günzel 2013, p. 94). The extraction can occur *periodically*. Different time-critical data can be transmitted at different periods: monthly, daily, or even more frequently. Periodic extraction is very often used. In addition, data can be transferred in an *event-driven* way, e.g., when a certain number of changes has occurred, or, in the extreme case, be *immediately* transmitted when a change occurs, but this is rarely used.

The extracted data can, for example, be provided in the form of files of a certain structure (see Sect. 10.2 for more details).

(b) *Transformation*

Identical data can exist in different forms in the various transactional systems. Some obvious examples (similar to Egger et al. 2004, p. 32):

1. Date: 01APR2025, 2025-04-01, 01042025, and 25091 (the 91st day of the year 2025) all describe the same date, April 1, 2025. They could, for example, be mapped to the target format 20250401 (year, month, day). This is simply a format transformation.

2. Gender: {m, w, d}, {male, female, diverse}, and {0, 1, 2} all represent the value set with the elements "male," "female," and "diverse." In the analytical system, the target format could, for example, be given by {m, f, d}. This transformation of values is called *recoding*.

3. Material number: In different transactional systems, this could be stored in the different data types `char(10)`, `num(12)`, and `integer`. `char(10)` is a string of length 10, and `num(12)` is a numeric string of length 12. We map them in the analytical system to "the least common multiple," here `char(12)`, assuming that only integers are actually used, which fit in `char(12)`.

4. Quantity unit: Instead of `double pack`, `p` and `pc` just `pc` is chosen (both p and pc stand for "piece"). This transformation rule also includes a conversion from double pack to pc.

In addition to cleaning up *syntactic problems* using format conversions, there are less obvious transformation rules. For example, if no value is recorded for a period—a *semantic problem*—depending on the use case, the rule "take the value of the previous period" (for stock data) or "value = 0" (for flow data) may be sensible (Baars and Kemper 2021, p. 28). Such an adjustment must be chosen deliberately such that analysis deliver correct results. Otherwise, it seems sensible to move the transformation into the data cubes (Zitzelsberger 2011).

Overall, this results in the following essential types of transformations (cf. Willinger and Gradl 2007, p. 48 ff.):

- *Transformation at value level*: The transformation refers only to a single value of the source and target structure. There are subtypes of this:
  - Transformation of values (recoding)
  - Format adjustment

– Assignment of a target structure field with a fixed value
- *Transformation at structure level*: The source structure differs not only at value level from the target structure. Rather, the target structure could, for example, be less or more nested than the source structure.

An important use case is the cleaning or unifying of addresses and, more generally, master data (cf. Sect. 8.3). A problem can arise for the key of business data. It can be different in the transactional systems, e.g., the customer number in the CRM system may not match that in the ERP system. In this case, the business data is stored with a key in the DWHS and the other keys as attributes, to not lose the reference.

Sometimes, the *automatic handling* is not possible or at least prone to errors (Baars and Kemper 2021, p. 29). Then the only option is to have the transformation performed by a human expert, which of course takes some effort. Examples of problems are *synonyms* (different words are used for one term) and *homonyms* (a word has a different meaning depending on the context). (What problems can arise here?) In such a *non-automatic handling*, the following cases can occur:
- *Automatic detection*: The exception is at least automatically detected, e.g., when a value is outside the defined value range. Maybe the value is already incorrect in the transactional system and should be corrected there too. Or a value is not anticipated in the transformation rules, so the transformation rule needs to be adjusted.
- *Non-automatic detection*: The exception is only recognized by an expert and will be corrected accordingly by him.

The transformation, i.e., a data cleanup (*data cleaning, data cleansing*), takes place in the staging area of the DWHS. There are a number of techniques and tools for this.

(c) *Loading*

The loading and the components used for storage are described further above.

4.2.3 Multidimensional Data Model

4.2.3.1 Data Cubes with Dimensions and Facts

In data modelling, it is usual to distinguish between semantic, logical, and physical data models. In traditional database systems, these roles are taken by the entity-relationship model, by relations, and by database system-specific physical models. The semantic data model in a DWHS, on the other hand, is usually *multidimensional*.

It is easy to illustrate it graphically in the case of two and three dimensions. Let's first look at the simpler case of two dimensions (Fig. 4.5).[5] In the example, we want to analyze how often a material was ordered in a period. We can visualize this in a

---

[5] The idea of illustration is taken from Snapp (2010, p. 65). Consistently, we also choose an example from purchasing here. We save the "classic" "sales data" for Exercise 4.2.

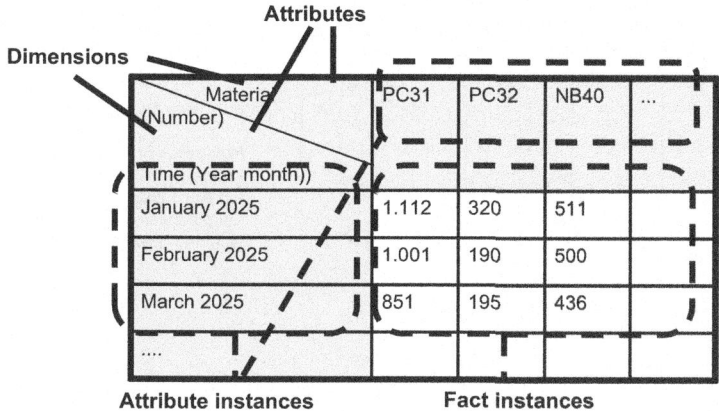

Fig. 4.5 Multidimensional data model: attributes and facts

table, well-known from spreadsheet programs. The two *dimensions* are the material and the time. Each dimension has characteristics, usually just called *attributes*. In the example, each dimension has only one attribute: The material has the material number, and the time has the month of a specific year. Later we will also look at multiple attributes per dimension. For each value combination of attributes (e.g., material = "PC31," time = "January 2051"), there is a numerical value, *fact*, also called *measure* or *key figure*, here 1112 (pieces). We assume that the data is only stored monthly, not daily. The attributes are thus the row and column labels, and the facts are the numerical values of the table. We could distinguish more precisely between *attribute* (like "year month," type level) and *attribute instance* (like "January 2025," instance level), likewise with facts.

Facts are *quantitative data*, measurable things, i.e., numbers. We are interested in these for the analysis, and we calculate with them. For example, we add up when we condense data (see below dimension hierarchies and aggregation).

The facts are organized according to the *dimensions*, which have descriptive meaning; they are *qualitative data*. We usually do not calculate with the dimensions. They are the criteria by which we want to analyze. (Can you tell from the data type whether data are facts or attributes?)

The data in the DWHS is almost always historized (see Sect. 3.3.1), i.e., time is one of the dimensions. There are only differences in granularity, i.e., how fine-grained the temporal resolution is. Often this is not monthly, as in our example, but daily.

If you want to distinguish more precisely, you could define a *key figure* as a fact or a number derived from facts (Marx Gomez et al. 2006, p. 13). Key figures can basically be calculated already when loading the data into the data cube or later during the analysis. In (Mehrwald 2010, p. 199 ff.), criteria for the decision are listed.

With three dimensions, we get a *data cube* (see Fig. 4.6). Strictly speaking, it is a cuboid, as the length ratios are open. As another dimension, we have added the purchasing organization.

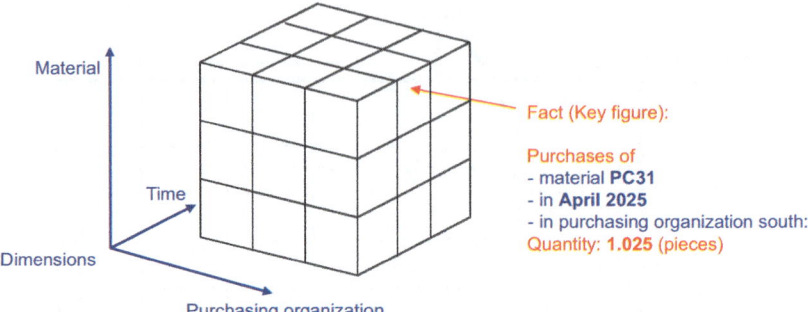

Fig. 4.6 Multidimensional data model: data cube

In fact, more than three dimensions are used in typical data models, but usually not too many, about five to eight. More than 15 would be unusual. Perhaps this limitation is due to the fact that it would otherwise be too complex for humans, or perhaps it is sufficient for practical questions (Baars and Kemper 2021, p. 112 f.). Even in the case of more than three dimensions, we call it a data cube.

4.2.3.2 Dimension Hierarchies and Aggregation

Unlike the typical x–y coordinates of school mathematics, usually *hierarchies* occur in the dimensions, and there is a corresponding *aggregation* of the facts. Let's look at an example (Fig. 4.7).

Often an analyst wants to analyze facts according to a coarser granularity than the most fine-grained, e.g., by material groups instead of materials or by months instead of days. This results in condensed, aggregated data. Several materials can be grouped into a material group, several material groups into a material area, and "all materials" together finally result in the coarsest condensation. We speak of a *dimension hierarchy*, also called *classification hierarchy* (Bauer and Günzel 2013, p. 119) or *aggregation hierarchy*. A subordinate entry is thus situated always under exactly one superior; the structure is a tree. The tree comprises several (*hierarchy, aggregation, condensation*) *levels*; they correspond to different degrees of condensation. Within a dimension, there can be more than one hierarchy, called *parallel dimension hierarchies* (Vaismana and Zymányi 2014, p. 99, where various hierarchy types are presented). In the example, the material could be assigned to a line of business, which is independent of material groups.

The hierarchy levels are additional attributes of a dimension. Whenever there is a functional dependency between attributes, e.g., the material group depends on the material, the attributes are usually put into the same dimension.

What happens to the facts when we aggregate multiple values of the cube? In our example, the individual order values should of course be added: The addition includes the order values of all those materials that belong to the same material group. So, if we go one hierarchy level higher in a dimension, the corresponding facts are aggregated, here added. Moving up in the hierarchy (an operation on attributes) results in an aggregation (an operation on facts). But addition is not in every

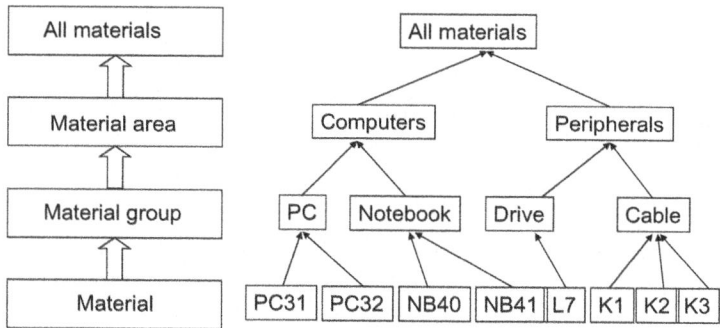

Fig. 4.7 Aggregation

case the appropriate aggregation operation. Think of a fact "average order value." In this case, computing the average of the order values would be the right operation. With any aggregation, it must therefore be specified which arithmetic operation is used for the facts. The standard aggregation functions in SQL92 are SUM, MIN, MAX, AVG (average), and COUNT. Other possibilities are the median, the standard deviation, "the N largest values," "the N smallest values," and "the N most frequent values." The functions have different algebraic properties (Plattner and Zeier 2011, p. 120). (Could different aggregation operations also be useful for a specific fact?)

So far, our assignment of attributes to dimensions was chosen for didactic reasons, i.e., for the sake of clarity. The dimensions were chosen independently of each other, and each dimension comprises related, dependent attributes. However, in practice, data cubes are constructed just for efficient analysis. Therefore, dimensions and the assignment of attributes to the dimensions are actually chosen for *technical* reasons, such as how many different values are there for an attribute; from a business perspective, only the set of attributes is fixed (Mehrwald 2010, p. 55; Wolf and Yamada 2010, p. 303). Mehrwald (2010, p. 190) states as a principle that the sum of the records of all dimensions should be as small as possible and gives an example of different divisions (Mehrwald 2010, p. 188). There are some rules on how to distribute attributes across dimensions for better performance. For example, in $N{:}M$ relationships of two attributes, distribution into different dimensions makes sense while in 1:N relationships, however, into the same dimension (Mehrwald 2010, p. 191). Unfortunately, results from theory show that automatically creating an optimal data cube is not an option. This is because this problem is as difficult as solving the travelling salesman problem: It is not provable to this day whether a solution is optimal (Mehrwald 2010, p. 192). While for the travelling salesman problem algorithms exist that at least produce "good" solutions, there are no comparable ones for data cube modeling today (Mehrwald 2010, p. 193).

4.2.3.3 Mapping to Relational Data Models

The multidimensional data model is a semantic data model. The question now is how it is mapped to a logical data model. One possibility is to use a database system that directly supports the multidimensional data model. This is called *MOLAP*

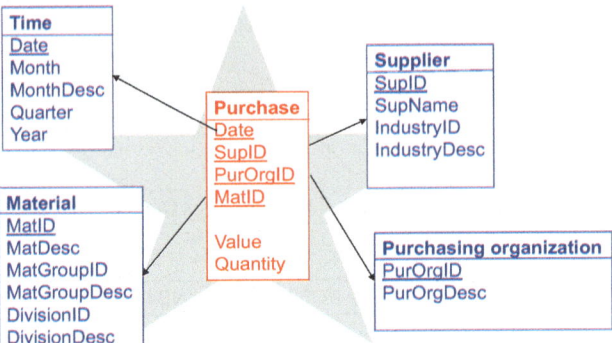

Fig. 4.8 Star schema

(*Multidimensional Online Analytical Processing*). More often, however, the multi-dimensional data model is mapped to a relational one: *ROLAP* (*Relational Online Analytical Processing*).[6] There are two pure forms for this, with many variants in between in practice:

• Star schema
• Snowflake schema

In both pure forms, the modeling of the facts is the same, and differences arise in the modeling of the dimensions, more precisely the dimension hierarchies (Bauer and Günzel 2013, p. 2 ff.).

(a) **Star Schema**

In the *star schema*, each dimension is assigned exactly one *dimension table* (Fig. 4.8). As primary key, the most fine-grained attribute could be chosen. So, if you want to be able to analyze on a daily basis, the primary key of the time dimension could be the date—if it should be monthly, the month of a year (e.g., 05_2025). However, *surrogate* (Neo-Latin, a substitute) keys are usually used for dimension tables, usually a four-byte integer. This will usually need less storage (Vaisman and Zymányi 2022, p. 110). According to Plattner and Zeier (2011, p. 180), the advantage of surrogate keys is less storage consumption in the fact table with only a slightly higher one in the dimension tables. In addition, joining the fact tables with the dimension tables, which is necessary for analysis, is simplified.

The more coarse-grain attributes for aggregation appear as non-key attributes. In the example, these are month, quarter, and year in the time dimension and material groups and divisions in the material dimension.

In the example, besides the attribute IDs, the corresponding designations (descriptions, texts) are stored in the dimension tables. For example, the mate-

---

[6]According to Bauer and Günzel (2013, p. 241), the terms ROLAP and MOLAP are misleading, as not only OLAP tools have to be used for analysis.

rial group ID 47 could have the designation "cable." These attributes are shown in the user interface of the analysis—a user usually does not want to see the technical ID 47 but the descriptive designation "cable." For simplicity, we assume that the designations are maintained in only one language.

We see that the dimension tables are not normalized (i.e., denormalized), i.e., they contain redundancies. This improves runtime performance (less joins), but it increases storage consumption.

At the center is the *fact table*. The composite primary key of the table is derived from the primary keys of the dimension tables. The non-key attributes are the facts. The fact table is normalized (Bauer and Günzel 2013, p. 246). (Why?)

Because different key figures are often analyzed according to different dimensions, there will be several stars next to each other, which is called a *galaxy* (Bauer and Günzel 2013, p. 248). If a dimension is relevant for different facts, it can be reused. If all dimensions match, these facts can be stored in the same fact table. Further down, we see that condensed data can be stored redundantly in aggregated fact tables to increase performance. A galaxy that also contains aggregates is called a *fact constellation schema* or just a *constellations schema* (Vaisman and Zymányi 2022, p. 108).

(b) **Snowflake Schema**

In the pure form of the *snowflake schema*, all dimension tables are normalized. We only deal with the simplest case; complex aspects such as time and language dependencies and performance issues are not considered here. In addition to the pure snowflake schema, there are mixtures between a normalized and denormalized representation.

A table is provided for each hierarchy level. The 1:N relationship between two hierarchy levels is represented by a foreign key relationship in the more fine-grained hierarchy level. In Fig. 4.9, for example, the "material" dimension contains the "material group" table, in which the material group designations are stored without redundancy. Multilingual designations can also be easily implemented with this approach. The snowflake schema requires more join operations than the denormalized representation of the star schema. This is more expensive in terms of performance, as it involves multiple reads from persistent storage (Plattner and Zeier 2011, p. 13).

(c) **Method for Setting Up a Snowflake or Star Schema**

With the following steps, we obtain a multidimensional data model for a simple scenario, implemented in a snowflake or a star. The method is illustrated using the purchase order scenario. This corresponds to the step-by-step construction of Figs. 4.8 and 4.9. For simplicity, we assume that the modeling is determined only by business aspects, not by performance.

1. *Clarify analysis possibilities*: A multidimensional data model is based on the desired analysis possibilities. We assume that these are known beforehand. If they change over time, this may require a different data cube. The problem can be solved with little effort if the enterprise data warehouse already contains the required data.

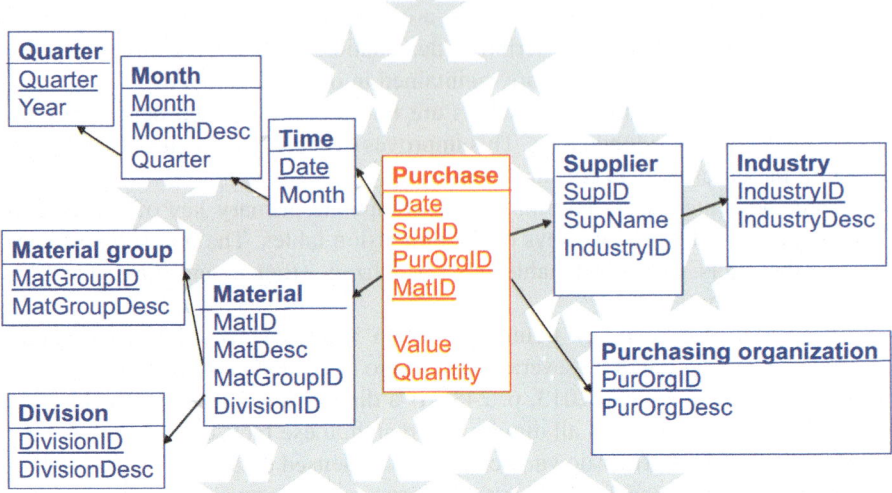

Fig. 4.9 Snowflake schema

In the example, we want to analyze purchase orders according to time, material, material group, division, supplier, industry, and purchasing organization. The analysis according to time shall be possible on a daily, monthly, quarterly, and annual basis. The condensation levels are therefore already fixed. We are interested in both the value (amount of money) and the quantity in the orders.

2. *Facts*: What numbers should be determined? Facts are quantitative data, i.e., numbers. If there are several numbers, it must be checked whether they should be analyzed under the same conditions, i.e., the same dimensions. For the fact or several of them, if they have the same dimensions, a fact table is modeled. The non-primary key field, the fact(s), is now known. The primary key fields are still open (see step 4).

   In the example, since we are interested in both the value and the quantity in the purchase orders, these two numbers are the facts.

3. *Dimensions*: The dimensions result from the desired analysis possibilities. The dimensions are independent of each other. For example, if we want to analyze materials and material groups, we do not need two separate dimensions, as the material group depends on the material. If, in addition to the materials, we want to analyze suppliers, these are independent dimensions, because a material could be procured from different suppliers. There are indeed relationships between materials and suppliers, but the supplier is generally not functionally dependent on the material. It should be noted that data with similar names sometimes do not belong to the same dimension. For example, if we have a creation date and a payment date, both are time related, but they are independent of each other.

In the example, the desired analysis options result in the independent dimensions time, material, supplier, and purchasing organization.

4. *Most fine-grained attribute*: For each dimension, it is necessary to check what the most fine-grained granularity is that should be analyzed. This could be chosen as the primary key of the dimension table in the star schema and in the snowflake schema as the primary key of the dimension table of the most fine-grained hierarchy level. In particular cases, several primary key fields for a dimension table can be combined. For example, the analysis should be based on the month of a year as the most fine-grained granularity. One option is a primary key field "month of the year," with values like 05_2025. A non-key field was then the month, e.g., 05, and another the year, e.g., 2025. An alternative approach would be to use two primary key fields "month," with value, e.g., 05, and "year," with value, e.g., 2025, resulting in fewer fields. Instead of the most fine-grained attribute, as mentioned, an artificial key is usually preferred, especially in the star schema.

   In the example, we choose the date for the time dimension, the material ID (MatID) for the material dimension, the supplier ID (SupID) for the supplier dimension, and the purchasing organization ID (PurOrgID) for the purchasing organization dimension.

5. *Dimension hierarchies*: Analysts generally also want to condense, aggregate values. The dimension hierarchies with hierarchy levels need to be determined. A "hierarchy" can also consist of just one higher level. In the star schema, each hierarchy level becomes a non-primary key field of the dimension table. In the snowflake schema, a separate table is used for each hierarchy level. The 1:N relationship between the more coarse-grained and the more fine-grained level is represented by foreign keys. It should be noted that there can be parallel dimension hierarchies.

   In the example, for the time, we have the dimension hierarchy day (date)-month-quarter-year. For the material, we have two parallel dimension hierarchies: one is material-material group, and the other is material-division, because the division is largely independent of the material group. For suppliers, we only have a simple hierarchy supplier-industry. The purchasing organization has no hierarchy. In the star schema, there is therefore exactly one table for each dimension. In the snowflake schema, there could be four tables for the time. But since the year has no attributes, there are only three tables. For the material, there are three tables, with a parallel dimension hierarchy. For the supplier, there are two tables, one for the hierarchy. For the purchasing organization, it is only one table because there is no hierarchy.

6. *Designations (Descriptions)*: The field values of the dimension attributes are so far only IDs. However, for analysis, meaningful designations should be available. For each ID, we need a corresponding designation as a non-primary key field. To simplify, we assume that the text only needs to be available in one language. While in the star schema all designations appear in the corresponding dimension table, in the snowflake schema, the designation is found in the table of the associated hierarchy level.

In the example, we have designations for almost all IDs, e.g., for the material. Only for the quarter and the year none is given, as they are self-explanatory.

For which dimensions a stronger normalization makes sense can depend on the following criteria (see Bauer and Günzel 2013, p. 247 f., where further criteria appear):

- The larger the number of hierarchy levels, the greater the redundancy in the star schema.
- If there are frequent changes in the dimensions (see below slowly changing dimensions), the snowflake schema is better, as the maintenance effort is lower.

4.2.3.4 Slowly Changing Dimensions

The individual facts are stored with a time reference and do not change anymore. However, attributes of the dimensions can change. Since this happens less frequently than write accesses to transaction data, the term *slowly changing dimensions* is used. Examples are name or address changes of business partners and product renaming, viz., master data changes. We look at some mechanisms to deal with this, and a more detailed presentation can be found in (Vaisman and Zymányi 2022, p. 124 ff.) or in (Baars and Kemper 2021, p. 67 ff.), which the following explanations are based on:

- Storage of only the current value: The attribute is not historized. This can be applied, for example, when the last name of a customer changes due to marriage. The "old" sales data are then shown using the new name, which will be adequate in this case.
- Snapshot historization: This is the opposite of the previous method. The dimension values are fully historized, i.e., just like the facts, even if no changes have occurred at individual points in time. Just looking at the storage consumption shows that this method should be avoided. It should only be used in exceptional cases.
- Delta historization: The idea is to store different time-related versions of an attribute only when its value has actually changed. There are several variants for this. The first one is key extensions: when the attribute changes, the new value is stored with a new key value with incremented version number (e.g., 3.01 is incremented to 3.02). This version number becomes a new key attribute, and the time of extraction is stored. In the fact table, the new dimension key is then used from this point in time. If you also store a "current" flag (1 = current, i.e., is the latest value; 0 = not current, applies to all old values), the current attribute value can be quickly determined without date comparison. If the time of extraction is too imprecise for analyses, a validity interval can instead be stored in the dimension records.

4.2.3.5 Operations on the Data Cube

OLAP operations on a data cube are:

- *Slicing*: Cut a "slice" of data records from the data cube. One of the dimensions is set to a fixed value (filter). Thus, the resulting sub-cube has one dimension less.
- *Dicing*: Setting filters, possibly for more than one dimension. However, no dimension is narrowed down to only one value (see slicing). A sub-cube is created. The number of dimensions remains the same.
- *Drill-down*: Display detailed information, e.g., instead of displaying the sum value for the whole year, which is an aggregated value, display the detailed monthly values.
- *Roll-up*: Reverse of Drill-down, i.e., going from detailed to aggregated.
- *Pivoting* (*Drill-across*): Swap dimensions; visually, this means rotating the cube.

4.2.4 Techniques for Performance Improvement

Various techniques for performance improvement are used in the DWHS.

(a) **Aggregates**

Suppose we have many materials, but the analysis is often only according to the material groups. Then performance can be increased if, in addition to the "purchase order" fact table, another fact table "purchase order by material groups" is created, which is updated in parallel to "purchase order." This table is called an *aggregate*. The difference in structure is only that instead of the material, the material group is a primary key field in both the material dimension table and the fact table. In the facts, the aggregated, condensed order values are updated. Advantage is faster access time, while the disadvantage is redundant data storage.

An aggregate is similar to a database view. However, not only the view definition is stored but the view instance. This is referred to as a *materialized view*.

(b) **Partitioning**

When database tables become very large, this can lead to poorer performance. One solution is to partition the data into different tables, usually according to value ranges of attributes (*range partitioning*). On the one hand, this allows for parallel reading from the partitions. On the other hand, depending on the query, access can be limited to only a few partitions of smaller size (Mehrwald 2010, p. 147). Partitioning can occur at the logical level or at the database level. If you want to use partitioning in a particular DWHS product, you need to check which restrictions exist, e.g., it might be possible only with certain attributes.

(c) **Clustering**

This is closely related to partitioning. There are s variants for this. In *index clustering*, data records that belong to the same database index value are stored adjacently. In single-column clustering, only one clustering index is possible per table. Multi-column clustering, on the other hand, is based on a combina-

Row		1	2	3	4	6	7
Industry	Car	0	0	0	0	1	1
	Airplane	0	0	1	1	0	0
	Mechanical engineering	1	1	0	0	0	0
Purchasing organization	North	1	1	0	1	0	1
	South	0	0	1	0	1	0

Fig. 4.10 Bitmap index

tion of several field values, e.g., month and sales value (Vaismana and Zymányi 2014, p. 45).

(d) *Caching*

Since the DWHS is usually only accessed in read mode, another obvious approach is to store query results in a cache memory of the DWHS.

(e) *Bitmap Indexes*

In addition to the usual treelike database indexes useful for fields with many possible values, *bitmap indexes* are used for fields with only a few values (Vaisman and Zymányi 2022, p. 247; Fig. 4.10). The value 1 indicates whether the attribute in a table row has the corresponding value. In the example, for table row 1, the attribute industry equals "Mechanical engineering," while the attribute purchasing organization equals "(Purchasing organization) North." It is also advantageous that these indexes allow to be compressed efficiently in database systems (Vaisman and Zymányi 2022, p. 271).

4.2.5 In-Memory Computing

In-Memory Computing (or *in-memory databases*) could be considered another technique for performance enhancement in analytical systems. But in fact, it is going much further; it is a new architectural principle for enterprise information systems. We will read more about it in the technology-focused Chap. 5 (Sect. 5.1.3.2). The basic idea is to store the complete (structured) company data in the main memory (RAM) instead of that on magnetic disks or SSDs that are common in database systems (Plattner and Zeier 2011). The separation between transactional and analytical systems, which is largely motivated by performance, could thus be abolished: only one system for both transactional and analytical purposes. (Which measures to increase performance become rather superfluous as a result?) This also allows analyses that include both historical and current data.

An in-memory database allows row or column storage of data records: While column-oriented databases (columnar databases) are generally more suitable for analytical systems and row-oriented databases are more suitable for transactional systems, a hybrid technique seems sensible for combined systems (Plattner and Zeier 2011, p. 81). The reason is that analytical systems access a large number of data records, but not all attributes are equally of interest in an analysis. (Do you have an example?) With transactional data, usually exactly one data record is processed, and all or many attributes are displayed, perhaps also changed. (Example?) The aim is automatic partitioning, which achieves the optimal mix. Plattner and Zeier (2011, p. 81) report a performance improvement of up to 400% compared to pure row- or column-oriented storage.

Another advantage offered by in-memory databases is parallel work with multi-core CPUs and multiprocessors: A multicore CPU has many computing cores on one chip. This is based on the observation in computer science that in the future, performance increases will no longer be achievable through higher clock rates, as limits are being reached, but through parallelization. Especially with the set-oriented language SQL, parallelism can often be effectively utilized.

With in-memory databases, aggregates need not be stored separately (saving storage) but can be efficiently calculated "on the fly" in main memory (Plattner and Zeier 2011, p. 164).

In my view, Plattner and Zeier (2011) do not sufficiently address another argument for analytical systems: the unification and integrated analysis of data from different sources. As a solution, views are suggested that bring together data from different in-memory database systems and thus allow a comprehensive analysis (Plattner and Zeier 2011, p. 184).

Many of the concepts presented for (disk-based) DWHS are equally relevant for analytical systems with in-memory databases, for example, the multidimensional data model (although not the same form of storage; see Sect. 4.2.6.2), the ETL process when multiple data sources are integrated, or the OLAP operations (Sect. 4.2.3.5).

4.2.6 Examples: SAP HANA, SAP BW/4HANA, and Pentaho

4.2.6.1 SAP HANA

SAP HANA was already mentioned as an in-memory database system in the section about the ERP system SAP S/4HANA (Sect. 3.7.1). In fact, SAP HANA is more than a database system. It can be used as a stand-alone application platform. Here we primarily consider the possibilities that SAP HANA (Bavaraju 2019) provides for data warehouse system analysis. In addition, there are many other aspects, even the development of complete application program with presentation and application logic is possible.

Analyses can be carried out in SAP HANA by modeling special views, so-called Calculation Views. Or they can be created by programming, especially with the HANA-specific language SQLScript. Modeling is an easily accessible but functionally limited way of creating analysis compared to programming.

The Calculation Views are actually views in the sense of database systems. That is, no new tables (as in the cubes of a data warehouse system) are created, but relationships between the existing database tables are defined, fields from those selected, and, if necessary, also new fields calculated from existing data. During analysis, the relationships are evaluated, and the calculations are carried out, which is sufficiently fast due to the in-memory technology: The idea is to store less (redundantly) and calculate more. There are views that resemble the star schema in a data warehouse system: A table with key figures is usually connected with dimensions, which generally represent master data. However, the data is not copied into data cubes (materialized) as in a conventional DWHS but only kept "virtually" as a view. For re-use, the dimensions are also represented by views. Views can be combined into a multi-level calculation process, which results in another hierarchical view. This is mainly used to combine key figures that are stored in different tables. With calculated fields, new fields can be calculated from existing table fields when the view is called at runtime. An important example is currency conversion: Amounts of money are not converted into different currencies when inserted into the tables but when executing the analysis. Views are modeled graphically ("drag-and-drop" technique).

SQLScript is an extension of SQL. It allows a combination of declarative and imperative programming, organized as stored procedures. In declarative programming, datasets are specified using SQL queries. Relationships between the datasets are defined, including variables, e.g., for (virtual) tables. Such datasets can then be further processed with the tools of imperative programming with the usual instruction types (assignment statements, conditions, loops).

Development, both modeling and programming, is done with the software development environment SAP HANA Studio, which is based on the development environment Eclipse, common in the Java environment, or with a Web-based development tool.

The database tables are almost exclusively stored in column-wise stored tables. The alternative is the row-wise storage, and mixtures (see Sect. 4.2.5) are currently not provided. They are stored in a compressed form, for which various techniques are used. One of them is dictionary compression, which is particularly suitable for character-like data. The distinct string values of an attribute that occur in the table are stored in a "dictionary vector." In the database table, only the row number of the vector is then stored in the corresponding table field.

There are interfaces to other SAP software, especially to applications in SAP's own programming language ABAP.

4.2.6.2 SAP BW/4HANA

Long before SAP HANA, the data warehouse system SAP Business Warehouse (SAP BW) has been available. Just as SAP HANA has a strong influence on the current ERP system SAP S/4HANA (see Sect. 3.7.1), so too on SAP BW/4HANA, the latest BW product (Lüdtke and Lüdtke 2020; Anane Adusei et al. 2018). In fact, many companies today do not use SAP HANA directly as a data warehouse system but some version of SAP BW (like SAP BW/4HANA) or carry out analysis directly in SAP S/4HANA (Anane Adusei et al. 2018, p. 265). SAP BW usually offers application objects that are "richer" from a business perspective than those of SAP

HANA (Anane Adusei et al. 2018, p. 187), plus "Business Content" (extractors, data model, example reports) (Anane Adusei et al. 2018, p. 335). We focus on the aspects of data modeling and business content.

(a) *Data Modeling*

The modeling objects have changed somewhat in SAP BW/4HANA compared to earlier SAP BW versions. For example, the main modeling object, the InfoCube, as a representation of a multidimensional data model, no longer exists. Instead, there are advanced Data Store Objects of several types and templates. For example, the template "Data Warehouse Layer-Data Mart" corresponds to a standard InfoCube (Anane Adusei et al. 2018, p. 218 ff.).

The characteristics (just called "attributes" above) of the dimensions and the key figures are modeled by *InfoObjects*, which already existed in earlier SAP-BW versions. Roughly, these are elementary data types. For example, "Material" and "Calendar Year" are InfoObjects of the type "Characteristic," and "Quantity" is an InfoObject of the type "Key Figure." In addition to the data type (such as "10-digit string" or "Currency field"), additional components can be specified for InfoObjects. For InfoObjects of the type "Characteristic," these are:

- Texts: You can create textual descriptions of different lengths (short, medium, long), which are language dependent. In analysis, users want to see such readable texts in their login language, as the attributes themselves are technical IDs.
- Hierarchies:[7] For aggregation, hierarchies can be defined, including parallel ones. In the hierarchy definition, the assignment of instances of a finer hierarchy level to the coarser one can be defined in SAP BW, but it can also be taken from the source system. Standard extractors from the ERP system, such as for cost centers or profit centers, fill the hierarchies.
- Attributes: Characteristics can have attributes (do not confuse them with the "attributes" mentioned above), i.e., dependent characteristics. In this way, master data is modelled. For an attribute, it can be determined whether it is only displayed or can be used for navigation in analysis like the characteristic of a dimension itself.

All these components can be defined as time dependent if necessary (see above slowly changing dimensions).

InfoObjects of the type "Key Figure" have additional components besides the data type:

- Currency/Quantity Unit: If it is clear that the key figure has always the same currency or quantity unit, this can be specified as a constant. Otherwise, a characteristic of the dimension "Unit" determines what the currency or quantity unit is.

---

[7] In addition to so-called external hierarchies, there are other ways to represent hierarchies, namely, via master data or dimension attributes. The advantages and disadvantages are described in Mehrwald (2010, p. 194 ff.).

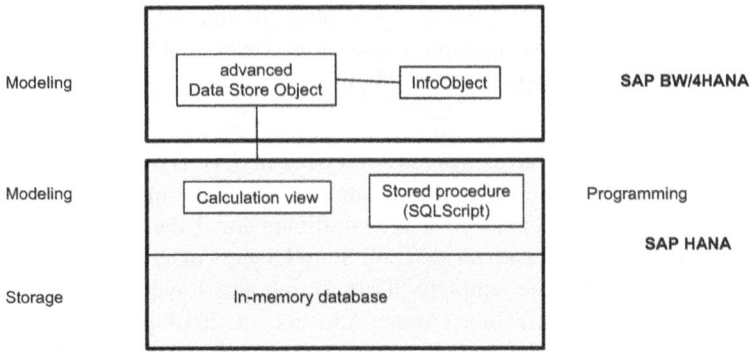

Fig. 4.11 SAP HANA and SAP BW/4HANA

- Aggregation: It is stored how the key figure is aggregated, that is, a standard aggregation and an exception aggregation can be specified. Possibilities are in particular "Sum" (the most common aggregation rule), "Average," "Count" (the number of values), and "Maximum/Minimum."
- Flow/Stock data: Associated with the aggregation is the indication of whether it is flow data (period-related data) or stock data (point-in-time data) (see Sect. 3.3.1).

A Calculation View in SAP HANA can be generated from an SAP BW object (Anane Adusei et al. 2018, p. 192). The relationship between SAP BW/4HANA and SAP HANA is shown in Fig. 4.11, where only the mentioned terms are shown.

(b) ***Business Content***

SAP Business Content provides predefined data models, extractors in the transactional SAP systems, and reports that can be used as templates. In practice, it turns out that especially the extractors of the Business Content are used, for which special plug-ins are provided in the SAP source systems. On the other hand, the data models for analysis are usually not used directly. The reason for this is probably that the companies' requirements vary very much and the data models have a major influence on performance. This may happen if data is put into the data cubes at a finer granularity than required or if time-dependent attributes are not required by the company.

4.2.6.3 Pentaho

Pentaho (Bouman and van Dongen 2009; Müller and Keller 2015) is probably the most well-known open-source business intelligence software. A while ago, it has been taken over by Hitachi. It originated from a series of open-source projects. It is developed in Java and can run on multiple platforms. In addition to the free "Community Version," there is an "Enterprise Edition" that contains additional features and offers maintenance support.

A functionally rich area is the "Data Integration" for the ETL process. Processes with transformation steps are defined graphically. There are 140 types of transformation steps, and you can also develop your own ones (Müller and Keller 2015, p. 90). Jobs are used to control the transformation processes.

There are both tools to create reports with little interaction possibilities (e.g. setting filters via parameters) and those for interactive OLAP analyses. Some tools are aimed at users, using "drag and drop"; others require deeper knowledge, sometimes programming or SQL knowledge. In dashboards, various analyses can be combined on one screen. Dashboards are an example where the difference between the Enterprise version and the Community version shows: In the Enterprise version, there are the Enterprise Dashboards, with which users can easily create dashboards. In the Community version, on the other hand, there are only the tools (also usable for the Enterprise version) that are aimed at developers; however, they can be used to design more complex dashboards (Müller and Keller 2015, p. 230).

A special feature is the integration with Big Data software (see Sect. 4.4, including Hadoop). Thus, Pentaho is a common platform for business intelligence and Big Data analysis. With Pentaho Data Integration, even MapReduce jobs can be designed that are executable on Hadoop clusters (Müller and Keller 2015, p. 117).

The data mining functionality is based on an open-source project from the University of Waikato in New Zealand. It includes, for example, methods for classification and clustering (see Sect. 4.3), and it allows scripts in the programming language R for statistical applications to be executed (Müller and Keller 2015, p. 134).

Information on Pentaho's authorization concept can be found in Sect. 16.3.3.

4.3   Data Science: Statistical Methods and Machine Learning

4.3.1   Concept

Data warehouse systems and business intelligence can be considered classics, so we now turn to newer topics. One of them is machine learning, a part of so-called Data Science. In recent years, this term has become popular for data analysis with statistical methods and especially methods of machine learning, a branch of artificial intelligence (Haneke et al. 2021). Even a job profile has been established, the data scientist, who should also have knowledge of computer science and the application domain, usually business.

Applying statistical methods has long played an important role in business, but machine learning also has a tradition: "Artificial intelligence" has existed since the mid-1950s. In the 1980s, it had a heyday, especially with rule-based expert systems. Also neural networks were already known. A neural network is a graph model, modeled after human connected neurons, which has parameters that are set to suitable values through training with training data ("learning"). After the training, the model is used for analytical calculations. Resuming our view on history, a quiet time followed for artificial intelligence, probably also because its promises were too high. Then, in recent years, especially machine learning (including Deep Learning) based on neural networks regained momentum. Successes are reported, and it remains to be seen what its potential is this time. For technology has changed: more powerful hardware, such as multi-core architectures and graphics cards, which are particularly suitable for matrix operations, as they typically occur in neural networks.

In Sect. 4.1.3, we saw that the analysis methods of this section belong to the category "heuristics for a 'good' solution." Depending on the task, it is necessary to select which analysis method is appropriate in view of quality requirements. According to Kauermann (2019), statistical methods and neural networks both have their advantages and areas of application: statistical methods for interpretation of what is present and neural networks as an "algorithmic black box" for recognizing "what comes next." The range of analysis methods is large—and methods from other areas should also be considered (see Sect. 4.1.3).

We also need to clarify whether a question can be answered from the existing data at all. Missing data may be a problem, such as temporal gaps in the captured data. In some cases, this is harmless, viz., if the missing data does not distort the situation, but just a smaller dataset is available. But in the case of "missing not at random," you might not be able to judge whether an analysis is valid. Even if not entire data records are missing but only certain crucial attributes, problems can arise. Both cases are discussed in (Kauermann 2019, p. 390).

As is usual in data analysis, all learning methods require data preparation and transformation. According to estimates, this can represent 80% of the effort of a project for machine learning (Trahasch and Felden 2021, p. 67). Here especially good programming skills are required (Riedhammer 2020).

4.3.2   Application of Learning Methods in Companies

Expectations of machine learning in information systems are:

- Better decisions, the main aspect of analytical functionality in general
- A stronger automation of applications (see Sect. 3.4.2)
- More usable software

Applications of machine learning are often found in classification, e.g. (Elsner et al. 2018, p. 138 ff.):

- A pre-evaluation of applicants for a position to support selecting applicants in human resources (comparing the candidates' characteristics with the requirements of the position).
- Service ticket classification: Classify a service ticket using text analysis, in order to route it to the responsible processor. Similarly, proposals for solution from a solution database can be found.

We want to take a closer look at another classification example, *predictive maintenance* (see (Huber 2021, p. 225 ff.) for the following). The aim of predictive maintenance is to prevent a decrease in production performance or product quality as well as machine failure. Unnecessary maintenance should be avoided, and the lifespan of the machines should be exhausted without accepting defects in the product quality. For this purpose, the machine condition is recorded, i.e., characteristics such as vibration, temperature, acoustics, images (captured via a camera), wear particles, or the condition of lubricants. The data is collected via sensors and transmitted to an analysis program (see Sect. 3.7.3). Classification methods then determine whether maintenance is necessary. The maintenance measures must then be carefully planned. On the one hand, they should be bundled; on the other hand, downtime and costs should be kept low. Even the scheduling is possible with analytical functionality, in this case mathematical optimization (see Sect. 4.5).

4.3.3 Integration with Enterprise Systems

We now have a basic understanding of machine learning and how it is applied in business. How do we integrate such applications with enterprise information systems? The following questions arise:

(a) **Who creates the applications?**
   - Vendors of standard business software: Applications of machine learning can be an integral part of standard business software.
   - The implementing company: It could also be an in-house development (see Chap. 15) by a company that uses an enterprise information system.
   - Software houses: As with other application software, software houses may offer additions to standard business software.
(b) **In which systems are they created and provided?**
   There are two approaches that may be combined (see (Braun 2021, p. 249)):
   - Integration into an enterprise system.
   - Function call (see Chap. 11) to a dedicated system for machine learning.
   In the first approach, a machine learning model becomes part of an enterprise information system, i.e., the functionality can be invoked like other algorithmic functionalities. This makes in particular sense if machine learning is closely integrated with the standard business logic.
   In the second case, an enterprise information system calls a model as a function or "service" in another system, which is dedicated to machine learning. For example, a service for image recognition could return a list of pairs of the type "label" (identification, e.g., "Material 17")—probability (e.g., 97%). Reasons for integration via a function call can be technical or organizational:
   - The second system is better suited for machine learning, an argument we have already seen similarly in Sect. 4.1.2.
   - A stable standard enterprise information system is organizationally separated from a more experimental and innovative system with company-specific extensions and new developments (see Chap. 15), such as machine learning.
   In both cases, it may be worth considering not to start a fresh call of the model (prediction) in any case but to use pre-calculated results. Thus, long waiting times in the user dialogs can be avoided. Braun (2021, p. 250) proposes this for

recommender systems in online retail. It is similar to aggregates in data warehouse systems (see Sect. 4.2.4).

(c) **How is the functionality developed?**

A system for machine learning can provide the following:

- A software development environment for creating new machine learning
  models, which is company-specific in-house development (Chap. 14), e.g.,
  Jupyter Notebooks (2024) and the open-source libraries TensorFlow (2024)
  and PyTorch (2024), often used for neural networks.
- Already trained models (built-in standard functionality).
- Retraining already trained models.

We will look at an example with both variants of item (b), integration and function call.

4.3.4   Example: Machine Learning in SAP S/4HANA and SAP Leonardo

In SAP software, there is on the one hand an integration of machine learning functionality into the system SAP S/4HANA (cf. Sect. 3.7.1). On the other hand, the
cloud software SAP Leonardo is available for innovative applications, including
machine learning. The functionality of the cloud software can be used in other systems via function call (via the SAP Cloud Connector).

In the SAP S/4HANA, there are some applications that use machine learning,
such as:

1. Digital Assistant: In SAP S/4HANA, the digital assistant SAP CoPilot is used,
   similar to the digital assistants from Apple (Siri) and Amazon (Alexa): It communicates in natural language with the user to support him and uses machine
   learning. It knows the context in which the user is working, e.g., the business
   object currently being processed on the screen (Elsner et al. 2018, p. 136).
2. Semi-automatic matching of customer payments: Customer payments are
   assigned to invoices based on previous data. More precisely, a probability is
   determined which invoice(s) may be relevant, and a suggestion is made to the
   clerk. The benefit is particularly evident in payments that cannot be assigned
   from the outset, such as when no purpose is entered for the payment (Elsner
   et al. 2018, p. 140 f.).

Machine learning support is also found in SAP Leonardo, SAP's "digital innovation
platform," which includes technology for other current topics such as the Internet of
Things, blockchain, and Big Data. Functionality is available on different levels,
comparable to components, assemblies, and end products: "functional services,"
"business services," and applications (Elsner et al. 2018, p. 73). Both built-in models in SAP Leonardo can be used, and new models can be implemented. An example
of a "business service" is the pre-selection of applicants: It checks how well an
applicant fits a job posting. Resume matching algorithms are used, which are based
on previous applicant data and job postings (Elsner et al. 2018, p. 140). A list of
candidates is determined, which is presented to the HR representative.

4.4 Big Data

4.4.1 Concept

Most of the data in data warehouses come from the company's transactional systems. Hence, the quality of the data will usually be quite good. Any deficiencies in the recording quality and differences between different data sources are eliminated during the "T" of the ETL process. Primarily, these are structured data and master and transaction data, specifically recorded for data processing in the company.

Today, however, much larger amounts of data are being generated by the increasing spread of information technology in many areas of life, often referred to as "digitization." A lot of data are generated that are not intended by the data generators for analysis: texts and administrative data from emails; similarly data in social media, Twitter, and Internet blogs; data in search engines (today especially one); data that reflect the navigation behavior of people on Web sites; data generated by mobile phones, including conversation partners, durations, and perhaps even the content of the conversation, as well as the current location of the owner (GPS data); and images from surveillance cameras. Other data are intended for analysis, but are not entered by humans but are automatically generated by "things," namely, sensor data, transmitted via the Internet of Things (see Sect. 3.6.3), or RFID data. Not all data have the same accessibility; many are initially stored by only a few providers (Internet corporations, telecommunications companies). While business transactions were the focus of data warehouses, here, it is the events of "digitized" social and economic life and the "digitized" actions and states of things.

At least theoretically, we can imagine the large amount of data that results from all of the sources mentioned above. Let's call it the "world data volume." We add to this the comparatively small amount of all structured data that we already know how to analyze. The large amount of data can be seen as a digital image of reality. In contrast to the system-model relationship, the image (corresponding to the model) is not consciously and methodically designed. The semantics of the data (let us, for a start, take the database schema as the semantics of structured data) is not explicit or at least does not have the same quality as for structured data. The data is not "complete"—not all statements and opinions will appear on social media, and not every movement is captured. Data can be contradictory or "false" (think of deliberate false ("fake") reports on the Internet). In other words, the data quality varies, and the effort of analyzing the different kinds of data and the results vary very much (as in the case of video data). And the amount of data evolves: New data is constantly being added, while existing ones are hardly changed.

We have gotten a bit general now. Our focus is on enterprise information systems. What do these have to do with the "world data volume?" Companies, but not only these, are at least interested in parts of the world data volume, selected according to the company's benefit. It is obvious that some data will have a greater significance (or any significance at all) for a company. And a selection is already given for reasons of processability and the accessibility of the data. But since it is not known which insights can be drawn from the data and, thus, which is the precise amount of data needed for the purpose, the desire prevails to collect as much data as possible.

The term "Big Data" is used for the analysis of large amounts of data of different types and origins, sometimes in legally and ethically problematic ways (see below). Conventional techniques of data analysis are no longer sufficient, and new techniques and technology are required (Meier and Kaufmann 2023). It is not a closed dataset; rather, new data is constantly being added. The dataset contains structured, semi-structured, and unstructured data. Some data, from the Internet of Things, come in more or less regular data streams, often requiring fast processing, almost in real time ("streaming").

Legal regulations (e.g., the right to informational self-determination and the European Union General Data Protection Regulation) impose the principle of data minimization, which is in conflict with Big Data collections. In particular, the purpose of data recording must be clear at the start (Kayser and Zubovic 2021, p. 179). Conflicts with data protection law can already arise during the creation of prototypes, where it is first tested which insights can be derived and for which purpose the data is used accordingly (ibid., p. 184). In research, the field of "privacy preserving data mining" deals with the anonymization of data (ibid., p. 181). Also, a certain minimum number of cases should make it difficult to draw conclusions about individuals.

"Big Data" is therefore often associated with surveillance and commercial use of all available (potential) customer data in marketing and sales. Besides these rather negatively perceived purposes, others also play a role, e.g., in medicine, the data analysis for diagnostics, or fraud detection in financial transactions. We see that data protection and, more generally, ethics are particularly important here.

4.4.2 Architecture

4.4.2.1 Overview

As business is not the only application domain of Big Data systems, their architecture is more general (see Fig. 4.12).

Similar to data warehouse systems, data is collected from a variety of data sources and stored in a so-called data lake. However, unlike in data warehouse systems, the data is stored just in raw form, and the transformation ("T") takes place afterward. The idea is to provide data quickly. Transformations can be made depending on the type of analysis (Freiknecht and Papp 2018, p. 19). However, it is also possible to provide preprocessed data in a data lake, which offers quality and

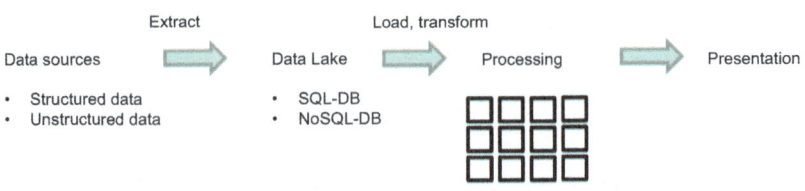

Fig. 4.12 Big data system architecture

performance advantages. Therefore, data referring to the same content can be stored redundantly with different levels of preprocessing in a data lake.

As described, the data can be structured and unstructured. For the structured data, relational database systems are common, as with data warehouse systems. For unstructured data, new storage forms have emerged, NoSQL databases, which we will discuss further below.

Regarding the processing, Fig. 4.12 indicates that it takes place on computer clusters to provide the required performance.

Platforms have been developed for storage and processing that can be used for various purposes. In many cases, this is open-source software. Several platforms are described in (Freiknecht and Papp 2018). Their development is quite fast-paced and heterogeneous: Constantly, there is further development going on, there are a number of software products for similar purposes, the products can often be combined with each other, and extensions and add-ons are offered in the "ecosystems" of the products. In addition to pure open-source software, there are also service-enhanced commercial products. Products can quickly become outdated, so newer products will be preferred. Different versions may use different methods. This results in a big effort for their operation and maintenance. Accordingly, there has been a recent trend toward cloud offerings (see Sect. 6.1). Cloud providers are both the aforementioned service providers and companies that already offer other cloud products and are now expanding their offerings to include Big Data functionality.

Next, we will take a closer look at data storage for implementing a data lake. Then we will discuss data processing.

4.4.2.2 Data Storage with NoSQL Databases

While conventional database systems using the SQL language have their advantages for structured data, Big Data often utilizes NoSQL database systems ("not only SQL") (Meier and Kaufmann 2019, p. 16). They are particularly well suited to the characteristic of frequently adding data but rarely changing them. In addition, they do not have a fixed schema for the data records, only an implicit one. In this way, different data records for a data type can have different attributes. More precisely, the schema is not defined at definition time, but only at runtime, called "schema on read" in Kleppmann (2017, p. 39). It is similar to the distinction between static and dynamic typing in programming languages, with corresponding advantages and disadvantages.

There are document-oriented databases, graph databases, and key-value databases. Interestingly, many of the ideas behind these can be found in early data models that were in use before the relational model: the hierarchical data model (as in IBM's IMS database system), similar to the model of document-oriented databases, and the network data model (promoted by the CODASYL organization), similar to graph databases (see (Kleppmann 2017, p. 38 and p. 60)).

Document-oriented databases like MongoDB or Apache CouchDB are particularly suitable for semi-structured data. Data is stored as hierarchies, i.e., trees: 1:N relationships are stored in the parent data record, not in separate data records. This provides a high degree of locality, unlike the relational model, where related data is in separate tables linked by foreign keys. Accordingly, access is fast when all parts of a data record need to be accessed. N:1 and N:M relationships are mapped similarly to relational databases—instead of foreign keys, there are document references. Documents are usually stored as strings, encoded in XML, JSON, or a binary variant (Kleppmann 2017, p. 41). Current relational database systems usually also support XML or JSON, so a certain convergence can be observed (see (Kleppmann 2017, p. 41)). We will get a good impression of the granularity of such datasets when we look at the XML and JSON formats in Chap. 10. Business data, according to our model from Chap. 3, is thus mapped to a data record, a document.

Graph databases like Neo4j or ArangoDB excel at mapping relationships between data. We saw in Chap. 3 that business data in transactional systems often has a lot of relationships to other business data. In addition to hierarchical relationships (1:N, conversely N:1), there are often also N:M relationships, which are represented more naturally in a graph model than via foreign key relationships or similar mechanisms and can be handled more easily than in document databases.

Key-value databases like Apache Cassandra or Google's Big Table store data as pairs of a key and a value, the actual data. There are in-memory and persistence-based variants.

4.4.2.3 Processing

Large computer clusters are used for data processing to provide the necessary high computing power. Analyses can also use methods of data science (see Sect. 4.3), and the fields are interrelated.

The rapid evolution of Big Data technologies is unfavorable for a textbook that is supposed to last for some time. For this reason, we will look at the "classic" in this area, Hadoop (Sect. 4.4.3.1), and a currently popular framework, Spark (Sect. 4.4.3.2). They are related to each other, as Spark can be used on a Hadoop cluster.

For processing, the so-called Lambda architecture (Marz and Warren 2015) is suggested if both batch processing and streaming processing are needed for incoming data. In batch processing, data is stored persistently, fail-safety is important, and processing is rather slow. Aggregation processes run periodically and can take hours, and the results are provided to the serving layer, responsible for returning the data, in a key-value store (Freiknecht and Papp, 2018, p. 461). The speed layer serves for immediate, fast, and continuous processing of data streams, especially from the Internet of Things and social media. Users communicate with the system via the serving layer, which uses the services of the other two layers.

The remarks from above on cloud computing apply here in particular. Thus, the software described below can be offered as a cloud product. Parts of the software can be integrated into other cloud products.

4.4.3 Examples

4.4.3.1 Apache Hadoop

Since the early days of Big Data processing, Apache Hadoop has been known, a Java-based open-source software. It uses Google's MapReduce algorithm and now also directed-acyclic-graph methods. A special file system is used.

The software runs on computer clusters and can be scaled accordingly. Depending on the performance requirements, a system can scale from a few nodes to thousands. The nodes are computers, but also virtualization may be utilized. Normal hardware is used, not necessarily supercomputers and multiprocessors.

The MapReduce algorithm uses the "divide and conquer" principle: A dataset to be analyzed is broken down into fragments in the first phase ("divide"), each of which is assigned to a similar "Map Task." The intermediate results of the Map Tasks are calculated in the second phase to the result ("conquer"). Accordingly, developing an analysis consists in breaking it down into suitable, parallely executable Map tasks and implementing the analysis-specific Map and Reduce functionality. According to the MapReduce programming model, the developer has to implement three methods: A Map method, a Reduce method, and a third method that runs a MapReduce job and provides the information that Map and Reduce method are used.

The data to be analyzed is provided as a file. Files are the norm, but other input and output options are available (Freiknecht and Papp 2018, p. 116). Larger files are broken down into different parts ("splits") and assigned to individual nodes for parallel processing (Freiknecht and Papp 2018, p. 116). Map and Reduce steps use lists of key-value pairs as data structures. In a job, after the input (for which the input data format has to be specified), the Map phase takes place, which generates a key-value list. In an internal step, the Combine phase merges data with the same key. The Reduce phase is then carried out multiple times, namely, once for each key, where the data stored for that key is "reduced." An introductory example can be found in (Freiknecht and Papp 2018, p. 46 ff.). From a set of grade reports for students, the year (key) and the grade (value) are extracted; in the Reduce step, the average grade is calculated from all grades for 1 year (key).

With this programming model, a developer is limited to problems whose solution can be (easily) expressed in Map and Reduce steps. A certain flexibility exists in running several different Map-Reduce jobs as a pipeline. The output of one job is the input for the next (Freiknecht and Papp 2018, p. 99 ff.). Not only sequential execution is possible. With the help of various frameworks, diverse control flows can be represented (Freiknecht and Papp 2018, p. 114), so in our parlance, Map-Reduce background business processes. The greatest flexibility arises when the YARN (Yet Another Resource Navigator) middleware is used (Freiknecht and Papp 2018, p. 130 ff.). Here, one is not limited to the Map-Reduce programming model but can provide any processing logic. However, the resource usage also has to be programmed, so the development effort will exceed that of the Map-Reduce model. It can be observed that the design of resource usage will be similar in many cases. So there seems to be potential for a solution by configuration, and the programming effort, as is usual with standard software, could be limited to the necessary.

4.4.3.2 Spark

In Hadoop, only the Map-Reduce method is directly supported as a programming model, while for others, additional programming effort is needed. In contrast, Apache Spark is a framework for many forms of processing, a so-called "General Purpose Processing Engine": Batch and streaming processing, machine learning, and SQL-like access logic, all in one framework. This was new at the time of its creation in the field of fragmented Big Data software (Freiknecht and Papp 2018, p. 462). It is realized as a program library that encapsulates the different processing forms. Spark can run on a Hadoop cluster, but other forms of deployment are also possible. Spark offers interfaces for that, up to independent execution on a Spark cluster. Diversity is thus offered both in the software on which Spark can be based and in the functionality that it offers.

In Spark, more complex processing is defined as a pipeline, consisting of "transformations" (mappings, filters) and "actions" (results are made persistent or returned to the client). A pipeline is a process that can be represented as a directed acyclic graph, i.e., there are no steps back. For Big Data processing, pipelines are often sufficient. For the most efficient execution of such a process, intermediate results of the steps are passed on in the main memory, and there is a cost-based optimizer.

The diversity continues with the usable programming languages: Programs can be written for Spark in various programming languages: Python, Java, Scala, and R (Freiknecht and Papp, 2018, p. 467).

For Spark, there is an extensive "ecosystem," with APIs among others for machine learning and SparkSQL for data querying. With SparkSQL, large amounts of data are searched as a whole, and performance is mainly achieved through parallel work in the cluster and in-memory computing. Unlike conventional relational database systems, no indexing system is used.

4.5   Planning

Planning functionality can be integrated into transactional systems in the same way as analysis/reporting functionality. Or dedicated *planning systems* can provide it. Long-, medium- and short-term plans can be created, such as sales or production plans. These plans can then be executed by the transactional systems, especially ERP systems. There are different ways of planning:

- *Data entry*: The planner enters the plan data at his discretion.
- *Extrapolation*: The plan data is extrapolated from past data.
- *Optimization*: Plan data is calculated from past and current data using mathematical optimization methods or heuristics.
- *Combinations* of the previous methods.

Supply Chain Management Systems (SCM systems) are an important form of planning systems, which offer all of the mentioned planning possibilities. Therefore, we want to study SCM systems in more detail as an example. Some SCM functions, like certain optimization methods, require such computing power that they are not practically executable in ERP systems and therefore are not provided. Or they are at least not suitable for larger problems, like many resources or production orders.

The vision of supply chain management is to optimize the entire supply chain, from raw material producers to manufacturers of components, assemblies, and semi-finished products, the manufacturer of the finished product, through wholesalers, retailers, to the end customer. In Exercise 4.5, we consider what obstacles arise in this comprehensive view. In practical cases, planning therefore largely refers to a single company or two companies in successive stages in a supply chain.

The SCM system is only responsible for *planning*, so a better name would be "supply chain planning system." The term *Advanced Planning System*[8] is used too. Planning needs, among other things, master data (like materials, suppliers, customers, production sites, warehouses) and transaction data (e.g., stock data) of the ERP system. The plans can then be handed over to an ERP system and executed there, possibly with some modifications (see Sect. 8.3 for a system landscape with an SCM system).

According to the above SCM vision, one might naively think that an SCM system automatically generates an optimal plan (e.g., a production plan) at the push of a button based on given input data (e.g., customer orders). If a new customer order was added, this could trigger a replanning into a changed, again optimal production plan. And due to cross-company cooperation, the planning could be based on already quite precisely determined sales and delivery data of the business partners. However, it is sobering to note that although there are functions of automatic planning, in practice, one is far from comprehensive fully automatic planning. So SCM systems offer improvements in planning compared to ERP systems, but automation only exists in parts. Planning functions are actually present in the following way:

- *Interactive planning*: The planner interactively creates a "good" plan, not necessarily the optimal one. For example, during capacity planning, he graphically sees the utilization of resources over time. He can now look for gaps where he can best schedule an operation. He can move operations, which then triggers the planning system to move adjacent operations. Analytical functionality therefore mainly consists of visualizing a set of data and some calculations.
- *Automatic planning*: *Optimization programs* are used, as we know them from operations research, e.g., linear optimization methods. For many optimization problems that occur in practice, the exact optimal solution is not achievable, either because there is no method for it in principle or because the search for the optimal solution would be too computationally intensive. Therefore, one usually settles for *heuristic methods*, like the *constraint propagation programming* (a search method in which found partial solutions narrow down the search space) or *genetic algorithms* (a stochastic search method) (Balla and Layer 2010, p. 267). Due to the use of more complex calculations, analytical functionality is thus more involved than in interactive planning.
- Often there are combinations of interactive and automatic methods.

---

[8] Snapp (2010, p. 32) distinguishes between *Advanced Planning* and *Supply Chain Planning*, with the latter standing for the execution of the logistics chain in an ERP system. The word "planning" is, just like with Enterprise Resource Planning, therefore context dependent.

At first glance, optimization methods may seem to be the preferred approach as they promise the optimal solution. In practice, however, interactive methods are often preferred because:

- The planning result is comprehensible.
- The planner's experiential knowledge is incorporated.
- In many companies, the data necessary for optimization (e.g., detailed cost data) is not available, and the costly introduction of these methods is not justified (Snapp 2010, p. 82). So again, the question of data availability and quality arises (see Sects. 4.1.3 and 4.1.4).

Another reason might be that many "optimization methods" are merely heuristics that do not guarantee finding the optimal solution. When Advanced Planning Systems came onto the market, optimization methods were seen as an important selling point, but now the main focus is no longer on this (Snapp 2010, p. 35).

While data are paramount in analytical functionality, also business processes are involved. In the SCM system, the most important business process is the *planning run*. It usually consists of several steps, each of which involves a planning function. Therefore, the definition of the steps and the selection of the functions are planning tasks. We look at this using an example from production planning, based on Balla and Layer (2010, p. 279 ff.).[9] What is important to us here is less the exact technical content than the example of a business process, which links planning functions (methods of business objects). (What would be the classes here?)

- Multi-level infinite demand planning of the materials according to the disposition level method. "Infinite" means that the limitation of resources (such as machines) is not yet taken into account; this is done in a later step. Regarding the disposition level method, the material is a hierarchical multi-level assembly. At the lowest level are the elementary materials ("raw materials" from the perspective of manufacturing). In a disposition level method, the bill of materials levels are planned from top to bottom (Gulyássy et al. 2009, Sect. 1.3.1).
- New planning of the operations on the bottleneck resource with the fine planning function "reschedule." This is capacity planning. However, this is (initially) not carried out for all resources but only for those known to be "critical" (bottleneck resources).
- Optimization run for the remaining resources. Here, optimization programs are actually used.

SCM systems often offer a rich selection of planning functions. In fact, many companies only use a few of the functions; three to four are already considered intensive use today (Snapp 2010, p. 46). The planning functionality can range from supply and sales planning to production and detailed planning.

---

[9] In Balla and Layer (2010), due to the functioning of the planning system and its interaction with the ERP system, a determination of the disposition levels is added in advance, which we will not go into further here.

For the complex calculation methods, hardware support may be available, especially an in-memory database. In addition, the set of available optimization methods can be kept open for expansion. An example for all these aspects can be found in (Pradhan 2016).

4.6   The Three-Layer Model in Analytical Systems

We recall the three-layer model of a (transactional) enterprise information system: business data, objects, and processes (see Chaps. 2 and 3). Is it also applicable to analytical systems? The answer would be yes, even though the focus is on data (see ETL process, Sect. 4.2.2). For example, interfaces are mainly used in the data layer.

In analytical systems, we can distinguish between analyzing and analyzed business data, objects, and processes—"analyzing" mostly as components of the analytical system, "analyzed" as references to transactional systems:

- *Analyzing business data and objects*: The analyses themselves can be considered business data or objects. The associated methods are the individual analysis methods. Analyzing business objects makes statements about a variety of analyzed business data (see below). But also all other functions of analytical systems, such as transformation steps or data transfers, can be seen as methods of business objects.

- *Analyzing business processes*: Examples of regularly occurring business processes are the ETL process and the distribution of standard reports. The irregular ones, such as ad hoc analysis (usually one-step business processes) and data mining, are less standardized. At definition time, the design process for the various types of analysis should be mentioned, especially the preparatory steps, such as the Enterprise Data Warehouse and the multidimensional data model in data warehouse systems or learning models in data science.

- *Analyzed business data and objects*: These are the analyzed data, such as purchase order and sales values. In master data analyses, there are, e.g., material and purchasing organization. Instead of business objects (with methods), only business data are considered. In addition, the analyzed data often do not reflect individual business transactions but include several condensed ones. Customizing and master data are used in the dimensions; part of the transaction data becomes facts. We can distinguish between stock and flow data (see Sect. 3.3.2).

- *Analyzed business processes*: Business processes can be analyzed at the activity and process level, e.g., average process durations, deviations from planned process durations, which activities take particularly long time (dwell times). In my view, however, rather, the results of the business processes are usually analyzed, e.g., orders or contracts as business data, as opposed to the order or contract processing processes.

4.7   Exercises and Proposed Solutions

(a) Exercises

Exercise 4.1 (System Structure)
A company wants to use ERP and data warehouse functionality. What central and decentralized approaches to system structure can you imagine for this?

Exercise 4.2 (Multidimensional Data Model)

(a) Create a star schema for a multidimensional data model for "sales revenue."[10] This shall allow sales data (quantity, amount of money) to be analyzed over time (month, year), by products and product groups, by customer groups (an analysis by individual customers is not necessary), by branches, and (aggregated) by sales areas.

(b) Expand the model so that in addition to the actual quantities and sales, the planned quantities and sales are taken into account. Consider different variants of modeling.

(c) Assume you have 5 product groups, 2500 products, 6 customer groups, 4 sales areas, and 25 branches. For which parts could it make sense to store aggregated data in fact tables instead of creating the aggregates "on the fly" at runtime? What does your expanded model look like?

(d) What would a star schema look like that also has language-dependent designations for the attributes?

(e) Is a solution with only one dimension table theoretically possible?

Exercise 4.3 (Optimization of the Supply Chain)
In the literature on supply chain management, you may often read a characterization like "optimization of the entire supply chain, from the raw material producer to the end consumer." Consider why this somewhat striking vision appears exaggerated in today's SCM systems.

Exercise 4.4 (Central System with In-memory Database)
In Sect. 4.2.5, it is noted that with in-memory databases, the boundary between transactional and analytical systems could be abandoned. Do you think it is conceivable that the planning functionality could also be integrated into such an integrated system? What advantages and what problems could there be?

---

[10] The "classic" question for data warehouse systems, covered in almost every data warehouse book; our example is based on the much more extensive case study by Baars and Kemper (2021, p. 70 ff.).

(b) Proposed Solutions for the Exercises

Exercise 4.1 (System Structure)
System structures from ERP systems and data warehouse systems can be combined, each of which can be central (one instance) or decentralized (multiple instances). Important cases are listed in (Davidenkoff and Werner 2008, p. 87):

- ERP system and DWHS both central: There is one instance of each system type. The DWHS is responsible for analyzing historical ERP data.
- ERP system decentralized, DWHS centralized: The DWHS analyzes the data of several decentralized ERP systems.
- ERP system and DWHS both decentralized: Like the first case, only there are several combinations of ERP-DWHS running parallel to each other.
- ERP system and DWHS both decentralized, plus a central DWHS. This is a combination of the second and third cases.

Exercise 4.2 (Multidimensional Data Model)
(a) and (b) see Fig. 4.13.

Regarding notation: The table names are **bold**, the key fields are <u>underlined</u>. Technical identifiers are marked with "ID" (e.g., ProdID) and non-technical designations (texts) without ID (e.g., "Product").

Actual and planned figures could alternatively also be modeled with an additional dimension "Actual/Plan." The key attribute would have, e.g., the values "0" for "Actual" and "1" for Plan.

(c) Due to the numerical ratios, it might make sense to use an aggregate for the sales per product group. The additional fact table would have the same dimensions as before, except for the product, replacing prodID by prodgroupID.

(d) Each dimension would have the designations as attributes (one designation per attribute) and an additional primary key field for the language code (e.g., EN for English, DE for German). This key field does not go into the fact table—numbers are not language dependent. This results in an exception to the rule of how the key fields of the fact table are derived. The question is rather theoretical; in practice, this would be solved by a snowflake schema.

Fig. 4.13 Star schema "sales"

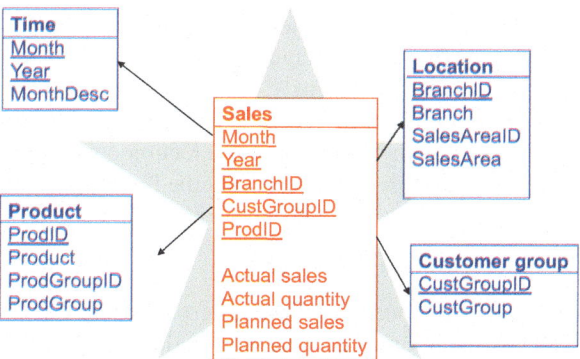

(e) Theoretically yes. This would then contain all attributes. The composite primary key would be derived from the primary key fields of all previous dimension tables. The content of the dimension table would be large, up to the cross product of the previous dimension tables. Moreover, it would not correspond to our guideline of "business modeling." This would only be practically applicable if several smaller dimensions were combined in order to reduce the number of joins.

Exercise 4.3 (Optimization of the Supply Chain)

- A company, e.g., an automotive supplier, is typically involved in several supply chains at the same time. The optimization of one supply chain will often conflict with the optimization of another (competing goals).
- The optimization is based on the fact that the companies in the supply chain, e.g., again the automotive supplier, disclose figures about their own capacity utilization. However, in addition to cooperation in the supply chain, there is also competition, so a company will withhold such figures.

Exercise 4.4 (Central system with In-memory Database)
Reasons for this:

- No data exchange between the systems necessary
- Data always up to date

Problems to be solved:

- Feasible in terms of complexity?
- Is it easy to reconcile different performance requirements (data access, calculations, write accesses to business data)?

4.8   Self-Assessment

4.1 General

1. What is the difference between a standard report and an interactive analysis? How do you access them?
2. Is a data warehouse system (DWHS) beneficial for a small company?
3. What are the disadvantages if transactional and analytical functionality are operated in separate systems?
4. Which SQL operations occur in transactional and analytical systems, in what form, and with what temporal selection conditions?
5. What data sources can you imagine for analytical systems?

4.2 Data Warehouse Systems

6. What is the purpose of the Enterprise Data Warehouse in a DWHS?
7. How many times is some data (redundantly) stored in the DWHS?

8. What criteria would you use to provide data marts?
9. Describe ways for extractions during the ETL process!
10. Why are data transformed during the ETL process?
11. Are there more transformations for master data or for transaction data?
12. Do you have ideas on how you can identify faulty data during a transformation?
13. Where are data loaded in the DWHS during the ETL process (step "L")?
14. Explain the difference between dimension, fact, attribute, and key figure!
15. What is the relationship between dimension hierarchies and aggregation?
16. Consider Fig. 4.4. Would aggregates be possible there? At which point?
17. What does the content of a dimension depend on?
18. What influence does the "business modeling" have on the design of the dimensions?
19. What does the term "materialized view" mean? What is another term for it?
20. What is the difference between a "normal" database index and a bitmap index?
21. Why can query processing in an in-memory database system be much faster than in a conventional database system?

4.3 Data Science: Statistical Methods and Machine Learning

22. How do statements made with statistical methods differ from those made with machine learning using neural networks?
23. What are the differences between the ETL processes in DWHS and those in machine learning (to be understood in a figurative sense)?
24. What data could be used for training the mentioned application for applicant pre-selection?
25. What advantages are expected from predictive maintenance compared to fixed-time maintenance schedules?
26. What reasons are there for providing applications with machine learning in a separate cloud system?

4.4 Big Data

27. Compare the terms "staging area," "Enterprise Data Warehouse," and "data lake" in DWHS and in Big Data applications, respectively.
28. Where does process control play a role in Big Data?

4.5 Planning

29. Does an ERP system have planning functionality?
30. Why are there planning systems?
31. How does the type of data processing we have learned for a DWHS differ from that of an SCM planning system? Are there similarities?
32. Why is it difficult to plan an entire supply chain?

References

Further Reading

The material covered on data warehouse systems is largely "standard content", accordingly it is extensively presented in various textbooks, particularly in detail in:
Vaisman, A., Zymányi, E.: Data Warehouse Systems: Design and Implementation, 2nd edn. Springer, Berlin (2022)

Further Cited Literature and Sources

Anane Adusei, D., Rötting, I., Yamada, S.: SAP HANA—Datenmodellierung. Rheinwerk, Bonn (2018)

Baars, H., Kemper, H.-G.: Business Intelligence & Analytics, 4th revised and extended edn. Springer Vieweg, Wiesbaden (2021)

Balla, J., Layer, F.: Produktionsplanung mit SAP APO, 2nd edn. Galileo Press, Bonn (2010)

Bauer, A., Günzel, H. (eds.): Data-Warehouse-Systeme, 4th revised and expanded edn. dpunkt, Heidelberg (2013)

Bavaraju, A.: Data Modeling for SAP HANA 2.0. Rheinwerk, New York (2019)

Bouman, R., van Dongen, J.: Pentaho Solutions. Business Intelligence and Data Warehousing with Pentaho and MySQL. Wiley, Indianapolis (2009)

Braun, M.: Analytics im Online-Handel. In: Haneke, U., Trahasch, S., Zimmer, M., Felden, C. (eds.) Data Science. Grundlagen, Architekturen und Anwendungen, 2nd revised and expanded edn, pp. 239–254. dpunkt, Heidelberg (2021)

Davidenkoff, A., Werner, D.: Global SAP Systems—Design and Architecture. Galileo Press, Bonn (2008)

Egger, N., Fiechter, J.M., Rohlf, J.: SAP BW Datenmodellierung. Galileo Press, Bonn (2004)

Elsner, M., González, G., Raben, M.: SAP Leonardo. Konzepte, Technologien, Best Practices. Rheinwerk, Bonn (2018)

Freiknecht, J., Papp, S.: Big Data in der Praxis, 2nd edn. Hanser, Munich (2018)

Gulyássy, F., Hoppe, M.N., Köhler, O., Vithayathil, B.: Materials Planning with SAP, 3rd updated and expanded edn. Galileo Press, New York (2009)

Haneke, U., Trahasch, S., Zimmer, M., Felden, C. (eds.): Data Science. Grundlagen, Architekturen und Anwendungen, 2nd revised and extended edn. dpunkt, Heidelberg (2021)

Huber, M.: Predictive Maintenance. In: Haneke, U., Trahasch, S., Zimmer, M., Felden, C. (eds.) Data Science. Grundlagen, Architekturen und Anwendungen, pp. 255–274. dpunkt, Heidelberg (2021)

Inmon, W.H.: Building the Data Warehouse, 1st edn. John Wiley, New York (1993)

Jupyter: jupyter.org/ (2024). Accessed 1 Oct 2024

Kauermann, G.: Data Science – Einige Gedanken aus Sicht eines Statistikers. Inform. Spektrum. **42**(6), 387–393 (2019)

Kayser, V., Zubovic, D.: Data privacy. In: Haneke, U., Trahasch, S., Zimmer, M., Felden, C. (eds.) Data Science. Grundlagen, Architekturen und Anwendungen, 2nd revised and extended edn, pp. 177–190. dpunkt, Heidelberg (2021)

Kleppmann, M.: Designing Data-Intensive Applications. O'Reilly, Sebastopol (2017)

Lüdtke, T., Lüdtke, M.: SAP BW/4HANA 2.0. Rheinwerk, New York (2020)

Marx Gomez, J., Rautenstrauch, C., Cissek, P., Grahlher, B.: Einführung in SAP Business Information Warehouse. Springer, Berlin (2006)

Marz, N., Warren, J.: Big Data: Principles and Best Practices of Scalable Realtime Data. Manning Publications, Shelter Island (2015)

Mehrwald, C.: Datawarehousing mit SAP BW. 7.5. corrected edn. dpunkt, Heidelberg (2010)

Meier, A., Kaufmann, M.: SQL & NoSQL Databases, 2nd edn. Springer, Cham (2023)

Müller, S., Keller, C.: Pentaho und Jedox. Hanser, Munich (2015)

Plattner, H., Zeier, A.: In-Memory Data Management. Springer, Berlin (2011)

Pradhan, S.: Demand and Supply Planning with SAP APO. Rheinwerk, New York (2016)

PyTorch: https://pytorch.org/ (2024). Accessed 1 Oct 2024

Riedhammer, K.: Private Communication. 22 Dec 2020 (2020)

Snapp, S.: Discover SAP SCM. Galileo Press, Bonn (2010)

TensorFlow: tensorflow.org (2024). Accessed 1 Oct 2024

Trahasch, S., Felden, C.: Grundlegende Methoden der Data Science. In: Haneke, U., Trahasch, S., Zimmer, M., Felden, C. (eds.) Data Science. Grundlagen, Architekturen und Anwendungen, 2nd revised and extended edn, pp. 65–100. dpunkt, Heidelberg (2021)

Willinger, M., Gradl, J.: Datenmigration in SAP, 2nd edn. Galileo Press, Bonn (2007)

Wolf, F.K., Yamada, S.: Datenmodellierung in SAP NetWeaver BW. Galileo Press, Bonn (2010)

Zitzelsberger, A.: Private Communication. 20 Oct 2011 (2011)

Application Platform

5

Summary

The core of the application platform is represented by the three-tier client-server architecture with database, application, and presentation layers. Special attention is paid to issues of performance and fail safety. It is shown how the layers can be distributed over more or fewer tiers.

Learning Objective

- Get to know the three-tier client-server architecture.

5.1   Three-Tier Client-Server Architecture

5.1.1   Overview

In this chapter, we deal with the platform of enterprise information systems in the sense of Chap. 2, i.e., the application-independent software that is part of the enterprise information system. We distinguish this from the system software and hardware, which are sometimes also referred to as "platform" (software platform, hardware platform).

© The Author(s), under exclusive license to Springer-Verlag GmbH, DE,
part of Springer Nature 2025
R. Weber, *Enterprise Information Systems*,
https://doi.org/10.1007/978-3-662-71718-9_5

We focus on the currently widespread technical architecture of an enterprise information system, the *three-tier client-server architecture*. In addition to the client-server architecture, the application platform includes other application-independent components. Some of them are addressed in other chapters. Below are examples:

- Software development environment
- Workflow management system
- Interfaces to additional software (document management, archive system, electronic data interchange, communication)

The application programs run on *application servers*. Several of them are usually connected via fast local TCP/IP networks to exactly one *database server* that provides access to the database (Fig. 5.1). For the moment, we assume that each layer runs on its own computer (i.e., tier; see also Sect. 5.2). (What is the exact difference between a "database system" and a "database server?")

The users work on workstations, mostly personal computers, which are connected to the application servers. They are called *presentation servers* because they provide the users with the presentation of the user dialogs. In common jargon, they are called *clients*. For the connection between application and database server, faster networks may be used for performance reasons than for connecting the presentation servers, as the figure suggests. We thus recognize three *layers*, which include the respective servers. The database layer is also called *persistence layer*.

Larger enterprise information systems have hundreds or thousands of users. In addition to application programs for *dialog users*, there are those without user interaction. They are called *batch jobs*. Examples are the creation of payroll statements and data archiving. Since multiple users and background jobs have simultaneous processing requests, dispatchers are needed, between the computers and within a computer. A dispatcher is part of the client-server architecture and usually runs on the application servers.

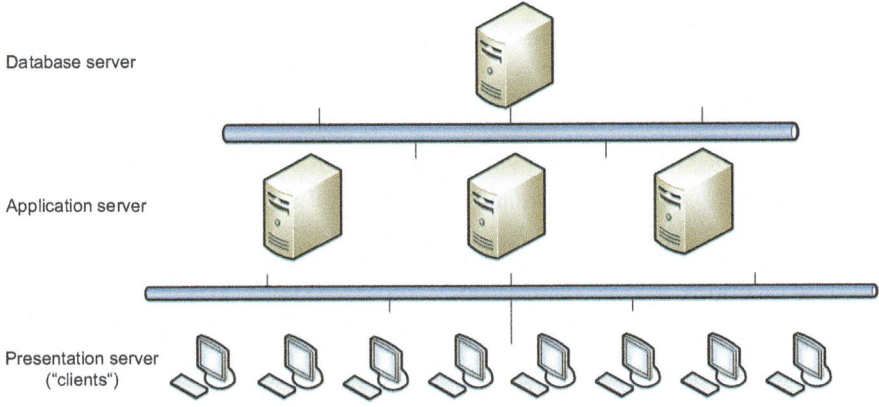

Fig. 5.1 Three-tier client-server architecture

Why multiple networked application servers instead of just one, with sufficient computing power? The architecture emerged for enterprise information systems in the early 1990s and was able to establish itself because of the low costs compared to mainframes: A mainframe, then common in business data processing, was significantly more expensive than several interconnected smaller computers. Initially, these were Unix computers; today, Windows and Linux are also used. In addition, performance can be increased by *scaling*, i.e., adapting the performance to an increased load: If more performance is needed, especially when the number of users grows, one or more additional application servers can be added. Thus, not the entire system, such as a mainframe, needs to be replaced by a new one. More precisely, this is called *horizontal scaling* or also *scale out*, in contrast to *vertical scaling* (*scale up*), where additional processors or memory are added to a computer.

In recent years, due to increased computing power and better cost-performance ratio, there has been a trend toward centralization: fewer, more powerful computers, which particularly reduces administrative effort.

In addition to scaling, this architecture offers another mechanism for performance control, *load balancing*: When a user logs into the system, he can automatically be assigned to the currently least loaded application server. The assignment can be made for the entire login time. The alternative would be to assign each user interaction individually. (Which approach involves more effort?)

The architecture also offers a certain *fail safety*: If an application server no longer functions correctly, users can log in to another one—the functionality of the overall system is not threatened. One of the critical points (*single point of failure, SPOF*) is the database server because there is only one.

Let's now take a closer look at the three layers.

5.1.2 Application Server

The application programs, also called "business logic," run on the application server. Usually, each application server can run all application programs, i.e., there is no functional specialization like "accounting runs on server 1, purchasing runs on server 2." Application servers can buffer data to relieve the database, which is a bottleneck in the classic architecture.

As described in Chap. 3, application programs can run in user dialog or in the background, often in batch processing. Accordingly, application servers offer support for both types. The performance of dialog programs can be measured by the response time perceived by the user. In addition to the average response time, the median or more generally a percentile can be used. A percentile is specified by a percentage, e.g., 95%, abbreviated p95. For such percentiles, like p95, a response time is given, e.g., 1 s. This means that 95% of the requests are answered in at most 1 s. (How can the median be given as a percentile?) For background programs, throughput can serve as a performance measure, such as the number of processed data records per second or the execution time for a job of a certain data size (for performance data, see Kleppmann 2017, p. 13 ff.).

5.1.3 Database Server

5.1.3.1 The Classic Approach

The database server establishes contact with the database system and thus the database. It can be seen as an application server with additional functionality. There is a subtle difference between a database server and a database system, in the sense of software (see Sect. 5.2). The database server is part of the application platform, while the database system is part of the system software. They can be products of different software vendors (see "platform independence" below). The database server is thus in a layer above the database system and accesses its services.

In principle, some database systems would allow multiple database servers, but this is not common practice (Schneider 2018, Sect. 1.2). While from the perspective of the enterprise information system there is only one database server, the internal structure can indeed have a distributed architecture, e.g., a particularly powerful database system on a multiprocessor architecture with mirroring of disks to increase fail safety.

Some database servers only support a single database system. For others, there is platform independence, i.e., different database systems can be used. In that case, a neutral database interface is useful in order to isolate the programs running on the application server from the interface of the specific database system. The database interface provides uniform access to different database systems but uses the respective native database interface to achieve the best possible performance. Performance problems in application programs often concern the database server, as data access is expensive (access via the network, access time to persistent storage). Therefore, a carefully designed database interface is important for the performance of the overall system. In addition, various programming techniques and buffering mechanisms serve to increase performance.

When using a database system, costs for the runtime license usually arise if the database system is not part of the enterprise information system.

All master, transaction, and customizing data (see Sect. 3.3) are kept in the database. In contrast to technical data, master, transaction, and customizing data are often organized in clients (see Sect. 3.3.3).

5.1.3.2 In-Memory Computing

(a) **Concept**

So far, the still common, traditional approach for a client-server system with a conventional database system has been described, i.e., the database is solely in a persistent memory (magnetic disk, solid-state-drives (SSD), where the term "drive" is somewhat misleading because there is no physical movement as with hard disks). A newer approach with great potential for business data processing is *in-memory databases*, also called *in-memory data management* or *in-memory computing* (Plattner and Zeier 2011, p. 14). As the name suggests, in an in-memory database, the content of the entire database is kept in main memory. The persistent storage only serves as a means of secure data storage (backup,

Table 5.1 Comparison of access times and data throughput

Storage medium	Access time (ns)	Data throughput (MB per second)
RAM	15–90	20,000
SSD drive	10,000	500
Magnetic disc	7,000,000	200

recovery). In-memory databases can be used for transactional and analytical functionality, with the main benefit being in the analytical (see Sect. 4.2.5).

As Rechenberg (2006, p. 275) points out, major advances in computer science are usually driven by hardware (e.g., PC, mobile devices), which computer scientists, mostly software oriented, do not always like to perceive. With in-memory databases, these advances are the ever larger and cheaper memory chips and multicore architectures. The concept of in-memory databases goes back to the 1980s, but only with today's technology does it become realistically usable (Plattner and Zeier 2011, p. 14). Due to the significantly faster access time and parallel processing, a performance increase for enterprise information systems can generally be achieved. In Hecker et al. (2016, p. 22), figures for access time to data and data throughput are given, i.e., how much data can be transferred per unit of time (see Table 5.1).

The following concepts are the basics of in-memory databases technology:

a. Data storage in main memory (RAM).
b. Only insert operations in the database: Changes are represented by validity flags and timestamps (Plattner and Zeier 2011, p. 109 ff.). Reasons are, for one, the historization but also the concurrency control. The advantage is that read transactions do not have to lock resources and therefore do not block other transactions (Plattner and Zeier 2011, p. 112).[1]
c. Row and column storage of data records (see Sect. 4.2.5).
d. Multicore CPUs and multiprocessors (see Sect. 4.2.5).

Various techniques are used for implementation:

a. Processing logic close to the database: While in a classic client-server architecture the application servers should take over as much processing logic as possible to relieve the bottleneck database, a lot of application logic is integrated into the database system in in-memory databases (Plattner and Zeier 2011, p. 155).
b. Data compression: Memory chips can store large amounts of data today, but without compression, the storage requirements would be too large (several PB in larger companies). Therefore, different forms of data compression are used (Plattner and Zeier 2011, p. 68).
c. No aggregates: Aggregates (see Sect. 4.2.4) are not stored separately (saving storage) but are efficiently calculated "on the fly" in memory (Plattner and Zeier 2011, p. 164).

---

[1] This concept is not mandatory for in-memory databases.

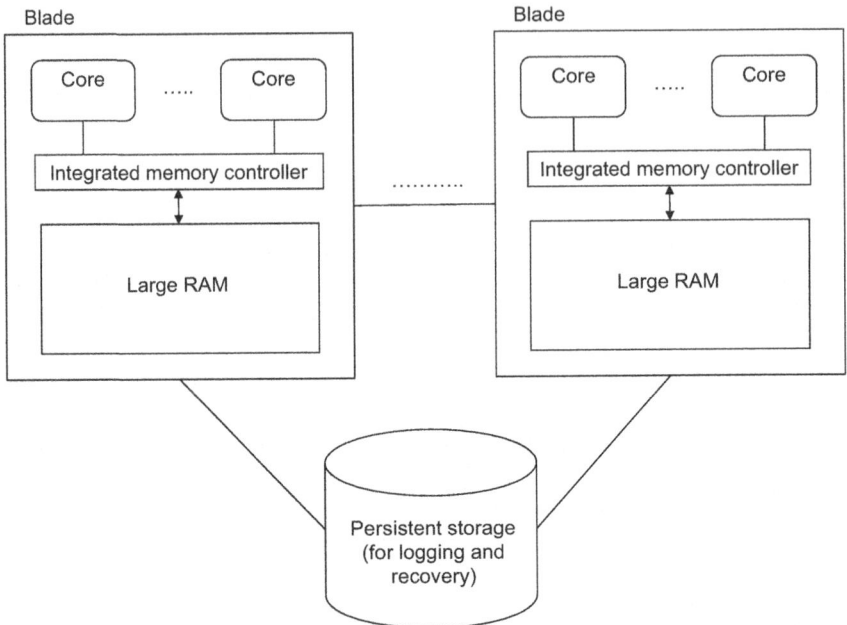

Fig. 5.2 Structure of SanssouciDB. (After Plattner and Zeier 2011, p. 34 f.)

Figure 5.2 shows the structure of the prototypical in-memory database system SanssouciDB (figure after Plattner and Zeier 2011, p. 34 f.). The computer consists of several parts, called *blades*. A blade has many computer cores (up to 64), which work in parallel on the same main memory (with 2 TB). It is connected to a persistent storage, which however only takes over the tasks of logging and recovery in case of failure. Ideally, one would like to install all the main memory and the computer cores on one blade, but size restrictions of currently available blades do not allow this. Therefore, several (like 25) blades are interconnected. In this way, a mixed shared-memory and shared-nothing architecture is created in the terminology of database systems.[2]

The following advantages are expected from in-memory databases (Plattner and Zeier 2011, pp. 3 and 22):

a. Reduced complexity of the enterprise information system: Fewer layers and components, thus easier administration; as a result, lower total cost of ownership (TCO).

b. Good response times for transactional and analytical applications (below 1 s, to retain the user's attention). This allows for better and faster decisions. Trial-and-error analyses, as commonly used with Web search engines, are made possible by the fast response times (Plattner and Zeier 2011, p. 9).

---

[2] Since the persistent memory is only used for logging and recovery in case of failure, it is not a shared-disk system.

   c. Data-intensive tasks can be performed close to the data source, thus not burdening other parts of the system.

   d. Computationally intensive tasks with mass data are accelerated. According to Plattner and Zeier (2011, p. 31), most of the data in an integrated enterprise information system (including a data warehouse system) is handled by mass data processing.

   e. New application functions are possible: In enterprise information systems, many tasks are so performance intensive that they are not performed in real time but in background processing overnight. An example is the reconciliation of invoices and payments, such as in mobile phone companies (Plattner and Zeier 2011, p. 162). Since mobile phone customers can be blocked for (allegedly) unpaid invoices, real-time reconciliation can lead to a better service for customers.

(b) **Comparison with the Classic Model**

The technology available in a client-server architecture influences the scope of a layer. In the "classic" client-server architecture, i.e., not using in-memory databases, the database is the bottleneck. There is only one database server, and the access times to the persistent memory are much greater than those to the main memory. Accordingly, most of the business logic is performed in the application server (see Fig. 5.3, left part). Often, larger amounts of business data are loaded from the database into the application server, processed, and written back to the database. The database server itself reads and writes the data, but does not change it.

With in-memory databases, on the other hand, the aim is to put as much processing logic as possible into the database. The means are stored procedures, viz., procedures that run on the database server. The database system provides a programming language for this. The role of the application server, on the other hand, decreases; in the context of a model-view-controller concept for dialog applications, it primarily acts as a controller between view and model and coordinates calls to stored procedures in the database server (see Fig. 5.3). Another advantage is that as few data as possible flow between the application server and the database server (Plattner and Zeier 2011, p. 156).

This shows that application programs for the different architectures must be written differently. We are still far from automatically distributing business

Fig. 5.3 Three-tier client-server architecture— without and with in-memory database

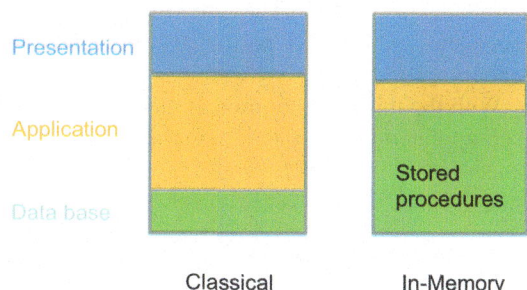

Presentation

Application

Data base

Stored procedures

Classical   In-Memory

logic, depending on the underlying technology. A program written for the "classic" architecture can be run on an in-memory architecture. However, the capabilities of in-memory computing are not used well, and performance is then solely improved through faster access times to the database system. For platform independence in in-memory computing, a standardization of programming language constructs for stored procedures with parallel execution would be necessary.

5.1.4 Presentation Server

The distribution of functions between the application server and the presentation server can be designed differently:

- *Thin client*: The client only takes on a few tasks, for example, mainframe terminal, terminal server client.
- *Fat client* or *rich client*: The client takes on more tasks, for which a separate program is installed on the presentation server. An example is a Java applet.

The advantage of Web browsers as presentation servers is mainly that no additional program needs to be installed and maintained (software patches) on the workstations.

Web browsers are usually seen as thin clients. However, this actually depends on the respective Web applications: In some, only content is presented in the Web browser, and the processing logic runs solely on the application server. Others use extensive scripting with JavaScript, so a larger portion of the computing power is on the client side.

Mobile applications are also significant today. The currently widespread mobile devices (smartphones and others) are small in size but technologically powerful computers and, depending on location, well and quickly networked. Accordingly, they may be presentation servers. Limitations exist due to the size of the screen. Nevertheless, some business applications are suitable for processing by mobile devices, e.g., simple decision-making tasks or notifications ("alerts"). It then makes sense to write applications tailored to these devices. Two approaches are currently in use: a thin client in the form of a Web browser for applications, possibly adapted to mobile devices. And a fat client in the form of an application that runs on the mobile device ("app"). The latter has the advantage that less network interaction is necessary, which is particularly helpful at locations with low network performance.

With the thin client approach for mobile devices, care is taken when writing the Web applications to make them "responsive," i.e., the screen mask adapts to the properties of the mobile device, for example, by hiding menus when there is not enough space.

For creating mobile applications using the fat client approach, two platforms dominate today: Apple iOS on the one side and Android on the other side for non-Apple devices.

In addition to these technical aspects, ergonomics plays a role ("user experience," abbreviated "UX"): Handling conventions and interfaces have emerged, some of which result from the physical properties of the device (screen size, virtual keyboard, not easy to handle with ten fingers). For user acceptance, this has to be taken into account when creating business applications.

5.1.5 Sizing

When setting up an enterprise information system, the question of how much performance is to be provided in total is crucial before the question of how many and which computers are used. The calculation of the system size is called *sizing*. Vendors of standard software may provide tools to calculate hardware requirements from given business requirements (number of simultaneous users in different application areas, how many customer orders or deliveries occur in a time interval, etc.).

The configuration of the computers is also important, e.g., how many processes are configured, and how is the memory allocated to different resources?

5.1.6 Hardware Consolidation

It must be decided whether to use a smaller number of powerful computers, possibly even just one (*hardware consolidation*) or more less powerful ones. Both opposing trends currently play a role (Schneider 2018, Sect. 2.4). Computers are becoming more and more powerful, so more centralization is possible, unlike in the early days of client-server architectures. Virtualization, i.e., the installation of several logical servers or even systems on one computer, also has an influence. The decision is mainly based on costs and availability. Both options can achieve a powerful system (Schneider 2018, Sect. 4.3). Maintenance, an important cost category, will be less complex with a smaller number of computers.

5.2 Architecture Variants

We have looked at the three-tier client-server architecture as the main representative for today's enterprise information systems. The three *logical* layers of software, presentation, and application and database layer can in fact be distributed over the three *physical* tiers of computers in different ways (see Alonso et al. (2004, p. 5) for the distinction between layer and tier). The layers are conceptually contained in any enterprise information system, although they are often closely interlinked and difficult to isolate in the software architecture.

In Alonso et al. (2004, p. 5), the database layer is more generally referred to as the *resource management layer*, to include other data sources besides the database, e.g., a file system or access to other enterprise information systems from where to dynamically read data. A similar idea is found in Sect. 4.2.2 in an example in the form of *virtual data cubes*. Since a database system is common for storing business data in enterprise information systems, we use the more specific term.

The presentation layer is usually related to the graphical user interface. But the view can be broadened to include other "clients," e.g., programs on another computer (Alonso et al. 2004, p. 4 f.). In this sense, serialization/deserialization in remote function calls (see Chap. 11) can be seen as "presentation logic."

Distributing the layers across different tiers results in various architectural variants. The following representation is based on Alonso et al. (2004, p. 9 ff.); the corresponding illustrations are slightly modified. Layers are represented in square boxes and tiers (i.e., computers) in boxes with rounded corners; the dashed box represents the software of the enterprise information system. A special case is the terminal in the first picture; this octagonal box is a device, not a computer.

5.2.1 Single-Tier Architecture

The entire enterprise information system, i.e., all three layers, is located on one computer. The users interact with "dumb" terminals. It is a central system (see Fig. 5.4, left), not a client-server architecture.

This case is predominant in the mainframe world. It used to be the standard case for business applications. Well-known and still widespread are *mainframes* from the manufacturer IBM. A so-called transaction processing monitor (*TP-Monitor*; a typical example is CICS from IBM) distributes user requests to programs and ensures

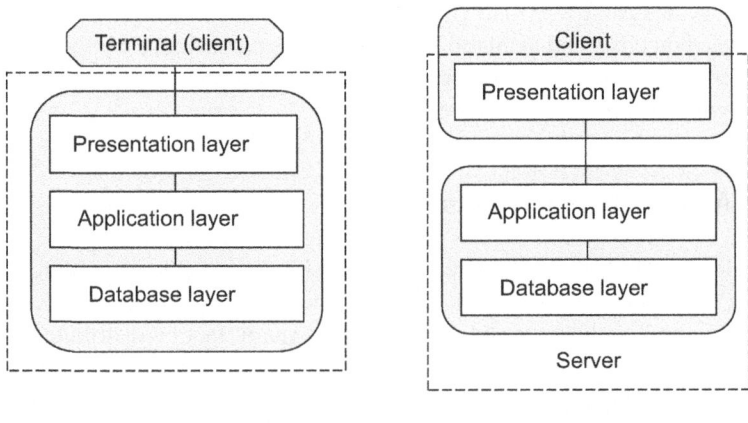

One-tier architecture   Two-tier architecture

Fig. 5.4 Single- and two-tier architecture

transactional execution. The data is stored in a database. (What is the difference to an application server?)

Often the separation of the layers was only conceptual, not in a strict software architecture ("monolithic systems"), as is frequently the case today.

5.2.2 Two-Tier Architecture

This coined the term "client-server architecture" (see Fig. 5.4, right). The server takes over the tasks of the application and database layer and the client those of the presentation layer. A part of the enterprise information system's software is thus installed on the client. In addition to this usual separation ("thin client, thick server"), the division of presentation and application layer on one side and database layer on the other side is possible ("thick client, thin server").

With two-tier architectures, a performance problem can easily arise, as a single computer, usually much less powerful than a mainframe, can only serve a limited number of users (Alonso et al. 2004, p. 14).

5.2.3 Three-Tier Architecture

We already know this case. Since there are now three types of computers, the terms "client" and "server" (see Fig. 5.5, left) are no longer sufficient. Usually, the application server also takes over a small part of the presentation layer by sending the user interface screens to be processed by the presentation server; this argument of course also applies to the two-level architecture.

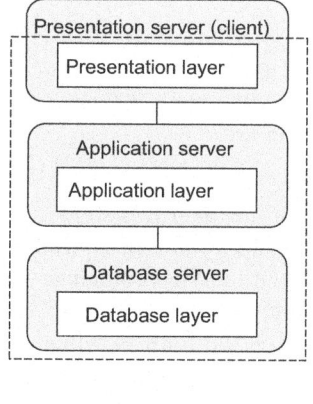

Three-tier architecture

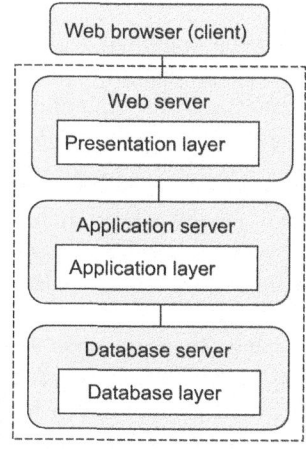

Four-tier architecture

Fig. 5.5 Three- and four-tier architecture

5.2.4   Four-Tier Architecture

In Alonso et al. (2004, p. 19 ff.), various types of *N*-tier architectures are described. This also includes the idea of considering a large enterprise information system as an *N*-tier architecture that integrates many smaller enterprise information systems. However, we represent this as a system landscape (see Chap. 8), in which various integration techniques (Part II of the book) are used.

The most important four-tier architecture today is probably the one that includes a Web server. The tasks of the Web and application server are distributed across two computers (see Fig. 5.5, right); in a three-tier architecture, they are merged ("Web application server"). The client does not contain any presentation layer specific to the enterprise information system but only a generic one in the form of the Web browser. The presentation layer is essentially the responsibility of the Web server, which generates the HTML pages that are only displayed by the Web browser. At this point, you can clearly see that the presentation layer cannot always be identified with the "client," in our case, the Web browser, unlike, for example, Java applets.

In general, it can be observed that with each additional tier, flexibility increases, but so does complexity, while performance decreases, as communication between the tiers requires performance (Alonso et al. 2004, p. 22).

5.3   Examples

5.3.1   Java Enterprise Edition

The *Java Enterprise Edition* (*JEE*) is not a product but a standard that sets requirements for application servers.

JEE defines two things:

- Interfaces to be complied with: The application programs must comply with these interfaces so that they can run on a JEE application server.
- Provided interfaces: Programming interfaces (APIs) that a JEE application server provides and that the application programs can use.

(a) **Interfaces to Be Complied with**
   In Fig. 5.6, the three-layer architecture according to JEE is shown. In the middle, we see a JEE application server. It provides a runtime environment that is divided into two parts: the EJB container and the Web container. In JEE, the term *container* means a runtime environment.

   EJB stands for *Enterprise Java Bean*. It is the form in which application programs for JEE are written. An EJB is a class that provides certain interfaces. The execution of application programs on a JEE application server is event based: certain events or state changes occur in the application server, e.g., the state change from `Passive` to `Method-Ready`. It is stipulated that the methods marked with the annotation `@PreActivate` are then called. This is called *inversion of control*—an EJB method is called at the right time, e.g., when a

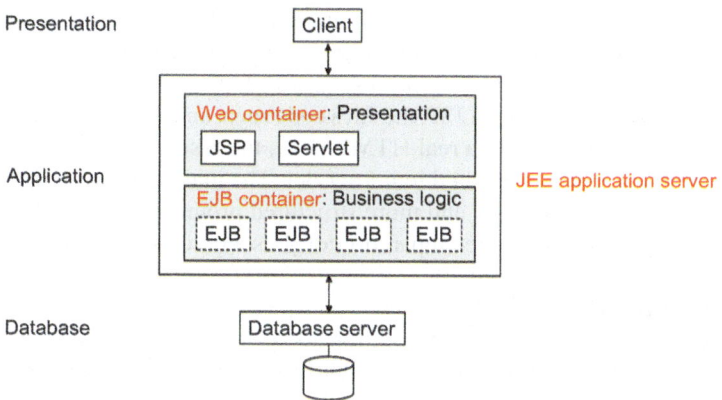

Fig. 5.6 Layer architecture according to JEE

request arrives—or the Hollywood principle: "Don't call us, we call you" (Gamma et al. 1994, Chap. 5, p. 55). EJBs can also be "put to sleep" temporarily and reactivated later.

There are different types of beans:

- *Session bean*: It is used for a client session. A typical use case is a shopping cart in an e-commerce system (Alonso et al. 2004, p. 106), where the session, which consists of several interactions, must store the state; this is referred to as a *stateful* session bean. In addition, there are *stateless* session beans for "one-time actions."
- *Entity bean*: It can be used to map persistent objects (see Sect. 3.4). The persistence can be managed by the entity bean itself or by the container.
- *Message-driven bean*: It can be used to implement message-based communication (see Chap. 10).

An EJB is an example of a *component* of a *component model* in the sense of software engineering (Burke and Monson-Haefel 2006, Chap. 1). As with many concepts in computer science, there is no clear definition but a common basic understanding of a component: a larger software building block, which encapsulates objects, provides interfaces, can be composed with other components, and runs in a runtime environment, usually an application server.

The *Web container* is the runtime environment for the display of user dialogs. In fact, there are "application servers" that only offer the Web container. The most famous is probably the Jakarta Tomcat Server. In this case, it is not a "real" application server but just a Web server.

Servlets run in the Web container. Servlets are, simply put, programs that accept an HTTP request and return an HTML page as an HTTP response. Thus, the program contains both the processing logic of the HTTP request (e.g., retrieving product information from a database) and the presentation logic (e.g., creating an HTML page from the product information, which presents the product information appealingly). (For which Web pages do you need servlets—or similar, for which not?)

Since this is somewhat tricky to program, there is another, higher-level programming interface: *Java Server Pages* (*JSP*). You can imagine this as an HTML page, in which at some places, Java code is inserted, a kind of HTML template. When accessing a JSP, the Java code runs, and from the result together with the HTML template, a real HTML page, the response page, is generated. Technically, a JSP is translated into a servlet. The main advantage of JSP compared to servlets is simpler and more structured programming of Web applications. This is due to a better separation of presentation (HTML) and business logic (the sprinkled Java code).

(b) **Provided Interfaces (APIs)**

The second aspect of JEE, in addition to the runtime environment and the related interfaces, are the programming interfaces that JEE servers provide. According to Alonso et al. (2004, p. 105), you can divide them into the usual three layers. In addition, the interfaces to be complied with are included and marked with a (*) to get a complete picture of the JEE interfaces.

- Presentation and communication:
  - Servlets (*)
  - Java Server Pages (JSP) (*)
  - JAXP (Java API for XML processing)[3]
  - JavaMail: interface to the email service (SMTP, POP3)
  - JAAS (Java authentication and authorization services)
- Application integration:
  - Enterprise Java beans (EJB) (*)
  - JTA (Java transaction API): for component-controlled transactions
  - JMS (Java messaging service): interface to message-oriented middleware (asynchronous communication) (see Chap. 10).
  - JNDI (Java naming and directory interface): access to name and directory services
- Database and general resource access:
  - JDBC (Java database connectivity): access to relational databases
  - JPA (Java persistence API):[4] to support persistent objects, especially object-relational mapping (see Sect. 3.4)
  - JCA (Java connector architecture): uniform access to other enterprise information systems

---

[3] We remember: According to Alonso et al. (2004, p. 4 f.), "presentation" for a client is broader than just for graphical user interfaces. Accordingly, the methods for the XML representation and, in terms of communication, the email to a client are also subsumed.

[4] JPA is used in recent JEE specifications, although it is rather a general-purpose approach and thus not limited to JEE (Bauer and Gregory 2016, Chap. 1).

5.3.2 Application Server in SAP Software

The SAP NetWeaver Application Server ABAP is the application platform for programs in SAP's own programming language ABAP (Advanced Business Application Programming Language) (for ABAP see Sect. 15.9.4). The application server contains several so-called work processes of different types. We look at some of them.

A *dialog work process* is responsible for the processing of programs with user dialog. When processing a dialog program, the user's thinking and typing take up most of the time. The "computing" in the broader sense, i.e., the execution of the application program on the application server, is only short, e.g., a tenth of the user time. Therefore, a dialog work process can process a whole series of dialog steps of different users in a short sequence.

A background processing work process (*batch work process*) on the other hand executes background programs, scheduled as batch jobs. Scheduling can occur at specific times, often periodically, or event driven (Föse et al. 2012, Chap. 7). Different operating modes can be set for an application server: for example, more dialog processes can be made available during the day, and more batch work processes at night. The switch between operating modes happens automatically.

The *enqueue work process* is used to lock data that shall be written to the database. It ensures that multiple users cannot change data at the same time and thus create inconsistencies. In fact, SAP does not (only) use the lock logic of the database system but has developed its own, which spans work processes and application servers. With such a lock, records of several tables, e.g., header and line-item table (see Sect. 3.3.1), may be locked together. Since the locked data can be processed in several dialog steps, which can be executed by different dialog work processes, the lock must span work processes.

The *message server* process (technically not a work process) runs on exactly one application server. It is responsible for communication between the application servers. It is used for load balancing and locking: Since there is only one enqueue work process, which runs on one of the application servers, the application servers contact the enqueue work process via the message server when they want to set a lock.

5.4 Exercises and Proposed Solutions

(a) Exercises

Exercise 5.1 (Performance in the Client-Server Architecture)
A company has acquired another one. Accordingly, more employees are now working with the ERP system, and performance problems arise. What options do you have in the three-tier client-server architecture to solve these problems?

Exercise 5.2 (Distribution of Tasks in a Client-Server Architecture)
A user displays a table content. There are about 300 rows. He wants to interactively sort the table by different attributes. At which tier of the client-server architecture would you locate the sorting functionality?

Exercise 5.3 (Buffering)
What data would you buffer to relieve the database server?

Exercise 5.4 (In-Memory Databases)
Why are in-memory databases useful in a platform for analytical systems?

Exercise 5.5 (Web Application Server)
What reasons could you think of for using two separate servers (Web and application server) instead of a combined Web application server?

(b) Proposed Solutions for the Exercises

Exercise 5.1
One option is to check the configuration of the application servers. Perhaps the problem can already be solved at this level. Another option is to set up another application server for better load balancing. More powerful hardware is of course still another option, such as providing not an additional application server but replacing an existing one by a more powerful one.

Exercise 5.2
The presentation server is suitable in this situation to relieve the application servers (avoid "round trips"). The prerequisite for this is of course that a sorting program (e.g., scripting in a Web browser) can run on the presentation server.

Exercise 5.3
Data that changes infrequently but is frequently read. This could be organizational units, for example. It is more difficult with master data—Why?

Exercise 5.4
Analytical systems read large amounts of data. Reducing access time improves the performance of the analytical applications. In addition, SQL's set-oriented access goes well with parallelization.

Exercise 5.5
There could be security reasons (firewalls), as well as performance reasons.

5.5   Self-Assessment

Three-Tier Client-Server Architecture in General

1. What makes a computer a presentation server, and what makes it an application server?
2. What are the critical points ("single point of failure") in the three-tier client-server architecture?
3. You change a material master record. How do the three layers of the client-server architecture work together in this case?
4. Where does the payroll accounting take place in the client-server architecture?
5. What is the difference between a layer and a tier (in the terminology of the book)?
6. What is the role of a terminal server in the client-server architecture of an enterprise information system?

Application Server

7. Why can there be multiple application servers in a client-server architecture?
8. In which case is more RAM consumed: With one application server with $n * m$ bytes or with n application servers each with m bytes? Why?
9. In the example of SAP software, what determines how many work processes there are in an application server?
10. You are writing a Web shop application with Java and want to run it on a JEE server. What does your development methodology look like? Which interfaces will you use?

Presentation Server

11. A Web browser seems to be the presentation server of an enterprise information system with a Web-based user interface. Why is the Web browser then not part of the presentation layer in Fig. 5.5?

References

Further Reading

The client-server architecture, including its historical development, is described in chapters 1 and 2 and Sect. 4.3 of:
Alonso, G., Casati, F., Kuno, H., Machiraju, V.: Web Services. Springer, Berlin (2004)

Introductions to client-server technology and JEE can be found in many other books, for example, in:
Tanenbaum, A., van Steen, M.: Distributed Systems, 2nd edn, Pearson new international edition. Pearson, Harlow (2014)

The development of Enterprise Java Beans is comprehensively described in:
Burke, B., Monson-Haefel, R.: Enterprise JavaBeans 3.0. O'Reilly Media, Sebastopol (2006)

Further Cited Literature and Sources

Bauer, C., Gregory, G.: Java Persistence with Hibernate, 2nd edn. Manning, Greenwich (2016)
Föse, F., Hagemann, S., Will, L.: SAP NetWeaver AS ABAP—System Administration, 4th edn. Rheinwerk, New York (2012)
Gamma, E., Helm, R., Johnson, R.: Design Patterns. Elements of Reusable Object-Oriented Software. Pearson, London (1994)
Hecker, D., Renner, T., Jacobs, B., Sylla, K.-H., Wohlfrom, A., Kötter, F.: Marktübersicht In-Memory-Systeme. Fraunhofer-Verlag, Stuttgart (2016)
Kleppmann, M.: Designing Data-Intensive Applications. O'Reilly, Sebastopol (2017)
Plattner, H., Zeier, A.: In-Memory Data Management. Springer, Berlin (2011)
Rechenberg, P.: Was ist Informatik, 4th edn. Hanser, Munich (2006)
Schneider, T.: SAP Performance Optimization Guide, 8th edn. Rheinwerk, New York (2018)

Deployment Forms

6

Clouds oder auch
Lageredeinedatenhierduidiotdamitwirsiealleaufeinmalabgreifenkönnen
Sybille Berg (GRM. Brainfuck,
first edition, Kiepenheuer & Witsch, Cologne,
2019, p. 405. Translated:
Clouds or also Storeyourdatahereyouidiotsowecangrabthemallatonce.)

Summary

An enterprise information system can be operated by the using company itself (on-premises) or by a service provider ("in the cloud"), with access via the Internet. A second aspect of deployment is the granularity in which application software is developed and operated: as a monolithic system or as a composition of fine-grain, largely independent services, as is intended with microservices. Further aspects are the types of content of an enterprise information system and who develops and provides the system.

Learning Objectives

- To be able to compare the currently common deployment forms of enterprise information systems: on-premises and cloud
- To be able to assess microservices as an alternative to monolithic systems
- To be able to classify further aspects such as "business content" and open-source systems

6.1   Cloud Computing

6.1.1   Concept

So far, we have implicitly assumed that in order to use an enterprise information system, a company acquires software licenses and installs and operates the software *on-premises*. This is still the most common case today. But especially in recent times, there is a big growth in cloud computing.

Cloud computing is based on the idea to not provide information processing services yourself but to rent them. More precisely, cloud computing has the following characteristics (Chellammal and Pethuru 2023, p. 40 ff.):

- *Rental model*: The software is not purchased and installed, but access to it is rented (*on demand*). The software or its use is then referred to as a *service*.
- *Multi-tenancy*: From the operator's side, pools of resources (computers, data storage, networks, software) are provided for a large number of companies and users (multi-tenancy) (Chellammal and Pethuru 2023, p. 42 f.). As with large rental houses, some communal contents can be cost-effective (Chellammal and Pethuru 2023, p. 42 f.). (Which parts are used communally? Which are company specific?)
- *Elasticity*: The potentially usable amount of resources is so large through dynamic scaling that the user gets the impression of infinite, not limited resources. This is referred to as elasticity, where resources can be added or removed on a fine-grained and short-term basis as needed (Chellammal and Pethuru 2023, p. 43).
- *Usage-based billing*: The billing of the service is usage dependent, i.e., depending on the number of users, time related or quantity related, such as according to computing power or storage amount ("pay per use").
- *Network access*: Access to the service is via the Internet or an intranet.

A common comparison is that of IT performance and electrical power: "IT from the socket," for which the term *utility computing* is used (Chellammal and Pethuru 2023, p. 18). For the user of cloud computing, it does not really matter which implementation is chosen for service provisioning. Usually, it is a centrally managed distributed system. In detail, differences can of course become important, e.g., with regard to the system's fail-safety or legal data protection regulations. (Is the move as easy as with electricity—i.e., from one cloud to the next?)

A related approach to cloud computing is *grid computing*. In grid computing, computing resources are bundled for a common task (see Chellammal and Pethuru (2023, p. 23 f.) for a detailed distinction). Chellammal and Pethuru (2023, p. 34) see cloud computing as a combination of grid computing (for the technical aspect of providing computing resources) and utility computing (for renting computing resources "on demand").

For the provider of cloud services, economies of scale arise from providing services to many companies. Advantages are already apparent on the hardware side: Large purchase quantities reduce the purchase prices, and many customers result in efficient resource utilization (Repschläger et al. 2010, p. 13). Furthermore, he can attract new customers by offering services, e.g., small businesses and medium-sized enterprises, which shy away from the investment and operating costs of large enterprise information systems.

6.1.2 Variants

(a) **Classification by Software Layers**

Cloud computing can be used at different layers (see our layer model in Chap. 2; Chellammal and Pethuru 2023, p. 36):

- *Infrastructure as a Service (IaaS):* system infrastructure
- *Platform as a Service (PaaS):* (Application) platform
- *Software as a Service (SaaS)*: applications

An overview of which layers are provided in what type of cloud software, also compared to an on-premises system, is shown in Fig. 6.1, based on (Chellammal and Pethuru 2023, p. 53 ff.).

In the case of infrastructure, generic resources are provided, e.g., storage or computing power. Companies like Amazon use a powerful hardware infrastructure to handle their online business even during peak times, such as before Christmas. The idea is to use such resources profitably for other purposes during times of lower utilization. This led to the creation of various system infrastructure services from Amazon. Providers today sometimes offer services at different layers (Repschläger et al. 2010, p. 8). Major providers for IaaS and PaaS besides Amazon are Google, Microsoft, and IBM, but there are also open-source developments.

The platform in PaaS is a development and runtime environment (Chellammal and Pethuru 2023, p. 36), plus usual supporting functionality such as application servers, called middleware in Fig. 6.1. (Is there a difference to the application platform according to Chap. 5?)

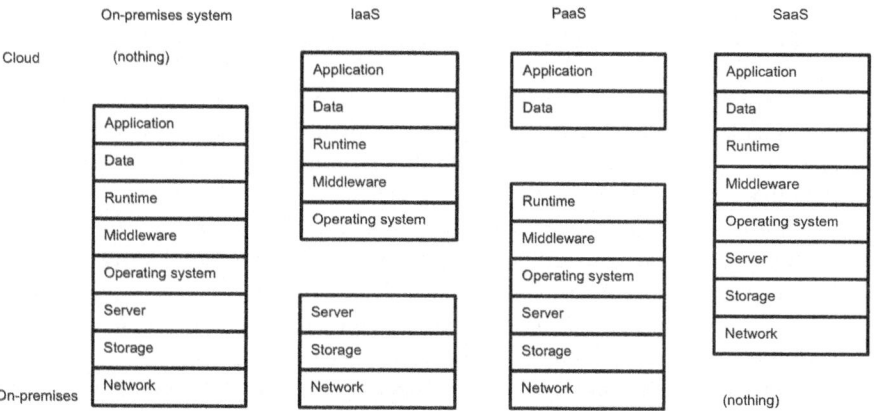

Fig. 6.1 Distribution of software layers in different types of cloud software. (After Chellammal and Pethuru 2023, p. 53 ff.)

The most interesting for us is the application level, Software as a Service. The idea behind this is to take over the hosting of applications. An earlier term with a slightly different focus for this was "Application Service Providing (ASP)," which, however, did not establish itself in this form. According to Repschläger et al. (2010, p. 7), the main difference between ASP and SaaS is the better customization possibility of SaaS.

An early well-known example for business cloud software is the CRM service salesforce.com (Chellammal and Pethuru 2023, p. 69). Nowadays, many software systems are offered both in an on-premises and a cloud version. They are usually operated by the software vendor. In theory, there should be no difference in how to make use of the software, especially the adaptability (see Chap. 15). But in practice, there are often more restrictions with cloud software. This may be for cost reasons—by limiting customization options, operating costs can be reduced, or more revenue can be generated from the sale of software licenses (on-premises). On the other hand, companies using the cloud product will often use a more up-to-date version than when using on-premises systems. This is because service providers are quicker in switching to a newer version and in applying bug fixes.

(b) **Location of the Cloud**

Distinctions arise according to the following questions:

Question 1: Are computing resources used exclusively for one company?

In a *private cloud*, the cloud software for one company runs separately from that for other companies, i.e., specific computing resources are assigned to only this company. In a *public cloud*, this need not be the case. The operator of the cloud software can thus use the same hardware and software for multiple companies in a public cloud, which reduces costs.

The separation in a private cloud achieves better data isolation. And it results in more individual performance control for the company. The private cloud can be operated by the company itself or by a service provider. In the first case, it is similar to the on-premises approach. This is referred to as an *internal cloud*. (What is the difference?) Access is securely provided via a virtual private network (VPN) over the Internet.

Question 2: Does a company use multiple cloud services?

Question 2.1: Are the cloud services used in a mixed form?

If a public cloud is used for some applications and a private one for others, this is called a *hybrid cloud* (a mixed form). In this case, business-critical applications could run in the internal cloud, non-critical ones in the public (Chellammal and Pethuru 2023, p. 50).

Question 2.2: Are the cloud services from different providers?

A company can also use a combination of different cloud software, combined even with on-premises systems. This is referred to as a *multi-cloud* (Chellammal and Pethuru 2023, p.306). A similar term is *hybrid IT*: the mix or simultaneous use of on-premises and cloud systems.

Especially with public clouds, companies may have concerns about data security (data loss) and data protection (unauthorized access to data or passing data to other parties). Cloud providers try to gain confidence by taking measures and informing about them (cf. Saueressig et al. 2023, p. 490). Examples are biometric access controls to buildings, uninterrupted power supply, and encrypted data backups in separate data centers. Security certificates, based, e.g., on ISO standards for information security management systems or the American National Standards Institute, serve to testify the security measures. Another measure are penetration tests by external ethical hackers. Companies may have particular concerns about data protection when the data center is located in a country with reservation concerning confidentiality or it is not even known in which data center (among several possible ones) the data actually is. Against such concerns, a data center can be operated in European Union Access Mode, where operation, maintenance, and support exclusively come from countries of the European Union.

6.1.3 Architecture

Technically, cloud software providers extensively use virtualization to efficiently utilize their systems and achieve elasticity. (What advantages do companies gain from using a cloud?)

Figure 6.2 illustrates the relationship between physical computing resources, virtual computing resources, and their allocation to the users (tenants) of cloud software.

The physical computing resources $p_1, \ldots, p_n$ represent the actual existing computers, storage media, and networks. They can be heterogeneous and located at geographically distant places. A virtualization layer makes these appear uniformly as virtual resources $v_1, \ldots, v_m$. This is done using a mapping that will also include mergers and divisions (not shown in the figure). It is managed by a virtual machine monitor, also known as a hypervisor. A virtual machine is a "container" with an operating system and applications. This allows multiple operating systems to run simultaneously on a physical machine, each in separate virtual machines (Chellammal and Pethuru 2023, p. 82). Depending on the type of computing resource, the effect is slightly different: For servers, it means that several virtual machines share a physical server. According to Chellammal and Pethuru (2023, p. 119), 30 virtual servers can be configured on one physical server. For storage media, it means that several heterogeneous storages can be seen as a single logical storage. The amount of virtual resources can finally be allocated to the tenants

Fig. 6.2 Physical and virtual resources and their allocation

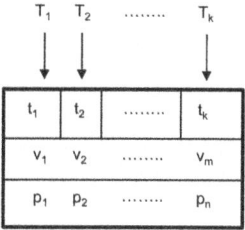

(Tenants) $t_1, \ldots, t_k$. This should happen dynamically, i.e., if a tenant's performance requirement changes, more or fewer resources can be quickly allocated ("dynamic provisioning"). This is the elasticity mentioned in Sect. 6.1.1, and as it is short term, it is even "rapid elasticity." The sets of resources allocated to the tenants are disjoint for security reasons. If the sum of all tenants' resources is below the physical resources deployed at a given time, this works well. If it were exceeded, additional physical resources would have to be activated to meet the performance requirements (response times, throughput). In a certain sense, this resembles the theoretical model of a Turing machine, which also has no performance limitation, there regarding storage, as storage can be expanded at any time.

Another form of virtualization is through *containers*. The operating system is dynamically divided into isolated containers—only one operating system for separate runtime environments. This is also referred to as operating system virtualization. This form of virtualization is particularly efficient, as the effort for creating and destroying a container is low (Chellammal and Pethuru 2023, p. 243).

For the provider of cloud software, the flexible provision of resources with extensive use of virtualization means that manual configuration will no longer be manageable. Instead, tools are used (cloud management platform tools) to carry it out programmatically (Chellammal and Pethuru 2023, p. 269). For example, there is software-defined networking for managing virtual networks, with which all network components are configured programmatically and abstracting from provider-specific network details (Chellammal and Pethuru 2023, p. 97).

6.1.4 Evaluation

Let's look at the advantages and disadvantages or risks for companies using cloud services:

Advantages:

- No large initial investments are required as with software licenses and infrastructure in the case of on-premises systems. Especially for small and medium-sized companies, particularly start-up companies, this can be an important argument. The idea is thus to replace fixed costs with variable ones.
- Only the required performance is purchased. In contrast, an on-premises enterprise information system is typically set up for peak load, while on average, a much lower performance was necessary.
- Long-term capital commitment and IT competence are not necessary. The contract terms are short (Repschläger et al. 2010, p. 9).

Disadvantages or risks:

- Many companies have less experience than with the operation of on-premises systems. It may therefore seem uncertain how well the approach works in the company.

- Since business data processing is handed over to others, great trust is necessary. This concerns not only the question of availability but also data security and confidentiality (see above).
- Today's cloud services are largely proprietary; there are no standards. Therefore, a quick switch to another provider is difficult. This is referred to as *vendor lock-in*. However, the situation with on-premises systems is similar.

6.2 Microservices

Up to now, we saw an enterprise information system as a monolithic installation unit with many interwoven ("integrated") functions and data, grouped in business objects and used in business processes. If you want a newer, enhanced version of just one part of it, one service, a new version of the entire system, is required.

With microservices, on the other hand, the view of application software is a multitude of largely independently developed "services" ("microservices," to emphasize the granularity—the service is not a whole system but a smaller unit) (Newman 2021, Chap. 1). It is both a development concept and an operating model. (What is the difference between a cloud service and a microservice?)

Approaches to services have been around for some time. A popular term in the 2000s was "service-oriented architecture" (SOA). In recent years, the aim has been to further develop the service idea with microservices. For a better understanding, let's take a brief look at the predecessor, the service-oriented architecture.

The motivation for the *service-oriented architecture (SOA)* was flexibility and reusability. Regarding flexibility, it is argued that today's business processes must be able to change very quickly so that a company can act and react quickly in the market. If the application functionality is available in the form of individual services, a business process can be designed quickly. (Does the argument also apply to microservices?) Regarding reusability, it should be noted that in large companies, largely similar or even the same functionality is often implemented in several places, in several systems. The goal is now to define reusable services that can be utilized in all places.

Accordingly, a basic idea of a service-oriented architecture is to first identify services and define their interfaces in such a way that they are reusable. Only in a second step it is considered how and in particular in which systems the services are realized.

Microservices are less about reusability than about modularization of application functionality: A microservice should represent a delimited business task of a certain size. A microservice is thus much smaller than an enterprise information system. The size is indirectly given by the size of the development group for its realization, namely, five to ten people. More extensive application functionality is therefore divided into small parts that can be developed and installed independently. It is agile software development, and microservices are mostly used for business custom software. In Schwartz (2017), examples of large Internet, trade, and financial companies are mentioned. The development group should not only develop the microservice but also operate it.

Each microservice should have its own database, either different instances of the same database or even different database systems, but at least separate database schemas (Schwartz 2017, p. 592). The microservices are developed independently of each other. For each microservice, a separate programming language, a software development environment, and a database product could be chosen. A microservice runs on a platform called "macro architecture" in the context of microservices—this in contrast to the structure of a microservice, the "micro architecture." The platform provides, e.g., load balancing or monitoring of the correct execution of the microservices.

The communication of the microservices with each other is done via APIs, technically usually implemented as REST-based Web services (see Sect. 11.8). For better performance, a microservice could make copies of data from another microservice (see Chap. 10). To keep the copies consistent, polling or the "publish-and-subscribe principle" can be used or more general events for notification of state changes (see Chap. 10).

In its basic form, microservices are therefore a distributed system of hierarchically equal fine-grained software components. An additional structure can be introduced as "self-contained system" (Schwartz 2017), consisting of several parts, which can be microservices. This brings us closer to modularly developed monolithic systems. According to Newman (2021, Chap. 14), this approach is currently less common.

It remains to be analyzed for which scenarios microservices are advantageous and for which the "classic" system approach or intermediate stages. In Schwartz (2017), this is discussed a little, and the example of the online service StackOverflow with a monolithic architecture and yet short development time is pointed out.

Generally, a few critical words concerning architectural styles and development methods in information systems (especially in practice) should be added: In my view, there is little scientific investigation of the superiority of one or other approach. Mostly there are just anecdotal experience reports, "success stories." They are far from a systematic investigation as we know it from other areas, e.g., systematic experiments in the natural sciences, studies on drugs, or, more generally, in evidence-based medicine. The statement that a method or an architecture was successful in a number of companies or projects cannot yet be considered a scientific proof. (What would such a scientific proof look like?)

6.3   Types of Content

In Chap. 2, we saw that an enterprise information system is application programs plus their company-specific customizing. The application programs are based on an application platform. We want to call the "content" of the enterprise information system everything that is added to the application platform. This can vary, depending on the type and specific form of an enterprise information system. An ERP system contains many directly (after customizing) usable application programs. In contrast, in a data warehouse system, there is only generic software for the definition time (e.g., design of data cubes, basic functions for data cleaning) and the runtime (e.g., aggregation support, buffering mechanisms).

Let's now look at a classification scheme for the content of an enterprise information system to address further types of content. The scheme uses three dimensions, each with a value range, which we will use for our classification examples:

1. Type of Content (T)
   - *Program objects* (p): This comprises all "things" in the enterprise information system of program type in the broader sense. ("Object" is not meant in the sense of object-orientation here.) This includes of course the source code of the business application programs and screens of the user interface but also database tables and globally usable data type definitions or business processes realized as workflows (see Chap. 12). Negatively characterized, it is everything that is not data (customizing, master, and transaction data). The value p can be refined by the program objects occurring in the respective enterprise information system, e.g., in database table, screen, and application program.
   - *Data* (d): Here too, a refinement is possible, for example, in customizing master and transaction data.
2. *Usability* (U)
   - *Immediately usable* (i): This content can be used immediately, without adaption.
   - *Copy template* (c): The content cannot be used immediately but serves as a copy template. A copy is then modified, adapted to the company's needs.
3. *Creator* (C): The creator of the content is indicated.
   - *Standard* (s): It is a standard object or data, i.e., the creator is the software provider.
   - *Add-on* (a): The enterprise information system has been extended with additional functionality, e.g., by a software development partner.
   - *New, company-specific* (n): The company that uses the content also created it.

With this scheme, we can classify content by triples (T, U, C) where T, U, and C take the respective values of their dimension. Let's look at some examples. (Think about why the given values make sense.) We start with the obvious and then discuss further possibilities.

1. A standard function, e.g., in an ERP system, has the value (p, i, s).
2. Master and transaction data in a production system (see Chap. 15). (What is the value of the tuple (T, U, C)?)
3. A currency unit has the value (d, i, s). It makes sense when standard software provides such content because every company needs a subset of the currency units.

4. In some enterprise information systems, a "model company" with demo data is available to familiarize yourself with the software using a test or training installation. The content of such a model company is (d, i, s).

5. Some systems provide "business content," proposals for certain standard cases. In a data warehouse system, this could be a data cube for evaluations in sales. Such "business content" has the value (p, c, s).

6. A standard role (see Chap. 16) in a business system has the value (d, i + c, s). Here we see that a value can serve different purposes: The standard role could in some cases (e.g., some companies) be used immediately and in others serve as a copy template.

7. A company-specific role (see Chap. 16) has the value (d, i, n).

(Can you find a combination possibility (T, U, C), for which there is no practical use case?)

6.4   Open-Source Systems

Another distinction of enterprise information systems results from their origin: Is a system a commercial product, an open-source system, or a custom development? Most common in this area today are commercial products. In contrast to custom developments, this is mainly due to economic reasons. In contrast to open-source systems, this may be due to limited availability of suitable open-source systems for the company type and size and probably also due to stability considerations. In certain areas, e.g., Big Data and machine learning software, open-source software is widespread.

With open-source software, two types of offers can be observed: On the one hand, a free "community edition," which many people think what open-source software is, and, on the other hand, a commercial "enterprise edition," which includes services for maintenance but often also additional functions. So here we see a hybrid form between commercial and (according to the common conception of pure, free) open-source software. There can be competing enterprise editions of different providers for an open-source software.

6.5   Exercises and Proposed Solutions

(a) Exercises

Exercise 6.1 (Multi-Tenancy)
What are the advantages and disadvantages of the following forms to realize multi-tenancy in cloud software: separate database, separate table, and same table?

Exercise 6.2 (Internal Cloud)
What reasons could there be for an internal cloud, as opposed to on-premises systems?

Exercise 6.3 (ERP and Microservices)
Assume you implement ERP functionality with microservices. Which microservices would you design? Would the microservices need to communicate with each other? In what way?

Exercise 6.4 (Microservice Development)
Each microservice could have its own programming language and database. What are the advantages and disadvantages of this?

(b) Proposed Solutions for the Exercises

Exercise 6.1
Separate database: high data isolation, full customization, separate performance control. Separate tables: full customization, table name calculation necessary for SQL accesses. Same table: easy access, customization options limited.

Exercise 6.2
Above all centralization, proliferation is thus prevented. Also, advantages that apply to other clouds (e.g., public) play a role, e.g., better hardware utilization through shared use.

Exercise 6.3
An option would be the granularity of business objects. If the microservices have their own data storage, communication takes place via method calls (interfaces). Would this approach make sense in a tightly integrated and standardized ERP system?

Exercise 6.4
The advantages and disadvantages of the programming language are similar to Best-of-Breed and Best-of-Suite (cf. Chap. 8). In addition, the skills of the development teams should be taken into consideration. As for the database, performance is also an issue (cf. the considerations in Chap. 5).

6.6   Self-Assessment

6.1 Cloud Computing

1. What skills are no longer needed in a company if only SaaS cloud products are used? Which ones do you still need?
2. How can the phrase "on demand" be interpreted in the context of cloud products?

3. Does an internal public cloud make sense?
4. What is the difference between a multi-cloud and a hybrid IT?
5. How is elasticity achieved in a cloud architecture?
6. Do cloud applications need interfaces?
7. Think about whether the term "application platform" introduced in Chap. 2 relates to IaaS or PaaS!

6.2 Microservices

8. Compare an API of an enterprise information system with a microservice. What is similar, and what is different?
9. Is it sensible to implement an ERP system as a set of cooperating microservices?

6.3 Content Types

10. Who provides "program objects" in an enterprise information system, who "data"?
11. Are there quasi-copy templates that can be used directly? Example?

6.4 Open-Source Systems

12. What is the advantage of providing open-source software in a cloud system (e.g., Big Data software)?

References

Further Reading

A comprehensive presentation of cloud computing is offered by:
Chellammal, S., Pethuru Raj, C.: Essentials of Cloud Computing, 2nd edn. Springer Nature, Switzerland (2023)

Microservices are comprehensively treated in:
Newman, S.: Building Microservices, 2nd edn. O'Reilly, Beijing (2021)

Further Cited Literature and Sources

Repschläger, J., Pannicke, D., Zarnekow, R.: Cloud Computing: Definitionen, Geschäftsmodelle und Entwicklungspotentiale. HMD Prax. Wirtschaftsinform. 275, 6–15 (2010)
Saueressig, T., Stein, T., Boeder, J., Kleis, W.: SAP S/4HANA—Architecture. Rheinwerk, Boston (2023)
Schwartz, A.: Microservices. Aktuelles Schlagwort. Informatik-Spektrum. **40**(6), 590–594 (2017)

Part II
Integration

Overview of Part II

7

Old Wall! *Pause.* Beyond is the … other hell.
Samuel Beckett (Endspiel Fin de partie Endgame,
first edition, Suhrkamp Paperback 171,
Frankfurt a. M., 1974, p. 40)

Summary
This chapter serves as a framework for the following chapters, which deal with integration techniques for enterprise information systems in a system landscape at all levels of our modeling view: the integration through data exchange at the level of business data; the integration via the user interface and the integration via the application logic using function calls, both at the level of business objects; and finally the integration using process management systems at the level of business processes.

Learning Objective

- To introduce the term "system landscape" and gain an overview of the integration techniques, which will be described in detail in the following chapters.

(a) **System Landscape**

Already in Chap. 3 with the interfaces of transactional systems, even more in Chap. 4 with the ETL process, and finally in Chap. 6 with microservices, we have seen that several enterprise information systems need to work together; they need to be integrated. In large companies, these can be hundreds of systems. Some or even all of them could be available in a cloud. Not everyone will be coupled with every other. Nevertheless, the integration effort is considerable.

The result is a *system landscape*. Figure 7.1 picks up a part of Fig. 1.1 from the introduction. The systems are now darker. We no longer look into the individual systems or system types in detail but treat them as black boxes. We will deal with the system landscape, the coupling of a company's enterprise information systems (dark parts), in Chap. 8. The following chapters are dedicated to the arrows of the image, the various integration techniques (Chaps. 9–12). Let us take a first look at these arrows.

In Chap. 2 and more specifically in Chap. 3, the modeling levels business data, business objects, and business processes were introduced. Furthermore, business interfaces for integrating the enterprise information systems of a system landscape were addressed. In fact, the integration can be carried out on all three levels (Fig. 7.2).

Let's look at the typical schematic structure of application programs (Fig. 7.3). We distinguish therein the levels of user dialogue, application logic, and data access (cf. the three-tier client-server technology in Chap. 5). Applications without dialogue, of course, lack the top level. (What replaces it?) For the following classification, this view is sufficient (cf. however the remarks on the presentation layer in Sect. 5.2). The various forms of integration can be illustrated according to this scheme.

(b) **Integration Through Data Exchange**
With this approach at the level of business data, data is ultimately exchanged between the databases of the application programs or systems (Fig. 7.4). In fact, this integration involves test and transformation logic in the receiving system in

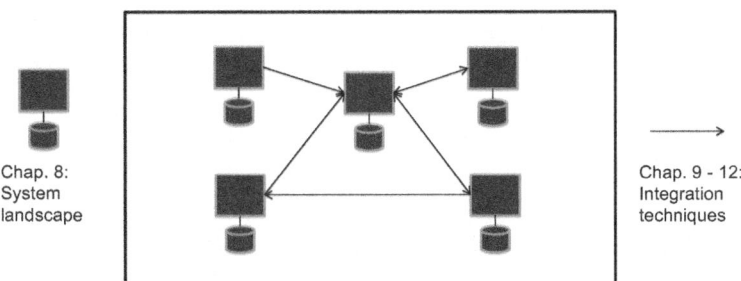

Fig. 7.1 Overview

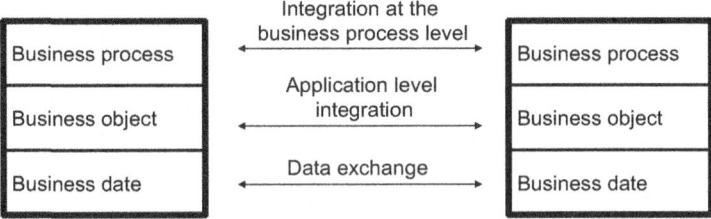

Fig. 7.2 Integration options

Fig. 7.3 Structure of an application program

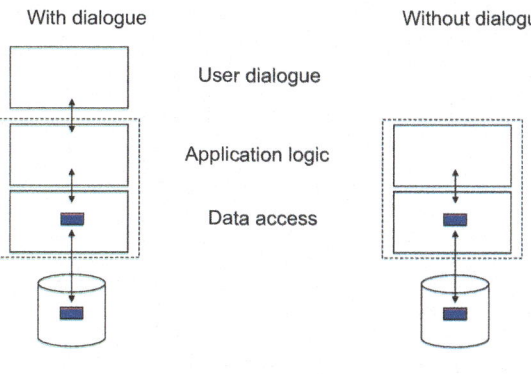

With dialogue

User dialogue

Application logic

Data access

Without dialogue

Fig. 7.4 Integration at the level of the business data

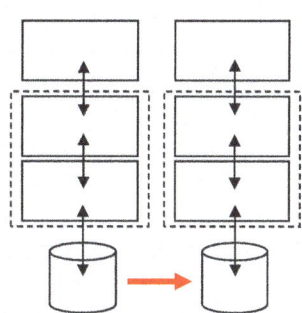

order to maintain data consistency. Also, data is usually not simply extracted from the database and sent in the sender system's format or, conversely, transformed into the recipient system's format. Rather, often a neutral data exchange format is used. This is why the trigger on the sender side is in fact the application layer. The difference to integration via the application logic is that here the intended use (i.e., the method, such as "create," "change") of the transmitted data is only implicit; only data is sent.

Usually, one of the systems is the "owner" of certain data (cf. Sect. 8.4), and the data is only provided to the other system as a copy, often with read-only program logic. This approach was used in Chap. 4. The transmission format must at least be agreed upon between the sender and recipient system. However, a standard that is understood by many systems is better. (Why?) XML is often used as the base technology. The technical implementation is discussed in Chap. 10.

At the business object level, there are two integration approaches: via the user interface and via the application logic (Fig. 7.5).

(c) **Integration via the User Interface**

On the one hand, you can use an integration software (a third software, in addition to system 1 and 2) such as a Web portal, from whose user interface dialog methods of the two systems can be called. This is referred to as *frontend integration*. This is in contrast to *backend integration*, also called *Enterprise Application Integration* (*EAI*), which is achieved through data exchange or via

Fig. 7.5 Integration at the level of business objects

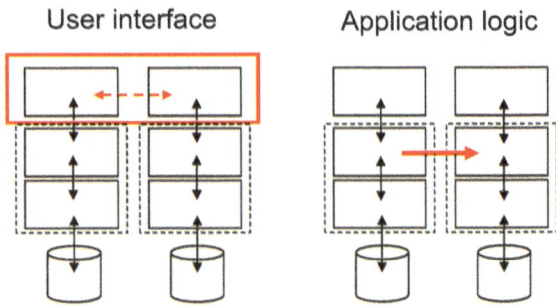

the application logic. A Web portal is in fact the typical form to integrate via the user interface. It may integrate many application programs from several systems but also other information sources. In addition to the mere juxtaposition of applications, a certain simple form of data transfer via the user interface is possible. This approach is discussed in Chap. 9. For the user, the result looks like just one enterprise information system; he does not see that the functions are running in different systems.

(d) **Integration via the Application Logic (Integration Through Function Call)**
A method of a business object is called in another system, usually without user dialog. In computer science, this corresponds to a procedure call or a function call, which is why we choose the term *integration through function call* (Chap. 11). A special feature is that the application programs can be developed in different programming languages, which requires a cross-language function call. From classic remote procedure call to Web services, there are various techniques for this. We have already discussed an example in Chap. 6, microservices. With microservices, an external system function or service call is not the exception but the rule for coupling application logic. (Why is it the rule there, but not in the "classic" approach?)

(e) **Integration at the Business Process Level**
At the level of business processes, there are also two possibilities (Fig. 7.6):

- **Orchestration**: A central business process carries out method calls in the various systems of the system landscape. (Is integration by means of data exchange or function call also necessary for this?)
- **Choreography**: In this case, decentralized business processes in the systems of the system landscape communicate with each other. Virtually, this also results in a system-wide business process. (What do the arrows between the two processes mean?)

In Chap. 12, the focus is mainly on orchestration using business process management systems.

While our considerations primarily refer to the integration between systems of a company's system landscape, the integration techniques are generally also applicable to the integration within just one system and between systems of business partners:

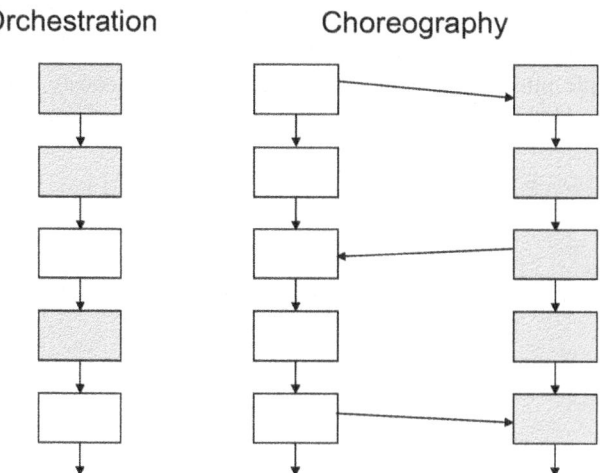

Fig. 7.6 Integration at the level of business processes

Within one system:

- Business data level: In an integrated application system, this will hardly occur, as communication takes place via the common database (in distributed systems, this is called "communication by *shared memory*").
- Business object level: Local function or method call.
- Business process level: Both of the mentioned forms are also possible in only one system, namely, orchestration using a process management system and choreography using event control (see Chap. 12).

Between business partners:

- Business data level: Inter-company integration through exchange of business documents such as EDI messages or XML documents.
- Business object level: Both of the mentioned forms are possible: an enterprise portal for suppliers as an example of an integration via the user interface and the use of Web services in the system of the business partner as a form of integration via the application logic.
- Business process level: Here, choreography is particularly relevant, although not as widespread as, e.g., EDI, which can be seen as an implicit choreography.

7.1 Self-Assessment

1. Electronic Data Interchange standards define business data and corresponding formats that can be used for intercompany integration. Is this merely an integration at the business data level or also at other levels?

2. What problems would arise if business data were exchanged directly between the databases of the involved systems?
3. Can multiple integration techniques be used simultaneously between two systems? Example?

System Landscape

8

It's too much for one man.
Samuel Beckett (Warten auf Godot En attendant Godot Waiting for Godot,
first edition, Suhrkamp Taschenbuch 1,
Frankfurt a. M., 1971, p. 28)

Every man his speciality.
Samuel Beckett (Endspiel Fin de partie Endgame,
first edition, Suhrkamp Paperback 171,
Frankfurt a. M., 1974, p. 20)

Summary

A system landscape comprises the enterprise information systems of a company and their connections. Usually, there are many in large companies, even more if also smaller individual application programs are taken into account. The systems must work together and therefore need to be integrated. We look at the difficulties that arise in integration, as well as approaches to solve them. For documentation, but also for system administration and data exchange between the systems, system landscapes are depicted in a model. In addition to common box diagrams, there are digital versions.

Learning Objectives

- To be able to assess the current situation of a system landscape with a variety of different systems.
- To get an overview of types of systems and what their specific tasks are.
- To get to know problems and possible solutions for the diversity.

© The Author(s), under exclusive license to Springer-Verlag GmbH, DE,
part of Springer Nature 2025
R. Weber, *Enterprise Information Systems*,
https://doi.org/10.1007/978-3-662-71718-9_8

8.1   Motivation

A company uses additional enterprise information systems alongside an ERP system mainly because they provide specialized functionality (see Exercise 8.1). This argument is particularly valid for larger companies, and we have already encountered it in the chapter on analytical systems. In fact, there are often hundreds of larger and smaller software systems and programs in companies that work together. They can be on-premises or in the cloud, and any mixture is possible, such as systems in different clouds (multi-cloud; see Sect. 6.1).

To motivate such *system landscapes*, we first look at what theoretical options there are, starting from a single enterprise information system (like an ERP system) to expand the application functionality. The starting point is therefore an enterprise information system S1 with its database DB1. The additional functionality is S2, which requires additional persistence DB2 (new tables or additional fields in existing tables). Various models are possible (see Fig. 8.1):

(a) *Further development*: The first idea is to add the functionality S2 to the system S1 and accordingly extend the database DB1 by DB2. Let's call this extended database DB1+2 (see Fig. 8.1a). In this approach, S2 is not an independent software component or even a system but simply additional functionality in the existing system. S2 can use S1, e.g., access tables from DB1 or call functions from S1. DB1 and DB2 are actually just subsets of the database DB1+2. S1, on the other hand, will not access DB2 because S1 does not yet know this new part: S2 is developed with knowledge of S1, but S1 has no knowledge of S2.

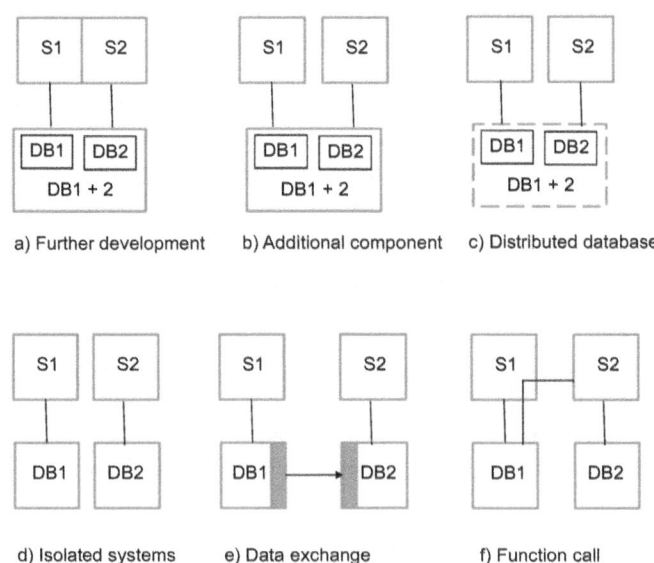

Fig. 8.1 System extension: options

(b) *Additional component*: A somewhat stronger separation is found in Fig. 8.1b. As before, there is a common database, but S2 has a greater independence from S1. It has not become a part of S1 but can be installed separately from S1. This approach is found today, for example, in "add-ons," which are installed and operated with an existing system. S1 and S2 use the same runtime environment.

(c) *Distributed database*: The separation has become stronger: S1 and S2 run in separate runtime environments; they are already separate systems. Each has a database, DB1 or DB2. However, they actually access a larger, distributed database DB1+2. According to our assumptions, this actually only applies to S2, because S1 is not aware of S2 and its database DB2. S2 can access DB1+2 similarly to (b). Internally, however, the protocols of a distributed database system run (see, e.g., (Connolly and Begg 2015, Chap. 24) or (Lemahieu et al. 2018, Chap. 16)). A distributed database system DB1+2 is a distributed system where the actual database systems DB1 and DB2 communicate to achieve a virtual larger database system DB1+2. While distributed database systems were probably designed exactly for this purpose, they do not really occur in practice today. One reason may be that both systems (or at least S2 according to our assumptions) need to know the database schema DB1+2, so there is a dependency on the database schema from DB2. Therefore, the database schema DB2 would have to be an interface of S1. Interfaces, on the other hand, are nowadays more likely to be provided at the level of data exchange and function call (see Chaps. 10 and 11).

(d) *Isolated systems*: This means, in fact, a step backward, compared with the previous models: The two systems and databases formally have nothing in common. They might have an indirect coupling via other systems though. We present this case especially for the systematic transition to the following more practically relevant models.

(e) *Data exchange*: Complete isolation is hardly conceivable, but a considerable independence may apply. It might be the case that both systems need certain common master data, e.g., suppliers. Each accesses its own supplier data, so on the system landscape level, there is redundancy. Even if the table names, field names, and their data types differ, from a business point of view, it is the same supplier. If a supplier was therefore created by S1 in DB1, it must be copied. Instead of re-entering "by hand," data exchange (see Chap. 10) is preferable. In Fig. 8.1e, the gray area in DB1 signals that this part was copied to DB2. This case occurs frequently in system landscapes of enterprise information systems.

(f) *Function call*: As an alternative to data exchange, a request from S2 to S1 can occur when data is needed. The line between (e) and (f) is not sharp. After all, S1 does not know what S2 does with the transmitted data. Are they stored (definitely or at least temporarily buffered), i.e., yielding a result similar to (e)? Or are only parts of it stored, perhaps in a modified form? (What is the purpose of the storage?) The pure case would be to store nothing and to make a (new) request for data each time it is needed.

The model of function call frequently occurs in practice. We discuss it in more detail in Chap. 11. It is particularly utilized in microservices, where each service should have its own data storage to be largely independent of others (see Sect. 6.2).

The models can also occur in combination: For some functions or data, one model is chosen and for others a different one.

It should be noted that in the above models (d–f), it is crucial for the separation of the databases that at least the database *schema* of DB1 is separated from that of DB2. If two separate logical databases were running on the same server, they would still be separate databases according to our model.

Let's now look at a small example of a system landscape.

System landscapes are usually depicted by diagrams like Fig. 8.2. We see different systems: At the center is an ERP system. It uses an EDI system to exchange Electronic Data Interchange (EDI) messages. Accordingly, there is an interface between the two systems. Engineers create technical drawings with a CAD system, which is also connected via an interface. We have discussed interfaces of this kind in the chapter on transactional systems. SCM systems and data warehouse systems were discussed in Chap. 4. What is new is a Customer Relationship Management (CRM) system, which we will look at in detail a little later. And finally, there is a custom analysis program written in-house, a spreadsheet program for controllers. Many controllers have a preference for such analysis.

We can distinguish different system categories:

- *Enterprise*: ERP, data warehouse, and SCM we have already met. Another one, CRM, follows below.
- *Technical*: CAD, time recording, EDI.
- *Document-oriented*: content management, archive, document management.
- *Office*: spreadsheet, word processing, project system, email.
- *Internet*: Web server, firewall, proxy server. Such systems are often omitted in diagrams of the system landscape and are considered technical subsystems of other systems.

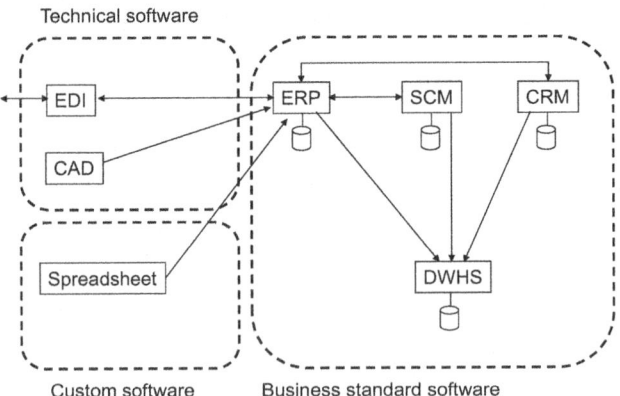

Fig. 8.2 A system landscape

We discuss in Exercise 8.1 why there may be even multiple systems of the same type in a company, usually ERP.

At the overview level, each system is represented just as a "box." In fact, a single system can already have a richer structure. (Example?)

8.2 Problems and Solutions

The following description is based on on-premises systems. Considering the concepts of "multi-cloud" and "hybrid IT" (see Sect. 6.1.2), there are many similarities with cloud products and mixtures with on-premises systems. In Exercise 8.4, we will address this.

(a) *One System Versus a System Landscape*

Let's compare the situation where a company only uses one system (which is of course unrealistic for larger companies—What kind of enterprise information system will that be?), with that of a many systems. The following differences are noticeable:

- There are multiple systems that need to be installed separately in the case of on-premises systems.
- The systems can come from different vendors. Especially then they have a different "philosophy," which is expressed in many ways, from different user interfaces (handling of the system) to differences in the correction of software errors (system administration). (Examples?)
- Each system usually has its own data storage. For enterprise information systems like ERP, SCM, and CRM, this is a database.
- The systems may require different operating systems, so the IT infrastructure of on-premises systems can be heterogeneous. This difference occurs in cases, for example, when a particular system component is currently only available for Microsoft Windows operating systems.
- The version changes of the systems are carried out separately at different times. (Why?)
- The systems are interconnected via connections and interfaces. These interfaces can be of different nature and quality: Some are part of the standard software, and interoperability tests have at least been carried out with other systems of the vendor. Others have been developed by the company using the system. However, not every system will be directly coupled with every other.
- The management of the systems is often decentralized.
- A system type, e.g., ERP, can occur multiple times, for example, there may be country-specific systems.

(b) *Problems*

Due to the differences, some problems arise, which do not occur when using only a single system:

- In the case of on-premises systems, more installations need to be carried out.

- As a rule, more computers are needed, unless virtualization is used.
- A diverse know-how is needed, in particular for system administration and system implementation.
- Integration effort when implementing the systems.
- Integration problems during runtime, e.g., when a system is temporarily not accessible.
- A separate login is required for each system, which can be remedied or mitigated by approaches such as single sign-on (see Chap. 9).
- Data inconsistency due to data redundancy is possible. This mainly affects master data. (Example?)
- After a version change of a system, it must be checked whether the interaction with the other systems still works. (Why might it not work anymore?)
- In the case of strong decentralization, a proliferation of systems, system settings, and different business processes can occur. Strong centralization, on the other hand, can be inflexible and bureaucratic.
- Some systems might only be poorly used: You only need a specific part of the system, but in the case of on-premises systems, you have to install and operate the entire system.

(c) *Solutions*

For the above problems, there are some solutions, which can at least alleviate the problems:

- Instead of a very heterogeneous system landscape where you choose the "best" system for each task (*best of breed*), some companies prefer to use a *best-of-suite* approach to reduce integration effort: That one software vendor is chosen who solves the company's problems best with his product range (suite). The integration effort between systems of one vendor is rightly estimated to be lower than between systems of different vendors.
- Related to this point: Choose products from as few software vendors as possible. Choosing just one vendor will usually not be possible, as no software vendor offers all the types of software needed in a company.
- Use of integration techniques.
- Centralization, fewer systems, e.g., not using a separate system for each area/region. If this is currently the case, try to merge the systems.
- Use of powerful computers and virtualization, so that in the case of on-premises systems, at least overall fewer computers need to be administered, e.g., one powerful application server instead of several less powerful ones, always considering cost-effectiveness (see Chap. 5).
- Check which software components are actually being used (logging), and turn off unused parts. These will not be whole enterprise information systems but parts within an enterprise information system. Often, these parts are unnecessarily maintained from one version to the next (see Chap. 15).
- Migration of legacy systems to a uniform software (of one vendor).

8.3 Patterns in System Landscapes

As in geographical landscapes, certain constellations occur repeatedly in system landscapes, which we would like to call *patterns*. In geographical landscapes, these are, e.g., industrial agglomerations, denser settlement along the coasts or rivers. In system landscapes, it occurs in situations such as close cooperation of related functions, common use of data, and comparing data from different organizational areas. Let's look at some examples.

(a) **Data Consolidation for Analysis**

We already know this pattern from analytical systems (see Fig. 8.3): Data from different sources is consolidated to analyze them together. The comparison of data from different sources is of particular interest. We could call it data integration. However, we avoid this term in order not to confuse it with data integration in ERP systems (access to a common database).

(b) **Central Master Data Management**

A specific solution approach to data inconsistency (see Sect. 8.2) is found in master data management. Master data is created in several systems, sometimes copied to others or—worse—maintained manually twice. (Example?) A solution is a specific system, which manages all master data centrally and thus provides consistent master data to other systems (Fig. 8.4). (A paradoxical situation at first glance: A problem that exists due to the involvement of too many systems is solved by yet another one.)

In our diagram, all master data of two ERP systems as well as an SCM and a PLM system (Product Life cycle Management, a system for managing all data in the life cycle of a product) are maintained in the master data management system and then distributed to the respective systems. This will go smoother if the systems are from the same vendor. (Why?) Ideally, such a system would provide a check logic for master data maintenance, which is compatible with that of the enterprise information systems. This will not be quite simple, because the check logic in the enterprise information systems can depend on system

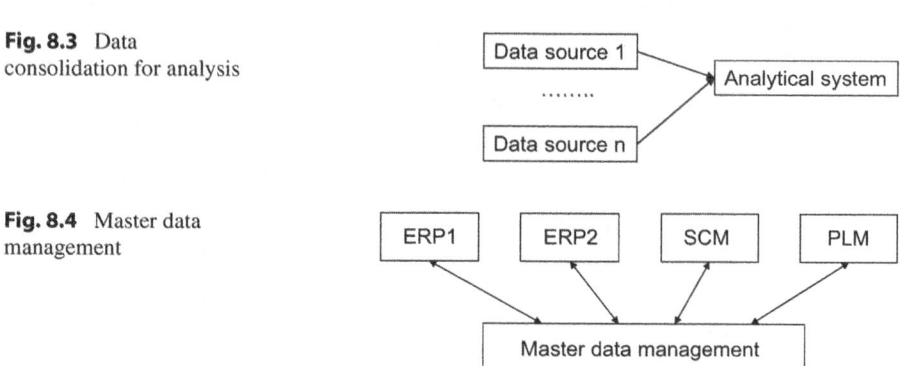

Fig. 8.3 Data consolidation for analysis

Fig. 8.4 Master data management

settings (customizing), and the question arises how exactly this can be replicated in the master data management system.

A weaker integration is not to maintain the master data in a central system but only to analyze and transform (clean) the data there and then distribute the "cleaned" data back to the enterprise information systems. The data transformation resembles that which we have seen in analytical systems (see Sects. 4.1.4 and 4.2.2).

(c) **SCM System Structure**

SCM (see Sect. 4.5) is typically operated in the company in the system structure shown in Fig. 8.5 (according to Bartsch and Teufel 2000). In addition to the SCM system, there is an ERP system and a data warehouse system.

The division of tasks in such a system structure is:

- The SCM system is responsible for *planning*, for which it requires master data (such as materials, suppliers, customers, production sites, warehouses) and transaction data from the ERP system. It also uses analysis data from the data warehouse system, particularly sales data from the past for sales planning. The planning can be imagined as a "proposal," which does not necessarily have to be accepted in its entirety. For this reason, transaction data must be transmitted from the ERP to the SCM system so that the latter knows how the plans were actually carried out.

- The ERP system is responsible for the *execution* of the supply chain. It receives the planning data from the planning system, e.g., a sales plan or a production plan, and implements them. Of course, the ERP system also continues to perform tasks in other areas (accounting, human resources).

- The data warehouse system receives, as shown in Chap. 4, the operational data relevant for evaluation purposes. The data warehouse system also fulfills other tasks, such as in sales or controlling.

(d) **CRM System Structure**

A similar picture emerges with *CRM* (*Customer Relationship Management*). At the center is a CRM system, which offers special functions for marketing, sales, and service (*operational CRM*). Extensive amounts of customer data are collected, which can be analyzed in a data warehouse system (DWHS) (*analytical CRM*).

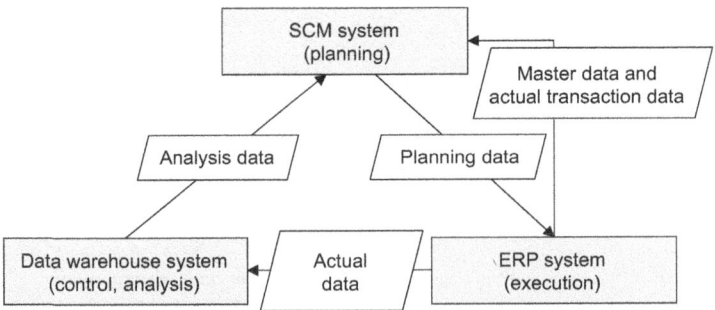

Fig. 8.5 Supply chain management system structure (Bartsch and Teufel 2000)

Fig. 8.6 CRM system structure

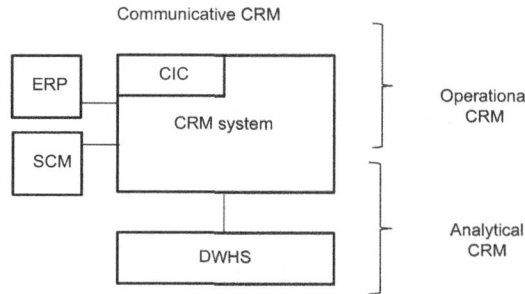

Employees working in the *customer interaction center* (*CIC*), a kind of extended call center and part of the CRM system, have specialized, easy-to-use user interfaces (usually Web interfaces), with which they get a unified view of the customer data, including transaction data such as orders. They can communicate with customers via several communication channels such as conventional telephone as well as Internet chat and telephony *(communicative CRM,* a part of the operational CRM).

A connection also exists to the ERP system, where sales orders are processed. And finally, there can be a connection to the SCM system. An example: A customer wants to find out whether a certain product can be delivered at a certain time. In difficult cases, in addition to a simple availability check on the stock in the ERP system, an extended availability check in an SCM system may be necessary. Not listed in Fig. 8.6 is the *collaborative CRM* to connect business partners and their systems.

8.4   Structural Features

We can further abstract from the patterns of the previous section to structural features, i.e., regularities that are abstract and independent of the specific applications. Some of these are already visible in the graphical modeling; some only become apparent when the systems and their connections are examined in more detail.

(a) **Data Owner**

Certain data, usually master data, is used by several systems. Often, some master data is only maintained in one system. This is then the *data owner* of this master data; the other systems just receive read-only copies.

Example 1:	Let us recapitulate our example of supply chain management (see above): The master data of the ERP system is transmitted to the planning system. However, the ERP system remains the data owner of this master data. The planning system only receives a (possibly renamed or restructured) copy of the master data. In some cases, these can be supplemented with SCM-specific attributes.
Example 2:	Two regional areas of a company use separate ERP systems. Many master data only concern one of the areas and therefore will not leave the respective system. This system is thus the owner of this master data.

(b) *Data Flow*

Related to the feature "data owner," certain data flows from one system to certain others.

Example:	Again, the example of supply chain management: master data flows from the ERP to the planning system.

(c) *Cluster*

Often particularly close relationships can be identified between parts of a system landscape, which can be referred to as *clusters*.

Example:	One more time, the example of supply chain management, now in a system landscape, which includes other systems: The supply chain management system structure, consisting of a planning system, an ERP system, and a data warehouse system, is such a cluster. The ERP system and the data warehouse system can have roles in different clusters. The data warehouse system could, for example, provide analysis for SCM as well as for the analytical CRM.

(d) *Leading System*

This structural feature tells how important a system is in (part of) a system landscape. In the introductory example of the system landscape (Fig. 8.2), the ERP system is the *leading system*, the spreadsheet program for data analysis, and the EDI and the CAD system are downstream systems.

8.5 Modeling

Just as it has proven useful in business process management to model a company's business processes to gain an overview and a common understanding of the processes, system landscapes are modeled as well. And here too, there are more or less formal approaches. The simplest are intuitively understandable but not standardized "box diagrams," such as the diagrams shown above. More sophisticated forms are digital and use standards for recording the system properties.

Such models describe the IT architecture of business data processing. While an *IT architecture* only maps a system landscape and the enterprise information systems contained therein, an *enterprise architecture* includes the human and the organization. Methods and models for enterprise architectures usually describe information systems from various perspectives.

For maintenance reasons, it seems sensible to distinguish in a model between:

- The *role* of the system, e.g., "CRM system," regardless of which product is used.
- The *system* itself, e.g., "the system CRM_central," which will be a specific product with a specific product version.

This can be represented by a hierarchical model: at the top level, only the roles of the systems are visible; at the details level, there are system, product, and product version. The reason for the distinction is that product versions will change from time to time (see Chap. 13), but these changes do not fundamentally affect the system landscape. An exception is if a version offered significantly expanded functionality with the effect that connections to other systems change. In rarer cases, a product can even be replaced by another. Example: A CRM system with ample functionality (but also corresponding complexity) could be replaced in a system landscape by a lightweight, custom-developed mini-CRM system, if only a small part of the CRM functionality is used. In this case, the role "CRM system" remains, and the underlying product and, consequently, the product version are changed.

A model of a system landscape can be used for various purposes:

- *Documentation*: The documentation of the existing system landscape helps in better understanding it. This provides the opportunity for analysis and further development of the system landscape.
- *Administration*: The aim is to gain an overview of which product versions are used where, for considerations of version changes and troubleshooting.
- *Models of cross-system business processes*: The exchange of data between systems can be described in a simpler way. For example, the model of an SCM scenario could just state that data is sent from the ERP to the planning system, only referring to the roles. If the planning system is replaced by another one with a new name and a different computer, the current system can be addressed automatically. It makes sense to use a digital model of the system landscape for this purpose. An example of this can be found in (Hengevoss and Linke 2009).

8.6   Exercises and Proposed Solutions

(a) Exercises

Exercise 8.1 (Reasons and Design Options for Multiple Systems)

(a) For what reasons might a company use multiple ERP systems (Tips: Security, languages, industries)? What are the alternatives?
(b) For what reasons might a company use additional enterprise information systems beyond an ERP system?

Exercise 8.2 (ERP and Component-Oriented Architecture)
In the past, vendors of business application software often only had an ERP system as a product offering, which was supposed to cover the needs of a company. Later, other products, such as CRM or SCM systems, were added. Not only does a CRM system offer functionality on the topic of "customer," but functions in the area of "sales" are already available in the ERP system.

- What are the reasons for the development and use of a CRM system as an additional system?
- What are reasons for extending an ERP system with CRM functionality?

Consider the interests of both the software vendor and the companies that use the application software.

Exercise 8.3 (Merging of Systems)
What problems could arise when merging systems, e.g., after a company merger.

Exercise 8.4 (System Landscape with Cloud Usage)
Which of the phenomena and problems mentioned in Sect. 8.2 also exist in the case of cloud systems?

(b) Proposed Solutions for the Exercises

Exercise 8.1 (Reasons and Design Options for Multiple Systems)

(a) Reasons for multiple ERP systems:
   - "Grown structures," politics.
   - Different business processes at different locations, so that the systems must be implemented differently. However, we should check whether this difference cannot be incorporated into one system, e.g., through organization-specific customization.
   - Individual systems in the individual countries, e.g., because the character sets are different and a system could not use all character sets at the same time in the past; this has been fundamentally solved with Unicode.
   - Data protection: a separate human resources system separated from the rest, so that no "accidental" access to sensitive personal data is possible. This is safer than protection by permissions.
   - Industry solutions (specialized ERP systems) or Best of Breed per area.
   - Performance increase, especially in earlier times, when powerful servers were much more expensive.

   Design options for ERP systems (cf. Davidenkoff and Werner 2008, p. 29):
   - "Single Box," i.e., a central system with a global database and several application servers, i.e., everything in one.
   - Decentralized systems without a shared database, i.e., everything is separate.
   - Decentralized systems with centralized development. This involves providing a template that is used for the common processes; decentralized additions, i.e., a mix of decentralized and centralized.

(b) Reasons for additional systems:
   - Special functions are not offered in the ERP system but in a specialized system (e.g., CRM, SCM).
   - Connecting heterogeneous systems, i.e., not all from the same vendor: Best-of-Breed approach. Or specialized but inexpensive systems are connected with the ERP system.
   - Use of different version cycles for the systems used. This argument applies to both the software vendor and its customers.
   - In addition to transactional systems, analytical systems (e.g., a data warehouse system) can be used; these have different structure and performance characteristics (more details in Chap. 4).

Exercise 8.2 (ERP and Component-Oriented Architecture)
Separate system:

- Specialized system
- Best-of-Breed approach
- Separate version changes possible

  Extension of the ERP system:

- Better integration
- Simpler administration
- Lower costs (?)

Exercise 8.3 (Merging of Systems)
When the enterprise information systems are different products, the business data can, in principle, differ (data structures). Even with the same product, there are problems: different number ranges, different customizing. (Examples?)

Exercise 8.4 (System Landscape with Cloud Usage)
Phenomena 2, 3, 5, 6, 7, and 8 (here possibly multiple tenants at the same cloud provider) and problems 3 (partially) and 4–8.

8.7   Self-Assessment

1. What does the statement "Each system has its own database" mean? What impact has it on the integration of different systems?
2. What can cause data inconsistencies in systems of a system landscape?
3. Why are version changes in systems of a system landscape often carried out separately, at different times?
4. Explain the terms "Best of Breed" and "Best of Suite."
5. What problems can arise when merging systems, i.e., instead of two systems (e.g., ERP systems) using only one?
6. What is meant by "analytical CRM?" What requirements on the system landscape does it impose?

References

Bartsch, H., Teufel, T.: Supply Chain Management mit SAP APO. Galileo Press, Bonn (2000)

Connolly, T., Begg, C.: Database Systems, 6th edn. Pearson, Boston (2015)

Davidenkoff, A., Werner, D.: Global SAP Systems—Design and Architecture. Galileo Press, Bonn (2008)

Hengevoss, W., Linke, A.: SAP NetWeaver System Landscape Directory. Galileo Press, Bonn (2009)

Lemahieu, W., vanden Broucke, S., Baesens, B.: Principles of Database Management. Cambridge University Press, Cambridge (2018)

Integration via the User Interface

9

> As you all know
> you can't just believe everything you are seeing here, can you?
> Now if you'll excuse me, I must be on my way
> *Jimi Hendrix: EXP (Axis: Bold as Love,*
> *LP Track/Polydor, 1967)*

Summary

We get to know enterprise portals as the common representative for integration via the user interface in enterprise information systems. A portal not only integrates business applications in the narrower sense. It also covers knowledge management, collaboration, and office functions as a central workplace. With a role concept, this workplace is designed user specifically so that users see portal contents tailored to their role in the company.

Learning Objective

- To see what degree of integration is possible via the user interface using the example of enterprise portals and, in addition, get to know other aspects of portal systems (role model, single sign-on, access to information, and collaboration).

9.1   Concept

A portal for an employee is a Web application that provides him with a unified access (*single point of access*) to—in the optimal case—all information and applications he needs for his daily work. The information can be stored in different storage systems like file servers and Web servers; the applications can run in different systems. However, due to the unified access, this distribution remains largely hidden from the user. Even though we consider the portal in terms of integration via the user interface, it is primarily a means of integrating people into cross-system business processes: An employee should be able to perform all dialog tasks that arise for him in business processes from the portal.

Portals can be divided into different categories (Großmann and Koschek 2005, p. 29 ff.), e.g., whether they are open to all people or only to a certain group of people (open and closed portals) and which group of people, such as employees, suppliers, or customers.

We are interested in *enterprise portals*, i.e., closed portals that are intended for the employees of a company or for business partners. Business partners, such as suppliers, can access the portal via an extranet (an access to an intranet via the Internet). Related to portals is the term "intranet," an internal Web application providing links to internally used Web sites and sometimes also applications. In contrast to a portal, an intranet usually does not offer personalized access and no linking of the applications among each other (Nicolescu et al. 2007, p. 36). In the following, we briefly call an enterprise portal just *portal*.

In Fig. 9.1, you find the motivation for application integration via the user interface. The clerk operates selected applications in an ERP and a supplier relationship management system (SRM). Without a portal, she would have to log in to two systems. The user IDs and passwords could be different. Likewise, the access (e.g., via different fat clients) to the two systems may differ from each other, especially if they are not from the same software vendor. In a portal, the two applications appear as "links" on its Web-based user interface, and she can work with both of them. The illusion is created that both applications are part of the portal. The applications are separate in the portal; a direct interaction between them does not have to be provided, but that is possible in a simple form (see "portlet" below). (What kind of interaction could this be?)

Fig. 9.1 Portal:
motivation

9.2 Portal Contents

Among the business applications integrated in the portal, there are *self-service functions*, such as vacation or travel requests. They are available to all employees and are intended to help reduce administrative costs. Moreover, portals offer access to further functionality, which is briefly mentioned here.

(a) *Information*

In addition to structured data, accessible through application programs, a portal contains a lot of information in unstructured data, usually stored in files. We speak of *documents* or *content*, and *document management systems* and *content management systems* (*CMS*) manage them. They offer, for example, different versions of a document or the orderly editing of a document by only one user at a time. Besides administrators, also users can be given the permission to change documents in a portal. Content includes any multimedia data (text, image, audio, video), not just "traditional" documents.

Some of the documents can be considered *knowledge* of the company, i.e., information that is necessary to fulfill a task or helps perform it better. Accordingly, we speak of *knowledge management*. Functions such as a search across all documents in the portal helps in accessing the knowledge. For knowledge management in addition to accessing information, the portal can provide surveys, discussion forums, user profiles, or notification services, e.g., about changes to a document (Nicolescu et al. 2007, p. 29 f.).

(b) *Office Environment*

The daily work naturally also includes the office environment, which is why functions such as email, calendar, and lists of tasks to be processed should be accessible via a portal.

(c) *Collaboration*

In addition to the functions of an office environment, which can also be used for collaboration between users, a portal can provide more specific functions: support of groupware systems, instant messaging, chat, application sharing, virtual meetings, and collaboration tasks.

9.3 System Structure

The portal architecture essentially corresponds to the three-tier client-server architecture that we learned about in Chap. 5. Instead of data storage, we prefer to speak of *backend systems*. These are the enterprise information systems and other data sources connected via *connectors*.

In the presentation layer, you usually find Web browsers. The applications are mostly equipped with a Web interface, so that they can be easily integrated into the portal. In principle, they can also be invoked independently of a portal in a Web browser.

The interesting part is the application layer. The application server is called *portal server* here. It includes, on the one hand, functions for application visualization and, on the other hand, basic services. These provide the structure management for the structure and navigation in the portal, the layout management for the preparation of the portal pages, and the functions of single sign-on, user administration, and personalization, which we will address below (Nicolescu et al. 2007, p. 33 f.). The portal server usually also contains application modules for the above-mentioned functions information, office environment, and collaboration, although they could in principle also be provided by backend systems.

An application runs in the portal in a virtual window, informally called "tile"; a technical term is *portlet* (Nicolescu et al. 2007, p. 33). Portlets are an extension of servlets (see Chap. 5). Unlike a servlet, the result is not a whole Web page; rather, several portlets together constitute a Web page, here a portal page. Programming interfaces for Java-based portlets are defined in a Java standard (Java Community Process 2003, 2008) defines version 2.0 of portlets, which supports event-based communication among portlets. The current version is 3.0 (Java Community Process 2017). While the applications usually run separately from each other, a limited form of interaction is possible. More complex forms of interaction are reserved for other integration approaches.

We remember: In a JEE application server, the runtime environment is called *container* (see Chap. 5). In a Java-based portal server, an extension of a JEE application server, there are two such containers: on the one hand, the *portlet container*, in which the individual portlets run, and, on the other hand, the servlet container, where the contents that the individual portlets deliver (*fragments*) are assembled into a portal page (Großmann and Koschek 2005, p. 212). The goal of the portlet standard is that portlets can run on any Java-based portal server. The approach *Web Services for Remote Portlets* goes one step further: Via a Web services interface (see Chap. 11), a language-independent call is possible (Großmann and Koschek 2005, p. 213 ff.; OASIS 2008).

In order for the portal user to get the impression of a seamless system, the individual applications running in the portal should have a similarly structured user interface. With different applications of the same software vendor, this is more likely due to style guidelines than with applications from different vendors.

After a user logs in to the portal, he should be able to execute all applications without further explicit login to the backend systems. The mechanism of *Single Sign-on* (*SSO*) is typically used in portals for that purpose. This relies on the *user management* of the portal to assign the portal user the access data of the backend systems and authenticate him there (Nicolescu et al. 2007, p. 28). The portal uses its portal certificate, which contains a public and a private part. The process for the implicit login in a target system (backend system) from the portal system can proceed as follows:

1. The portal generates a message with the following data: the system ID of the portal and the user ID in the target system (backend system), encrypted with the (secret part of the) portal certificate.

2. The portal sends the message to the target system.
3. The target system decrypts the information contained therein with the public part of the portal certificate. The public part of the portal certificate must have been previously stored in the target system.
4. The target system uses the user ID for login (without password!). The received system ID must be registered as a trusted system in the target system. (Why does this work without password?)

9.4   Role-Based Access and Personalization

The applications and information should be tailored to the portal user. There are two possibilities that may be combined for this purpose (Großmann and Koschek 2005, p. 94 ff.):

- *Role-based access* by the administrator: The administrator provides one or more *roles* for each portal user. The roles determine which portal contents the user sees and the corresponding portal-specific permissions. Unlike in the backend systems (see Sect. 16.2), roles in the portal are important for the provision of applications and information as well as for navigation. The permissions in the backend systems are independent of this, i.e., the user needs additional appropriate permissions to execute the application in the backend system. Examples of roles are "Purchaser," in which purchasing-specific applications are summarized, and "Self-Service" with the self-service functions that should be available to every employee.
- Personalization *according to personal settings*: Here, each user can adapt the user interface to a limited extent, e.g., the arrangement of the applications.[1]

9.5   Implementation in the Enterprise Information System

After having learned how an integration technique works, we have to think about how it can be implemented in enterprise information systems and which methodological steps are necessary. It may work "out of the box," and just some configuration needs to be done. Or—often—it may require software development of different types (cf. Chap. 15). So, near the end of each integration chapter, we will deal with that issue.

In the case of the portal, we want to integrate two (or more) applications that can be located in different systems. The two applications are dialogue methods that may have a close relationship (e.g., refer to the same supplier), but they do not have to (e.g., vacation request forms next to purchase requests).

---

[1] In addition, there is *implicit personalization*, where depending on the user's behavior, information is displayed or hidden (Großmann and Koschek 2005, p. 95).

The interaction of two applications via the portal is symmetrical, i.e., both applications have the same interaction principle (no division into active and passive; see Sect. 3.6.2). Therefore, the requirements for them are the same. It is necessary that the methods are implemented as Web applications. (We leave out the somewhat awkward call of another GUI from the Web browser.) If the methods are closely related in content and therefore a simple form of data interaction makes sense, portlets are advantageous for a good "user experience." If these are not yet available, development effort is required. Likewise, more comfort is achieved if the two enterprise information systems are connected to the portal via connectors and offer Single Sign-on.

The Web applications or portlets just have to be included in the portal system and assigned to the appropriate roles.

9.6   Integration Application

Another approach should be mentioned, which could be considered integration via the user interface due to its designation: a new application developed for integration with a new user interface (screen mask). The application internally accesses data of the systems to be integrated via APIs and presents them a unified view, possibly including editing (Fig. 9.2). (What could this look like, e.g., in master data display?)

Technically, however, this is not an integration via the user interface in the sense of this chapter but a new application (e.g., a company-specific in-house development; see Chap. 14), which uses integration via function call (see Chap. 11).

Fig. 9.2 Integration application

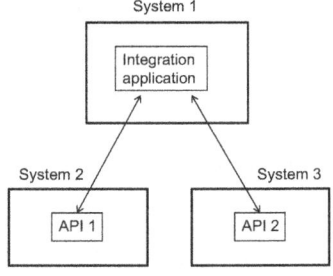

9.7   Exercises and Proposed Solutions

(a) Exercises

Exercise 9.1 (Suitability of Applications for Portals)
The portal should be the unified access point for a user to all applications. Can you think of applications that are less suitable for portal integration?

Exercise 9.2 (Maintenance of Permissions in the Portal)
In Sect. 9.4, it was mentioned that the user's permissions must be maintained in the backend systems. Would it be possible, in your opinion, to maintain these permission in the portal instead?

(b) Proposed Solutions for the Tasks

Exercise 9.1 (Suitability of Applications for Portals)
There is no absolute, theoretical obstacle, but, for example, graphics-intensive software with a corresponding special user interface can be problematic for portal integration. More generally, this applies to legacy software, which cannot simply be provided with a Web user interface. One solution is calling the application with its non-Web-based user interface from the portal.

Exercise 9.2 (Maintenance of Permissions in the Portal)
The user permissions refer to customizing data of the enterprise information system. Accordingly, maintenance must be coupled with the enterprise information system.

9.8   Self-Assessment

1. What is the difference between a "normal" Web application and a portlet?
2. What types of data can be transferred by a portlet, and which cannot?
3. A portal typically offers single sign-on. Does this work for all applications displayed in the portal?
4. Which aspect of a portal provides integration between enterprise information systems?

References

Großmann, M., Koschek, H.: Unternehmensportale—Grundlagen, Architekturen. Springer, Berlin (2005)

Java Community Process: JSR-000168 Portlet Specification. https://www.jcp.org/ja/jsr/detail?id=168 (2003). Accessed 3 Nov 2024

Java Community Process: JSR-000286 Portlet Specification 2.0. https://www.jcp.org/en/jsr/detail?id=286 (2008). Accessed 3 Nov 3, 2024

Java Community Process: JSR-000362 Portlet Specification 3.0. https://www.jcp.org/en/jsr/detail?id=362 (2017). Accessed 11 Oct 2024

Nicolescu, V., Klappert, K., Krcmar, H.: SAP NetWeaver Portal. Galileo Press, Bonn (2007)

OASIS: Web Services for Remote Portlets. Specification v2.0. http://docs.oasis-open.org/wsrp/v2/wsrp-2.0-spec-os-01.html (2008). Accessed 3 Nov 2024

Integration Through Data Exchange

10

I've always hated packing
but also unpacking
we have to unpack again
everything we pack
Thomas Bernhard: Am Ziel (Die Stücke,
first edition, Suhrkamp 1969–1981, 1983, p. 1006, translated)

Summary

Scenarios of data exchange in a system landscape are described, and XML is presented in detail as an example technology for data exchange formats. After introducing the elementary concepts of XML, namely, elements and attributes, namespaces and the data type definition using XML Schema are discussed. As an alternative, JSON is briefly described. It is reflected on what insights can be drawn from the "XML case study" for integration through data exchange. A message broker is a special communication channel that is used in particular for data exchange. We look at associated concepts such as asynchronous communication and the publish-and-subscribe principle.

Learning Objectives

- To learn about integration through data exchange using XML.
- To be able to define an XML document and an XML Schema document for a task.
- To be able to assess the services of a message broker.

10.1   Distributed Business Objects

In a transactional system, application programs are integrated with each other by accessing the common database (see Chap. 3). If the application programs run in different systems, i.e., with separate databases, the data needed in common could theoretically be copied from one database to another, usually requiring data transformation. (Why?) To achieve the same degree of integration as in a single system, extensive precautions would have to be taken: It would have to be ensured that the programs can access the data both for reading and writing, and the accesses would have to be synchronized. However, equal access and the associated effort are usually not necessary. We recall supply chain management (SCM; see Sect. 8.3), where master data is copied only for read access, or analytical systems, where data is generally accessed only for reading after it has been written (see Chap. 4).

Let's look at common scenarios where data from a sender system (source system) is needed in a receiver system (target system) (Fig. 10.1). On the left is a business object in the sender system S and on the right a business object in the receiver system R, which results from the sending process. At the moment, we are considering only one business object and later also a set of business objects. Shown are stylized class diagrams to indicate attributes and methods of the business objects. However, it should be noted that these are business objects, i.e., instances, which are sent, not classes. What is sent is a copy of the business object in the sender system (see Sect. 3.4.1). For simplicity, we can imagine this as the attributes of the business object, called business data in Sect. 3.3.

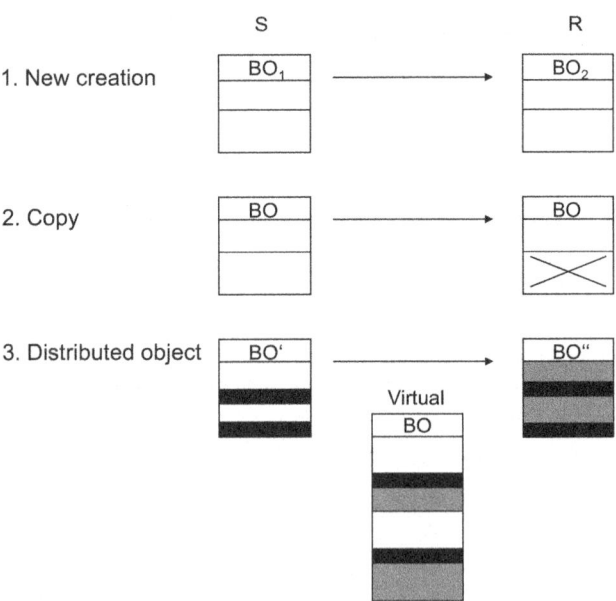

Fig. 10.1   Data exchange scenarios

1. *New, independent object*: In this case, a copy of the business object BO_1 is made in S and sent to R. From the template BO_1, a new business object BO_2 is created in R. BO_2 could, in terms of content (i.e., independent of technical implementation details, which can also exist), belong to a different class than BO_1. For example, BO_1 could be a purchase order and BO_2 a sales order—the purchase order is a sales order from the supplier's point of view. The scenario particularly reflects inter-company data exchange.
2. *Copied, fully dependent object*: A copy of the business object BO is created in R. Normally, S remains the data owner (see Sect. 8.4) of BO; changes occur only in S. Therefore, the methods in the picture are shown as crossed out. The scenario is used, for example, for the exchange of master data, as in the case of SCM (see Sect. 8.3). However, it often does not appear in its pure form but in an extended form according to scenario 3.
3. *Distributed, partially dependent object*: In S, BO' is sent to R, which creates a new object BO'' from it, usually of the same content class. The difference is that in both systems, some attributes and methods will be the same (in the figure drawn in black), but there can be additions of system-specific attributes and methods. In the case of master data exchange in SCM, for example, the material master in the ERP system could have additional ERP-specific attributes, e.g., concerning accounting. In the SCM system on the other hand, SCM-specific attributes could be added, e.g., for the so-called pegging: It is used in SCM to assign material receipts to requirements. Virtually, i.e., in our imagination, this can be seen as a new business object BO, which includes all the attributes and methods of the two systems. The critical case is when a common attribute in the two systems has different values (data inconsistency; cf. Sect. 8.2).

All scenarios have in common that we need an exchange format for data transmission that both systems understand, even though the object representation in the systems can be different. The mentioned scenarios, especially 2, are related to *data replication* (see, e.g., (Kleppmann 2017, p. 151 ff.)), as we know it from distributed systems. What is different, besides the different object representation, is that the purpose is not increasing fail safety and performance, at least not directly.

10.2   Data Exchange Between Enterprise Systems

Figure 10.2 shows the data exchange from a sender system S to a receiver system R. We consider the case that data referring to only one business object (like one order) is sent; the case of several business objects is similar. In S, structured data is

Fig. 10.2 Integration via data exchange

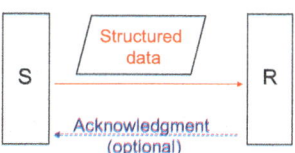

created from business data such as an order in a data exchange format for sending and transmitted to R. R receives it and performs an input processing: It checks the data; transforms it into business data, like an order; and stores it in its database. Usually, for traceability, error correction, and asynchronous processing (cf. Sect. 10.5), both the original message (e.g., order data packaged as a message) and the derived business data (e.g., an order in the corresponding tables) are stored, the original message usually both in S and in R. (Why?) Depending on whether the transmission is reliable, a receipt acknowledgment may be useful or omitted (cf. Sect. 11.6). The further processing of the received data, e.g., the order processing, takes place only after the storage of the business object. This could, for example, occur in a business process, which is initiated by the creation event (see Sect. 12.1).

Two things are required for communication:

- *Data exchange format*: The data must be transmitted in a format that both S and R understand. That means S must be able to generate (encode) it. R must be able to decode it and know what to do with the data.
- *Communication channel*: The data is sent over a communication channel that connects S and R.

So, S must pack the business data into the exchange format before sending, and R must unpack it and, above all, perform the input processing. Let's now look at the exchange format and the communication channel in more detail.

10.2.1 Data Exchange Format

In our scenario, only S and R need to understand the data. The data format could therefore in principle be individually agreed between them. But S will probably communicate with many similar receivers and likewise R with many senders. Also, it is usually standard software, which only wants to support a small number of common formats. Therefore, it makes sense that the structured data is encoded in a *standard format*. With the format, we must distinguish between the technical and the content data format. The *content data format* determines how the data structure looks like, i.e., which attributes are there. The *technical data format* determines how the data structure is encoded, e.g., using XML (cf. Sect. 3.6.2).

For example, in a very simplified order, the content data format has two fields, "material" and "quantity," here with the fixed and therefore omitted quantity unit "piece." As technical data formats for the order "three pieces of material 1400," we could, for example, choose.

```
0000001400;3
```

or

```
Material:0000001400;Quantity:3
```

Common technical data formats are:

- *Simple bit, byte, or character format*: This specifies which bits, bytes, or characters have which meaning in the order they appear. For example, "the first ten characters are the order number, followed by the order date in the format year-month-day, …" The advantage of such a format is very compact data transmission. The disadvantage is that the data order must be meticulously kept. And rules must be established for what happens with optional data.
- *Comma-separated values (CSV)*: A delimiter is set between the data values. The delimiter can be the comma, as the name suggests. Often a different character is used that must not appear in the raw data or is transmitted in a special form. This is why CSV can also be read as *character-separated values*. In this sense, the tab character is preferable to the comma or semicolon because the latter two appear more frequently in raw data (Finkbohner et al. 2024, p.420). When an optional data value is not transmitted, two delimiters appear directly next to each other. Leading non-significant zeros could be omitted, as they can be reconstructed by the delimiters. This format is often used in practice.
- *XML (eXtended Markup Language)*: XML is a markup language, which we will discuss in detail in the following section.
- *JSON (JavaScript Object Notation)*: A language for representing objects, part of the scripting language JavaScript (see Sect. 10.4).
- *EDI-formats*: *EDI (Electronic Data Interchange)* is an older, established method for transmitting business data in inter-company integration. In fact, there are several EDI standards. The most well-known are EDIFACT, more commonly used in Europe, and ANSI X.12, more commonly used in the USA. EDI standards not only define the technical but also the content data format.
- *Database table entries*: An obvious approach would be to send data directly as database table rows from S to R. The conversion of the structured transfer data into table rows in the receiving system could thus be omitted. The idea is a more or less direct write access to the database tables of the target system. But there are several pitfalls. For one thing, the exchange format would be the database schema of the target system. Even though this is a precise description of the transmitted data, it is not suitable as a cross-platform standard. And even if the source and target system use the same software, even in the same version, the data must be validated (checked) before being stored in the target system, just like with any other approach by the way. This is because the system states (especially customizing and master data) of the sending and the receiving system will be different. A certain amount of validation logic can be formulated in database systems, which prevents many errors such as format errors or implausible values. However, it is a much more extensive content validation and transformation that takes place in enterprise information systems. (Example?) The validations to be run through must be the same as those when entering data via the user interface. Therefore, this approach is avoided. When migrating legacy data (see Chap. 14), database table entries of the sender system are often provided and then transformed, e.g., with the following approach.

- *Simulation of user inputs*: Continuing the argumentation with "database table entries," the structured data could be sent in a format that allows them to be imported into R by simulating user inputs. This ensures that the received data undergoes the same validation logic as data entered via user interfaces. Disadvantages of this approach are that it is not a standard format and that the data structures depend on the current state of the user interfaces. When these are changed in a new version, the previously used data structures can no longer be used, and they must be adapted to the new user interfaces.
- *Function call for creating data*: At this point, the types of integration, "Integration through data exchange" and "Integration through function call," meet. We therefore discuss this approach in Chap. 11.

10.2.2 Communication Channel

Depending on the application scenario, different communication channels are suitable. They only have a technical, not a content-related, character.[1] Some examples are:

- *File directory*: There may be an agreement between S and R that S places a file periodically, e.g., at night, in a specific file directory where R picks it up later.
- *Email*: Especially in early EDI systems, S transferred data to a secured mailbox, where it was available for R.
- *HTTP*: S can transmit the data to R via the HTTP-POST method. R must provide a program on his Web server, which receives and processes the data.
- *Message broker* (more generally: message transmission system, message-oriented middleware): We will treat this approach in more detail in Sect. 10.5.
- *Storage medium exchange*: Data can be transferred via storage medium exchange (CD, DVD, USB stick, formerly often magnetic tape).

Different scenarios have different requirements for the quality of the transmission. In addition to the obvious performance, these are requirements regarding transmission problems: transmission errors, connection interruptions, and unauthorized access. The requirements concern the safety of the transmission, both in terms of error handling and access protection. Especially in inter-company integration, it is important to ensure that the communication channel is secure. This includes that the transmitted data is not read by others without authorization, that they are not falsified, and that R can assume that really S and not someone else has sent them.

10.2.3 Use Cases

Important use cases for integration via data exchange are shown in Table 10.1. Some we have already learned in earlier chapters:

---

[1] An exception is possible with message brokers; see Sect. 10.5.2.

Table 10.1 Data exchange scenarios

	Inter-company integration	Data exchange between in-house systems (EAI)	Offline synchronization	Legacy data migration	ETL
Data volume	Mostly low	Low to medium	Low	Very high	High
Data format	EDI, XML	XML, file (CSV, special format)	Special format	CSV	CSV, special format
Communication channel	Internet, VPN, mailbox, file	File, function call for data transmission, message-oriented middleware	Middleware, file	File	File, function call for data transmission
Examples	EDI: mostly transaction data such as order or invoice	SCM: master and transaction data such as material, bill of materials or order	CRM: Mobile sales: transaction data such as orders	Majority of the master and (partially) transaction data	DWHS: sales data

- Data exchange between in-house systems: The master and transaction data transfer in SCM (see Chap. 8)
- ETL (see Chap. 4)

The row "data volume" indicates how much data is transferred in a single data exchange. For example, in inter-company integration—one can imagine the transfer of an order via EDI—often only one business object, i.e., a small amount of data, is exchanged in a single transmission. In contrast, the legacy data migration transfers a very large amount of master and transaction data at once, namely, at least all those needed for business transactions in the new system. Legacy data migration takes place when an old enterprise information system is replaced by a new one and the legacy data must be made at least partially available in the new system (see Chap. 14). (Why is this useful?) In the case of a high data volume, usually, only spot checks and plausibility checks are carried out to verify the data.

"Data format" lists some typical data formats; it is not a complete enumeration. For example, files are common in legacy data migration. It is important to distinguish *tabular* files, where all lines have the same structure, from *sequential* files, where this is not the case (Finkbohner et al. 2024, p. 420).

10.3   The Data Exchange Format XML

We use the language XML to study concepts of data exchange formats exemplarily, as a case study. Of the abovementioned use cases, inter-company integration and data exchange between in-house systems are particularly relevant. We will later see that exchange formats also play a role in integration through function call (see Chap. 11). Accordingly, we will continue the case study there when it comes to Web services. XML has diverse applications, not only for business applications.[2] They can be divided into text-oriented and data-oriented; we will only deal with the latter in the following, as they are relevant for data exchange.

10.3.1 XML Documents

XML stands for *eXtensible Markup Language*. It is a standard of the *World Wide Web Consortium* (short, *W3C*). The origin of XML goes back to the markup language *SGML (Standard Generalized Markup Language)* from IBM, a very comprehensive and complex language that did not find wide application.[3] XML is very much reduced compared to SGML.

What a markup language is in general and XML in particular is best explained with an example (Fig. 10.3). The "structured data" here is solely the name of a supplier. Our XML document consists of one *element*, namely, supplier, which has the value Whipsnade Ltd. The value or, in XML terminology, the *content* of the element begins after the *start tag* of the element, <supplier>, and ends before the *end tag* </supplier> of the element. *Tag* originally means label; in computer science, it is used for "marking." The tags describe the data. Overall, XML is a text-oriented language, because both the elements and the values are text. The Unicode character set is used. If you wanted to integrate binary data, they need to be encoded as text.

Let's look at a larger, more realistic example (Fig. 10.4). For the supplier, the address is given in addition to the supplier number and the name. It is a complex data structure, as there are sub-elements. The address is again a data structure, consisting of street, postal code, and city.

Essential to this document, and to XML documents in general, is:

- There is exactly one *root element*, here supplier.
- The value of supplier is again, as in the first example, everything between start and end tag. Only this time, the type of the value is not a string but has a structured, "complex" content. The value of an element can therefore be simple (string) or complex (structured data type, nesting).[4]

---

[2] XML is widely used, even for the definition of programming languages, cf. XSLT.

[3] The history of XML and its predecessors can be found in Sebestyen (2010, p. 18 ff.).

[4] Here we simplify a bit, as there is also a mix of both, which we do not consider.

Fig. 10.3 A small XML
document

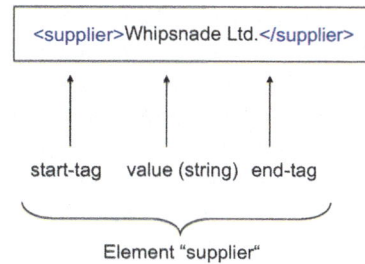

```
<supplier>Whipsnade Ltd.</supplier>
```

↑   ↑   ↑

start-tag   value (string) end-tag

Element "supplier"

Fig. 10.4 An almost
realistic XML document

```
<supplier>
    <number>4711</number>
    <name>Whipsnade Ltd.</name>
    <address>
        <street>60 Pepperday Avenue</street>
        <postalCode>12345</postalCode>
        <town>Lompoc</town>
    </address>
</supplier>
```

- An element may have sub-elements. Supplier has `number`, `name`, and `address` as sub-elements. `address` has `street`, `postalCode`, and `town` as sub-elements. A superordinate element is called *parent element*, the directly subordinate ones *child elements*, and they are among each other *siblings*.

XML does not specify which elements there are. They can be largely freely chosen, similar to identifiers in programming languages. Therefore, XML is also called a *meta-markup language*: a language, with which XML languages for various areas, including purchasing, can be formulated. These are referred to as *XML applications*. This is the meaning of the "X" in "eXtensible Markup Language." This distinguishes XML from HTML, where only fixed elements with a predefined meaning, e.g., `html`, `body`, and `h1`, are used. In contrast to HTML, XML uses semantic (meaning-bearing) tags, not physical (printing technical, e.g., `font`, `b`) or logical (concerning the structure, e.g., `h1`, `strong`) (Sebestyen 2010, p. 26). However, the meaning is not defined in XML itself but must be documented separately.

It would be nice if there was a uniform standard for orders and similar common business data. However, this is not the case today. Long-term experience with EDI standards shows that this goal is unlikely to be achieved in the medium term, as in EDI regional and industry-specific standards such as EDIFACT, ANSI X.12, and Odette coexist.

Not used in the example document but possible:

- An element may have *attributes*. If you want to classify suppliers, for example, the element could have the attribute `category`: `<supplier category="regular">`. Like for elements, XML allows freedom of choice for attribute names. The value of an attribute is always a string. If you want to add more extensive attribute information, you need to use multiple attributes.

With attributes, there is some freedom: An element can have several; the order is irrelevant. An attribute can be written in single or double quotation marks. Spaces can be before and after the equals sign. There is no rule whether some data should be represented as an attribute or as a sub-element. Although stylistic recommendations can be given, ultimately, it seems a matter of taste. You will find both attribute-heavy and element-heavy XML documents.

- Elements may be empty, i.e., have no content: `<remark></remark>`. To simplify writing, `<remark/>` is used synonymously in this case.
- An element may be optional, i.e., omitted. If, for example, the element `remark` can be empty, it might make sense to keep it optional and omit it when it is empty.
- An element (except for the root element) can occur multiple times. Example:

```
<suppliers>
  <supplier>
  ...
  </supplier>
  <supplier>
  ...
  </supplier>
  ...
</suppliers>
```

This is a list of several suppliers. For each individual supplier, there is the element `supplier`.

- An XML document may have an XML declaration in the first line. This specifies in particular the character encoding of the document:

```
<?xml version="1.0" encoding="UTF-8"?>
```

In this case, it is a Unicode encoding with variable length. Other possibilities are, for example, US-ASCII or ISO-8859-1, an ASCII extension, which, among other things, contains umlauts.

- Comments are framed with `<!--` and `-->`: `<!-- This is a comment. -->` XML contains some other possibilities like processing instructions, which are less important for our consideration and are therefore omitted here.

10.3.2 Rules

Various rules apply to XML documents. They concern:

- *Well-formedness*: These rules must be followed in order to be "correct XML" at all.
- *Stylistics*: Stylistic rules have been established in practice, enhancing processing and readability.
- *Validity*: If we want to check whether an XML document is, for example, a correct order, not just correct XML, additional rules must be followed.

(a) Well-Formedness

These rules must be followed by all XML documents. If a document violates such a rule, it is not a well-formed XML document ("syntax error"). You can easily test the syntactic correctness by putting the content into a file with the `.xml` extension and opening it with a Web browser. Web browsers usually have an integrated XML parser, so error messages (more or less understandable) will be shown if the document is not a well-formed XML.

- There is exactly one root element (already known).
- The elements have a "bracket structure," as we know it, from arithmetic expressions in programming languages. Every beginning tag must therefore have an end tag. And elements must not overlap. Therefore, something like `<x><y>123</x></y>` is forbidden, as the elements x and y overlap.
- Attributes are strings and thus have simple content (already known).
- Elements, as well as attributes, follow the syntax for identifiers in programming languages ("XML names"; see below), and they contain in particular no spaces.
- The character "<" may only occur at the designated places like the beginning of a tag. Otherwise, it must be `&lt;`[5]

XML names in detail: Alphanumeric characters are allowed, from any languages, including ideograms and umlauts, and also underscore, hyphen, and dot, the colon only for namespaces (see later). The name must start with a letter, an ideogram, or an underscore. Spaces are not allowed in names. Names are case sensitive. The word "XML" may not, in any combination of upper- and lowercase, be included.

From the rules of well-formedness, it follows that XML documents have a tree structure. The tree for our example document is shown in Fig. 10.5.

(b) Stylistics

XML documents are primarily intended for machine processing. Nevertheless, it makes sense to choose the definition so that it is easily readable by humans. This helps for understanding XML schema documents (see later) or when troubleshooting during the development process. Readability for humans is one of the design goals of XML; brevity is not highly valued (Sebestyen 2010, p. 25). Other stylistic rules concern rather the easy machine processing and composition of documents.

- *Intelligible identifiers*: Elements and attributes should have intelligible identifiers—the argument is like in programming. So `postalCode` is preferred to `p` or `pc`.
- *Structuring through nesting*: In principle, a data structure could be represented as a flat list of elements, each with a string value. For readability, however, nesting makes sense. In the example, `address` is nested in `supplier`, as `address` encapsulates related information. We will see later that XML documents are "assembled" from components, which are defined separately. This is similar to when a more complex material is built from individual

---

[5] Such a sequence of characters is called *Character Entity Reference*. There are a few more: `&amp;` for the character &, also `&gt;` `&quot;` `&apos;` Also so-called *CDATA* sections serve for easy integration of any text.

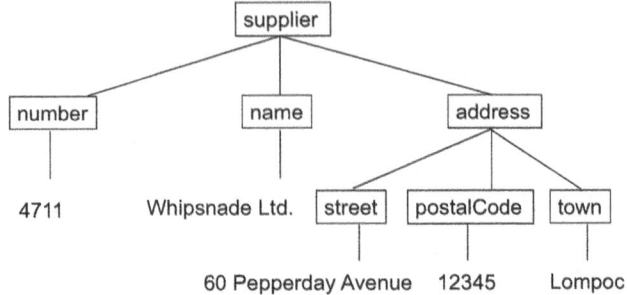

Fig. 10.5 XML tree structure

standard assemblies, which in turn contain standard components. Moreover, such structuring is beneficial for processing. In this sense, `street`, `postalCode`, and `town` should not appear directly as sub-elements of `supplier` but below `address`. If business data has, e.g., a header/line-item structure, this should be reflected in the XML document.

- *Parent element for repeating elements*: Further above we saw the repeating element `supplier`, which appeared below the parent element `supplier`. Such a superordinate element should always be defined for easier processing.

- *No numbering for repeating elements*: In the same example, it should be mentioned that the repeating elements do not get an index, i.e., it should not be written as `supplier1`, `supplier2`, ... or `supplier[1]`, `supplier[2]`, ... The index is only implicitly present by the order of the elements. Elements with different names, like `supplier1` and `supplier2`, are different and need to be defined separately. All occurrences of `supplier`, on the other hand, refer to the same element definition.

- *Mixed-case instead of underscores*: `postalCode` (mixed case) is more usual than `Postal_Code`, `postal_code`, `POSTAL_CODE`, or even `POSTALCODE`.

(c) Validity

We could specify informally (natural language) how an XML representation of a particular data structure, e.g., a supplier, looks like. For example, we could state that the root element for describing a supplier is `supplier`, followed by the elements `number`, `name`, `address`, etc. But a formal description with a schema description language (see below) has many benefits. (Do you know other languages for syntax definition from computer science?) An XML document is valid if it complies with the specification. We will consider validity rules in the context of XML Schema (Sect. 10.3.4).

Fig. 10.6 Namespace:
motivation

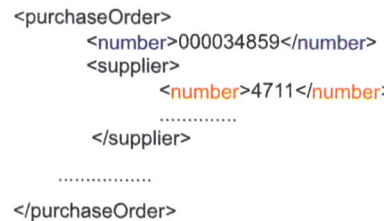

```
<purchaseOrder>
      <number>000034859</number>
      <supplier>
              <number>4711</number>
              ..............
      </supplier>

            .................

</purchaseOrder>
```

10.3.3 Namespaces

To motivate namespaces, let's look at an example (Fig. 10.6).

The element number appears twice, but with different meaning and different format (data type). In the first case, it is the order number, in the second the supplier number. For the reader, the context is clear from the parent element. However, for simple processing and for easier definition (see below), the distinction should be made at the element level, not through the context. The problem of elements with the same name arises especially when documents use separately defined "assemblies." For example, many business data include addresses, bank details, and personal information, which are defined once and then reused. In the initial "assembly," inconsistencies could still be uncovered. But if they are developed separately, this becomes difficult. Especially with frequently used terms like name, number, and type, a name collision is easily possible. The attempt to make it unambiguous through longer designations like purchaseOrderNumber leads to unnecessarily long designations and still does not offer complete security that collisions are ruled out.

The solution is *namespaces* (Fig. 10.7). The idea is also common in programming languages. In Microsoft .NET languages like C#, they are also called *namespaces* while in Java *packages*.

- Each element is assigned a namespace: number in the namespace "purchase order" is distinguished from number in the namespace "supplier."
- A namespace is represented by a *URI* (*Unique Resource Identifier*; the best-known subtype are *URLs, Unique Resource Locators*). The namespace "purchase order," e.g., could be represented by the URL http://www.mycompRW721.de/ns/po. The URI (or URL in our case) need not be a link to a document, i.e., you might not be able to use it in a Web browser. It is considered only a unique name, not necessarily with content.
- In order to assign a namespace to an element, you could think of prefixing the element with the URI. However, since the URIs are long, a shorter form is used.[6]

---

[6]Another argument is that URIs usually contain characters (/, %, ~) that are not allowed in XML names.

Fig. 10.7 Namespace: example

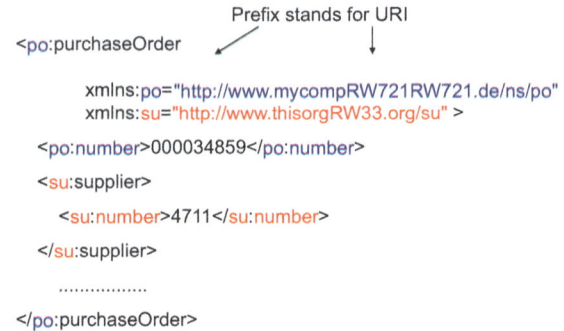

A prefix is assigned to a namespace, as a nickname, which applies in the present document. This is done in our XML document by `xmlns:po= "http://www.mycompRW721.de/ns/po"`. `xmlns` stands for "XML Namespace." The prefix `po` stands for the URL `http://www.mycompRW721.de/ns/po`. Prefix designations are usually one to three-character strings.[7] Note that the prefix only applies to this XML document. In another XML document, a different prefix could be used for the namespace. `po:number` is called a *qualified name*, with prefix `po` and local part `number`.

- As a precaution, the rule is applied not only to "critical" designations (like `number`) but to all.

Another argument for namespaces is that elements and attributes belonging to an XML application are grouped together. This can help in XML processing. For example, an XML document could be transformed in a processing pipeline in several steps (see Sect. 10.3.5). In each step, elements and attributes of a certain namespace could be processed (Sebestyen 2010, p. 65). There is often a one-to-one relationship between namespaces and XML applications.

10.3.4 XML Schema

(a) Type and Instance
When a system receives an XML document that is supposed to be an order, it must check whether the content actually corresponds to an order. If the recipient were a human, he could interpret the XML document, based on intelligible identifiers. However, an XML document is intended for processing by a program. The program needs a precise description of the structure of an XML document for an order. In principle, the description could be informal, in natural language. A developer could create a check program from it. However, it is more convenient if the validation logic can be automatically derived from a formal description. This is the purpose of

---

[7] For identification, only the namespace counts: if `p1` and `p2` refer to the same namespace, then `<p1:number>` and `<p2:number>` refer to the same declaration of number. For prefixes, the syntax rules of XML names apply, only that the colon may not be part of a prefix.

XML Schema, a language to define types of XML documents.[8] Like XML, XML Schema is a W3C standard. A validating *XML parser* gets an XML document i ("instance"; see below) and an XML Schema document t ("type") as inputs, and it checks whether i corresponds to the definition specified in t. If not, the validation errors are indicated. It corresponds to the syntax check of a program by a compiler or a parser. The best-known XML parsers include Microsoft XML Core Services (MSXML) and Xerces. A list of XML parsers can be found in Sebestyen (2010, p. 58 ff.).

Strictly speaking, XML Schema can perform a comprehensive, but not a complete, business logic check whether an XML document represents a valid order. For example, a material that does not exist could occur in a supposed order. XML Schema checks at the type level, i.e., the *possible* material numbers allowed by the data type. It does not check the *actual* material numbers, which result from the content of the enterprise information system. This problem arises particularly with master and transaction data. The receiving system must perform these checks after the schema validation. The check for some customizing data, e.g., currency units, is theoretically a borderline case: one could create an enumeration type for it with XML Schema, but pragmatically, one would delegate the check to the enterprise information system. (Would this theoretically also be possible for master data? And practically sensible?)

An XML Schema document thus describes a *type* or a set or class of *instances*, here XML documents, called *XML instance documents* or *XML instances*. This is similar to how a data type (e.g., Integer) describes a set of numbers (whole numbers within a range) and an object-oriented class describes a set of possible object instances.

(b) Syntax
An XML Schema document is itself an XML document. That is, the same language is used for the meta-level (the descriptive level) as for the described level.

Let's look at two examples of the XML document instances presented above. First, the one for the simple XML document, which only contains a supplier name (Fig. 10.8).

XML schema documents make extensive use of namespaces. The first line states that the XML document is an XML schema document. This distinguishes XML schema documents from other, "normal" XML documents. In the second line, the type of the supplier document is set. Only one element with name supplier and type string is declared.[9] string is a built-in type of XML Schema, as indicated

---

[8] A language for describing the type of XML documents that was already available with the introduction of XML (and thus before XML Schema) is *Document Type Definitions* (*DTDs*). Their syntax is not XML, and they are less expressive than XML Schema. Today, XML Schema is preferred.

[9] It is noticeable that elements (of the schema document, not the instance document) are written with namespace; the attributes are written without namespace. The reason is that the attributes of the XML schema namespace are not declared globally (i.e., directly below the schema element) but locally. If they were defined globally, they would have to appear with namespace specification. Local attributes can, depending on the specification of the form attribute at the declaration or also of the attributeFormDefault attribute of the schema element, be specified without namespace specification (Walmsley 2002, p. 51 and p. 152).

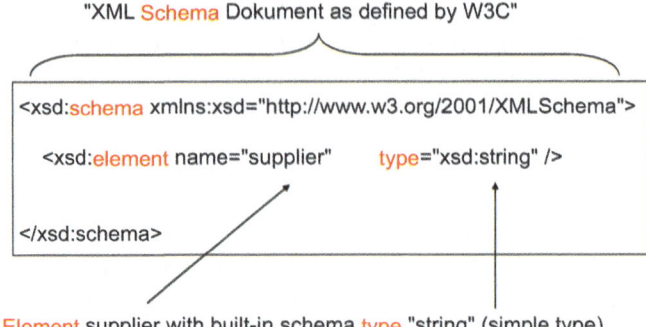

"XML Schema Dokument as defined by W3C"

```
<xsd:schema xmlns:xsd="http://www.w3.org/2001/XMLSchema">

    <xsd:element name="supplier"        type="xsd:string" />

</xsd:schema>
```

Element supplier with built-in schema type "string" (simple type)

Fig. 10.8 XML schema for the simple XML document

```
<xsd:schema xmlns:xsd="http://www.w3.org/2001/XMLSchema">

    <xsd:element name="supplier">                      Complex
      <xsd:complexType>                                elements
       <xsd:sequence>                                  (sequence)
         <xsd:element name="number" type="xsd:string" />    Simple
         <xsd:element name="name"   type="xsd:string" />    elements
         <xsd:element name="address" >
             ......
       </xsd:sequence>
       <xsd:attribute name= "category"  type ="xsd:string" />    Attribute
      </xsd:complexType>
    </xsd:element>
</xsd:schema>
```

Fig. 10.9 XML schema for the slightly more complex XML document

by the namespace prefix xsd. In addition to string, many simple data types are already built into XML Schema, e.g., Boolean, byte, integer, float, double, duration, and dateTime.

Our second example, supplier data including number, name, and address (Fig. 10.9), shows how complex data types are defined. A word on terminology: Elements and attributes are declared, and types are defined (Sebestyen 2010, p. 116).

One way to represent the complex type of supplier is to not specify a type name, but to nest the type definition directly afterwards. First it is said to be a complex type (complexType). Then it is said what kind of complex type it is; here, it is a sequence. Because there are different kinds, like:

- sequence: Several elements one after another. The order must be kept. An element can of course be nested. This type is often used.
- all: Several elements occur, but the order does not matter.
- choice: One of several elements. (Which two of the three are similar in terms of their use?)

In our example, most of the elements of the sequence have simple types, so the built-in type is used as an attribute. Only `address` has a complex type, defined again using `complexType` and `sequence`.[10]

According to XML Schema, an element is considered complex not only when it has a nested type instead of a simple one but also when it has an attribute. It is a little bit complicated to describe an element with a (seemingly) simple type and an attribute in XML Schema. Therefore, in this introductory text, we use attributes at most with elements of complex type. Our example of a supplier with categorization would look like this:

```
<xsd:element name="supplier">
  <xsd:complexType>
    <xsd:simpleContent>
      <xsd:extension base="xsd:string">
        <xsd:attribute name="category" type ="xsd:string"/>
      </xsd:extension>
    </xsd:simpleContent>
  </xsd:complexType>
</xsd:element>
```

XML schema is a rich language with diverse type description possibilities, e.g., enumeration types, where the individual elements of a set are enumerated. We have only looked at a small part of it.

(c) Use of Namespaces

Figure 10.10 shows how to define XML documents that use a namespace. A target namespace is specified, which is used in the XML instance for the elements. `elementFormDefault="qualified"` and `attributeFormDefault="qualified"` express that all elements and attributes use the namespace (they are then referred to as "qualified elements"). Otherwise, some elements could be used with, some without a namespace, which is usually not what you want.

The counterpart to the XML schema document (type) is an XML document (instance) that refers to that XML schema document (Fig. 10.11). The namespace declaration is used intensively, which is why it may appear a bit cryptic at first glance. Let's look at it line by line:

- From `po:purchaseOrder`, we see that a namespace is declared for `purchaseOrder`, for which the prefix `po` is used.
- `xmlns:xsi=`... introduces a namespace for XML instances. This namespace declaration is a helper construct, which is only needed for the following line.

---

[10]An alternative formulation works with *named* (*complex*) *types*. The declaration is `<xsd:complexType name="supplierType">`. If complexType does not appear at the highest level, but nested under element, no explicit name is given, and an anonymous type is created.

Fig. 10.10 XML schema
with Namespace (1):
schema

```
<xsd:schema
   xmlns:xsd="http://www.w3.org/2001/XMLSchema"
   targetNamespace="http://www.mycompRW721.de/ns/po"
   elementFormDefault="qualified"
   attributeFormDefault="qualified">
      .....
</xsd:schema>
```

```
<po:purchaseOrder
   xmlns:xsi="http://www.w3.org/2001/XMLSchema-instance"
   xsi:schemaLocation="http://www.mycompRW721.de/po  po_ns.xsd"
   xmlns:po="http://www.mycompRW721.de/ns/po"            Namespace
   po:category= "n">
................
</po:purchaseOrder>
```

Fig. 10.11 XML schema with Namespace (2): XML document with prefixes

• There, the attribute schema location (`schemaLocation`) is specified, which may be given for XML instances, but it is not mandatory. Its value looks at first glance like a URL.[11] In fact, there is a space before `po_ns.xsd`, so the string consists of two parts. The front part is the namespace (`http://www.mycompRW721.de/po`); the back part is a reference to the file with the XML schema document, in our case just the filename as a relative path (`po_ns.xsd`). This expresses that the declarations for the namespace `http://www.mycompRW721.de/po` are in the file `po_ns.xsd`, which is located in this case in the same directory as the file of the currently processed XML instance document. The `schemaLocation` attribute is a hint for the schema processor where to find the schema document. Alternatively, the schema processor could offer parameters for specifying the XML instance document and the XML Schema document.[12]

• In the line `xmlns:po=`..., as in an earlier example, the namespace for orders along with the prefix is set. Before that, it was already used for the element declaration `purchaseOrder`. Even though the namespace declaration appears here textually after its use, it is considered "simultaneous": It was set at the element `purchaseOrder` and can be used for that element and all sub-elements.

• In the line `po:category="n"`, the namespace with prefix `po` is used for an attribute declaration.

Figure 10.12 shows an alternative for the XML document; it has the same meaning. If you want to save the effort of writing the same prefix in an XML instance docu-

---

[11] Analogously, there is the attribute `noNamespaceSchemaLocation`, which is used for XML documents without namespaces and only refers to the location of the schema.

[12] If multiple namespaces shall be used, they must be described in different schema documents, because a schema document describes (at most) one namespace (Walmsley 2002, S. 59). The various schema documents can then be imported into a higher-level schema document using the `import` element.

```
<purchaseOrder
   xmlns:xsi="http://www.w3.org/2001/XMLSchema-instance"
   xsi:schemaLocation="http://www.mycompRW721.de/po   po_ns.xsd"
   xmlns="http://www.mycompRW721.de/ns/po"      Default namespace
   xmlns:tns="http://www.mycompRW721.de/ns/po"   Namespace for
   tns:category= "n">                            attributes
   ...............
</purchaseOrder>
```

Fig. 10.12 XML schema with Namespace (3): XML document with default namespace

ment again and again, you can set a default namespace. For this default namespace, the "empty" (or no) prefix applies. A peculiarity of XML Schema is found here: The default namespace only applies to elements, not to attributes. Since the attribute poType has a namespace, you must use the prefix for the attribute.

(d) Repeating Structures and Optional Elements
An element can occur multiple times (the example supplier within suppliers) and can be optional. So it can occur from zero to any number of times. The attribute minOccurs determines how often an element occurs at least and maxOccurs how often at most. Both attributes have the default value 1. They only need to be specified for deviating numbers. An optional element is indicated with minOccurs="0". For maxOccurs there is the special value unbounded, which means "any number of times."

10.3.5 Processing of XML Documents

In an exercise, you can create a small XML document with a text editor. There are also specialized XML editors, a list can be found in Sebestyen (2010, p. 60 ff.). For the exchange of business data, however, other methods are used. XML documents are generated and processed by programs. We distinguish the translation between business data and XML from the transformation of XML to XML, i.e., how an XML document is transformed into another.

(a) Programming Techniques for Processing
• *String processing*: Since an XML document is character based, it could be generated and processed by string processing. In simple cases, this is feasible, especially generating XML data. In general, however, it is complex.
• *Programming interfaces*: There are standards for XML programming interfaces, and implementations in common programming languages are available. The best known are the *Document Object Model* (*DOM*) and the *Simple API for XML* (*SAX*). For DOM, the entire XML document is built as a tree structure in main memory, so it can be written and read. DOM contains, e.g., functions such as "create an element below another element." The memory consumption is high for large documents, which is why SAX is preferred for reading access. Here, the

parser generates predefined events when reading an XML document, for which event handler routines can be written.

- *Translation of XML into objects or data structures*: The automatic translation of XML into objects or data structures of a programming language makes it much easier for a programmer to process XML data. A class (or several linked by attributes) is generated from an XML Schema document at definition time. At runtime, an object of the class is instantiated. Its attributes contain the data, which correspond to the elements and attributes of the XML document. Methods do not play a major role; the object (or a network of objects) is used like a complex data structure. The transformation into data structures is similar. In both cases, the reverse direction is also possible: generate an XML document from an object or a data structure. The programmer can thus work with his usual concepts: classes, objects, and data structures. Internally, these generation mechanisms will use the abovementioned programming interfaces.

(b) Transformation from XML to XML

If the sender generates a different XML format than the receiver needs but the business data contained in the XML documents are the same, a transformation of the sender format into the receiver format is possible. Of course, the techniques mentioned above could be used for a transformation, also into a different format, e.g., PDF, RTF, or HTML. However, various other techniques have been established, which also could be combined:

- *Graphical mapping*: This will be the most pleasant method for the developer. In a graphical user interface, which, e.g., shows graphical representations of the XML schema documents for source and target, he draws arrows between source and target elements. Mapping (transformation) programs or XSLT programs (see below) are then automatically generated.
- *XSLT program*: XSLT (*eXtensible Stylesheet Language Transformations*) is an XML standard, in fact a small programming language, with which an XML document can be transformed into another one. An XSLT program is rule based and itself coded in XML. Experience shows that it takes some practice to write programs for complex transformations.
- *Mapping program*: These are custom-developed programs, which generally use the programming techniques mentioned at (a). A programmer might choose this technique in complex scenarios where graphical mapping is not sufficient and for pragmatic reasons he does not want to use XSLT.[13]

---

[13] Although XSLT is Turing-complete, thus all transformations could theoretically be carried out with it, and it may be easier for a developer to write a mapping program in his familiar programming language.

10.3.6 Findings from the XML Case Study

We have come to know XML as a common technology for exchanging business data. Technologies change, and there have long been related means for data exchange (EDI, CSV files). In this section, we want to reconsider what insights, beyond the specific technical design with XML, we can draw from this case study.

(a) Exchange of Business Data
Business data as treelike data structures: Business data are complex, nested, tree-like data structures. XML is particularly suitable for this structure. An entire business object can appear in one document, unlike in relational databases, where one business object is usually stored in several tables, such as for header and line-item data.

Only attributes of business objects: In data exchange, only attributes of business objects are considered, no methods or functions. The receiver must know which function to execute with the sent data. This is clear with business data like "invoice"—the invoice shall be created in the receiving system, and follow-up actions, checking and booking, shall be initiated. An intermediate position is taken by data such as "quotation change," which causes the receiver to update the quotation data. Here, not only the business date "quotation" but also the method is communicated, which already resembles a function call (see Chap. 11).

Media independent: Exchange formats can be media independent. XML does not specify the physical medium: The data can be exchanged as a file or—more often—as runtime data. Finally, it would be possible to store business data directly in the XML format. In addition to native XML databases, also other database systems offer XML support.

Communication independent: Related to the previous point, it has so far been left out how XML documents are transmitted. The XML standards are independent of this. In the following sections, we will see what mechanisms there are.

(b) Standardization
Common understanding between sender and receiver: For data exchange, sender and receiver must have a common understanding of the exchanged data. This could be a bilateral agreement. For an ad hoc integration between two applications, this may be appropriate. But since many senders and receivers have the same data exchange needs, in particular in inter-company integration, standardization makes sense. XML itself is an infrastructure standard ("meta-markup language"). It does not define common business data such as orders or invoices. There are other standardization organizations that define data exchange standards based on XML. In fact, standards do exist, and they are used for data exchange. Even before XML, EDI standards have a long tradition. Still, there are some problems involved. So let's talk about some standardization problems in the following, which are based on experience:

- *Temporal availability*: Standards are usually created in committees, and voting is required. Accordingly, it takes time until a standard is available. If a company is looking for a solution to a problem, it may be the case that at that time there is no standard yet or at least no product that supports the standard.
- *Multiple standards*: If there are several competing standards for a task, the question is which one will endure. It is not an easy choice for a company. Using several standards at the same time usually does not make sense, as it is costly and increases complexity.
- *Poor quality*: Due to the process how standards are created in committees, where the standardizing companies pursue their own interests, the result of standardization is not always satisfactory. Typical weaknesses are that standards allow several variants, which result from provider interests or simply from lack of agreement. A standard is often a compromise, not necessarily the best solution. This makes some standards complex and difficult to implement. As a consequence, some providers may choose to implement only a subset (profile). When different products implement non-matching profiles, interoperability fails. In general, there are well-thought-out and widely used standards, like the IEEE Standard 754 for representation of floating-point numbers. But there are also standards that are practically not used, like the ISO-OSI standards for data communication.
  XML fulfills its purpose as a standard, but there are also points of criticism: the low performance imposed by the representation or the complexity of the XML schema standard (see also Sebestyen 2010, p. 35). For this reason, further alternative schema languages such as Relax, Relax NG, and Schematron were developed.
- *Different interpretation*: Syntactic properties can be precisely described and automated in computer science. Semantic properties are problematic, for which mostly no useable description formalisms are available, in many cases only an informal description in natural language. Especially then it may happen that different people have a different understanding of some part of a standard, e.g., what the meaning of a particular element in an XML standard is. Different standard implementations can therefore interpret parts differently, leading to interoperability problems.

(c) Design

We now look at some aspects that were designed in a certain way in XML but could also be solved differently for the purpose of data exchange.

Human-readable: XML documents shall be readable by humans, for example, by choosing descriptive names for the elements. Consequently, element names have a certain length. This is different in many EDI standards. It does not seem necessary in every case, because the standard use case of XML is machine processing. Furthermore, there are schema editors for easier manual handling. Especially for debugging purposes, however, human readability may be an advantage.

Performance: Performance is not a priority in XML. For example, it is a character-based language. Many data values could be encoded more efficiently than in characters; for the Boolean values "true" and "false," one bit would suffice.

Should element names be included in a data document, or should it contain just the raw data, i.e., the values of the elements?

10.4   The Data Exchange Format JSON

JSON stands for JavaScript Object Notation but is used in many programming environments (Friesen 2019, p. 187 ff.). The format also uses (nested, iterated) name-value pairs. But it is simpler than XML and deals exclusively with data structures, not text documents, which would also be possible in XML. Our supplier example looks like this in JSON (Fig. 10.13):

JSON knows three types of values: objects, noted in curly brackets ({ }), literal values (strings, numbers, Boolean values, null as null value)—these two types occur in the example—and arrays, noted in square brackets, [ ], and comma-separated. There is no distinction between integers and decimal numbers. The latter is found in the following example snippet (Fig. 10.14):

A brief description of JSON can be found at JSON (2024).

Namespaces and schema-based validation were initially not supported (Tilkov et al. 2015, p. 89). Now JSON Schema is intended for validation (Friesen 2019, p. 195), currently still in a draft version (JSON Schema 2024).

Fig. 10.13 Supplier data in JSON format

```
{
    "number":    4711,
    "name":      "Whipsnade Ltd.",
    "address": {
                    "street":      "60 Pepperday Avenue",
                    "postalCode":  12345,
                    "town":        "Lompoc"
                }
}
....
```

Fig. 10.14 Arrays in JSON

```
"products": [ {   "id":         1020,
                  "price":      20.00,
                  "currency":   "EUR"
              },
              {   "id":         1030,
                  "price":      40.00,
                  "currency":   "EUR"
              }
            ]
....
```

10.5 Message Brokers as a Communication Channel

Most of the communication channels mentioned in Sect. 10.2.2 are self-explanatory. Message brokers (more generally: message queuing systems) may be less familiar. Some aspects of transmission such as reliability, receiver determination (routing), and mapping can very well be illustrated by means of message brokers. The term "message" is used here in a more general/abstract sense than business data: *What* is transmitted in the message, the message content (e.g., business data), is not initially in focus (see Sect. 10.5.2). This allows message brokers to be used in the same way when calling functions (see Chap. 11). Some but by far not all companies use message brokers.

10.5.1 Queuing Systems

The messages that are transmitted on a communication channel can be persistently stored for transmission (*persistent* messages), or they only exist during the communication (*transient* messages). For transmission, *message queuing systems* can be used. Also the terms *message-oriented middleware* (*MOM*) and *message transmission system* are used. MOM offers additional functionality, such as an expiration date or a priority, which can be specified for a message (Alonso et al. 2004, p. 62). Although transient queuing systems are possible (Tanenbaum and van Steen 2014, p. 141 ff.), the persistent ones are common.

Let's take a closer look at how it works (Fig. 10.15): The sender sends a message to a *persistent* queue of the receiver. The receiver eventually takes the message from the queue and processes it. With this decoupling, the receiver does not have to be ready for processing immediately. He doesn't even have to be operational; his system could be temporarily unavailable, provided his queue is ready to receive. Persistent queues can therefore ensure reliable message transmission (see below). Therefore, they are also called *transactional* queues (Alonso et al. 2004, p. 64). (What is the content of the transaction?)

Message-oriented communication between people is familiar to us (email). When we hand a message over to the email system, we trust that it will be delivered. Experience shows that this works reasonably well, but not perfectly. For message-oriented communication between applications, however, we expect the highest reliability.

A variant is shown in Fig. 10.16. Here, several receivers share a common queue. The idea is that several receivers are intended as "processing units" for load distribution. Each of these receivers could process any message equally. The performance can be scaled by adjusting the number of receivers.

Fig. 10.15 Message-oriented communication

(Persistent) queue of R

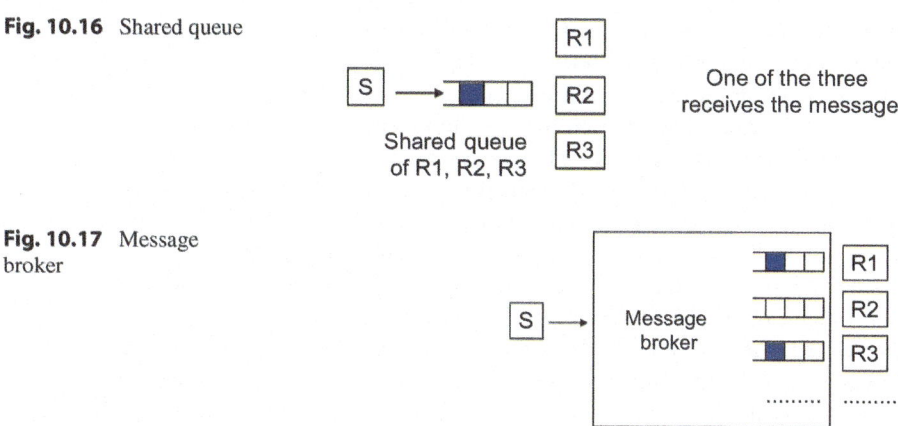

Fig. 10.16 Shared queue

Fig. 10.17 Message broker

It is possible to introduce intermediate nodes, called *routers* or *relays*, in addition to the queues of the applications and their queue managers. Thus, the communication mechanism store-and-forward is used. The routers can have the routing knowledge in a queue network with dynamic topology. The queue managers of the applications then only need to know their next router (Tanenbaum and van Steen 2014, p. 148).

Sender and receiver communicate with the MOM via an API. A common one is the *Java Messaging Service* (*JMS*) (Ferreira 2013, p. 50 ff.), which, however, does not say anything about the internal workings of the MOM or its communication with other MOM systems.

10.5.2 Message Brokers

In this variant of a MOM, a mediating component, the *message broker* (see Fig. 10.17), connects senders and receivers. The message broker is the central concept of *Enterprise Application Integration* (*EAI*). It is a queuing system with additional functionality. The senders do not address a receiver directly. Rather they address the message to the message broker. The message broker then determines for the incoming message which receivers it should be delivered to. This is called *routing*. A message may be delivered to several receivers (implicit multicast). The basis of the decision who should receive the message can in particular be the message type (e.g., "order") or even parts of the message content. (Example?) Of course, the receiver can also be explicitly specified, and the message is then simply passed through. In order for the message broker to be able to carry out the routing, it stores part of the application or integration knowledge. In this case, the broker does not only know technical communication rules but also business rules. For traceability and debugging, this distributed information is obstructive. The performance could also suffer—after all, the main task of a message broker is to distribute messages quickly (Alonso et al. 2004, p. 75).

A message broker can do more than just pass a message untouched to the appropriate receivers. It is possible that the sender and receiver use content-equivalent messages, but the message formats are different. (Example?) In this case, the message broker can convert the formats (*mapping*) (Fig. 10.18). Of course, it is important that the target information can be "calculated" from the source information. Various techniques can be used for mapping (see Sect. 10.3.5).

A message broker, mediating between senders and receivers results in a *hub-and-spoke-architecture* (Fig. 10.19), instead of point-to-point connections. The communicating systems are represented as small circles. With point-to-point connections, there are direct connections between the systems, but not every system has to be connected to every other. In the hub-and-spoke-architecture, all systems are directly connected only to the message broker. But indirectly, every system is connected to every other. Accordingly, this architecture is suitable for intra-company application integration. An internal company message broker can also send messages to partner companies (or, vice versa, receive them). But independent companies will usually not accept a central control of their applications with a common message broker (Alonso et al. 2004, p. 127).

With point-to-point connections, there is topologically a maximum of $n * (n − 1) / 2$ connections, with the hub-and-spoke architecture only n. However, this statement only applies to the *system connections*—and all systems are usually connected to the local internal network anyway. So this statement should be relativized. More importantly, applications (programs, processes) communicate between two systems, so several *application connections* may exist. (Example?) In Fig. 10.20, we see four application connections, which go through the message broker. Between sender and receiver 1, there are two application connections with numbers 1 and 2, e.g., for two different messages. The application connection number 3, on the other hand, goes from the sender to both receiver 2 and receiver 3; the black dot indicates

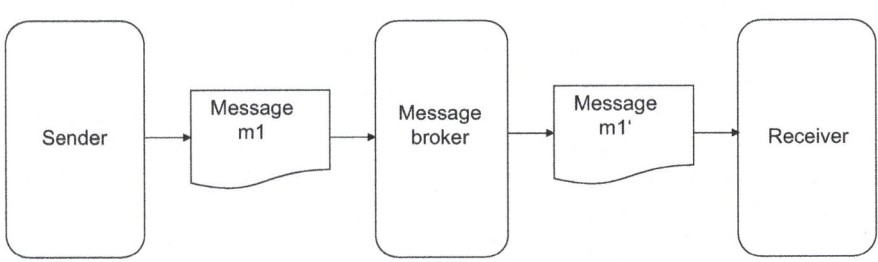

Fig. 10.18 Mapping

Fig. 10.19 Hub-and-spoke architecture

Fig. 10.20 Application
connections

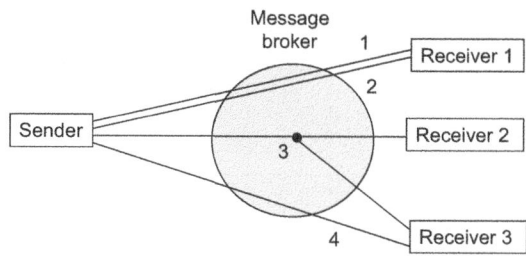

the split. Finally, there is a fourth application connection, this time between the sender and receiver 3. In this case, there are three point-to-point application connections and one that corresponds to a multicast.

The central position of the message broker can still bring advantages:

- It can be tracked which connections are used in a system network.
- All data is centrally logged.
- Communication administration can focus on the message broker.

If there are advantages of using a message broker even in scenarios of lower integration, what drawbacks are there (see also Alonso et al. 2004, p. 81 f.)?

- *Effort*: A message broker requires effort of various kinds: first of all, the software, hardware, and personnel costs (administration) for operating the message broker, and, in addition, the implementation costs, especially the design or adaptation (encapsulation) of the applications such that they can be used with the message broker. A single point-to-point connection involves usually less effort.
- *Performance*: Routing all messages through the message broker costs performance. On the other hand, logging can be useful, for example, in detecting errors.
- *Dependence on the message broker*: This does not only mean that the message broker is a "single point of failure" at runtime. The connection of an enterprise information system to a message broker and the developments in the message broker (e.g., mappings between messages) can be quite specific to a message broker product and must be updated when switching to another product.
- *Part of the application logic is in the message broker:* The disadvantage has already been mentioned above.

10.5.3 Publish and Subscribe

A concept that can be realized with message brokers is *publish and subscribe* (Fig. 10.21). A subscriber (usually a program) subscribes to a *topic*.[14] "Topic" is an abstract term. It could be, for example, a message type like "order," "order for

---

[14] This is the terminology of JMS. You could also call it "messages of a certain kind" but bearing in mind that a reference to an instance is also possible. Alonso et al. (2004, p. 76) distinguish between *type-based* subscription, where nested subtypes are also possible, e.g., `PurchaseOrder.newPurchaseOrder`, and *parameter-based* subscription of the kind "type=..." and "customer=..." and "quantity=...".

Fig. 10.21 Publish and
subscribe

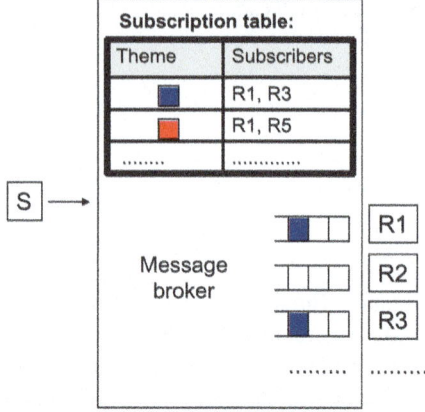

supplier 4711," or also "order 501." There is a *subscription table* in the message
broker for this purpose. There can be multiple subscribers for a topic. When a message with a specific topic arrives, all subscribers receive the message (or a copy of
it). (What is the difference from the case of Fig. 10.16?) If a subscriber is no longer
interested in a topic, he removes himself from the subscription table. The concept of
"publish and subscribe" is also used in communication via events (cf. Chaps. 3 and
12). The events correspond to the messages and the event handlers to the subscribers. In the literature, this is referred to as the "event-condition-action-paradigm,"
e.g., in Alonso et al. (2004, p. 263). Event handlers are therefore only triggered
when the condition formulated in the subscription table concerning the event parameters is met.

The topic can be at the type or instance level. The above example "order" is at the
type level: The receiver waits for any order. In contrast, "order 501" is at the instance
level: The subscriber only waits for a response to the order with the number 501;
others do not interest him.

The aforementioned JMS has, in addition to point-to-point operations, also
publish-and-subscribe operations in its API (Alonso et al. 2004, p. 76).

10.6   Implementation in the Enterprise System

A system wants to transmit data to another. Since the interfaces for this purpose in
the two systems are not symmetrical, we must distinguish between the sender system (active) and the receiver system (passive) (cf. Sect. 3.6.2).

(a) Sender system
    A function is needed that selects the data either in an event-driven (when the
    data to be transmitted is created or changed) or a time-driven way (e.g., every
    night), transforms them into an exchange format like XML or JSON, and trans-
    mits them.
        Such a function may already be built into the system, such as an extractor for
    a data warehouse system. If not, development effort is required on the sender

side. For the event-driven transmission, this may be an extension of the software (see Sect. 15.8) or a modification (see Sect. 15.9), if that is possible in the system at all. The advantage of event-driven transmission is that the data to be transmitted are already determined in the extension. The disadvantage is poorer performance when many such transmissions happen immediately, not bundled in a batch job overnight.

For the time-driven transmission, a company-specific custom development (see Sect. 15.7) may be required. The sender system should provide interfaces: an API to select changed data or, otherwise, access to the database tables or database triggers—the situation is similar to the step "extraction" in the ETL process (Sect. 4.2.2). Determining the data to be transmitted is therefore the main problem. Based on this, the conversion into the exchange format and the data transmission is programmed, for which certainly generic APIs are available.

In both cases—function already included in the system or newly programmed—finally, some configuration is necessary (activation, target system, etc.).

(b) Target system

A function is required that receives the data, checks, transforms, and writes them into the database. It can be already included in the standard software or developed in-house. For receiving the encoded data and unpacking, generic functionality may be available. More critical is whether there is an API for checking the data and transferring them into the database, maintaining data consistency. If not, less comfortable mechanisms are used, e.g., the simulation of data entry via user interfaces (advantage is integrated validation logic; cf. Sect. 10.2.1) or the elaborate and somewhat delicate design of one's own validation logic with subsequent direct access to the database tables. The processing of the received data could be event triggered—the data is processed immediately upon receipt—or time controlled: The sender could write the data into a file directory, from where they are, and then processed in batch jobs.

If the source and target systems offer data transmission and reception functions but the data formats do not match, a mapping is required. This can be done in different ways, for example, via a message broker (cf. Sects. 10.3.5 and 10.5.2). Message brokers in the source or target system can also be used independently of each other for other purposes, especially for reliable data transmission.

10.7 Exercises and Proposed Solutions

(a) Exercises

Exercise 10.1 (XML Documents)

The company "Rapid Transit Ltd." wants to create a product catalog to be used by its customer companies, e.g., in a Web-based procurement system (e-procurement).

For this purpose, data from a part of its own manufactured or externally procured products are included.

Rapid Transit currently stores the following product data in its inventory management system: product number, product description, cost center of manufacturing or procurement, quantity unit of the product (e.g., "piece," "kilogram," "meter"), manufacturing cost per unit, sales price per unit, current stock, storage cost per unit and fiscal year, source of supply (for externally procured products), quantity discount condition, and number of units sold in the current fiscal year.

(a) Provide the product catalog in XML format for transmission to the customer companies. Consider which of the existing information should be included in the product catalog.

Of course, a realistic product catalog contains many products. For our exercise, choose just two products.

(b) Provide an XML Schema document for the product catalog. Check the consistency between the instance document and the schema document (e.g., with Microsoft Visual Studio or with the tool available at the URL http://tools.decisionsoft.com/schemaValidate/, accessed on November 2, 2024).

Exercise 10.2 (Data Format for Legacy Data Migration)
A company is replacing its old enterprise information system and must migrate at least part of the legacy data into the new system. In which cases would you choose XML as the data format?

(b) Proposed Solutions for the Exercises

Exercise 10.1 (XML Documents)

(a) First, consider which information should appear in the product catalog. For example, the manufacturing costs should not be included (business part of the exercise). Then implement it with XML (technical part).

```xml
<?xml version="1.0"?>
<productCatalog>
  <company>Rapid Transit Ltd.</company>
  <version>2.1</version>
  <currencyUnit>EUR</currencyUnit>
  <products>
    <product>
      <ID>1938293232</ID>
      <name>E-Guitar HyperTap</name>
      <unit>p</unit>
      <price>345.00</price>
      <onStock>A</onStock>
    </product>
    <product>
      <ID>322394837</ID>
      <name>E-Guitar Cable KT-39</name>
```

```
            <unit>p</unit>
            <price>12.00</price>
            <discount>Ordering at leats 3: 7 percent discount
            </discount>
            <onStock>B</onStock>
        </product>
      </products>
</productCatalog>
```

The document has a header/line-item structure. In the proposed solution, only some data was included in the header, e.g., the currency unit, which applies to all line-items. Further attributes could be the validity interval and the language of the product catalog.

The discount is only informally represented in the proposed solution. A stronger formalization, e.g., graduated prices, is possible. However, it seems difficult and costly to formalize all possible discounts.

(b)
```xml
<?xml version="1.0"?>
<xsd:schema xmlns:xsd="http://www.w3.org/2001/XMLSchema">
 <xsd:element name="productCatalog">
  <xsd:complexType>
   <xsd:sequence>
     <xsd:element name="company"      type="xsd:string"/>
     <xsd:element name="version"      type="xsd:string"/>
     <xsd:element name="currencyUnit" type="xsd:string"/>
     <xsd:element name="products">
       <xsd:complexType>
         <xsd:sequence>
           <xsd:element name="product" maxOccurs="unbounded">
             <xsd:complexType>
              <xsd:sequence>
                <xsd:element name="ID"       type="xsd:string"/>
                <xsd:element name="name"     type="xsd:string"/>
                <xsd:element name="unit"     type="xsd:string"/>
                <xsd:element name="price"    type="xsd:string"/>
                <xsd:element name="discount" type="xsd:string"
                      minOccurs="0"/>
                <xsd:element name="onStock"  type="xsd:string"/>
              </xsd:sequence>
             </xsd:complexType>
           </xsd:element>
         </xsd:sequence>
       </xsd:complexType>
     </xsd:element>
   </xsd:sequence>
  </xsd:complexType>
 </xsd:element>
</xsd:schema>
```

It is important that the discount is optional (minOccurs="0") and the product is a repeating element (maxOccurs="unbounded"). In this simple solution, string is used for all elementary data types.

Exercise 10.2 (Data Format for Legacy Data Migration)

XML has some overhead compared to pure raw data, because the descriptive information is part of the data. Since the data structures of the source and target system are well-known during the legacy data transfer, the data structures do not comply with any standard, the transfer is done only once, and the data volume to be transferred is large, it seems sensible that the programs for data transfer do without the tags. XML could be used if the source or target system provides an XML interface for this purpose, because it can then easily be used.

10.8 Self-Assessment

10.1 Distributed Business Objects

1. What is the difference between the scenarios "New creation" and "Copy" in Fig. 10.1?
2. What can cause inconsistencies in a distributed object (see Fig. 10.1)? Could these be avoided?

10.2 Data Exchange Between Enterprise Systems

3. Where have we already encountered data exchange before this chapter?

10.3 The Data Exchange Format XML

4. Compare the formats XML and CSV: What types of data structures are used in the respective formats?
5. In what way is XML "stricter" than HTML, and in what way is it less strict?
6. What is the difference between an element and an attribute?
7. Are attributes necessary in XML?
8. What data type does an element have, and what does an attribute have?
9. How do you represent an array in XML?
10. What is the purpose of XML Schema? Is it necessary when using XML?
11. What errors can be found in a schema validation, and which ones cannot?
12. A customer has an outgoing XML interface for orders, a supplier an incoming for orders. Can they communicate without problems?

10.4 The Data Exchange Format JSON

13. Compare the ratio of raw data to total data between XML and JSON!

10.5 Message Brokers as a Communication Channel

14. What is the advantage of using a message broker for the integration through data exchange?
15. What is meant by "content-based routing?"
16. What is the purpose of mapping functionality in a message broker?
17. How could a message reach multiple receivers when using a message broker?
18. In an inter-company integration, message exchange can be used. Would there be one or two message brokers in such a scenario? Or none?

References

Further Reading

XML is covered more or less in depth in many books. A more in-depth treatment can be found for example in:
Harold, E.R., Means, W.S.: XML in a Nutshell, 3rd edn. O'Reilly, Sebastopol (2005)
XML: Chap. 2, Namespaces in XML: Chap. 4, XML Schema: Chap. 16 and as reference Chap. 21

For XML Schema, besides the standard, there is an easier to read introduction from the W3C:
W3C: XML schema part 0: primer, 2nd edition. http://www.w3.org/TR/2004/REC-xmlschema-0-20041028/primer.html (2004). Accessed 2 Nov 2024

Message brokers are extensively covered in:
Ferreira, D.R.: Enterprise Systems Integration. Springer, Berlin (2013)

Further Cited Literature and Sources

Alonso, G., Casati, F., Kuno, H., Machiraju, V.: Web Services. Springer, Berlin (2004)
Finkbohner, F., Höft, M., Roth, M., Kinold, J., Kuchelmeister, W., Widera, L.: Data Migration for SAP. Rheinwerk, Boston (2024)
Friesen, J.: Java XML and JSON. Apress, Berkeley (2019)
JSON: http://www.json.org/ (2024). Accessed 15 Oct 2024
JSON Schema: http://json-schema.org (2024). Accessed 15 Oct 2024
Kleppmann, M.: Designing Data-Intensive Applications. O'Reilly, Sebastopol (2017)
Sebestyen, T.J.: XML. Pearson, Munich (2010)
Tanenbaum, A., van Steen, M.: Distributed Systems, 2nd edn, Pearson new international edition. Pearson, Harlow (2014)
Tilkov, S., Eigenbrodt, M., Schreier, S., Wolf, O.: REST und HTTP, 3rd edn. dpunkt, Heidelberg (2015)
Walmsley, P.: Definitive XML Schema. Prentice Hall PTR, Upper Saddle River, NJ (2002)

Integration Through Function Call

11

Computer age—in harms way
We will prevail and perform our function.
Neil Young: We R in Control. (Trans, LP,
Geffen Records, 1982)

Summary
The integration through function call is illustrated using the example of Web services. The concept, the runtime process, the methodological approach at definition time, and the standards used, SOAP, WSDL, and UDDI, are discussed. The support by messaging systems for reliable transmission and other qualitative features are presented. In addition to the technical aspects, organizational ones are addressed. Web services are briefly compared with other approaches to integration through function call, especially REST.

Learning Objective

- To learn about integration through function call using the example of Web services.

11.1 Model

By integration through function call, we simply mean that a program C (*Client*) in one system calls a function f in a second system S (*Server*). It is the idea of the classic *Remote Procedure Call (RPC)*. See Sect. 11.9 for a classification of the techniques. Instead of as a server system, S can also be seen as a server function.

Fig. 11.1 Function call
over a communication
channel

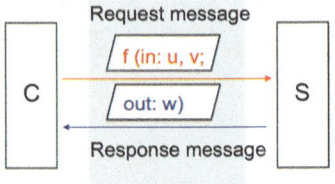

Figure 11.1 illustrates the model. C sends a request message over a communication channel, in which the function call is packed: in the example, the function name f and two input parameters u and v. In the server system S, the message is unpacked, the function f with the input parameters u and v is called, and the result, in our case an output parameter w, is computed. This is packed into a response message and sent back over the communication channel.

We look at the integration through function call using the example of Web services. Sometimes, the term "Web service" is interpreted more broadly: any form of service that can be called in the Inter- or intranet. In particular, Web pages would then be Web services. In this chapter on the other hand, the term is used more narrowly, as is common in computer science, only as program-to-program communication. And especially with the standards SOAP/WSDL (Sects. 11.1–11.4) or REST (Sect. 11.8).

We use Web services for the following reasons for illustration:

- The principles of remote function call are similar in other techniques (RPC, Java RMI, CORBA). One example is enough to understand the concept.
- Web services are widely used and available in many programming environments. They are today considered an important candidate for cross-platform function call. (What does "cross-platform" mean in this context?)
- Since Web services are based on XML, our XML-based representation, started with data exchange in Chap. 10, can be continued. (The same applies to REST-based Web services with JSON).

Already in Chap. 7, we saw that integration techniques both target internal enterprise integration (*Enterprise Application Integration*, *EAI*, or *Application to Application Integration*, *A2A*) and cross-enterprise or intercompany integration (*Business to Business Integration—B2B*). The concepts are similar in both cases, but in cross-enterprise integration, additional requirements arise, e.g., regarding security. In fact, Web services are mostly used internally or between closely cooperating business partners (see Alonso et al. 2004, p. 184), which in my estimation is still the case today.

Let's look at the model of Web services compared to business objects (see Sect. 3.4, Fig. 3.8). A Web service interface description only includes operations (Fig. 11.2), which are comparable to the methods of business objects, but have no attributes and events—the concept is not object oriented. Implementations of Web services on the other hand often use object orientation, in the sense that technical

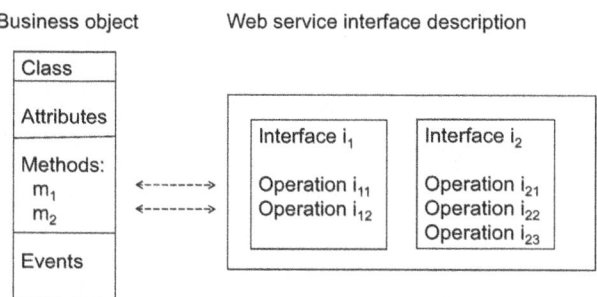

Fig. 11.2 Web service definition

server objects provide the operations. The operations are coarse grained like methods of business objects, also for performance reasons (less network traffic). Reading "attributes" is realized through read operations. A way to map events can be found in Sect. 10.5.3. The operations need to appear in an interface: Even if the Web service only offers one operation, an interface with this operation is necessary. Interfaces also fit into the object-oriented concept of business objects, although not explicitly mentioned in Sect. 3.4.

In fact, in this chapter, we prefer the term "function" instead of operation or method and use it synonymously in a broad sense: It can be a "function" in the narrower, programming language sense, i.e., a subroutine or a procedure of procedural programming. But we also use it for a method of object-oriented programming or of a business object.

For each operation of a Web service, a request and a response message are defined as well as their structure. The meaning (semantics) is only described informally.

A word on terminology: In a Web service, it is actually the operations that are called, not the service. Although sometimes you will read "call of the Web service," e.g., when it contains only one service operation. The client is also termed the *caller*, *sender*, or *consumer* of the service; the server is also called the *receiver* or *provider* of the service.

In the following, we focus on the common interaction pattern request-response. Other interaction patterns are discussed in Sect. 11.5.

11.2   Runtime Process

Let's now refine the process presented in the previous section using the example of Web services (Fig. 11.3). The client calls a very simplified order function: A material number is passed, and an order number is returned as a result. The simplification refers to the number and structure of the parameters. This is to keep the example small, resulting in small XML request and response documents.

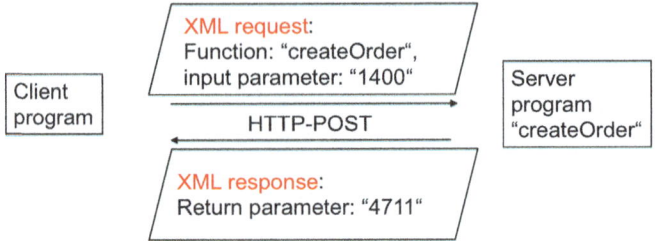

Fig. 11.3 Web service call

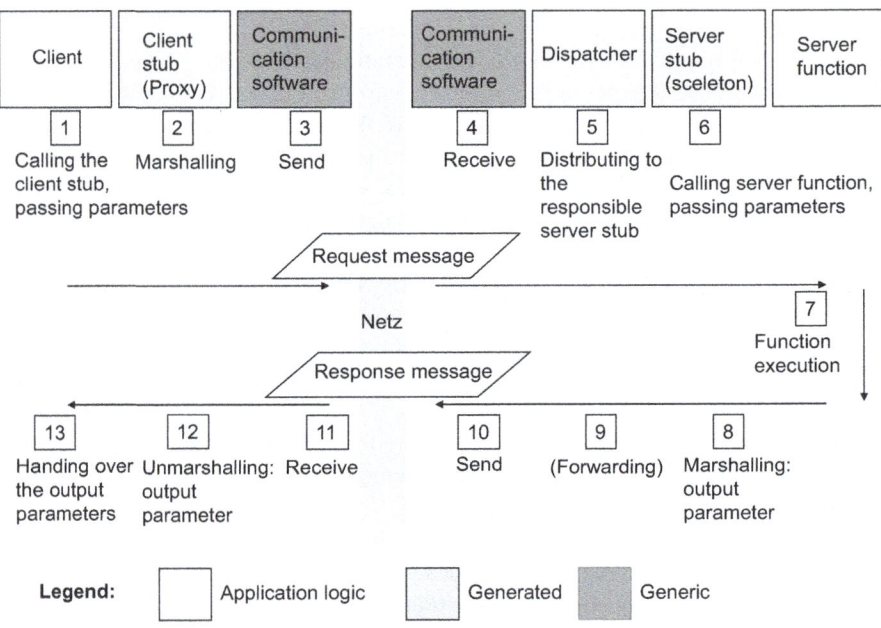

Fig. 11.4 Detailed process of the function call (Alonso et al. 2004, p. 163 f)

From a conceptual point of view, the function is the static method `createOrder` of the class `purchaseOrder`. The fact that it is a static method is typical for Web services. Although programs for Web services are usually developed in an object-oriented manner today, Web services are conceptually function oriented. (What could be the reason?)

The usual process is as follows (Fig. 11.4, similar to Alonso et al. 2004, p. 163 f.). We choose the HTTP method POST for communication, a synchronous communication. We will look at other options in Sect. 11.5. The illustration is designed to reflect the principle of any remote function call, i.e., it also applies to

RPC, for example. Web service-specific explanations concerning XML, SOAP (see below), and HTTP are found in steps 2, 3, and 5.

(a) *On the Client Side*

1. The client program triggers the function call. In fact, a *client stub*, a representative (also called *proxy*, *proxy procedure*, or *proxy object*) of the remote function, is called. The program call is therefore usually designed like a local function call. However, it is configured or specified in the program that the function is performed in the server system.

2. The client stub packs the function call based on the configuration information into an XML request document and passes it to the communication channel. In addition, another packing for the communication channel is carried out ("HTTP wrap"; cf. Alonso et al. 2004, p. 163), analogously when receiving the response document and when dispatching on the server side. The XML request document contains the name of the function and the input parameters. This packing is called *serialization* or *marshalling*.[1] The parameters are passed with the parameter passing mechanism call-by-value (for inputs) or call-by-copy/restore (for outputs), which is used as a replacement for call-by-reference. Call-by-reference is problematic because the two systems do not run in the same address space. With call-by-copy/restore, the passed parameter value is copied, the result is calculated, and the caller's parameter is overwritten with the result value (Tanenbaum and van Steen 2014, p. 127). The client stub can usually access generic functions, called *SOAP engine* or *SOAP processor* (Alonso et al. 2004, p. 163).

3. The request document is (usually) sent via HTTP to the receiver system, more precisely with the HTTP POST method. HTTP offers, for example, compared to the direct use of TCP/IP, the advantage that it can be tunneled through firewalls (Alonso et al. 2004, p. 152). The URL of the receiver system is provided as configuration information or is dynamically set in the client program.

The client program then waits for the response document. HTTP POST blocks during the call. The request and response documents are thus transmitted in the same HTTP method, not two separate ones. We see other communication possibilities in Sect. 11.5.

(b) *Continuation on the Server Side*

4. The server system receives the request document.

5. The dispatcher (also called *SOAP router*) distributes it to the responsible *server stub* (also called *skeleton*) while the analog to the client stub on the server side. The distribution can be based on the URL to which the message is directed or parts thereof.

---

[1] The terms are sometimes used synonymously. There is a subtle difference: Marshalling means packing data into a message of a certain format. Serialization transforms such a message into a byte stream (Alonso et al. 2004, p. 37).

6. The server unpacks the data (*deserialization* or *unmarshalling*): function name and input parameters. Then it calls the function with the input parameters.
7. It calculates output parameters, here the order number.
8. The server system packs this into a response document (again serialization/ marshalling).
9. It is passed on.
10. It is sent to the client system.

(c) ***Continuation on the Client Side***

11. The client receives the response document.
12. The client unpacks the data (*deserialization* or *unmarshalling*), the output parameters.
13. The output parameters are passed to the "local function call." The function call is thus completed.

The programs used have function-dependent parts. These must be provided by developers on the client and server side (application logic). There are function-dependent generated parts, which are automatically generated by the development environment (see Sect. 11.3). And there are function-independent parts of the infra-structure that are already available and can be used for all functions.

The remote function call should appear as local as possible. However, the differ-ence becomes clear at one point: communication errors are possible, and different measures, depending on the type of function, can be taken to deal with the errors (see Sect. 11.6).

With serialization/marshalling and deserialization/unmarshalling, it should be noted that the data formats in the client and server system do not have to match. For example, strings can be encoded differently in different systems, or the byte order can be different (Little Endian, Big Endian). The problem is discussed in detail in (Tanenbaum and van Steen 2014, p. 130), albeit in the context of RPC. The solution is to translate into a unique transmission format. The client encodes its own format into this transmission format; the server decodes the transmission format into its own format. In this way, a cross-language function call is made possible.

Request and response documents are encoded in the same way in Web services:

- Macro level:[2] This level concerns the outer shell, how the two documents are structured. The so-called SOAP format is used (Fig. 11.5), which is XML based. SOAP is a W3C standard. According to that standard, a SOAP message consists of an `envelope` (the root element of a SOAP message), an optional `header` (not necessary in our example, therefore omitted), and a `body`. In addition to this structuring of a message, SOAP also provides a format for exceptions in error situations.
- Micro level: There are a number of predefined possibilities how the encoding of the function name, the parameter names, and values can be done. Which of these possibilities is used is determined when defining the Web service.

---

[2] The terms "micro-level" and "macro-level" are my own, not predefined by Web services.

Fig. 11.5 SOAP message

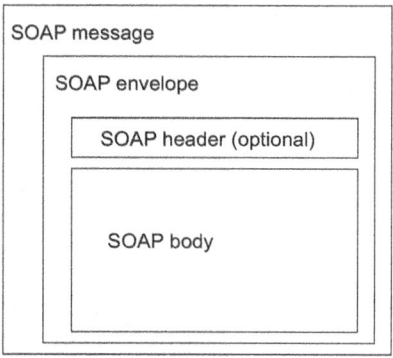

Details on the micro level: This is one of the trickier parts of Web services, and understanding it does not bring us much benefit. For curious people, however, a few words: When defining a Web service, it is determined which *interaction style* and which *encoding rules* are applied. Accordingly, the content of a SOAP message looks different. For the interaction style, there are the options *document* and *rpc*. With "document," each message is a document, agreed between sender and receiver; with RPC, the function signature is implemented by the SOAP middleware. As for encoding rules, there are the so-called SOAP encoding (but they are SOAP messages in any case), which determines how base types (e.g., integer, string) and complex types are encoded. The alternative encoding rule is *literal*, where an XML schema representation of the data structures is used (Alonso et al. 2004, p. 158 f.).

On the use of the header: In the SOAP model, it is assumed that a SOAP message can pass through multiple nodes. SOAP is independent of the transport protocol and also open for such a step-by-step transmission. We implicitly assumed that the message is transmitted directly from the sender to the receiver. The header is particularly important for this step-by-step transmission through multiple nodes but also for transactions as well as for authentication and authorization. For nodes, different roles can be defined that determine how they handle the header attributes (Alonso et al. 2004, p. 157).

Examples of a request and of a response document are shown in Figs. 11.6 and 11.7.[3]

In addition to the encapsulation as a SOAP message (Envelope and Body), the function name createOrder and the input parameter name number stand out. Both use the application-specific namespace of an order, here http://www.mycompRW721.de/ns/po/, which is used with prefix po. The number 1400 is the material number of the material to be ordered.

In the response document, there are two function-specific elements, createOrderResponse and createOrderResult. According to the encoding rules of the micro level, a Response is appended to the function name createOrder to signal that it is the response document. The aesthete will

---

[3] In the micro-level, the encoding document/literal is used here.

Fig. 11.6 Request in Web
service operation call

```
<soap:Envelope
 xmlns:soap="http://www.w3.org/2003/05/soap-envelope">
  <soap:Body>
   <po:createOrder
    xmlns:po="http://www.mycompRW721.de/ns/po/">
       <po:number>1400</po:number>
   </po:createOrder>
  </soap:Body>
</soap:Envelope>
```

Fig. 11.7 Response in
Web service operation call

```
<soap:Envelope
 xmlns:soap="http://www.w3.org/2003/05/soap-envelope">
  <soap:Body>
   <po:createOrderResponse
    xmlns:po="http://www.mycompRW721.de/ns/po/">
       <po:createOrderResult>4711</po:createOrderResult>
   </po:createOrderResponse>
  </soap:Body>
</soap:Envelope>
```

complain that it is not kept symmetrically, since no `Request` is appended to the function name in the request document. The function value is returned by appending `Result` to the function name.

The assignment of a response to a request document is here implicit, as HTTP-POST blocks when sending the request document until the corresponding response document is received. The address of the service is not included in the SOAP message. It is just used by HTTP-POST.[4]

11.3   Development at Definition Time

11.3.1 Definition with WSDL

Like the function call at runtime, the interface of the function call at definition time is also described independently of the programming language. This is done with the *Web Service Description Language* (*WSDL*), also a W3C standard. It exists in version 1.1 from 2001 and in version 2.0 from 2007, with a slightly different terminology.

In the standard, a function is called (*service-*)*operation*. In WSDL, not every operation is described in its own document. Rather, several operations are combined into a *service definition*. For structuring, a Web service definition is divided into several *interfaces* (somewhat misleadingly called *Port Types* in WSDL 1.1 and then *Interfaces* in WSDL 2.0). Each interface may include several operations.

---

[4] Similarly, routing information, i.e., a sequence of nodes to be traversed, is not included in the SOAP standard. These aspects are addressed by further Web service standards: *WS-Addressing*, which allows an address within a SOAP message to be specified; in addition to the URI, other referencing information can be used to identify the service instance object. With *WS-Routing*, SOAP paths of nodes can be specified in the header (Alonso et al. 2004, p. 191 f.).

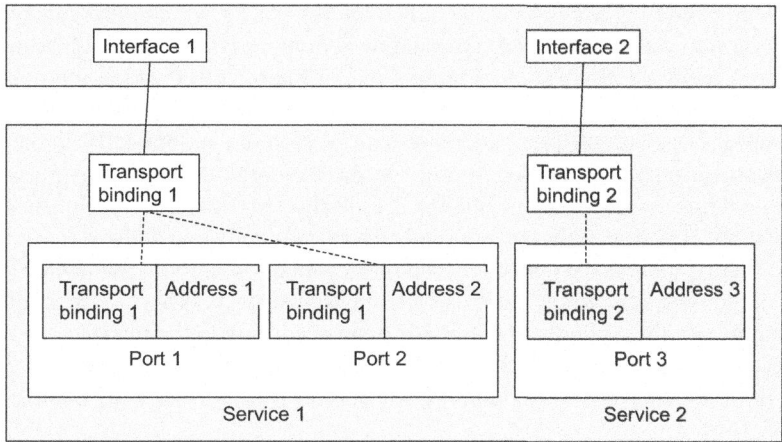

Fig. 11.8 Concrete part of a Web service

Each operation is defined by (depending on the interaction pattern, up to) two XML documents, a request and a response document. Each of the documents contains parameters in addition to the operation name, represented by *parts*. For each part, an XML schema data type is specified. In principle, type systems other than XML Schema are also possible in WSDL (Alonso et al. 2004, p. 167). Operations can have *exceptions* for error situations, which are also described in the WSDL definition.

The *abstract part* of a Web service (Alonso et al. 2004, p. 167), also called *definition part*, formally establishes its signature. What is obviously still missing is the address where the Web service can be called, e.g., a URL. This is found in the *concrete part*. It is somewhat misleadingly also called *implementation part*, because it does not contain, like the implementation part of a class, a program code that implements the Web service.

In fact, the concept is here more intricate, and therefore, it may be a bit harder to understand. Figure 11.8 represents the concept and the connection to the definition part.

The implementation part uses *transport bindings*: A Web service is today usually handled with the communication channel HTTP. In fact, it could also use other communication channels; theoretically, e.g., SMTP (email), the Web service standard at least leaves this open. This is determined in the transport binding.[5] A transport binding is defined for each interface of a Web service. In the figure, we see a Web service with two interfaces 1 and 2. For each interface, there is a transport binding.[6]

---

[5] A communication purist might take issue with the word "transport." It is used here in a broader sense.

[6] It could get a bit more complicated: For one and the same Web service, different *transport bindings* are possible. For example, the Web service could (theoretically) be accessed both via HTTP and via SMTP. Therefore, multiple transport bindings for an interface are possible.

Transport bindings can now be assigned addresses, for which *ports* (also called *endpoints*) are used. A port has a name and two components: a transport binding and an address (e.g., a URL). The operations of the interface for which the transport binding was defined are then accessible at that address. For the same transport binding, several ports with different addresses can be stored, e.g., one URL in the USA and one in Europe. (For what purpose?) In the example, there are two ports with different addresses for transport binding 1 (and thus for interface 1). But for transport binding 2, there is only one port and accordingly only one address.

And finally, there is the concept of the *service*, in my opinion, a somewhat unfortunate name when the whole thing is called a Web service. A service is a union of several ports. In the example, the union is done according to the interfaces.

The concrete part is new compared to other interface description languages, which limit themselves to the signatures of the functions or methods (Alonso et al. 2004, p. 166).

11.3.2 Methodical Approach

When developing and using a Web service, two questions arise:

1. Server program: How do I develop a Web service, and how do I make it available?
2. Client program: How do I call a Web service operation?

There are two methodical approaches (Fig. 11.9). They use functionality of today's development environments for Web services.

(a) **Bottom-Up (Inside-Out, Implementation First)**
    Here, one usually develops a Web service in the form of a class with (conceptually) static methods (Fig. 11.10), which, however, can technically be realized with an object instance of a server class. Annotations in the development envi-

Fig. 11.9 Top-down and bottom-up

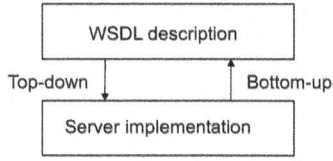

Fig. 11.10 Bottom-up

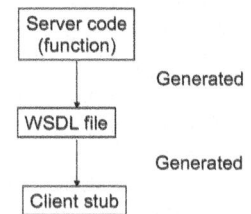

ronment indicate that the methods can be used as service operations.[7] From the source code, a WSDL description is generated on the one hand. On the other hand, the Web service can be published on a suitable Web server and thus made available for callers. Both the executable program code and the WSDL description are provided for them. "Suitable" means that the Web server provides a runtime environment for executing the Web service. You can see that the development and runtime platform is irrelevant for the caller, but not for the server developer: His development platform must match the Web server. The server development is completed with that.

The WSDL description is the basis for client development. It can be carried out on a different platform. For example, the Web service could be developed in a Java environment, but the client is implemented with Microsoft .NET. The WSDL document can be accessible on the Web server where the Web service was published, as described above. Or it can be provided in another way as a file. From the WSDL description, a *client stub* is generated. The client stub is used by the caller like a local function or method call. In fact, it hides functionality that handles the communication with XML request and response documents described in Sect. 11.1.

The advantage of this approach is that, theoretically, developers do not need to understand WSDL for either server or client development, as the conversion is carried out by the development environments. However, in practical cases, errors may occur where understanding WSDL can help, as the following paragraph shows. The approach is called "inside-out" because it works from the "inside" and the server implementation to the outside, the interface. The approach is called "implementation first" because we start with the implementation and then generate the WSDL description.

We have implicitly assumed that the WSDL description, which was generated by the server's development environment, is understood by the client's. In practical cases, this is not always the case. The reason is, in addition to software errors, which are always possible, that WSDL is a comprehensive standard and not all development environments use and understand all facets. To alleviate the problem, the Web Service Interoperability Organization (WS-I) has created profiles like the WS-I Basic Profile of different versions, i.e., subsets of WSDL, which should be understood by all development environments (Web Service Interoperability Organization 2010). This concerns restrictions, e.g., on transport over HTTP and on certain interaction patterns (van Lessen et al. 2011, p. 52).

(b) **Top-Down (Outside-In, Contract First)**

Here you start with a given WSDL description (Fig. 11.11). This could theoretically have been written "by hand," e.g., by a standardization committee. (Is writing "by hand" realistic?) Or it could have been created by a reference

---

[7] In JAX-WS (Java API for XML based RPC), annotations @WebService for a state-based session bean and @WebMethod for individual methods are used to indicate their use as Web service (operation). In addition, there are other annotations for various other aspects, e.g., the encoding style (JAX-WS 2006).

Fig. 11.11 Top-down

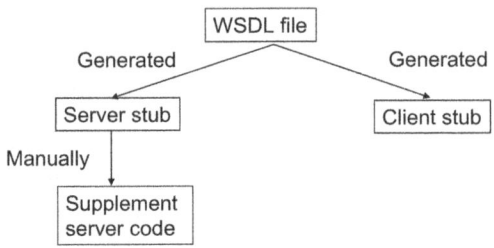

implementation of the Web service and thus technically like bottom-up. The goal now is to implement this Web service (or provide additional implementations besides the reference implementation). While the provider of the Web service dictates the interface in the bottom-up approach, top-down is used for standards that could be implemented by a variety of service providers.

The starting point is therefore a WSDL description. From this, a *server stub* can be generated. For example, a class with an empty method per operation with suitable parameters could be provided, the content of which now needs to be programmed. In terms of application logic, this is of course the crucial step. However, the programmer is freed from tedious and schematic tasks of encapsulation as a Web service, namely, XML and communication handling. As described in the bottom-up approach, annotations in the development environment ensure that executable program code is generated for the Web service on a Web server.

The approach is called "outside-in" because it starts from the outside, i.e., from the interface. In other words, the contract, i.e., the interface, to be adhered to is the starting point (contract first).

To keep the explanation simple, we have only considered the synchronous call of a Web service, which is very common. In Sect. 11.5, we will get to know other forms.

11.4 Directory

So far, we have assumed that the caller already knows the Web service to be used. With the basic Web service technology, as with other approaches to integration through function calls, there is another mediating component: a *directory*. Service providers publish services in such a directory, and service consumers search the directory for a suitable service.

There is the OASIS standard *Universal Description, Discovery and Integration* (*UDDI*) for this purpose. UDDI includes an API for publishing and searching for services and for communicating with other UDDI directories (Alonso et al. 2004, pp. 153 and 179). The API itself is implemented as a Web service. UDDI does not specify the exact form in which Web services are described in the directory. So the use of WSDL is not prescribed, although it is common. The standards are therefore complementary. Search terms must be assigned individually, and there is no predefined categorization, keyword list, or the like, as we know it from the yellow pages of a phone book. Web service standards only talk about technical, not content, aspects.

The search for services and establishment of communication between client and server (*binding*; Tanenbaum and van Steen 2014, p. 137) can happen at definition time, i.e., by the software developer (*static binding*[8]) or at runtime (*dynamic binding*). From my point of view, the dynamic binding is often overestimated in the literature: With dynamic binding, a calling program is supposed to dynamically determine the appropriate service in a directory at runtime. As Alonso et al. (2004, p. 188 f.) explain, this will only be possible in individual cases. Because two problems oppose the automatic finding, firstly, it must be understood what the service does and which parameters need to be passed. This is unrealistic for arbitrary services. For a limited case, however, UDDI offers a possibility: The service provides a reference to its description (WSDL specification) in a UDDI directory. This reference has a unique number.[9] If you know the number, you can search for all services that match the description, i.e., different implementations of the same service. (What would be a use case for this?) But even then, the second reason can prevent dynamic binding: In cross-company use, companies will not spontaneously call functionally matching services; the call must rather be preceded by a contractual agreement. Further obstacles are possible, such as services having the same interface but accessing different sets of data (e.g., different supplier groups). Various problems are addressed in Alonso et al. (2004, p. 300 ff.).

UDDI was initially strongly promoted for *public* directories. However, this did not catch on, and no public directories with sufficiently interesting content were created. Today, it is rather used for *private*, company-internal directories.

11.5 Asynchronous Call

In our previous consideration, we assumed that Web services are called synchronously via HTTP. The communication is *synchronous* in the sense that the sender waits until he receives the response message and only then continues his program.

Now we consider the asynchronous processing of a Web service (see Fig. 11.12). Here, message queuing systems again are used (cf. Sect. 10.5; the possibilities described there also apply here). The sender now communicates the request message *asynchronously* and transmits it to a *persistent* queue of the receiver. Once the message is stored in the queue, the sender's work is done for the time being. The receiver eventually takes the message from the queue and processes it, e.g., he executes the requested function call and generates a response message. In the same way as with the first message transmission, a second one occurs, in the return direction

---

[8] Binding here is understood in a different sense than the transport binding of a Web service.

[9] Formally, the description is stored in a so-called *tModel* (Technical Model) with this number (Alonso et al. 2004, p. 177). Different implementations of a Web service can reference the same tModel.

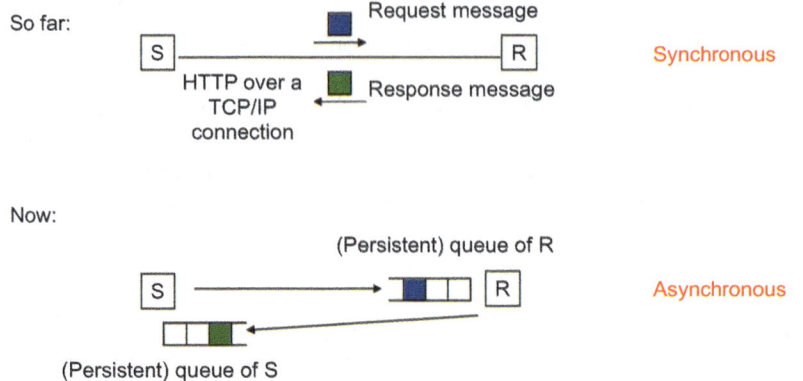

Fig. 11.12 Message-oriented communication

Fig. 11.13 Interaction patterns (1)

in this case. Since the two message transmissions are decoupled, it must be ensured that the response message is correlated with the request message, e.g., by a sequence number, as is common in data communication. In addition, the receiver must know the address of the sender (or of his send queue; each application has a send and a receive queue; Tanenbaum and van Steen 2014, p. 149), so that the response message can be sent back. With HTTP, this address was implicitly known while waiting for the response message. (How can the receiver know the sender's address?)

This communication is asynchronous: The sender transmits his request message and does not wait for an immediate response message. At some point, he will of course receive it in his queue and process it, but there is a temporal decoupling. This runtime advantage can result in higher complexity when creating applications at definition time, as this programming model is less familiar.

The request-response form is probably the most common interaction pattern in message-oriented communication in general and in Web services in particular. If we focus only on the message exchange, the integration via data exchange can also be seen in this context. Abstracting from the meaning of a message, we can therefore identify the following *interaction patterns* of message exchange for Web services (Fig. 11.13). In this respect, Web services can also be understood based on the concept of the message instead of the function call (RPC). The model thus goes beyond usual RPC-like models.

- *Request-response*: This interaction pattern is used in Web services for a function call: The request is followed by the response. The question arises whether the client blocks and waits for the response (*synchronous* call) or whether the response only occurs later in a separate communication (*asynchronous*).[10] The latter can also be expressed through one-way communication combined with a notification (see below).
- *One-way communication*: Only one message flows from the client to the server. This could be a data exchange (creating data, without receipt acknowledgment; see Chap. 10) or an asynchronous function call where there is no return value. (Example?)
- *Notification*: From the perspective of message exchange, this is the reverse to one-way communication. However, the content should only be information, not a changing operation like in one-way communication. This interaction pattern can represent the triggering of an event (see Sect. 3.4.3) or the result of an asynchronous function call, in connection with the interaction pattern one-way communication for the call.
- *Solicit response*: In this rather rarely used interaction pattern, client and server reverse their roles: The server initiates the interaction.

These interaction patterns are typically listed for Web services. In a WSDL document, the order of the listed messages determines the type of interaction (van Lessen et al. 2011, p. 47). The interoperability profile WS-I Basic Profile (Web Services Interoperability Organization 2010) only allows request-response and one-way communication (van Lessen et al. 2011, p. 84). Any number of additional interaction patterns can be found if we do not assume a maximum of one message in each direction (Fig. 11.14):

- *Session*: Multiple related messages flow from the client to the server. They are exchanged within a *session*. The service calls, realized through the messages, depend on each other and can access shared data held in main memory for this purpose (session state).
- *Arbitrary*: In this most general case, several messages are exchanged between the communication partners in a coordinated order. The roles "client" and "server" no longer seem appropriate in this free form of interaction. And finally, we can expand the communication from two to any number of communication partners. Often, this is broken down into a series of two-way communications. An important special case is the communication via a message broker (see Sect. 10.5.2).

---

[10] In fact, there are various possibilities in detail, as known from RPC. The client can wait until the server has accepted the call ("normal" *asynchronous RPC*) or respond immediately (*one-way RPC*). A special case is the *delayed synchronous RPC*. It consists of two asynchronous RPCs, the first from the client to the server and the second from the server to the client, to deliver the results. A variant of this is that the client asks for the result later (Tanenbaum and van Steen 2014, p. 134).

Fig. 11.14 Interaction patterns (2)

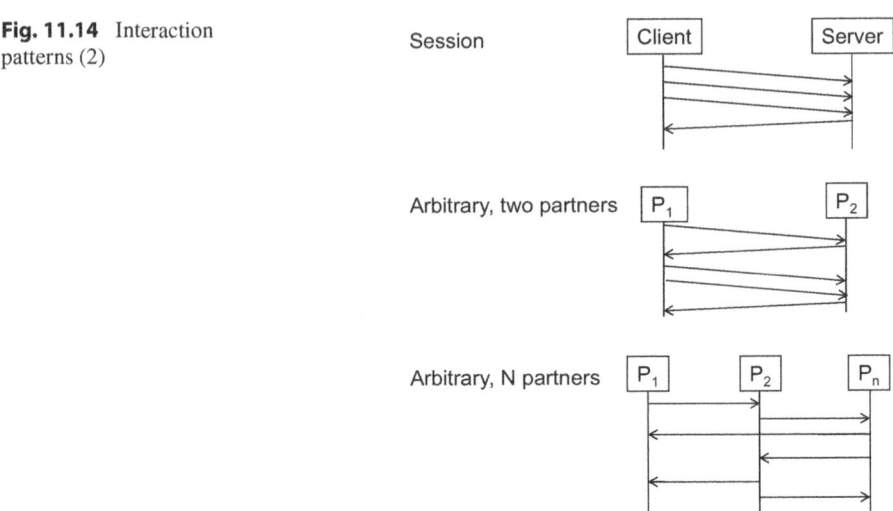

The interaction patterns "request-response" to "solicit response" can be seen as models of a method call of a business object or an activity in a business process. The interaction pattern "arbitrary" on the other hand represents a cooperative business process or a view of it. Here, two or more applications communicate within or between companies in several steps. The interaction pattern "session" is a borderline case: It could be seen as a composition of simpler methods or activities into more complex ones or as a business process. The composition and coordination of activities or services, especially with regard to business processes, will be discussed in Chap. 12.

The integration forms "data exchange," "function," and "business process" are thus closely interrelated. In computer science, we know the integration means "shared memory" and "message exchange" in parallel, distributed systems. We have learned about shared memory (in our case persistent) in the form of data integration in transactional systems as well as in analytical systems. Message exchange takes place in an intra-company system landscape as well as in inter-company integration. (Can you give an example of such inter-company integration?)

11.6   Service Properties

Sending a request message and receiving the response message (if necessary) can be referred to as a *service* or more precisely as a *service operation*. We can abstract from the type of service (data exchange, function call). Regulations can also be made for several service calls in a row (transactional, in the correct order). If we operate the service call with a MOM infrastructure, we can define *service properties*, which the infrastructure can guarantee or at least support. They reflect the criteria mentioned in the previous sections. The following representation is according to Huvar et al. (2009, p. 107 ff.):

1. *Interaction patterns*: We looked at these in Sect. 11.5.
2. *Blocking*: Does the sender block and wait for the response message (*blocking* or *synchronous*): Or does he continue immediately, usually with other tasks (*non-blocking* or *asynchronous*)?
3. *Session*: If several service calls take place one after the other, are these completely independent of each other (*stateless*)? Or is a session established in which several service operations take place one after the other and the state is maintained between the calls (*stateful*)?
4. *Reliability*: Is the transmission *unreliable*, i.e., is it possible that the message does not reach the receiver, for example, due to a communication error? Or is the transmission guaranteed (*reliable*, i.e., "exactly once" or even "exactly once in the correct order")?
5. *Transaction behavior*: This concerns the encapsulation of several consecutive service calls into a transaction. If the "transactional" property is set, either all or none of the service calls are executed.
6. *Commit handling*: Should a commit to complete a transaction be triggered automatically by the infrastructure or explicitly by the caller (*with commit/without commit*)? (What could be a reason for the caller to trigger it?)

For each service (actually for each service operation), these properties can be specified. However, not all combinations are possible or make sense. Correlations exist between:

- Interaction patterns and blocking: For request-response, "synchronous" is usually sensible, but not mandatory.
- Blocking and reliability: "Non-blocking" and "reliable" is usually a good combination.

The following service properties are based on the content, not on the configuration of a service:

- *Service content*: Is the service content *data* or a *function call*?
- *Addressing*: Is the receiver *directly* addressed or *indirectly* (e.g., identified via a message broker or according to the "publish and subscribe" principle)?

In Exercise 11.3, you can think about which properties are appropriate for different services.

We want to take a closer look at the property "reliability." Unlike with local function calls, communication errors can occur when transmitting the request or response message in remote function calls. Also, the client or server may not be available at times, namely, the server before or during the call or the client after the request has been transmitted. Accordingly, there are different "call semantics":

- *maybe (best effort)*: No error correction mechanisms are used. If everything goes well, the remote call behaves like a local one, except for the performance and limited options for parameter passing, e.g., no call-by-reference is used. For read access, this may be sufficient; if the call is not successful, the client will repeat it later if necessary.

- *at least once*: If the client does not receive a response, the call is repeatedly transmitted and executed until a response arrives, or it is estimated that there will be no response in the foreseeable future. For many functions, repeated execution is not sensible. The "textbook classic" is the transfer to an account, even though this is a rather unrealistic example. The difference to "maybe" is that the runtime system, not the client, takes care of the repeated transmission.
- *at most once*: This is similar to "at least once." However, duplicates of the call are detected and filtered out. The server stores the response message and transmits it multiple times if necessary, but does not execute the function again.
- *exactly once*: This is generally required in enterprise information systems for write access. The call semantics "exactly once" is achieved with the help of transaction mechanisms on the client and server side (separate transactions) as well as with the help of the Web service standard Reliable Messaging. By the transactions on the client and server side, the transmission of the call is persisted. The message transmission system can therefore repeat a call, even if the client, the server, or the message transmission system is temporarily unavailable (system crash). "Reliable Messaging" guarantees through repeated transmission that the message actually goes from the client to the server system. A detailed treatment of this, especially sequence diagrams, can be found in Huvar et al. (2009, p. 112 ff.).
- *exactly once in the correct order*: This concerns the interaction pattern "session," where the individual messages must be transmitted and processed in the correct order.

11.7   Organization

Up to now, our discussion was technical: How does a Web service work? And how do you develop it? However, typical difficulties in function-oriented integration are less technical in nature than content related: Suitable functions must be available, which can be called. At first, this sounds trivial. But the question of reusability of software has a long history in computer science, and the results are not always satisfactory. Only the technical mechanisms of how functions are provided have changed. They range from program libraries, over inheritance mechanisms in object-oriented programming, to component models. Typical aspects are (see also general aspects of interfaces in Sect. 3.6):

- *Function set*: The function set shall contain just the appropriate functions. None required for a task (business process) should be missing. And in order to reduce the effort (development, maintenance), the function set should also not be too large, i.e., it should not contain unnecessary functions.
- *Compatibility*: The functions must fit well together. For example, there should be the usual CRUD functions (create, read, update, delete), as well as more specialized functions (e.g., the release of business documents), to cover the life cycle of a business object completely. In addition, there should be further processing pos-

sibilities, e.g., converting quotations into orders, i.e., relationships between different classes.

- *Granularity*: The functions should have a suitable granularity: not too fine grained, as is common in object-oriented programming, because then many calls are necessary; the programming and runtime effort (round trips) can increase as a result; not too coarse grained, because then perhaps the detailed control of business objects is lost.
- *Function interface*: The functions must have the appropriate parameters. If an important parameter is missing, the usability may be forfeited. (What can a developer use as a guide when designing the interface?)
- *Uniformity*: The functions should be designed according to a uniform guideline, so that the understanding of one area can be transferred to the rest.
- *Understandability*: The functions must be understandable. Here, the understandability for different groups of people (employees from IT and business) must be considered, as they often use a different language. In addition, errors can creep in through poorly understandable functions. Understandability includes a sensible organization of the parameters, as well as good documentation.
- *Access*: The functions must be easy to find. For this, a directory helps, in which the functions are sensibly organized into areas and classes and documented.
- *Stability*: The functions should be released for the long term. Program changes should leave the interface unchanged. (How would you organize this?)
- *Transactionality*: This is particularly important for business application software. In a transactional control, several function calls are encapsulated together as a transaction—either all or none have an effect.

11.8 REST-Based Web Services

Another form of Web services is described in (Fielding 2000): "Representational State Transfer" (REST). The technique is increasingly widespread, for example, for implementing microservices (see Sect. 6.2). One reason may be that SOAP-based Web services at times seem clumsy. Thus, REST can be considered a lightweight alternative to SOAP-based Web services, similar as JSON to XML for data description.

Although theoretically independent of HTTP, it is today in practice used in conjunction with it. The basic idea is to use only the HTTP methods GET (read), PUT (modify and create), POST (create and special functions, beyond CRUD), and DELETE, which act on resources that are addressed by a URI. Compared to our model of business objects, the usual, ubiquitous CRUD methods are available. However, more specific methods require special treatment.

As for resources, one could think of business objects, and indeed the business objects will also be resources. But the resource concept is more general; other "things" can also be considered resources. In Tilkov et al. (2015, p. 36 ff.), among others, the following are mentioned:

- List: In our parlance, this would be a class.
- Sub-resource: A part of another resource, e.g., a supplier address or order line-items within an order.
- Filter: A subset of a list. In our parlance, these are objects of a class that have a certain property or a certain attribute value, e.g., released purchase requisitions.

Since each method is directed at exactly one resource, our business object model can in principle be reproduced. This is because REST has a more restricted method concept but as a compensation, a richer resource/business object concept. More specific change methods can be represented via the POST method, because its semantics is more open. Furthermore, special resources may be introduced, e.g., the method "cancel" (an order) could be represented as creating a new resource "cancellation" with reference to the order.

A resource could in principle be accessible with several addresses (URIs), and it can have several representations. In a service operation call, the favored representation can be specified. For this to work, of course, the representations must be implemented in the service. The usual representation will be JSON (see Sect. 10.4), in line with the lightweight design, but others are possible, e.g., XML, HTML, and JPEG. While JSON and XML seem best suited for machine processing, HTML (in conjunction with the GET method) can be used for displaying a resource in a Web browser. In addition to communication between systems, REST is also used in the implementation of Web applications.

Our example from Sect. 11.2 looks like this with REST, using JSON as the representation format. It is a POST to create a purchase order:

```
POST http://www.mycompRW721.de/purchaseOrders
```

The request message is

```
POST /purchaseOrders
Host: www.mycompRW721.de
Accept: application/json
{
     "number": 1400
}
```

In the header fields, in particular, the acceptable or desired representation format is specified. This of course only works if the service supports this format. The body in JSON format, in curly brackets, is brief for this simple example. We saw in Sect. 10.4 that much richer structures are possible with JSON, similar to XML.

The response document looks like this:

```
HTTP/1.1 201 created
Content-Type: application/json
Date: Mon, 13 Jul 2020 10:00:00 GMT
```

```
Location: http://www.mycompRW721.de/purchaseOrders/4711
Content-Length: 95
{
  "href": "http://www.mycompRW721.de/purchaseOrders/4711",
  "description": "Purchase order 4711"
}
```

The return value 201 indicates that a new resource (here a purchase order) has been created. The body indicates which one it is.

Relationships between resources are represented as links, familiar from HTML. JSON as a standard actually does not support links, but extensions have been defined (Tilkov et al. 2015, p.89 ff.). The relationships are similar to those we have seen with business objects (see Sect. 3.3.3) or in database parlance: foreign keys.

The methods used in REST should retain their properties defined in HTTP. This concerns the semantics (as far as defined for HTTP), the security (freedom from side effects), and idempotence: The methods GET and PUT are idempotent, i.e., if you perform them twice, the effect is like executing them once (provided no further methods were executed in between). The GET method is safe, so it has no side effects (reading should be strictly reading, apart from writing log entries). The creation of a resource can be done with the POST method to a list resource (comparable to a static method in business object classes) or with the PUT method to a resource of a business object, called primary resource in (Tilkov et al. 2015, p. 37). In the first case, the resource would be, e.g., "purchase orders," and during the creation process, a purchase order as primary resource with an internally assigned number is created. In the second case, the resource would be, e.g., "purchase order 1342," and the number would therefore have been determined beforehand. The POST method is the "most open" method, as its semantics is not precisely defined, and besides the creation, it can also be used for other purposes. Accordingly, it is the natural candidate for more specific change methods, with the specifics being passed as parameters in the POST call.

HTTP offers an extension mechanism: The standard methods can be supplemented with additional ones, with advantages and disadvantages (see (Tilkov et al. 2015, p. 63). A disadvantage is that clients then need to know the additional methods and implement them.

We have now learned almost all the basic principles of REST (Tilkov et al. 2015, p. 11): resources with unique IDs (URIs), links between resources, standard methods (from HTTP, with their usual meaning), and different representations. One principle is still missing: stateless communication. This does not mean that there must not exist any state between different method calls. In a dialog application, for example, a state is usual. However, the state should not be transient on the server. It should be either managed by the client, generally transient, or the resource state should be used, generally stored in the database. The advantage of this provision is that two requests do not have to be handled by the same server instance, and thus load distribution and (horizontal) scalability (see Sect. 5.1.1) can be realized more easily.

For the secure transmission of REST calls, on the one hand, communication via HTTPS can be used. On the other hand, encryption and signing methods of the individual representation formats, e.g., XML or PDF, can be utilized. A generic, standardized encryption or signing of HTTP requests and responses, on the other hand, is not available (Tilkov et al. 2015, p. 131).

For the description of RESTful APIs, there are various tools and languages, some with the ability to generate client and server code, comparable to techniques available for WSDL (see Sect. 11.3.2 (Tilkov et al. 2015, p. 161 ff)).

11.9 Other Techniques for Function Calls

Over time, various techniques for remote function calls have emerged, more or less prevalent in practice.

* *Remote Procedure Call (RPC)*: This "classic" introduced the principle in the early 1980s. Before that, the packaging and sending of a function call and the unpacking of the results had to be done "by hand" via lower communication interfaces. The mechanism is cross-language.
* *Java Remote Method Invocation (RMI)*: While the first techniques were procedural, this is an object-oriented mechanism in Java, therefore usable only between Java systems.
* *CORBA Method Call*: CORBA stands for *Common Object Request Broker Architecture*, a standard of the *Object Management Group (OMG)* for cross-platform method calls. "Cross-platform" is the same goal as in Web services. However, the calls are object oriented, while they are procedural in Web services. For various reasons, the technology has not established itself (van Lessen et al. 2011, p. 5).

A more comprehensive presentation can be found, for example, in Tanenbaum and van Steen (2014, Ch. and Sect. 4.2, 10 and 12).

Table 11.1 shows the similarities and differences between these mechanisms of function calls (call semantics according to Coulouris et al. (2005, p. 187 f.); for explanation, see Sect. 11.2).

11.10 Implementation in the Enterprise Information System

The task is that a function in the server system shall be called by the client system (the system that triggers the call), e.g., within a dialog method.

In fact, the case is similar to data exchange (Sect. 10.6), so we can keep the description shorter. Instead of sending data, the client system triggers a Web service call in the server system. The Web service call could occur event driven in an extension point (see Sect. 15.8) of the aforementioned dialog method. For example, when the user clicks a certain tab, the Web service queries data, and the data are then visualized in the dialog method. The extension point could also be used to adapt the user interface (e.g., an additional tab for displaying the transmitted data).

Table 11.1 Comparison between function call techniques

	Web Service	REST Service	RPC	Java RMI	CORBA
Interface	WSDL	Various languages	Interface Definition Language (IDL)[a]	Java interface	CORBA IDL
Runtime format (Data)	SOAP and encoding rules specified for Web services	URI, MIME	IDL	Java object serialization	Common Data Representation (CDR)
Communication channel	HTTP, message broker	HTTP	TCP/IP	TCP/IP, Java runtime environment	CORBA Object Request Broker
Development language	Many (independent)	Many (independent)	Many (independent)	Java	Many (independent)
Call semantics	Depending on implementation	Depending on implementation	"At least once"[b]	"At most once"	"At most once" and "best effort"

[a] In DCE RPC (*DCE* stands for *Distributed Computing Environment*, a standard of the Open Software Foundation, today Open Group), the Interface Definition Language (IDL) is used, which is based on the programming language ANSI C (The Open Group 1997). In RPC, the IDL is used not only for interface description but also for the mapping from one programming language to the runtime format (Alonso et al. 2004, p. 41)

[b] In Sun RPC

The server system must provide the Web service. It can already be included in the standard software. Or it is a custom development (see Sect. 15.7). An API that contains the appropriate method should be the basis for the Web service. The Web service then only encapsulates the API method. If the API method is not available, it is custom developed. Access to the corresponding database tables is needed for that purpose. Finally, the Web service still needs to be configured.

11.11   Exercises and Proposed Solutions

(a) Exercises

Exercise 11.1 (Various Types of Integration, Including Message Broker)
This exercise concerns all previously covered integration techniques.

A clerk wants to record, view, and search both customer master data and interactions. The data is located in an ERP and in a CRM system.

- What integration possibilities (user interface, application logic, data) between the two systems are conceivable, and what would they look like in this specific case?
- Would you use a message broker in this case? What speaks for and against it in our case?

Exercise 11.2 (Identifying Services)
Three systems are used in a company: ERP, CRM, and a data warehouse system. A new Web application shall be created, which uses the following services. The services should be provided by encapsulating functions of the enterprise information systems. Consider which systems are involved in the services and what runtime properties (regarding interaction patterns, blocking, reliability, commit behavior, and session) the services should have.

(a) Create customer master data.
(b) Query customer data.
(c) Create an order.
(d) Send invoice via EDI (Electronic Data Interchange).
(e) Sales statistics of customers for shorter periods (e.g., last week) and longer periods (e.g., the last 10 years).

(b) Proposed Solution for the Exercises

Exercise 11.1 (Various Types of Integration, Including Message Broker)

(a)
- User interface: The clerks maintain customer master data and interactions in the portal. Both applications appear side by side. The portal uses single sign-on, so that the clerks do not have to log in twice. After searching for customer master data, the clerks can see the associated interactions, if this is implemented, for example, via event-oriented communication (portlets).

- Application logic: For example, a new application is written in the ERP system. It reads the interactions via a Web service and displays them.
- Data: Customer master data is transferred from ERP to CRM, e.g., in background jobs. The technical format can be XML or a CSV file.

(b)

- For: Secure transmission of data (here customer data), incl. logging, openness for later integrations.
- Against: Overdimensioned solution, if it is really only this one integration task. This argument will prevail here.

Exercise 11.2 (Identifying Services)

	(a)	(b)	(c)	(d)	(e)
Involved systems	ERP, CRM	ERP, CRM	ERP	ERP	ERP, DWHS
Interaction pattern	One-way communication	Request-response	One-way communication	One-way communication	Request-response
Blocking	No	Yes	No	No	Yes
Reliability	Yes	No	Yes	Yes	No
Commit handling	Yes	No	Yes	Yes	No
Session	No	No	No	No	No/yes

11.12 Self-Assessment

1. What is the relationship between integration through function call and business objects?
2. What is the difference between a Web service and a Web application? What are the similarities?
3. What is the relationship between XML and Web services?
4. What information do you provide for a Web service operation?
5. Why could you say on the one hand that Web service operations are static methods, but not on the other hand?
6. What is a client stub?
7. What is the difference between a server stub and a server function (see Fig. 11.4)?
8. What does "generic parts" in Fig. 11.4 mean?
9. Which part of a Web service definition is important for software development: the abstract, the concrete, or both?
10. What is the relationship between XML Schema and WSDL?
11. Why should Web service operations be more coarse grained than methods often used in object-oriented programming?
12. What is meant by transactionality in the context of Web services?
13. Can you use a message broker for Web services? How do you correlate the request and the response message?

References

Further Reading

The concepts of SOAP/WSDL-based Web services are well described in:
Alonso, G., Casati, F., Kuno, H., Machiraju, V.: Web Services. Springer, Berlin (2004)

A benefit of the following book is the detailed presentation of a web service example:
Papazoglou, M.P.: Web Services: Principles and Technology. Prentice-Hall, Upper Saddle
    River (2007)

A brief introduction to REST can be found, e.g., in the first chapter of:
Varanasi, B., Belida, S.: Spring REST. Apress, Berkeley (2015)

Detailed information about the REST principles can be found in:
Richardson, L., Ruby, S.: RESTful Web Services. O'Reilly & Associates, Sebastopol (2007)
Concepts of remote procedure and method calls are extensively explained in some books, e.g., in:
Coulouris, G., Dollimore, J., Kindberg, T.: Distributed Systems, 4th edn. Addison-Wesley, Harlow
    and others (2005)
Tanenbaum, A., van Steen, M.: Distributed Systems, 2nd edn, Pearson new international edition.
    Pearson, Harlow (2014)

Further Cited Literature and Sources

Fielding, R.T.: Architectural Styles and the Design of Network-Based Software Architectures.
    Dissertation, University of California, Irvine (2000)
Huvar, M., Falter, T., Fiedler, T., Zubev, A.: Developing Applications with Enterprise SOA. Galileo
    Press, Bonn (2009)
JAX-WS: https://www.jcp.org/en/jsr/detail?id=224 (2006). Accessed 13 Mar 2025
The Open Group: https://pubs.opengroup.org/onlinepubs/9629399/chap4.htm (1997). Accessed
    18 Oct 2024
Tilkov, S., Eigenbrodt, M., Schreier, S., Wolf, O.: REST und HTTP, 3rd edn. dpunkt,
    Heidelberg (2015)
van Lessen, T., Lübke, D., Nitzsche, J.: Geschäftsprozesse automatisieren mit BPEL. dpunkt,
    Heidelberg (2011)
Web   Services   Interoperability   Organization: WS-I   Basic   Profile   (2010).
    http://ws-i.org/profiles/BasicProfile-1.2-2010-11-09.html. Accessed 2 Nov 2024

Integration Through Process Management Systems

12

HAMM Is it working? *Pause. Impatiently:* The alarm, is it working?
CLOV Why wouldn't it be working?
HAMM Because it's worked too much.
CLOV But it's hardly worked at all.
HAMM *angrily:* Then because it's worked too little!
Samuel Beckett (Endspiel Fin de partie Endgame,
first edition, Suhrkamp Taschenbuch 171,
Frankfurt a. M., 1974, p. 68)

Summary
The integration at the level of business processes is presented using the example of process management systems. Through process control, the methods of business objects are called in an order defined in the process (orchestration). Such a process can take place in a single enterprise information system or in several systems of a system landscape. Inter-company integration is also possible, usually with mutual coordination of business processes (choreography) instead of central control.

Learning Objective

- To get to know process-oriented integration using process management systems.

12.1 Process Management Systems

In Chap. 3, we saw that enterprise information systems provide business processes. There are also business processes in which several systems of a system landscape participate. Some business processes have implicit process control (partly defined in the software, partly organizational), while some have explicit (e.g., through a process management or, more specifically, a workflow system).

In this chapter, we are interested in explicit process control. This can be considered an integration of application functionality, because the methods of business objects are executed in a certain, at least to some extent, predetermined order by agents (people or programs). If all process steps take place in only one enterprise information system, it is a system-internal control and (partial) automation. If, on the other hand, the process steps are distributed over several enterprise information systems, it is a form of integration of enterprise information systems, i.e., in the focus of Part II of the book. In the latter case, also other, complementary integration techniques are generally used. (What would make sense here?)

Systems for business process control have a long tradition. While the ideas and concepts were retained and merely developed further, the names of these systems have changed over time. In the 1990s, the term *workflow management system* or shorter *workflow systems* was coined. Now also *business process management system* (*BPM system*) or, shorter, *process management system* is used. In the following, we use these two terms:

- *Workflow systems*: This is the narrower of the two terms. Workflow systems typically control processes that contain both dialog (even predominantly) and background activities. The dialog activities represent the "work" for the clerks (with enterprise information system support, thus partial automation); the background activities stand for complete automation.
- *Process management systems*: This more general term includes both workflow systems and systems that control processes consisting of only background activities (see, e.g., the ETL process, Sect. 4.2.2, in particular the data integration of Pentaho, Sect. 4.2.6.3, and Big Data pipelines, Sect. 4.4.3.2).

In practice, the two terms are often less strictly separated.

Let's first look at a workflow system and then see what differences arise with other process management systems.

In Fig. 12.1, we see the components that typically make up a workflow system. At definition time, workflow developers model a process, usually with a graphical modeling tool. Unlike other tools that only visualize processes, the result is a fully formally described executable *process definition* (also called *process model*). This may be executed by the *workflow runtime system* (also called business process engine or workflow engine). For the process to start, a *process instance* of the process definition is instantiated. The workflow runtime system ensures that the process instance runs exactly according to the process definition.

During runtime, the individual steps (*activities*) of the process definition are either automatically executed by programs[1] or, more often, by users executing application programs in dialog. In Fig. 12.1, we see four activities of a process, with the middle two activities in a loop. Except for the fourth activity, they are processed

---

[1] Here we simplify a bit. There are internal steps that the workflow system carries on its own, without an activity or a work item being involved, e.g., condition evaluations or waiting steps.

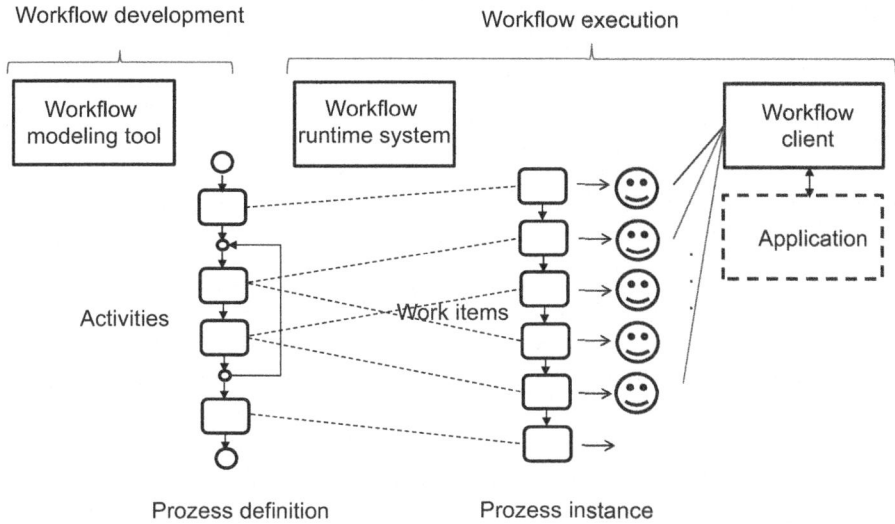

Fig. 12.1 Workflow system

by users in dialog. The workflow system generates a *work item* (also called *activity instance*) when the previous step is finished. We see that due to loops and conditions, there is a 0:*N* relationship between activities and work items. The workflow system assigns the work item to a user as an *agent* when the activity requires a user dialog, e.g., the release of a purchase requisition. The agent usually sees his work items in an inbox, which can also contain emails and other entries. From there he can execute the work item. This involves the *workflow client*, a functional part of the inbox. When the agent selects the function "execute" of the work item, the workflow client calls the corresponding application (in our model, the method of a business object) and gets results at the end of the call. If no dialog is necessary (background activity), the workflow runtime system initiates the automatic execution of the activity by an application program, e.g., sending an email to a business partner.

Process management with human interaction, mostly for decision steps or data entry, is called "human workflow management" in Freund and Rücker (2019, p. 6) and "human interaction workflow" in Weske (2024, p. 67). The extreme case of a process without human interaction is called "system workflow" (Weske 2024, p. 67) or "service orchestration," where the background steps are considered service operations (such as in Web services; see Chap. 11). Some process management systems (such as the one mentioned in Sect. 4.2.6.3 for the ETL process) only support processes with background activities. In such a system, the term "workflow" is simply replaced by "process," and the workflow client is of course omitted.

The workflow system realizes a *push principle*: The work to be done is transmitted, "pushed," to the users. The opposite is the *pull principle* for the users. It is common without workflow support: The user must collect his various tasks, such as approve vacation requests or purchase requisitions, check invoices, or read emails, at different places in an enterprise information system or even in several enterprise information systems. In this sense, workflow is another means of integrating people with enterprise information systems (cf. Chap. 9).

How does a process get started? Although processes can be started manually for testing purposes, the more comfortable and usual way is to use events (see Sect. 3.4.3): A start event, e.g., "purchase requisition created" can thus automatically start a process, in this case for purchase requisition release.

A process definition executable by a process management system is developed following a methodology of business process management. This could include the following three forms of process definitions:

- *Process sketch*: In Freund and Rücker (2019, p. 16), this is called *strategic process model*. The process is described from a bird's-eye view. It should fit on a sheet of paper. Process variants and error handling are omitted; you focus on a "happy-path view," i.e., the successful path through the process is chosen. In this process definition, which primarily serves for basic coordination in a company, semantic inconsistencies and gaps are pragmatically accepted. Brevity and comprehensibility are prioritized (Freund and Rücker 2019, p. 89). They mention, "Every process model is incomplete—but some are useful" (Freund and Rücker 2019, p. 100).
- *Conceptual detailed process*: Like the process sketch, this is modeled from a business perspective, but it is much more detailed. To achieve a "good" conceptual detailed process is a challenging and important task. After all, it will be of little use to support an inefficient process through process management. In (Freund and Rücker 2019, p. 16), this process corresponds to the *human process flow* in an *operational process model*.
- *Executable detailed process*: This process is executable by a process management system—the focus of this chapter. Executable process definitions are usually not created by the business department but by process developers. However, they are in close contact with the business department. The executable detailed process is tailored to the conceptual detailed process. In (Freund and Rücker 2019, p. 16), this corresponds to the *technical process flow* in an *operational process model*. They emphasize that it is advantageous to design the human and the technical process flow simultaneously due to their interaction (Freund and Rücker 2019, p. 18).

12.2   Process Definition

For the process control to be as automated as described above, the process definition must be machine executable. In Sect. 3.5, we learned about the parts of a process definition:

- Control flow
- Data flow
- Agent assignment

Now let's look at how these aspects are expressed in process management systems.

12.2.1 Control Flow

(a) **Language Constructs**

You can imagine a process definition that is executable by the runtime system of a process management system as similar to a program. It is also called "programming in the large." The activities correspond to the elementary instructions, which in process definitions are usually not assignment statements but method calls of business objects. The order is determined by language constructs such as sequence, branching, and loop. Language constructs that are less frequently used in programming, but play a significant role in process definitions, are parallel sections and events.

Parallel sections shorten the process throughput time. The number of parallel branches can be statically predetermined in the process model or only become known at runtime. The typical use case for the latter is that a branch should be executed for several instances of similar business objects, e.g., the review of several quotations, the number of which only becomes apparent during the process. With parallel branches, the merging can happen after all branches have completed. However, more sophisticated forms are also possible: The merging happens when M out of N branches are completed, e.g., when only the majority of decision-makers have to agree. Or a condition is formulated that must be fulfilled in order for the process to continue.

Events are used to synchronize data changes with the control flow: A process can wait for events. Or events can be generated in the process—explicitly in a dedicated process step or implicitly by triggering an event as a side effect in an activity. Such data changes also include the receipt of transmitted messages (cf. Sect. 10.5).

The above remarks about language constructs largely refer to *block-based* languages. In block-based languages, all language constructs have exactly one input and exactly one output. Thus, they correspond to the principle of structured programming. The counterpart are *graph-based* languages (e.g., BPMN), where connections (edges) are drawn between nodes. An arbitrary jump from one node to another ("goto") is not possible in a block-based language.

Process definitions generally have a version number. After all, a process, especially a workflow, has a long throughput time, usually days or weeks. If the process definition is changed during runtime, it must be ensured that the "old" processes are completed according to the old process definition. (Why?)

(b) **Graphical Modeling**

The control flow is usually defined with a graphical modeling tool, a component of the process management system. The motivation is that processes should also be understood by non-programmers. The graphical form is supposed to facilitate this. Since process definitions in practice have few steps compared to programs—processes on the order of 10–100 activities are common—this can be well accomplished with a graphical representation. Many process management systems use their own modeling language; some are based on notations like Event-driven Process Chains, UML activity diagrams, or BPMN. In the academic world, Petri nets and variants thereof, like workflow nets, are popular. An overview of notations is provided by Weske (2024).

(c) **Orchestration and Choreography**

Processes can run in exactly one system (local processes) or cross-system in a system landscape. In the latter case, it is possible that a central process takes control over the parts of the process running in the individual systems. This is called *orchestration*: The process management system determines the order, similar to how a conductor works with an orchestra. The central process is a *composition* of the business object methods used in the steps (see Sect. 12.6). Alternatively, multiple processes in different systems can communicate and synchronize with each other. This is called *choreography*. The analogy is ballet, where individual dancers coordinate with each other (see Fig. 7.6). It is a *coordination* between parts of the process or between the business object methods used in the steps. (See Alonso et al. (2004, pp. 250 ff. and pp. 276 ff.) for the relationship between composition and coordination.)

Orchestration is used for intra-company process control and choreography mainly for inter-company integration. In the latter, only the protocol between the cooperating business processes (collaborative business processes) is agreed upon. The focus is on message exchange. The cooperating processes will always include internal steps, which will be company-specific and therefore should not be made public. The messages can be physical, e.g., letters that are scanned, and the scanned documents may start processes or messages in the sense of Chap. 10.

12.2.2 Data Flow

The statements made in Sect. 3.5.3 apply particularly to process management systems. In fact, it is only in process management systems that the data flow is systematically and accurately modeled. In the analysis and concept phase for a process, the data flow is pragmatically often left out at first, though some clues result from the names of the activities.

Conditions, e.g., for controlling branches and loops, can be complex in processes. One approach is to describe such conditions with a language of its own and to separate these so-called business rules from the process definition (*business rules management*). This is based on the observation that processes can become confusing due to complex conditions and that the rules might change more frequently than the process definition. A simple technique for formulating conditions are decision tables. But there are also special business rules engines and decision engines (Freund and Rücker 2019, p. 171), and there is even an OMG standard for it: Decision Model and Notation (DMN) (Freund and Rücker 2019, Chap. 12).

12.2.3 Agent Assignment in Workflows

An automated background step is executed by the workflow system as in the case of integration through function call. This can be done by a local or remote function call, e.g., via a Web service. More specific for workflow is the assignment of users to dialog steps. Workflow systems support the forms of agent assignment as outlined in Sect. 3.5.3. What types of abstract agents are possible depends on the workflow system. However, users, user groups, and roles will always be included. The forms of dynamic agent assignment also vary. A common method to at least define agent assignments at the level of roles or abstract agents are *swim lanes*. The process definition is drawn in such a way that the activities to be performed by the same agent are on the same swim lane (see Fig. 3.9).

12.3   Flexibility

After we have learned the essential language constructs for processes, we now come to some more specific aspects. The first is flexibility in processes. This aspect plays a role in workflow systems. In principle, a process runs exactly according to its process definition. However, even with highly standardized processes, a certain flexibility at runtime is at times useful and therefore provided in process management systems. We look at such possibilities, structured according to the parts of the process definition.

(a) **Control Flow**

In highly standardized processes, we will not deviate from the control flow. However, there are also processes where the order is not so strictly predetermined or where some deviation is allowed in individual cases. This flexibility is called ad hoc *processes*. For example, steps could be omitted or additional ones inserted, possibly from a predetermined set of optional steps. The possibilities must be designed in such a way that the data flow is not endangered. For example, of course, no step can be removed that creates a business object that is processed in the following step. But there are also less obvious examples, e.g., that a step can only be executed when in a previous step a business object was set to a certain state. A special form of flexibility are *case management systems* (Weske 2024, S. 420): A set of activities is defined, and the order can be freely chosen by the agents, as long as they adhere to the defined data dependencies.

(b) **Data Flow**

In addition to the data flow defined in the process definition, users can add notes, attachments (e.g., text documents), and business objects (e.g., an object reference to a specific supplier) to the work items during work item processing. These are usually not accessed in the activity implementations. However, they are passed through the process and can be viewed and supplemented by subsequent agents.

(c) **Agent Assignment**

The possibilities shown in Sect. 3.5.4 already offer a certain flexibility: A work item can be delivered to abstract agents, e.g., some user group. Cooperative behavior is assumed, i.e., the agents distribute the incoming work items among themselves. Furthermore, a user could decide in a dialog step which agent from a predefined set of agents should execute the next step. A prerequisite is an activity for agent selection in the process definition. A third possibility is passing a work item to a statically determined set of agents if the dynamic agent assignment cannot determine a specific agent. The dynamic agent assignment is based on attributes or methods of business objects, which are supposed to deliver agents as a result. However, an exception could occur during the method execution, and no agent is found.

Regardless of the process definition, an agent may choose to forward a work item to another user. This may happen when an agent realizes that he is not suitable for executing a certain work item, e.g., because he is new in the company and has not yet processed such a task. A similar topic is *substitution*. The use cases are vacation and sickness. They are treated slightly differently (planned or unplanned absence), and a workflow system should allow two forms: On the one hand, an employee should be able to activate a colleague as a substitute (case vacation). On the other hand, the colleague should be able to take over the substitution for the employee or be assigned to it by a third person (case sickness). The process definitions do not need to be designed for this; the substitution happens at the organizational employee level. More sophisticated forms of substitution are conceivable, e.g., that only certain tasks are taken over by a colleague.

12.4 Business Objects in Processes, and Beyond

So far we assumed that business processes use data (attributes, method parameters), methods, and events of business objects only. In detail, a more varied picture emerges:

(a) **Data**

    (a1) *Business objects/data*: In the process, the primarily processed data are in fact business data or the corresponding business objects.

    (a2) *Control flow data*: In addition to business data, there are other data that are only used for the control flow, called "control flow data" in Alonso et al. (2004, p. 264), as opposed to "application-specific data." These are, for example, "flags" or agents that are stored for reuse in subsequent steps.

(b) **Methods**

    (b1) *Activity implementation*: As we know, methods of business objects are used for this purpose.

    (b2) *Dynamic agent assignment*: The dynamic agent assignment depends in some cases on just one business object, e.g., the person responsible for a certain material, the HR officer for employees with a certain initial letter of the name, or the superior of an employee. Then the agent may be just an attribute of a business object. However, in some cases, additional parameters may be necessary. Then the agent assignment is implemented as a method or a function, and the question is whether this method can conceptually be considered a method of a business object or rather some "helper object." The method's result is always a set of agents, possibly the empty set, if no agent can be identified. However, the complexity differs, from a table lookup to traversing the organization model.

(b3) *Boolean method/function in conditions*: Many conditions will just be formulated using expressions involving data, e.g., PurReq.State = 'R' ("released"). More complex conditions, however, may use Boolean methods or functions.

(b4) *Process-internal operation*: In addition to the activities implemented by business object methods, there are process operations such as assignment statements with control flow data (see above) or process control operations, e.g., cancelling an activity or the entire process. They could be considered methods of a process object—process dependent as in the first case (e.g., storing a release flag in the process data) or generic (e.g., setting the process state) as in the second.

(c) **Events**

(c1) *Business object event*: These are the events we mainly talked about (cf. Sect. 3.4.3). But there are others that may occur in processes.

(c2) *Message event*: The arrival of a message (cf. Sect 10.5).

(c3) *Time event*: The reaching of a deadline or the passing of a specified time.

12.5   Error Handling

As the saying goes: You often only appreciate health when you realize what you are missing during an illness. In a similar way, we want to take a look at "diseases," i.e., errors, in processes to better understand the technology. Before we systematically deal with errors and possible reactions, let us first look at Fig. 12.2 with some typical error situations in processes:

1. An event is supposed to start the process, but it is not triggered.
2. An error occurs during activity execution, e.g., a program crash.
3. An agent cannot be determined, e.g., because a position is not filled.
4. Data created in an activity is not passed on.
5. Data passed on to the process is not made available to a subsequent activity.
6. An activity has an unexpected result value, for which no subsequent activity is planned.

Errors can therefore occur in all parts of the process definition:

- Control flow, macro level: If the control flow is "wrong" (e.g., wrong order, one step too many or too few, a step which should be replaced by another), it will be a modeling error. It is fundamentally the "wrong process." It is necessary to cor-

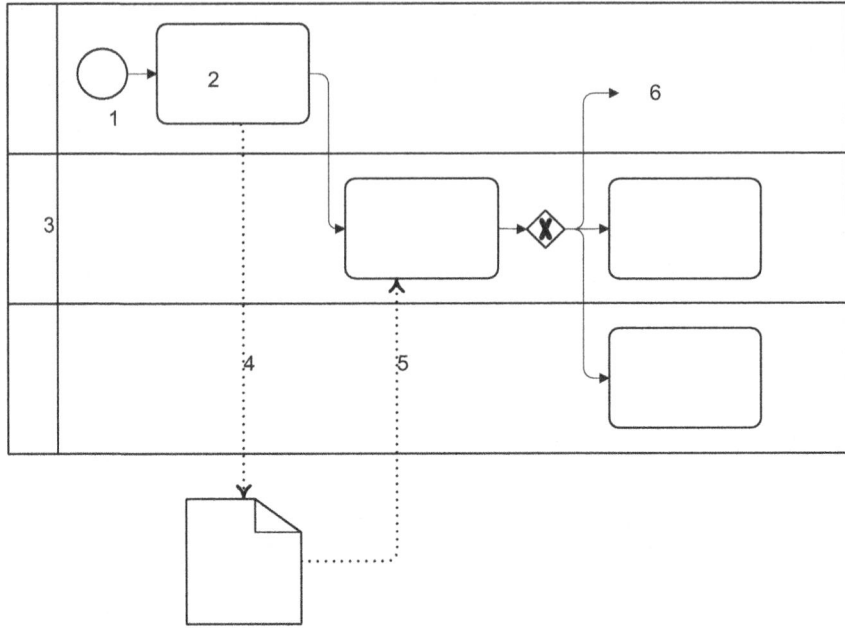

Fig. 12.2 Possible errors in process execution

rect the process definition. Such errors should be discovered during the testing of a newly developed process. Or the problem only affects a given process instance; then the above measures for flexibility can help. (How?)

- Control flow, micro level: This means that an error occurs during the execution of an activity instance. On the one hand, it could be a programming error in the activity implementation (method of a business object). In this case, the program error must be corrected. The work item is set to a correct state using an administration function and is executed again. Another case arises when a possible exception of the activity implementation was not caught in the process definition, perhaps with the motive that this exception does not occur or only occurs in rare cases. For pragmatic reasons (effort), often not for all exceptions is an automated handling provided in process definitions. Rather, it may have been decided that the exception will be handled outside the process. The work item is then handled with an administration function. Depending on the particular case, the work item could, e.g., be terminated, or certain data could be set.
- Data flow: This indicates an error in the process definition. The process should be corrected, and the activity instance should be set to a correct state using an administration function.
- Agent assignment: In this case, the process and often also the method for dynamic agent assignment are faulty. A problem could be that an abstract agent cannot be resolved to a concrete one. For example, an empty group of agents is determined, or a position is currently not occupied. Some of these errors vanish without

changing the process, e.g., if the position is only temporarily vacant during a reassignment.

Another category of "errors" are temporal deviations from the "normal," expected processing in workflows: Deadlines are not met. Deadlines can be set in the activities, such as "must be completed within two days at the latest." For delays, an escalation management can be defined in the process. In the simplest case, a certain person (often the superior) is informed about the delay. A more sophisticated form is an escalation sub-process, which is defined using the usual means of process definition. In this case, the escalation sub-process becomes active in addition to the "normal" process. The escalation sub-process can influence the "normal" process, e.g., declare particular steps obsolete.

12.6   Advantages and Disadvantages of Using Process Management Systems

To assess for which cases the use of process management systems is worthwhile, we compare the advantages and disadvantages:

Advantages:

- Automation: Business processes are at least partially automated. (What exactly does this mean?) If a business process consists only of background activities, even complete automation is possible.
- Increase quality (in workflows): By automating data flows, user input errors are avoided. Activity-specific instructions for work item execution reduce the error rate.
- Data transfer in cross-system processes: In this sense, a process management system also supports the integration forms through data exchange and function call.
- Reduce throughput time (in workflows): Process management systems offer various mechanisms for this. Let's look at the different time shares: Throughput time = transmission time + idle time + processing time. Agents get work items as early as possible, and the required data is provided. This affects the transmission time. The idle time is the longest and therefore the most critical part. (Why?) Deadline monitoring usually leads to decreasing idle time. Parallel branches in the process definition influence all parts of the throughput time. The provision of data, including notes and attachments, shortens the processing time.
- Analysis: An analysis of the processes with analytical systems is possible. The goal is process improvement. The prerequisite for this is the logging of runtime data. It is part of *business activity monitoring*.
- Guaranteed correct sequence: If a process is controlled by a process management system, it always runs according to the process definition. Exceptions were mentioned in Sect. 12.3.
- Traceability (especially in workflows): The process log shows the details of the execution. A workflow log records which steps of the process took place at what

times, who processed the steps, and much more. You may adjust which information is logged. Legal regulations and company agreements can set limits for this. (Why?) This particularly concerns systematic analysis (see below).

Disadvantages:

- Effort: A high effort is involved in developing executable process definitions and some effort in running them (administration).
- Inflexible: Although there are measures for flexibility, these should rather be the exception. Processes that are supposed to run differently each time are less suitable for process management systems.
- Dependence on the process management system: If the process management system fails, critical business processes must not come to a standstill. Accordingly, high availability is important. And it should be possible that humans control the processes temporarily when the process management system is not available.

This implies that process management systems are worthwhile for such processes which

- Are highly standardized, i.e., always run according to the same process definition, with little requirement for flexibility.
- Should be particularly traceable, e.g., in the sense that compliance with regulations, such as the four-eyes principle in certain approval steps, can be demonstrated

In practice, both "mini-processes" for small business processes or parts of larger business processes are used as well as processes with a multitude of steps.

12.7　Processes as Composition in Different Contexts

We can consider business processes a form of *composition* of business object methods or services. The same could be said about many application programs. Where is the boundary between a business process and an application program? Below, we look at the spectrum of composition possibilities:

- *Screen change*: In principle, an application program with several screens, possibly jumps to other application programs, could be seen or represented as a micro-business process (*frontend process* as opposed to *backend processes*, "page-flows"; cf. van Lessen et al. 2011, p. 53). The order could be graphically defined similar to using a process tool. Thus, there are similarities to process management systems, but the definition and runtime system will differ, e.g., no logging of process data and processing times is included. (Why?)
- *Transaction*: Several methods are composed according to the ACID principle. This is suitable for short-running programs, possibly across system boundaries (two-phase commit protocol; cf. Tanenbaum and van Steen 2014, p. 355), although the latter is less common in practice.

- *Business transaction*: If processes take a long time, such as hours or days, as business processes do, the representation as an ACID transaction does not make sense. A business transaction offers a weaker level, where no rollback is possible in case of failure. Instead, compensation operations must be provided. This topic has been extensively covered in research, but is not widespread in practice (Alonso et al. 2004, p. 272). Business transactions are also found in BPMN and BPEL.
- *Orchestration of methods and services*: The orchestration of service operations in a BPEL process can in many cases be seen as a program (if events or messages are not used). Similar cases are the transformation processes in Pentaho (Sect. 4.2.6.3) and MapReduce pipelines and processes in Big Data applications (Sects. 4.4.3.1 and 4.4.3.2).
- *Intra-company process with agent changes*: This case cannot be well represented as a program, as agent changes are not supported by programs.
- *Inter-company process with message flows*: Beyond the previous case, the message flows must be considered.

12.8   Cross-References from Process Management to Further Concepts

We have reached the end of the second part. Process management comes very close to a desire in information systems: the most extensive automation of business processes possible. (What does "most extensive possible" mean here? How could the limit be surmounted?) At this topic, all aspects covered in the previous chapters come together, including those from Part I. We review them and establish the connections to process management.

- *Transactional systems*: We learned the concepts business data, objects, and processes, which also apply to analytical systems. Workflows and processes without human interaction are business processes controlled by process management systems. They use methods of business objects in the activities, and their attributes are used in control flow. It is precisely the operational, always similar business processes that are particularly suitable for process management.
- *Analytical systems*: Analysis of process data, such as throughput times, is possible. An advanced approach is the detection of implicit processes through data mining (Process Mining; see van der Aalst 2016). These implicit processes could be turned into explicit ones to increase automation. With analytic functionality, optimized control of resources is theoretically possible:
  - *Human agents*: For example, the least burdened agent suitable for a task could be assigned. Also the context could also be taken into account, e.g., that an agent is the usual contact for a particular customer or that he is experienced in planning a certain material (dependency on runtime data, here the processed business object).

- *Computers*: The distribution of background activities on computing resources can be optimized, as in cloud computing (see Sect. 6.1).
- *Business partners*: The suitable business partners, e.g., a supplier for a purchase order, could be determined. The selection decision can include the conditions, the security, or the idea of diversification (risk reduction).
• *Integration* via *the user interface*: A comprehensive inbox in a portal may contain work items but also other tasks and information such as emails. The execution of the work items appears in the Web interface of the portal; for the agent, it is thus hidden in which system the work items are actually executed.
• *Integration through data exchange*: Data is exchanged in inter-company business process integration in the form of messages. The order of the messages is determined by choreography, already available in EDI, even though the name "choreography" was not yet common.
• *Integration through function call*: The process orchestrates a series of function calls, e.g., Web services.

12.9   Examples

12.9.1 SAP Business Workflow

SAP Business Workflow is the established workflow system in software like SAP S/4HANA (Dutta et al. 2024). It is primarily intended for system-local business processes, with the activity implementations being predominantly SAP applications. Process definitions are block based. SAP Business Workflow corresponds to the concepts presented, but some special features should be mentioned.

• Integration with organizational management: So-called organizational objects serve as abstract agents. These are objects of organizational management, not in the object-oriented sense. They include organizational units that represent departments, project groups, and business areas. Other organizational objects are jobs, positions, persons (employees), and users (Fig. 12.3). A task assigned to the "Development Department" goes to the users Boss, Vinch, Loper, and Vellow, while a task for the "Architect" job position goes to Vinch.
• Events from applications: A variety of applications trigger events, which can be used for workflow start and for synchronization in workflows. In addition, custom-defined events can be generated via several mechanisms using customizing, i.e., without modifying the standard application programs (see Sect. 15.8).
• Customization concept: Various settings are provided for company-specific customizations, avoiding the need to modify the standard (see Chap. 15). For example, business objects can be extended with the concept of *delegation*.
• Task layer: Methods of business objects are not directly called in processes. Instead, there is an intermediate layer called *tasks*. They encapsulate as a reusable unit methods of business objects together with description texts and static agent assignments.

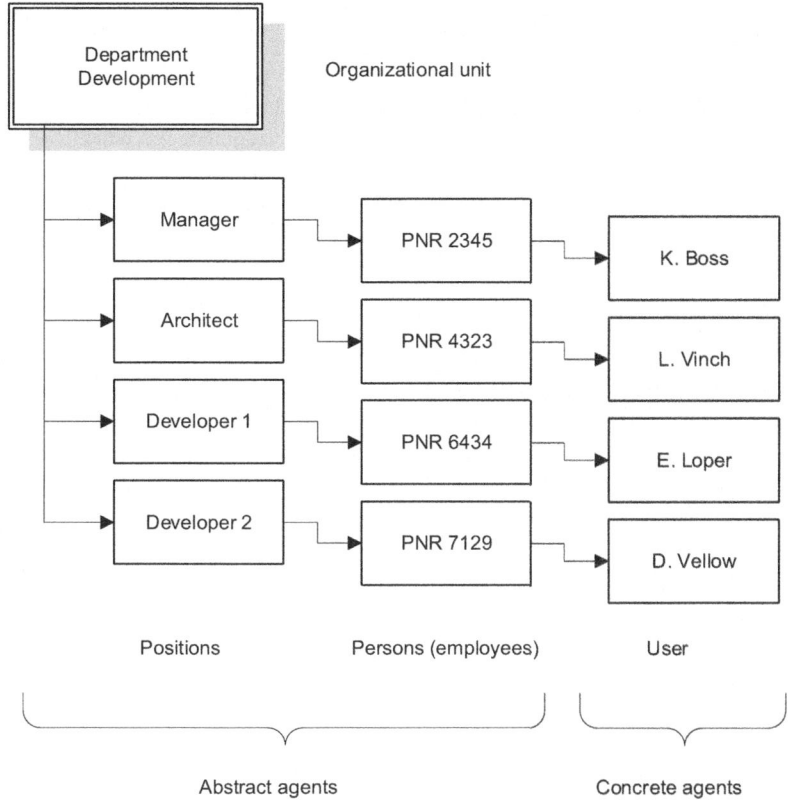

Fig. 12.3 Assignment via organizational management

- Standard *workflow scenarios*: SAP Business Workflow is part of several SAP systems. This allows companies that use systems like SAP S/4HANA to create their own workflows. In addition, each system already includes workflow scenarios that can be used by companies, just like application programs after customizing. A workflow scenario consists of one or more process definitions, the tasks used in the activities, and the classes or object types of business objects referenced there. The workflow scenarios can be adopted 1:1 or serve as a template for own workflows. The template is then copied, additional steps may be inserted, or steps are removed if they are not necessary for a company.

12.9.2 Workflow Functionality in Vtiger CRM

The Vtiger CRM system (see Sect. 3.7) includes some predefined workflows (Saledif 2014, p. 345 ff.). But new workflows can also be defined (see also Rossi 2011, p. 141 ff.). Workflows are closely related to the database fields of business data (called "modules" in Vtiger CRM).

A workflow is started by an event. This can be a time event, e.g., daily or on a certain day of the month, or an application event, e.g., every time a data record of the module is saved or whenever a data record of the module changes. A condition can be formulated using the fields of the data record as well as the fields of referenced master data such as "person" or "organization," whether the workflow should actually be started. In a condition, you may use comparisons such as "is equal," "contains," or "was changed to…." And finally, it is determined which function is executed, such as sending an email or assigning a specific employee a to-do.

12.9.3 BPEL

This is not an example of a specific process management system, but a notation that has been implemented in various systems. So it is a process notation, as are BPMN, discussed in Sect. 3.5, and *Event-driven Process Chains* (Scheer et al. 2005).

The *Business Process Execution Language (BPEL)* is a standard that builds on Web services and aims at their composition (van Lessen et al. 2011). BPEL defines a programming language, encoded in XML, where elementary instructions can call Web services (orchestration of Web services). BPEL can also be used for the choreography of such processes: Abstract models are formulated, which serve as protocols for inter-company processes, but exclude company-internal process steps (van Lessen et al. 2011, p. 54). The language is hybrid, in the sense that it contains block-based language constructs but also graph-based ones, which can be mixed. BPEL is intended for the special case of business processes:

- Which consist only of background steps.
- Where the background steps are implemented by Web services

Variables are part of the language. The activities can access global variables (implicit data flow). Table 12.1 shows some BPEL language constructs.

Table 12.1 Some BPEL language constructs

Language construct	Meaning
Receive	Wait for a message
Pick	Wait for one of several possible messages or a time event
Reply	Send message
Invoke	Call a Web service
Sequence	Sequence
If	Branching
Flow	Parallelism
While, repeatUntil, forEach	Loop
FaultHandlers	Error handling
Compensate	Compensation
Wait	Wait for a specified amount of time
Exit	Explicitly end process instance
Link	For graph-based modeling

A BPEL program consists of several files: BPEL for the process definition, WSDL for the invoked and the provided Web services (a BPEL process itself offers a Web service interface), and XSD (XML Schema) for data types, which are used in WSDL and BPEL. However, these files are usually not created with a text editor but in a development environment (modeling tool), which reduces the effort of XML and Web service handling.

By using only standards, a BPEL process could run directly in various BPEL runtime environments. Such runtime but also development environments are, for example, jBPM (2024), IBM WebSphere BPM Suite, or Oracle BPEL Process Manager (van Lessen et al. 2011, p. 199 ff.).

12.10 Implementation in the Enterprise Information System

Assume there is a process that has (at least) two activities. Each activity calls a method. In a cross-system process, the two methods are located in two different enterprise information systems, in a system-internal process in the same. The situation is structurally similar to the integration with portal systems (see Sect. 9.5): In addition to the two involved enterprise information systems, there is a third system, in this case, the process management system. And the interfaces of the enterprise information systems again are symmetric. Therefore, it is sufficient to consider only one enterprise information system and one activity.

Ideally, the enterprise information system will provide a method that can be called by the process management system, i.e., it is already "process enabled." How this interface exactly looks like depends on the specific process management system. Usual candidates for background methods are Web services (WSDL/SOAP or REST based) (see Chap. 11). For dialog methods, the situation is less obvious and specific to the process management system.

12.11 Exercises and Proposed Solutions

(a) Exercises

Exercise 12.1 (Comparison with a Programming Language)
What differences do you see between a process definition for a process management system and a program in a common programming language?

Exercise 12.2 (Process Definition for an Example)
What do you need to do to use the process definition of Exercise 3.4 in Chap. 3 in a process management system?

Exercise 12.3 (Workflow Definition in SAP Business Workflow)
This exercise requires access to an SAP S/HANA system.

Just as you learn programming best by doing it practically with a programming language, you learn workflow management best by using a workflow system. Developing a workflow would take a lot of time, so we just want to look at an existing workflow.

In the workflow builder (transaction SWDD), look at the workflow WS20000001 ("Release vendor data"). By double-clicking on the steps, you can see the details, e.g., for the step "Check general vendor data," you see the reference to the corresponding standard task TS20000002. With a double click on this standard task, you see the details, including the object method that is used.

(b) Proposed Solutions for the Exercises

Exercise 12.1 (Comparison with a Programming Language)

- Granularity: At the deepest level, there are not assignment statements but method calls ("two-level programming").
- Runtime: For a program, milliseconds are common and for a background process seconds to hours. For a workflow, it is often days to weeks.
- Persistent program state: A process "survives" even a system crash. In addition, the process is not continuously active: Often, long waiting phases arise until activities are executed, and the process may continue.
- So far, no standardized notation is generally used. This may change eventually with BPMN.
- Frequent use of parallel sections and events.
- Graphical notation is common for processes but rare for programming languages.
- Scope: Even extensive processes do not reach the size of typical business programs (measured by lines of code).

Exercise 12.2 (Process Definition for an Example)
All parts—control flow, data flow, and agent assignment—must be formally defined in the "language" of the respective workflow system.

Exercise 12.3 (Workflow Definition in SAP Business Workflow)
The description should already be sufficiently detailed.

12.12 Self-Assessment

1. Why does the term "integration" make sense for a process management system, even when the activities only take place in a single enterprise information system?
2. What other integration techniques could be used in conjunction with process management for cross-system workflows?
3. How is a process controlled when no process management system is used?
4. What is the difference between an activity and a work item?

5. How is a process optimized when it is implemented with a process management system?
6. How can the use of a workflow system shorten the idle time?
7. What things could be seen as process documentation when using a workflow?
8. How is dynamic agent assignment implemented in a workflow system?

References

Further Reading

The concepts of process management are extensively described in:
Weske, M.: Business Process Management, 4th edn. Springer, Berlin (2024)

The following book deals with BPMN and also describes how to embed executable process definitions in a of business process management methodology. It contains many tips and assessments from a practical perspective. In this sense, it bridges between a business view of process management, as is common in information systems today, and our more technical focus:
Freund, J., Rücker, B.: Real-Life BPMN, 4th edn. Camunda (2019)

Similarly, as mentioned in Chap. 3, the following books cover BPMN and its methodical usage:
Silver, B.: BPMN Quick and Easy: With Method and Style. Cody-Cassidy Press, Altadena, CA (2017)
Silver, B.: BPMN Method and Style, 2nd edn. Cody-Cassidy Press, Aptos, CA (2011)

Further Cited Literature and Sources

Alonso, G., Casati, F., Kuno, H., Machiraju, V.: Web Services. Springer, Berlin (2004)
Dutta, S., Ghosh, N., Goon, K., Jana, S., Mukherjee, A., Rao, S., Rao, Y., Sane, Y., Veshala, N., Viswanathan, S.: Workflow for SAP S/HANA. Rheinwerk, Boston (2024)
jBPM: https://www.jbpm.org/ (2024). Accessed 3 Nov 2024
Rossi, I.D.: vtiger CRM. Beginner's Guide. Packt Publishing, Birmingham (2011)
Saledif, T.: vtiger 6.0 Compact. Brain Media (2014)
Scheer, A.-W., Thomas, O., Adam, O.: Process modeling using event-driven process chains. In: Dumas, M., van der Aals, W., ter Hofstede, A.H.M. (eds.) Process-Aware Information Systems. Wiley, Hoboken, NJ (2005)
Tanenbaum, A., van Steen, M.: Distributed Systems, 2nd edn, Pearson new international edition. Pearson, Harlow (2014)
van der Aalst, W.: Process Mining: Data Science in Action, 2nd edn. Springer, Berlin (2016)
van Lessen, T., Lübke, D., Nitzsche, J.: Geschäftsprozesse automatisieren mit BPEL. dpunkt, Heidelberg (2011)

Part III

Operation

Overview of Part III

13

Something is taking its course.
Samuel Beckett (Endspiel Fin de partie Endgame,
first edition, Suhrkamp Paperback 171,
Frankfurt a. M., 1974, p. 24)

Summary

We look at the life cycle of an enterprise information system in a company. In the following chapters, we delve into four topics: the selection and implementation of standard business software, its adaption (customization), access control, and system administration. According to the perspective of the book, viz., that of a company using the enterprise information system, our life cycle begins after the "birth," i.e., the development of the enterprise information system by the software vendor. Its development is therefore not in focus, but some aspects can be found in the "in-house development" part of the chapter on adaptation.

Learning Objective

- To gain an overview of the life cycle of enterprise information systems.

Companies today no longer predominantly use in-house developed programs as in the past but standard software. Thus, you could consider the life cycle of an enterprise information system presented here as the phase model of "software engineering in information systems": Instead of focusing on new development, the focus is on the selection, configuration, and customization of the software. Software development also has its place in the context of additional development and extensions. Software engineering in the narrower sense, on the other hand, plays a role primarily in in-house custom-development. Agile methods are particularly worth mentioning here, as they are used for developing microservices (see Sect. 6.2).

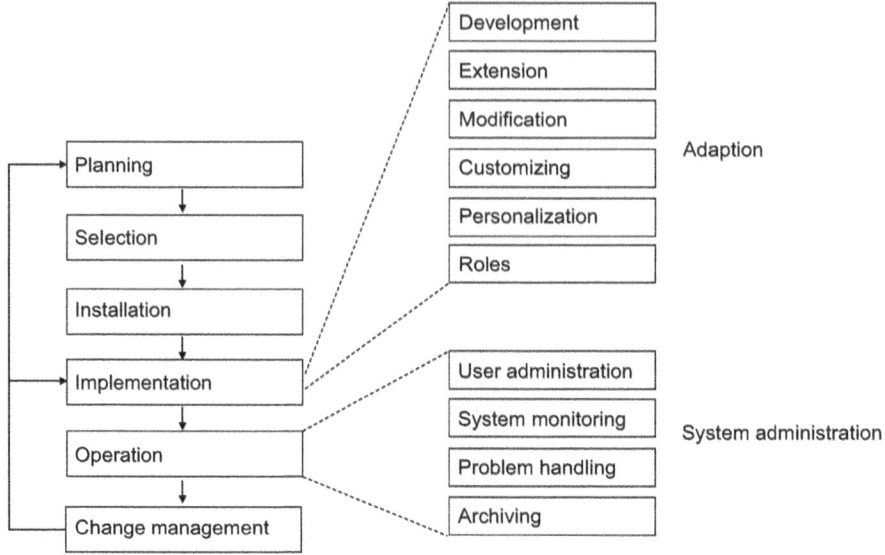

Fig. 13.1 Life cycle

From the perspective of a company using the software, the life cycle of an enterprise information system looks like this (Fig. 13.1).

(a) **Planning**

First, the system landscape and its enterprise information systems must be planned. Typical questions are:

- Which parts of the existing system landscape should be replaced by one or more new enterprise information systems? In the following, we assume that it is only one.
- What requirements does the enterprise information system have to meet in terms of functionality and integrability with the existing system landscape?
- Should it be an on-premises system or a cloud offer, or would both do?
- In what chronological order should parts of the system landscape be replaced?

(b) **Selection**

After planning, the company checks which enterprise information systems best meet the requirements and selects one or a combination of several. The software selection is covered in Chap. 14.

(c) **Installation**

The installation of a large application system is often not as straightforward as the installation of a small PC program. In particular, the installation volume and duration are orders of magnitude higher. This step is of course omitted for cloud software.

(d) **Implementation**

The most complex part follows: the implementation of the standard software in the company. This is the second topic of Chap. 14.

The aspect of adapting standard software to the company's needs is covered in detail in Chap. 15.

(e) **Operation**

After the implementation, the software can be put into operation. This is called *go live*. In ongoing operation, there are administrative tasks, in particular (Is there a difference between cloud and on-premises systems?):

- *User management*: Users master data must be created in the enterprise information system. They need the appropriate permissions (for permissions, see Chap. 16).
- *System monitoring*: The system must be monitored, as performance can decrease and system parts can fail. This is addressed in Chap. 17.
- *Problem handling*: Problems will arise during ongoing operation. Some of them cannot be solved by the system configuration; they are software errors ("bugs"). The main task is to ensure that the software corrections (patches) get into the system (see also Chap. 17).

(f) **Change Management**

Over time, additional requirements for the software may arise in the company, which need to be taken into account. Often it can be handled by further adjustments, including extensions. However, it can also lead to implementing new software or at least a new version of the software (see Chap. 14).

13.1 Self-Assessment

1. A company wants to use business application software. In what situations may in-house programming be necessary? Who will carry it out?
2. Can you imagine causes of why a company might want a new application software or at least a new version of the software used so far?
3. Which parts of the life cycle (Fig. 13.1) will run differently for a cloud product than for an on-premises product, and which will be the same or at least similar?

Selection and Implementation of Business Standard Software

14

Summary

The phases from the selection of a new business standard software till "go live" are presented. An important question today is whether a cloud product should be chosen.

> **Learning Objectives**
>
> - To gain an overview of the aspects that arise when implementing business standard software.
> - To review many concepts and methods that were discussed in previous chapters.

14.1 Selection of Standard Software

A company may intend to acquire a new enterprise information system for various reasons. Usually, an older existing system is replaced to better or more cost-effectively run business processes. In this chapter, we address all the activities required to put this into action—from planning to "go live" of the new system (see Fig. 14.1 for an overview).

© The Author(s), under exclusive license to Springer-Verlag GmbH, DE,
part of Springer Nature 2025
R. Weber, *Enterprise Information Systems*,
https://doi.org/10.1007/978-3-662-71718-9_14

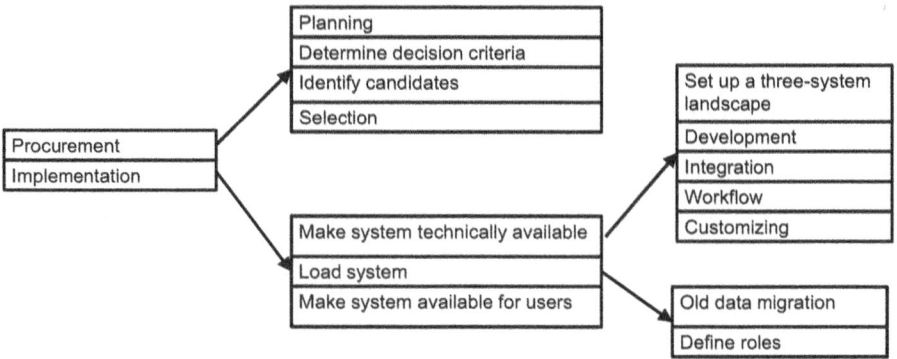

Fig. 14.1 Phases in the selection and implementation of standard software

14.1.1 Planning

The reasons for implementing a new enterprise information system are diverse. We can divide them into different categories. Some reasons have characteristics of various categories.

1. *Functionality*:
   (a) The new enterprise information system offers functions that the company needs, but the old one does not have at all or not in the quality or to the extent. For example, regulatory requirements may require new or expanded functions.
   (b) Related to this: An additional new, specialized system offers further functions (see Chap. 8). Example: extended functionality of a CRM system in sales while the existing ERP system only has basic functions in that area.
   (c) A smaller company implements an ERP system for the first time. So far, it has only used basic functions via a service provider, such as for accounting (see Chap. 1).
   (d) The new system offers functions that were up to now developed in-house (custom development, add-ons; see Sect. 8.1). Replacing them may save costs (see, below, total costs).
2. *Costs*:
   (a) A software provider makes a particularly favorable offer for his new product, perhaps also in connection with point 4b—a change would be necessary in the foreseeable future anyway.
   (b) High maintenance costs: These may have increased recently. Or a competitor's product is just cheaper in this regard (Fischer 2024).
3. *Performance*:
   (a) Business processes can be implemented more efficiently with the new standard software.
   (b) The existing system is not sufficiently scalable for company growth (for both (Fischer 2024)).

4. *Miscellaneous*:
   (a) Dissatisfaction with the current software or with its provider.
   (b) The old system should be replaced because the maintenance interval has expired. The maintenance by the software provider or a specialized company could become at least more expensive.
   (c) It would take a great effort to integrate the existing software with further required new software (Fischer 2024).
   (d) A corporation acquires a company, and an enterprise information system used in the subsidiary now needs to be integrated into the corporation's system landscape. This case is different, as a system selection and full-scale implementation are not necessary. The integration into the system landscape could be loose. For example, only data flowing into the corporation's balance sheet system could be transmitted (see Chap. 10). Or cross-company analysis could be accomplished in a data warehouse integration (see Sect. 4.2), while the transactional systems continue to run separately for the time being.

In fact, depending on which of the above reasons apply, the situation for system selection will be different:

1. *Provider open*: The company will check products of various providers for suitability. The previous provider may be included or may be excluded due to dissatisfaction.
2. *Provider fixed*: The company will choose a new product from the same provider. A question will be whether it should be a cloud or an on-premises product (see Sect. 6.1).
3. *Provider and system fixed*: It will be the new system version from the same provider (upgrade; see below).

The following steps will of course vary greatly with these three options. Our description is based on the most comprehensive case, the first one (see Fig. 14.2).

Finally, we look at the spectrum of changes in the software that are possible, ranging from updating an existing system to procuring a new one (Table 14.1).

The effort for a release change should not be underestimated, especially if the system contains modifications (see Sect. 15.9). (Is there a difference between cloud and on-premises systems?)

Result of this phase: The decision to introduce a new system or renew an existing one, a rough schedule for this, and an estimate of the effort and its financing.

14.1.2 Determine Decision Criteria

(a) **The Terms "Decision Criterion" and "Requirement"**
    As we have seen in Sect. 14.1.1, a company will have a number of requirements for new standard software, but there are also other aspects, especially costs. We therefore use the more general term "decision criterion." What is the difference between a decision criterion and a requirement?

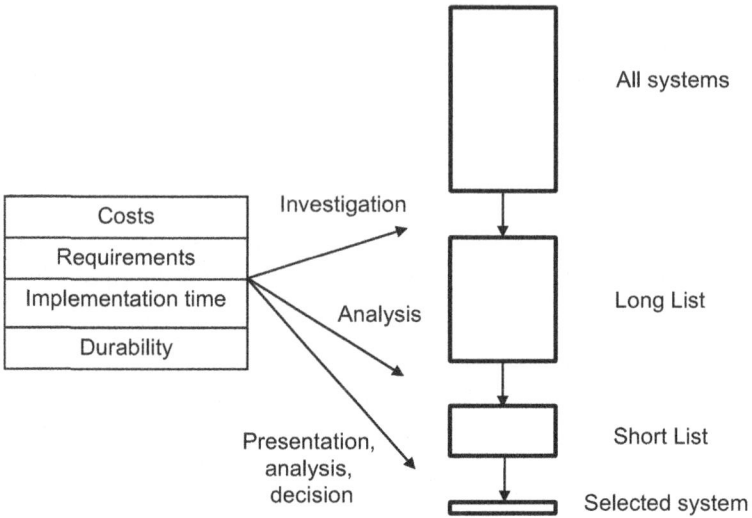

Fig. 14.2 Process of selecting standard software

Table 14.1 Degrees of change in business standard software

Designation	Content
First implementation of standard business software	Complete change of work methods
Change of provider	Completely different product
Release change (version change)	Very big changes, new main version
Upgrade	Major changes, new subversion
Update	Minor improvements within a version, often bug fixes

- A *requirement* is a property that must, should, or "can" be met—depending on the urgency attributed to it. If a must-requirement, also called a *criterion for exclusion*, is not met, the software is not taken into consideration. With a should-requirement, there is a little flexibility—functionality vs. costs. If a "can"-requirement is met, it is advantageous, but it can also be done without in a pinch. The word "can" may be a bit misleading because it seems too indifferent; hence, we used the quotation marks.
- A *decision criterion* is more general than a requirement. It is an aspect that will play a role in the decision. It often has a coarser granularity than a requirement: there will be many (detailed) requirements but only a few decision criteria. A requirement can be seen as a fine-grained decision criterion, which in its pure form is fulfilled or not fulfilled, so it is binary. Somewhat more general, the degree of fulfillment of a requirement could not only be set to 0 and 1, or 0 and 100%, but you could also estimate some value in between, e.g., 90%. This estimate will be according to the quantitative and/or qualitative degree of fulfillment.

Let us try to distinguish between decision criterion and requirement using an example, the costs of the new system. A typical requirement is that a certain amount (budget) is not exceeded—this is binary. A decision criterion, on the other hand, is that the costs are low. If several systems are within budget, we prefer a cheap offer. Definitely then, when the offers are otherwise approximately equivalent. This, however, is often not easy to judge. Complete equivalence will not exist anyway—at some points one product will have a strength, at others the other. Another decision criterion regarding costs is a good price/performance ratio.

At first glance, requirements seem more rigid and concise. However, we observe that business decisions, e.g., on budgets, are not immovable and that on closer questioning, a must-requirement can sometimes become a should-requirement.

A rough idea of the requirements will have already formed during the operation of the previous system. A detailed one will be developed after the decision for a new system has been made.

(b) **Categories of Decision Criteria**

Let us look at categories of decision criteria:

1. *Costs*

1.1 *Budget*

What budget is available for the implementation project and for the operation of the system?

1.2 *Software Costs*

These are the purchase (for on-premises systems) or rental costs (for cloud systems) of the products. With a purchase of the software, there are one-time license costs. There are various pricing models. A common one is based on the number of users who use the system (*named users*). In this model, it actually depends on the number of people, not on the number of user IDs. Thus, one person could have several users for testing purposes. There may be price differences for different user categories (e.g., developers or clerks). Another model is based on the number of users who can work in the system at the same time (*concurrent users*). Finally, load-dependent prices are possible, for example, according to the number of personnel master records or according to the transaction data volume (Lehmann and Buxmann 2009). Similar approaches apply to cloud products (Sect. 6.1). In addition, after a purchase, regular maintenance costs are incurred, to be paid to the software provider. They are often in the order of 20% of the license costs per year.

Maybe an expensive product meets the requirements better, but because of a large price difference, a company prefers the second-best product in terms of functionality.

1.3 *Total Costs*

During implementation and operation, the software costs will only make up a part. Rather, the *total cost of ownership* (*TCO*) should be decisive. These are the costs for the entire life cycle. Included are the implementation costs, for adapting the system to the company's needs, and a variety of costs, such as for personnel, maintenance, energy, and cooling of the hardware in the case of on-premises systems.

1.4 *Resources*

The question is whether the necessary resources for the system implementation are available at all (technically, organizationally, and financially) (Fischer 2024), an aspect that is particularly relevant for larger systems.

2. *Requirements*

2.1 *Functional Requirements*

The company's business processes should be (largely) directly covered, so there should be only as little company-specific custom development as possible (see Sect. 15.7).

2.2 *Non-functional Requirements*

These include usability, performance, scalability, security, integrability into the system landscape (see Chaps. 5 and 8), and integration into the existing system infrastructure (operating system, database system) (see Chap. 2).

3. *Implementation Time*

How much time will the implementation take? The time is usually correlated with the costs. Maybe for business reasons, a critical deadline must be met by when the system implementation is completed.

4. *Future Security*

This includes various criteria (Fischer 2024):

4.1 *Future Security of the Provider*

What is the market position of the provider? What about references, support, and services?

A reliable relationship with the software provider is important: Will the software provider remain in the market permanently? An enterprise information system is usually in operation for many years; 20 years or more are common. The company should therefore exist at least that long. How good is the support, for example, in case of problems or requests for product development?

4.2 *Future Security of the System*

An established system with continual further development will have an advantage over a new, barely known one. What about the availability of potential employees who can use, adapt, configure, and administer the software?

The project risk should also be considered: Is the system already used by other companies of similar size and industry? What is the experience regarding costs and implementation duration?

Products from the same software vendor integrate more easily with each other (lower integration costs, more stable operation). Thus, the company strategy may be to focus on just a few vendors and preferably choose these. According to the strategy *Best of Suite*, the vendor is selected whose products overall work best for the company, even if other vendors are more advantageous for individual products. With *Best of Breed*, the best product is chosen for each component.

There may be a conflict between the decision criteria "cost" and "(functional) requirements":

- A company might choose a more cost-effective system and adapt its own business processes to the product instead of the other way around (see Chap. 15; adaptation also incurs costs). In this sense, a cloud product that is cheaper in comparison to the on-premises product and that has fewer customization options might be considered. A perfect fit is hardly ever given anyhow. Therefore, the question is how much deviation from the target business processes is tolerable.
- Conversely, for a large corporation with a very high number of business transactions, it may be more economical to map exactly the target business processes, despite high customization effort. This is because the customization costs will amortize over time through the sum of many small time savings.

Hence, the question is: To what extent does the company adapt to the standard software, and to what extent is the standard software adapted to the company (see Chap. 15)? The total costs are decisive. However, some costs are difficult to estimate, for example, revenue losses when business processes are slowed down or when quality decreases.

The decision for a new system can affect several systems of a system landscape (see Chap. 8):

- The new system could replace the functions of several others, such as a standard system and a custom development.
- The integration effort with other products can vary depending on the chosen system.

Result of this phase: Decision criteria and requirements, more precise information on effort, budget, and schedule than in the planning phase.

14.1.3 Identify Candidates

Now the research begins which software products to consider, based on the decision criteria and requirements. A pragmatic approach in two stages is common:

1. *Long list*: A research with little effort per candidate results in a list of about ten fundamentally suitable enterprise information systems.
2. *Short list*: These systems are analyzed in more detail and with more effort. Some may be eliminated due to criteria for exclusion that were not apparent before. And some might appear far less attractive than others at second sight. The result is a second, shorter list of about five systems that will be examined in still more detail with even more effort per system in the next phase, "selection."

Literature, Web portals, consulting companies, and company contacts are the basis for research, especially in stage 1. In stage 2, requests for clarification to the software providers may be added.

Stage 1 can be particularly complex with ERP systems for small or medium-sized businesses. This is because it means a preselection from hundreds of systems that are on the market for this company category. There is a much smaller market for business standard software for large companies (cf. Sect. 3.7).

How do you find out whether a software should be included in the long list? Some criteria, usually criteria for exclusion:

- *Company size* for which the software is designed. This has already been discussed above.
- *Industry-specific requirements*: For example, in the food industry, batch tracking is necessary. Public enterprises may legally require cameralistics as an accounting method instead of the double-entry bookkeeping commonly used in the private sector.
- *Company-specific peculiarities*, which the company usually knows best. Such a peculiarity could have played an important role in the selection of the previous enterprise information system, and a large amount of customization may have been necessary.

Conversely, which approaches are less likely to achieve the goal?

- *Comparing function lists*: ERP systems often offer similar lists at this level, with differences only becoming apparent in detail. Such a detail might be with what organizational and time reference data can be recorded; the company might have specific requirements for this. On the other side, in a function list, you might notice that a required functional area is not included at all, such as production in an ERP software for commercial enterprises. However, this will usually already be apparent from a brief description of the software.
- *Comparing business processes at a high level of abstraction*: For example, if there are reference processes of the standard software and modeled business processes of the company (cf. Sect. 3.5.4), one might get the idea to align the processes. However, such models will appear similar at a higher level, and decisive differences will again only be found in detail. In addition, the comparison effort can be considerable.

So in many cases, one would have to look very closely at the software to fully assess the fit. Some questions will not be answered from publicly available information (e.g., from marketing-oriented product descriptions on the Internet) or only with big effort (e.g., with the online documentation of the software, if publicly available). It may make sense to ask the software provider or to postpone such questions to the detailed analysis (see next phase, "Selection").

Result of this phase: A short list of a few enterprise information systems, about five, which need to be examined more closely in order to finally select one of them.

14.1.4 Selection

Next is the detailed analysis of the systems that are still candidates in order to select one of them. So far, several systems seem to be suitable, and the existing information, usually from the Web sites of the software providers or software selection portals, does not yet provide a final picture. Certainly, some open questions will have arisen during the rough analysis of the previous phase, which now need to be clarified.

Therefore, the company now contacts the software vendors and asks for a presentation of the system, including clarification of the open questions. This will usually take place at the company's location. Salespeople from the software vendor will take on this task and take questions they cannot answer immediately in order to clarify them with internal specialists.

A clever presentation may mask weaknesses of the product or simply not addresses them. Therefore, a vigilant, critical attitude is sensible, and asking the "right" questions is important. Company employees who are competent in their respective functional areas should be present during the questioning. It is also useful to give the provider some use cases to map and demonstrate in the system ("proof of concept") (Fischer 2024).It is not an easy task to match the large functional scope of a software with one's own requirements in a limited time. The question is not only whether the requirements are sufficiently covered but also whether the product offers extensions to fill the gaps and what effort this involves. Because rarely will a system fulfill all wishes from the start. For every unfulfilled wish, the question arises whether the company waives it or accepts the effort for the adjustment.

Taking into account the requirements, the total costs, and the expected implementation duration, the company selects an enterprise information system, negotiates a price, and pays. Depending on the type of use—on-premises or in the cloud—it receives the system for installation or a network access to the cloud product. For an on-premises system, the hardware and software platform must be provided, i.e., computers must be procured, and operating systems and other system software must be installed. Sizing (see Sect. 5.1.5) is used to determine the performance of the hardware to be procured.

Result of this phase: An enterprise information system has been selected, access is available, the effort for the implementation is estimated, and a schedule is available.

14.2 System Implementation

Once a standard business software is purchased and installed, it is not immediately ready for use. It must first be adapted to the company's needs. This is part of the *implementation* of the standard software. This use of the term "implementation" in information systems differs from its use in computer science, where it refers to the realization of a concept or specification through software development. The organizational framework is the implementation project, some activities of which are presented in the following sections. Some of the activities, e.g., in-house development, will not occur in every implementation project. Always necessary, however, is customizing (parameterization), the company-specific adaptation in the narrower sense through configuration settings (Sect. 15.3). An implementation project is generally divided into sub-projects due to its size. In the case of an ERP system, this could be done according to functional areas (accounting, sales, warehouse management, production, human resources). Various people work on the implementation project:

- IT staff of the company: After all, they have to ensure that the system runs properly, and they have the IT expertise.
- Employees from the company's business departments: They bring the application know-how, especially the company-specific one. Some of them will only be used temporarily in the project, as they also have to carry out their daily business.
- Consultants: They either come from the consulting area of the software vendor or—more often—from larger or smaller consulting companies, often specialized in part of the products of a software provider. Therefore, they are less business consultants ("strategy consulting"); rather, solid knowledge of the applications and technology of the standard software is required, preferably also experience in the implementation of the standard software in other companies.

There are various strategies for the implementation:

- *Big-bang*: The introduction takes place in one big step.
- *Step-by-step implementation*: The software is implemented in several smaller steps according to functional areas, e.g., first accounting; then warehouse management, purchasing, and sales; and finally human resources. (What happens to the areas not yet implemented?)
- *Parallel operation*: The previous and the new system are operated in parallel for some time. This offers higher security (fallback option to the previous system in case of difficulties) but a huge effort due to double manual data entry.

A corporation that operates in several countries can organize the implementation according to the locations or countries (country-by-country implementation). In this way, the risk is limited to one national company at a time. Experience can be used for subsequent countries.

Vendors of standard software and consulting companies have developed *implementation methods*, in recent years also agile ones, in which essentially the activities mentioned below occur. Generally, the activities are organized in phases, such as:

- *Preparation of the implementation project*: The project team, the project plan, and the division into sub-projects are determined.
- *Design*: The target system is defined. The starting point are the requirements that were defined in the selection process (Sect. 14.1). However, it becomes more comprehensive and detailed, because the entire system behavior is defined, not

just points decisive for the selection. It is also determined: What can the standard software do directly (with system settings)? What needs to be supplemented by extensions or additional programs?

- *Realization*: Carrying out the design.
- *System start*: In jargon called "Go live."

The following are the activities that play a role in the design and realization. The presentation in this section may sometimes be shorter than in the previous one, when detailed aspects are explained in other chapters. Figure 14.3 gives an overview. Not all activities will occur in all implementation projects. The grey colors in the illustration give an assessment of this; darker ones are less frequent.

14.2.1 Make System Available

Before the system can go into productive operation, it must be set up and adapted to the needs of the company. This is done through software development (extensions, company-specific in-house development) and configuration, especially customizing (see Chap. 15 for all types of adaptation). Depending on the system type and the type of adaptation, not all of these activities take place or not to the same extent. Thus, we have seen in Sect. 6.1 that with cloud usage, there are often more limited customization options, even if it is the "same" software.

(a) **Set Up a Three-System Landscape**
     For the different forms of adaptation, especially when they involve software development, which will often be the case, a three-system landscape of development, test, and production systems should be set up (see Sect. 15.6). With cloud systems, there are corresponding options: tenants (see Sect. 6.1) may be created for these and other purposes, such as configuration (Saueressig et al. 2023, p. 471).

	Set up a three-system landscape
	Adjustment through development
	Detail aspect: analytical functionality
	- In the transactional system
Make system available	- In the analytical system
	Integration
	Support through process management systems
	Customizing
	Tests
Load the system	Legacy data migration
	Define roles (incl. permissions)
	Create users
Make available for users	Product training
	Company-specific training

Fig. 14.3 Contents of a system implementation

The activities mentioned below can partially overlap or even occur in a modified order.

(b) **Adaptation Through Development**

Here we consider adaptation through software development, i.e., company-specific extensions and in-house development (see Sects. 15.7–15.9).

(c) **Detailed Aspect: Analytical Functionality**

The approach differs depending on whether the enterprise information system is transactional or analytical.

(c1) **Transactional System**

With a transactional system, it must be decided which analyses (reports) should run in the transactional system and which should take place in a dedicated system like a data warehouse system (see Chap. 4). In the transactional system, the built-in data models can be used, but if the desired analysis is not already available as a standard report, development effort will be required.

(c2) **Analytical System**

In transactional systems, the application functionality is already largely present in the standard software (except for the abovementioned adaptations through development). In analytical systems, however, especially in data warehouse systems, data models for the analyses and the analyses themselves must be defined (see Sect. 4.2). In addition, ETL processes must be realized at point (d) (configuration or development).

In analytical systems that offer machine learning functionality, the models must be defined (if not already present) and trained specifically for the company (see Sect. 4.3).The activities can therefore differ, depending on the type of analytical system.

(d) **Integration**

Integration includes the various configuration and development activities required for coupling the systems of a system landscape, which we learned about in Part II of the book. If standard software from a software vendor is used, many integration options are already provided in the customizing of the systems. In many cases, however, development and configuration effort is necessary.

Integration will often go hand in hand with adaptation, for example, when a function of another system is called at an extension point (Sect. 15.8 combined with Chap. 11). Integration can thus require development activities in two or more coupled systems.

(e) **Control with Process Management Systems**

If certain business processes shall be controlled by process management from the start, development effort is also required here (see Chap. 12). However, this is often postponed until some time after the system implementation.

(f) **Customizing**

Finally, there is adaptation by configuration, i.e., customizing (see Sect. 15.3).

(g) **Tests**

The various activities, especially development activities, of course require tests. These are:

- *Developer tests* in the development system.
- *Tests by a test team*, not by the developers themselves, in the test system (i.e., tests in the narrower sense).
- *Integration tests* in the system landscape. A clean approach for this is a test system landscape with integrated test systems.
- *Load tests*: The tests mentioned so far usually involve only a small amount of selected data in a lightly loaded system. This is because the focus was on functionality. Load tests supplement by checking whether the programs will also perform well in real-life operation, with a multitude of simultaneously working users (usually simulated) and background processes.

Result of this phase: The system is installed, extended by programs, and integrated into the system landscape, and the customizing has been done. Tests of the development, integration, and configuration have been carried out.

14.2.2 Load the System

The system is now almost ready for operation. However, it still lacks the master and transaction data. (What about customizing data?) They usually (depending on the system type) have to be transferred from the previous system. Not all legacy data are required but those that are necessary for future operation.

A special category is the user master data. User master data must be assigned appropriate roles (or equivalent concepts), including the corresponding permissions (Chap. 16).

So the following steps are necessary:

(a) **Legacy Data Migration**
The occasion for implementing a new transactional system is rarely the company foundation. Rather, it will usually replace a predecessor system. At least parts of the existing data must therefore be transferred to the new system. Careful consideration is needed on which master data and especially which transaction data are migrated, e.g., only the balances, the individual items, or also balanced items (Willinger and Gradl 2007, p. 26). It becomes clear that legacy data migration is not a purely technical matter but includes business considerations, e.g., with regard to accounting for open items regarding the cross-entry (Willinger and Gradl 2007, p. 29 ff.) or the question of the order of data transfer, e.g., master data before transaction data and orders before goods receipt bookings (Willinger and Gradl 2007, p. 42).

Legacy data migration is a special case of integration via data exchange. So the basic techniques are used (Chap. 10). Unlike in the ETL process, data cleansing (step "T") should already take place before the migration, for example, to eliminate duplicates. A transformation with regard to the target format in the new system will however often additionally be necessary. Traditionally, legacy data migration is performed by programmers. This can be a bottleneck in an implementation project, as programmers are needed across various tasks and functional areas. But there are specialized tools that use techniques that avoid programming or only require it in a few places. So the task can also be taken over by other employees.

(b) **Define Roles (incl. Permissions)**
Roles were already briefly discussed in Chap. 9 (for portals, but roles are common in any enterprise information system), and they will be dealt with in more detail in Chap. 16, as they are used for access control.

(c) **Create User Master Data**
The appropriate roles must be assigned to the users.

Result of this phase: The system is technically operational.

14.2.3 Make Available to Users

From a technical point of view, the users could now get started. If it is a new system, however, training will be necessary beforehand. For this purpose, it makes sense to set up a training system or at least a training tenant (see Sect. 3.3).

(a) **Product Training**
There is general product training about the system architecture and the operating concept. And there are specific product trainings for respective functional areas of the users. It can take place at some training center, or trainers could teach at the company's location. Training can be done by the software vendor or by companies specialized in training the standard software.

(b) **Company-Specific Training**
In addition to this company-independent training, there will also be company-specific training, for example, to explain which organizational levels are used at the company or which customizing decisions were made. For that purpose, company-specific user documentation (different from the general documentation of the software vendor) is helpful.

Now the system is both technically accessible, and the users have the knowledge to operate it. So the company can start using the system ("Go live"): Clerks run business processes, and the system administration ensures smooth operation (see Chap. 17). During the first few days, it will make sense that the software vendor, key users, and the IT department provide special support in order to better manage initial problems. User feedback can be used for optimization (Fischer 2024).

Result of this phase: A (hopefully well) running system.

14.3   Exercises and Proposed Solutions

(a) Exercises

Exercise 14.1 (Legacy Data Migration)
Which legacy data would you migrate? Or, in other words, which not?

Exercise 14.2 (Version Change)

A company wants to switch to the new enterprise information system of the same software vendor, i.e., replace its outdated system. Which of the phases and activities described above will have to be gone through, and what do they look like in this case? Assume that the new version is a significant further development of the previously used standard software.

Exercise 14.3 (Simplification of the System Landscape)

Find examples of cases where a new enterprise information system could lead to a simplification in the system landscape.

(b) Proposed Solutions for the Exercises

Exercise 14.1 (Legacy Data Migration)

Active data (in the sense of Sect. 3.3) shall be migrated, including the referenced master data, to ensure consistency. When migrating further master data, a cleanup is useful: Which master data will still be used in future business processes? For example, business partners who are not referenced in migrated transaction data and with whom the business relationship has been terminated could be omitted.

Exercise 14.2 (Version Change)

All phases will have to be run through, but the effort in individual phases will be significantly less than when, for example, switching to a product from another vendor. This becomes particularly obvious in the phases "Identify candidates" and "Selection." Here, only a decision is necessary whether the system should be used on-premises or in a cloud variant. A detail question in the latter case is whether a public cloud or a private cloud is chosen (see Sect. 6.1). Customizing will probably only require delta and upgrade customizing (see Sect. 15.3). (Look for examples of further simplifications in the various phases.)

Exercise 14.3 (Simplification of the System Landscape)

Some ideas:

- The new standard software could include a function that was previously provided as an additional development (add-on, microservice, company-specific in-house development).
- The new transactional system is more powerful, so that certain analyses can take place directly in the system. A data warehouse system could become obsolete; at least part of the ETL process could be eliminated.
- The new system could cover industry functionality of various industries by installing corresponding add-ons. A conglomerate could thus do without various industry systems.

14.4   Self-Assessment

14.1 Selection of Standard Software

4. What is the advantage if a company can replace an in-house development when implementing a new enterprise information system? What is the disadvantage?
5. For what reason could a software vendor offer a particularly favorable deal for its new product to an existing customer?
6. Why might the parent company be inclined to let an acquired company continue to use its ERP system?
7. Is future security of a system a decision criterion or a requirement?
8. Do the strategies "Best of Suite" and "Best of Breed" also apply to cloud systems?
9. How does the selection of business standard software differ between smaller companies and large corporations?
10. What is meant by a "Proof of concept?" What is the benefit of it?

14.2 System Implementation

8. What is the advantage of a country-by-country system implementation in a multinational company?
9. Which activities are not necessary in an upgrade compared to the implementation of a system from another software vendor?
10. What is the difference between a product training and a company-specific user training?
11. What follows after the "Go live?"

References

Further Reading

Organizational aspects of an implementation project, but less technical, are addressed in:
Gadatsch, A.: Business Process Management. Springer, Wiesbaden (2023)

Further Cited Literature and Sources

Fischer, O.: Private Communication. 12 Sept 2024 (2024)
Lehmann, S., Buxmann, P.: Pricing strategies of software vendors. Bus. Inf. Syst. Eng. 1(6), 452–462 (2009)
Saueressig, T., Stein, T., Boeder, J., Kleis, W.: SAP S/4HANA—Architecture. Rheinwerk, Boston (2023)
Willinger, M., Gradl, J.: Datenmigration in SAP, 2nd edn. Galileo Press, Bonn (2007)

Adaptation of Business Standard Software

15

Cut twice and still too short, said the tailor.
Proverb

Summary

We look at the various ways to adapt standard software to a company and also to the needs of individual users and user groups. We distinguish between adaptation through configuration, which includes customizing, personalization, and the use of roles, and adaptation through development, namely, in-house development in a company, company-specific extension, and modification of the standard software.

Learning Objective

- To learn about the different adaptation options for business standard software.

15.1   Types of Adaptation

Here we gain an overview of the types of adaptation, which will be explored in more depth in the following sections. Often, the term *customization* is used instead of adaptation. In this book, we choose "adaptation" for two reasons. In the first place, the phrase "to customize software" is used by different people for different purposes, on the one hand, for adaptation in general, both by programming and configuration, and, on the other hand, just for configuration or parameterization, e.g., "customizing" in SAP software. "Adaptation" avoids confusion, in particular "customization" vs. "customizing." In the second place, our "adaptation" also includes personalization and the use of roles, which might not be generally considered customization.

© The Author(s), under exclusive license to Springer-Verlag GmbH, DE,   269
part of Springer Nature 2025
R. Weber, *Enterprise Information Systems*,
https://doi.org/10.1007/978-3-662-71718-9_15

Table 15.1 Configuration options

	Effect	Content	Carried out by
Customizing	Tenant, system (rarely); all users	Business functions	Specialists (consultants, organizers, etc.)
Role	User group	User interface, access permissions	Administrators, organizers
Personalization	User	User interface	Users for themselves

There are two categories of adaptation: configuration and development.

(a) *Configuration*

The settings are maintained in user interfaces. Table 15.1 shows the configuration options in more detail:

System-wide and tenant-wide settings of customizing affect the way the standard software works, e.g., which accounts can be booked. The settings for users or user groups, on the other hand, only determine which functions a user sees and is allowed to execute, as well as how they see them.

We learned about the role concept in Chap. 9. This assigns settings to groups of users. These settings only apply to these users, not to the whole company. Users can take on different roles, thus implicitly belonging to different, non-mutually exclusive user groups. Related to roles are authorization profiles (see Chap. 16).

(b) *Development*

This is adaptation of the standard software through programming. It always affects the entire enterprise information system, i.e., all tenants and all users. Development includes:

- *In-house development*: development of additional programs, i.e., in addition to the standard software.
- *Extension*: addition to the source code of the standard software at designated places.
- *Modification*: changing the source code of the standard software at any place (In which case is this possible?)

In the following, we will look at the different types of adaptation in detail. We start with the types of adaptation through configuration and then move on to those through development.

15.2 Customizing

Customizing (parameterization) is necessary in any case when implementing business standard software. It does not require any programming knowledge; rather, the settings are made via the user interface. It is related to the "options" that we know, for example, from word processing programs. The user interface in customizing is similar; only the options for business standard software are of a different magnitude. In addition, customizing requires both knowledge of the standard software and of the company's business processes. Many settings cannot be changed later or at least not easily. The customizing settings affect the company as a whole, not just individual users as in personalization. Like master and transaction data, the customizing settings are stored in the database of the enterprise information system.

Some types of customizing settings:

- The organizational structure of the company and settings for it, e.g., purchasing organizations and plants.
- Controlling parameters that influence which functions can be selected, for example, the material type determines, among other things, whether a material can be ordered.
- Field settings for the user interface: For some applications, you can set which fields from a given set should appear in an application program for users. More precisely, you can even set whether a field is only displayed or can also be changed, whether it is visible at all and whether data entry is mandatory.

We will look at some examples in Exercise 15.1.

The boundary between customizing and master data is sometimes fluid (cf. organizational units).

Just for clarity: Customizing does not exactly mean changing the standard behavior of the software. Sometimes, you might read something like that in the literature. Otherwise, a company would not have to do it, if it was satisfied with the standard behavior. However, it always has to be carried out. Rather, it means making company-specific system settings. Some settings are completely in line with the standard behavior, but the standard cannot provide default settings for those. (Why?) One example is defining the organizational units or the group currency. With other settings, one of several functional options is selected (e.g., which variant of accounting is used). With still others, details are determined, e.g., tolerances (see example below). To reduce the effort, predefined "packages" of customizing settings can be chosen in some products, where decisions have been made for common standard cases. These packages of course do not contain company-specific data, such as the names of the plants.

15.3 Personalization

In personalization, the user makes "harmless" but useful settings that support his way of working (user interface) and only apply to him. Typical cases are:

- Data representation: We have seen that business data is determined by a unique identifier; in addition, there is a language-dependent designation. A user may set whether only the designation, the identifier, or both are displayed. Another example is the date format, which depends on the cultural area (cf. internationalization). For example, April 1, 2025, is 01.04.2025 in Germany but 04/01/2025 in the USA.

- Default values for certain fields: User-specific default values can be automatically entered into certain screen fields. If a purchaser always orders for plant 1000, for example, 1000 can be entered into all plant fields. When necessary, the user overwrites it.
- Layout properties: This concerns, for example, the font size—easier readability versus more information per area.
- User-specific menu or favorites: As an alternative to the standard menu, with a multitude of functions that might confuse the user, he may configure a user-specific menu or user-defined favorites. This menu will just contain the functions frequently chosen by the user. It is similar to a role (see below), but unlike a role, it is individually set by the user.

15.4 Roles

We already learned about roles in Chap. 9. We will see more details about that in Chap. 16.

15.5 Three-System Landscape

We now come to adaptation through software development, for which there are again different forms. The three-system landscape is common for all forms.

When a company develops business software, also for its own use, it will sensibly not do this in the system in which the day-to-day business is conducted. We will look at the reasons in Exercise 15.3. The *three-system landscape* (Fig. 15.1) is recommended and established.

The development takes place in the *development system*, also called *integration system* (Föse et al. 2012, Chap. 4).

After developer tests, self-contained developments are transferred to a *test system*, also called *quality assurance system* or *consolidation system*, and tested there. The testers should not be identical to the developers. Detected errors are corrected

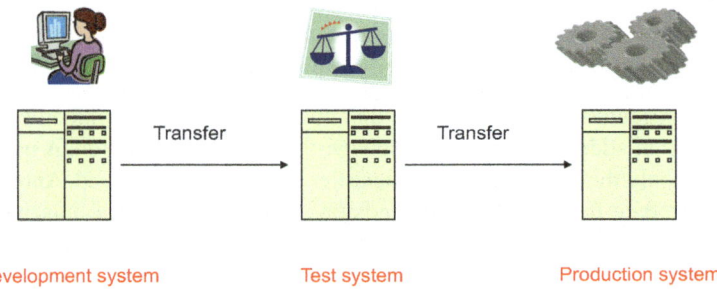

Fig. 15.1 Three-system landscape

in the development system, and the corrected programs are transferred again and retested. For a realistic test, it is important that the test data corresponds in structure, quality, and quantity to the production data. Since it is usually complex to generate artificial test data, production data is often used. Depending on the application, this can be problematic (e.g., human resources, salary data). So anonymized production data may be used as a substitute. In practice, there are often pitfalls in detail.

When the tests have been successful, the development objects are transferred to the *production system*, also called *delivery system* (Föse et al. 2012, Chap. 4), and run there (hopefully) well.

If a company uses several enterprise information systems (system landscape) and possibly carries out simultaneous developments for them, the three-system landscape looks more complex. It should be noted that a test system must also be available even if there is no in-house development for this system, but only the integration should be tested. After all, the test should not disturb the production operation, especially not access production data.

In addition to the mentioned systems, there can be training and demo systems.

15.6 Company-Specific In-House Development

By company-specific *in-house development*, we understand to create additional, company-specific software, usually related to the standard software. This development becomes necessary when the standard software does not contain a specific function or not in the desired form. The standard software often has development tools to accomplish this. "Software" is not just source code. It includes more generally *development objects*, "objects" not necessarily in the object-oriented sense. Some examples outline the spectrum of development objects:

- Application programs with user interface
- Object-oriented classes
- Database tables
- Data types of a data dictionary
- Web services
- Workflows

In some cases, an in-house development becomes superfluous in a later version of the standard software, when that version includes the function. In order to reduce maintenance costs (every created piece of software causes maintenance effort), it is advisable to migrate to the new standard function (see Chap. 14).

Rarely will an in-house development be completely independent of the standard software. Rather, individual functions of the standard software will be used, usually via a programming interface. (Example?) For a stable software development, it is important that such interfaces are released by the software provider, i.e., they are "official" interfaces.

An intermediate stage between standard software and company-specific in-house development are *add-ons*. These are additional developments by software houses and consulting companies, which are based on the standard software and fill known gaps (see Sect. 8.1).

15.7   Extension

In that case, the standard software does offer a function, but the function should be slightly adjusted. The easiest way for a company is the adjustment by customizing. Customizing means selecting one of several predefined adjustments. However, there are applications for which company-specific adjustment requests are extremely different. So a comprehensive selection list is not realistic. However, it can at least be known at which points of the application the adjustment makes sense. Then the concept of company-specific *extension* can be used: *Extension points* are offered, where company-specific program code can be "hooked in." An extension point can be imagined like a hole in the standard software, which can be filled with program code developed by the company. An extension point has a predefined interface (signature) that the company's program has to implement. (Why does this make sense?) Technically, a dynamic program call takes place—dynamic in the sense that the current content of the extension point is used. The provider of the standard software specifies (documentation) the extension points, including a description of its interface.

The special thing about the extension point is that it is stable with regard to new versions of the standard software. That is, when the company switches to a new version, the extension continues to work without further ado.

Another frequently used extension option is *database table extensions*. The use case is that in addition to the data fields available in the standard software, additional company-specific ones should be used in a database table. For this purpose, a company-specific table extension with those fields is defined. In addition, it must be ensured that the fields are filled, which usually happens by also extending screen masks. The additional fields are combined with the regular ones into the extended data record. This is written as a whole into the database, i.e., in the same database transaction.

15.8   Modification

We speak of *modification* when the company changes the standard software at points not explicitly intended for this. Company-specific extension and customizing also influence the behavior of the standard software, but they do not change the software. Modification is only possible in a company if the development objects of the standard software are available to the company and development know-how exists in the company. Usually, it is source code that is changed in a modification, sometimes combined with changes to screen masks and database tables. Modifications without source code changes are also conceivable, e.g., extending data field, which can affect data types, database tables, and screen masks, but not necessarily the source code. Skill is needed to find the places in the source code that should be modified. There are two risks with modification:

- Warranty: The provider of the standard software does not guarantee that the modified software runs correctly and—more importantly—does not change the correct behavior of the standard software elsewhere as a side effect.
- Stability against new versions: When a new version of the standard software is installed, the modifications are at risk. In that case, it must be carefully checked and tested whether the modification still works in the new version.

For these reasons, modification is warned against. It should be used only when other adaptation methods cannot be applied.

15.9 Examples

15.9.1 Customizing in SAP Software

The *implementation guide* (*IMG*) includes access to the customizing settings, which are carried out in *customizing activities*. The *SAP Reference IMG* contains all customizing activities that are possible in the SAP system (transaction SPRO). Related settings are presented in a sensible order. In addition to accessing the customizing activities, transaction SPRO offers possibilities for the management of customizing projects. Typically customizing activities are distributed to different project groups. In addition, a company-specific implementation guide can be defined, which contains the company-relevant subset of the reference guide.

The customizing activities are organized in a menu hierarchically by application areas. Directly next to each customizing activity is a description. Customizing activities are classified as "must" (no SAP default possible), "can" (the SAP default is to be checked), or "not required" (standard system). There is also a designation as "critical" or "not critical" (Föse et al. 2012, Chap. 6).

There is more or less validation logic for the data in the customizing tables. If only few checks are needed, the customizing activity is often a generated dialog program for table maintenance, which may be supplemented by manually created checking logic. This means, when entering a table or several dependent tables (e.g., header/line-item structures), a dialog program is automatically generated with which table entries can be created, changed, deleted, or simply displayed.

The customizing tables have different *delivery classes* for different categories of customizing data:

- C: Maintenance only by the company, no SAP import; this means that SAP does not provide proposed values. For example, the company structure is specific to the company, e.g., which production plants exist. This category is therefore closely related to master data (see Sect. 3.3.1).
- G: Maintenance by the company and SAP, but the company and SAP have separate namespaces. SAP provides values, and in a new software version, this list may change. It is generally sensible to only add values, as the company may have

used existing values. The company can enter its own values, which, due to the separate namespaces, are not overwritten by new SAP entries. Technically identical but content-wise different sub-cases can occur:

– The addition is the exception: Currency units, country codes, or units of measure can be adopted. While it is usually not sensible to add currency units, company- or industry-specific units of measure could be added by the company. Thus, all or many of the values predefined in the standard software are adopted by the company, although not all of them are necessarily used.

– The addition is the rule: The standard software provides some suggested values, which can be adopted. Company-specific additions are however common. They often are based on the proposed values of the standard software: Those are copied and modified.

In addition to these delivery classes for customizing, there are others for master and transaction data as well as system tables, e.g., for development objects.

15.9.2 Customizing the User Interface in Vtiger CRM

With the "Studio" software, the user interface in Vtiger CRM (see Sect. 3.7.3) can be customized to some extent without programming (Saledif 2014, p. 290 ff.; Rossi 2011, p. 116 ff.; Piepiorra 2007, Sect. 5.2.2). A "module" is selected, e.g., Lead, in which a block (category) is selected or a new one is created in order to add a new field. Finally, the properties of the field are defined: The data type of the field (e.g., "text," "decimal," "checkbox," "selection list") and its length are set. A selection list serves as value help for a field. Existing selection lists can be customized, i.e., new values can be added, and existing entries can be renamed (if not used by the system itself) or deleted (Saledif 2014, p. 304). The entries can be assigned to a role. In this case, only users who have been assigned this role or a role superior to it see the entry. (There is a hierarchy concept for roles in Vtiger CRM.) With a menu editor, menu items can be deselected, or additional menu items can be added.

15.9.3 Customizing the User Interface in Microsoft Dynamics 365 Business Central

The same applies to Microsoft Dynamics 365 Business Central. The system uses role-based clients. The user interfaces can be customized through settings. There is personalization and "configuration," which in this context means a change of user roles (Ebert and Hauptmann 2023, p. 11). Data fields, columns, and buttons can be arranged, shown, and hidden. Anything beyond can only be accomplished through programming. A role-specific start page, the "Role Center," is available. There are a number of pre-configured Role Centers.

15.9.4 Example: Custom Development with ABAP in SAP Software

The vast majority of application software in SAP systems is written in SAP's own programming language *ABAP* (*Advanced Business Application Programming*) (O'Neill and Perfiljeva 2020). For ABAP, SAP offers a development environment, the *ABAP Workbench*, and now there is an alternative, Eclipse-based, more conventional development environment. ABAP programs are interpreted, i.e., not compiled into machine code, and run in the ABAP runtime environment, a virtual machine. The source code can be accessed by a company (with exceptions for some products). Companies can even modify it (see however Sect. 15.8).

ABAP is a very extensive language with a large number of instructions, which may have various variants and additions. In other programming languages, more functionality is shifted to software libraries. Integrated into the language are SQL instructions and transaction control functions.

The programs are stored in the database. An ABAP programmer using the ABAP Workbench therefore does not deal with files. Development objects are grouped in *packages*. For example, in SAP S/4HANA, there are packages "Purchasing" and "Overhead Cost Controlling."

In the early days, ABAP was not object-oriented (ABAP/4, where "4" stands for "fourth-generation language"). *Function modules* were a concept for modularization, comparable to functions in other programming languages. They are still used today for remote function calls. Meanwhile, ABAP has been expanded to an object-oriented language (ABAP Objects). Since SAP S/4HANA uses the in-memory database SAP HANA, especially in newer functions, stored procedures are called (see Sect. 3.7.1). Data types are often not defined locally in a program but in the ABAP Dictionary, a collection of data types (among other things). Currently, the ABAP RESTful Application Programming Model (Baumbusch et al. 2023) is suggested, especially for SAP Fiori apps (see below) (for REST, see Sect. 11.8).

The technology for designing user interfaces is partly SAP specific. Most programs use *dynpros* (*dynamic programs*), which offer a page-oriented interaction behavior. The latest user interfaces, on the other hand, are Web-based and use the scripting language JavaScript. The design principle is called SAP Fiori, and the SAPUI5 framework is used (Saueressig et al. 2023, p. 68).

To distinguish company-specific developments from the standard software, *namespaces* are used. The names of development objects of the company must begin with Y or Z. Alternatively, companies can reserve their own namespaces at SAP. For example, the company Twillie Ltd. could reserve the namespace /twillie/. The development objects then start with /twillie/ instead of Y or Z. Exercise 15.2 addresses the benefits of namespaces for development partners and consulting companies.

15.9.5 Extension in SAP Software

Over time, various extension concepts have emerged in SAP software: *User-Exit*, *classic BAdI (Business Add-in)*, and *new BAdI in the expansion spot*. They exist today side by side. In Schwaninger (2011), from which we pick up the following example, you can find a comprehensive treatment of how these extensions can be used in materials management of SAP software, as well as an explanation of the concepts. What extension possibilities exist can be found in the SAP implementation guide, the documentation, or specialist literature about applications.

We look at the methodology using an example, the BAdI ME_POHIST_DISP_CUST. It influences how the purchase order history in purchase order line-items is displayed. The definition of the BAdI can be found in SAP S/4HANA in transaction SE18. The most important part of the BAdI is an ABAP interface, here if_ex_me_pohist_disp_cust. An ABAP interface describes the signature of class components, especially methods. It shows which methods exist, what parameters they have, and what their types are. In addition, there is documentation and a sample implementation that can serve as a template for company-specific implementation. The call of the BAdI in the SAP source code follows the following scheme:

```
DATA: l_badi TYPE REF TO ME_POHIST_DISP_CUST.

GET BADI l_badi.
CALL BADI l_badi->if_ex_me_pohist_disp_cust~fieldcat_change …
```

In the first line, a variable for the BAdI is declared. It is used for method calls similar to an object reference. In the second line, the BAdI implementation is determined.[1] In the third, the method fieldcat_change ("change field catalog") of the interface if_ex_me_pohist_disp_cust of the BAdI implementation is called. For simplification, the parameters are only indicated by dots. This is what SAP provides.

For the company-specific BAdI implementation, an ABAP class must now be developed, which implements this interface. In Schwaninger (2011, p. 34), the following simple sample implementation is given for our method fieldcat_change:

```
METHOD if_ex_me_pohist_disp_cust~fieldcat_change.
     DELETE ct_fieldcat WHERE fieldname = 'DMBTR' OR
                              fieldname = 'HSWAE' OR
                              fieldname = 'WRBTR' OR
                              fieldname = 'WAERS'.
ENDMETHOD.
```

---

[1] For simplicity, we assume that there is exactly one implementation of the BAdI. But more complex cases can also be represented.

ct_fieldcat is a changing parameter, i.e., a parameter that serves as both input and output for the method. Its contents is a list (more precisely, internal table) of field names with additional information ("field catalog"). The method deletes some entries of this list. Those fields are not displayed in the purchase order history.

A BAdI implementation consists in writing an implementation for all methods provided in the interface. If one of the methods is not significant, the implementation is left empty. A BAdI implementation must finally be activated to show effect. Conversely, it can be deactivated if it should at least temporarily be ineffective.

Organizationally, the new BAdIs are organized in *extension spots*. An extension spot groups related BAdIs. Our BAdI ME_POHIST_DISP_CUST is located in the extension spot ES_BADI_ME_POHIST.

In addition to this extension by software developers, there are extension possibilities for "key users" (Saueressig et al. 2023, p. 113 ff.). The terms *low-code* or even *no-code* platforms are used. With no-code platforms, it is not trained software developers that create program code but key users or "citizen developers". They use visual editors, which then generate programming objects. According to Banda et al. (2024, p. 496), the difference between "no-code" and "low-code" is that in "low-code" development, a traditional development environment is supplemented with a no-code platform.

Besides these "in-app extensions," there is also the "side-by-side extension" in the SAP Cloud Platform. The idea here is to leave the "stable core" (like the ERP system) unaffected. Instead extensions are carried out in a separate system. In this case, it is a cloud system, where development tools and interfaces are available (Banda et al. 2024, p. 163 and p. 527 ff.). According to our systematics, the extension application is technically a company-specific in-house development (Sect. 15.7).

15.9.6 Extension in Microsoft Dynamics 365 Business Central

In Microsoft Dynamics 365 Business Central, unlike its predecessor product, Microsoft Dynamics NAV, there is an extension concept (cf. (Demiliani and Tacconi 2018, chapters "The New Extension Model" and "Developing an Extension with AL and Visual Studio Code") for the following explanations). Previously modification (cf. Sect. 15.8) was possible and common, with the mentioned problems, especially the matching effort in a version change. Now tables (table object) and masks (page object) can be adjusted with the extension objects table extension object and page extension object. For example, a new field can be added to a table and made available in a mask. Properties of standard fields, however, can only be changed in a very limited way.

New development objects can be created, in addition to the mentioned ones, of course also program code (code units). In extensions, program code is called via events defined by Microsoft.

The development environment Microsoft Studio Code and the programming language AL are used, also this in contrast to predecessor products.

15.10 Exercises and Proposed Solutions

(a) Exercises

Exercise 15.1 (Customizing)
This exercise can be performed in an SAP S/4HANA system.

Customizing of materials management: Which customizing activity controls which views can be created for which material type? (Tip: Look at material types in customizing—transaction SPRO: This can be found in "Logistics general" in the basic settings of the material master. Take a look at the settings for the material types "Raw materials" and "Finished Product.")

Exercise 15.2 (Namespaces)
Why is it useful for consulting companies that want to offer add-ons to reserve namespaces at SAP?

Exercise 15.3 (Three-System Landscape)
What problems arise when company-specific in-house development takes place in the production system?

Exercise 15.4 (Modification)
We know a risk of modification: As a "side effect," parts of the standard software could be unintentionally affected. So a standard function might no longer work properly. Let's assume such an effect occurs and the company creates a problem report to the software vendor. With which mechanisms could the software vendor quickly find out that the problem actually originates from a modification?

(b) Proposed Solutions for the Exercises

Exercise 15.1 (Customizing)
Views for a material type: In customizing: Logistics - General→Material Master→Basic Settings→Material Types→Define Attributes of Material Types. The "departments" correspond to the views.

Exercise 15.2 (Namespaces)
New development objects can only be created in the namespaces Y* and Z* or a namespace reserved at SAP by companies. If the consulting company develops a software and creates a workbench request (the means to import software into an SAP system), it can lead to name collisions in namespaces Y* and Z* at its customers. This is avoided with a reserved namespace.

Exercise 15.3 (Three-System Landscape)

- Instability if development takes place during operation. In the worst case, programs could even return incorrect results.

- Performance restrictions.
- Developers have access to potentially sensitive production data (e.g., salary data).

Exercise 15.4 (Modification)
The problem solver must be able to quickly determine whether the software has been modified. A theoretical but slow way is source code comparison. It is faster via logging (administrative information of the programs), but in both cases, access to the company's software is necessary. A better option is to log the modifications (i.e., the fact that the program has been changed) at the software vendor's: Registered developers of the company register their changes, which is recorded by the software vendor. The problem solver then recognizes without direct access to the company's software whether it has been modified.

15.11 Self-Assessment

Configuration

1. Is it possible to delete a field from a user interface screen mask or at least make it invisible? If yes, why? If no, why not, or in which cases is it not possible?
2. What are the similarities between customizing data and master data?
3. You are implementing a new version of your standard software. Is a new customizing necessary?
4. What is the difference between personalization and customizing?

Software Development

5. Is in-house development independent of the standard software?
6. In what kind of system does in-house development take place?
7. Why could a software run correctly in the development system but not in the test system?
8. Why should not (only) developers take over the test? What role does the test system play?
9. What is the difference between in-house development and extension?
10. In which cases is a modification possible?
11. Why can modification be dangerous? Why is it then still done sometimes?
12. What are the advantages and disadvantages if a company-specific in-house development takes place in the enterprise information system to be adapted? And what are they if they take place in a separate system?

References

Banda, S., Chandra, S., Gooi, C.A.: SAP Business Technology Platform, 2nd edn. Rheinwerk, Boston (2024)

Baumbusch, L., Jäger, M., Lensch, M.: ABAP RESTful Application Programming Model. The Comprehensive Guide. Rheinwerk, Bonn (2023)

Demiliani, S., Tacconi, D.: Microsoft Dynamics 365 Business Central Development Quick Start Guide. Packt Publishing, Birmingham (2018)

Ebert, J., Hauptmann, C.: Microsoft Dynamics 365 Business Central, 2nd updated edn. Hanser, Munich (2023)

Föse, F., Hagemann, S., Will, L.: SAP NetWeaver AS ABAP—System Administration, 4th edn. Rheinwerk, New York (2012)

O'Neill, B., Perfiljeva, J.: ABAP. An Introduction, 2nd updated and expanded edn. Rheinwerk, Boston (2020)

Piepiorra, F.: vtiger CRM v5.x. bomots (2007)

Rossi, I.D.: vtiger CRM. Beginner's Guide. Packt Publishing, Birmingham (2011)

Saledif, T.: vtiger 6.0 kompakt. Brain Media (2014)

Saueressig, T., Stein, T., Boeder, J., Kleis, W.: SAP S/4HANA—Architecture. Rheinwerk, Boston (2023)

Schwaninger, J.: ABAP—Development for Materials Management in SAP: User-Exits and BAdIs. Galileo Press, Bonn (2011)

Access Control

16

If it tempts you so much, try it in spite of my prohibition.
But take note: I am powerful.
And I am only the most lowly gatekeeper.
But from room to room stand gatekeepers,
each more powerful than the other.
I can't endure even one glimpse of the third.
Franz Kafka: Before the Law
(*https://www.kafka-online.info/before-the-law.html*. Accessed on 01.10.2025)

Summary

Access is controlled in enterprise information systems through permissions. Roles are used in order to assign users precise permissions in the simplest possible way.

Learning Objectives

- To understand how the access to functions in business application software is technically controlled by permissions.
- To learn about the organizational approach to granting permissions.

© The Author(s), under exclusive license to Springer-Verlag GmbH, DE,
part of Springer Nature 2025
R. Weber, *Enterprise Information Systems*,
https://doi.org/10.1007/978-3-662-71718-9_16

16.1   Permissions

Access control in business standard software includes two aspects:

1. "Ask"[1]: The standard software includes permission checks in the program code. This is the task of the software creator—the software vendor in the case of business standard software and in-house developers in the case of company-specific in-house development.
2. "Bid": The users are assigned suitable permissions so that they pass the checks. The assignment of such permissions is the task of the company that uses the standard software. Roles are used to manage this organizationally.

According to Ferraiolo et al. (2007, p. 4) in addition to users and permissions, subjects, objects, and operations are the key concepts of access control. "Subjects" are the computer processes acting on behalf of a user. So at a specific moment in time, there may be several subjects for a user. The objects are the entities to be protected. In an ERP system, such an entity is, for example, material master data. And an operation is, for example, to create or update that material data. A *permission*, also called *privilege* or *authorization*, is a combination of an object and an operation.

A user should have exactly those permissions that he needs—not too many, not too few.

- Too few: He cannot perform tasks that he should carry out.
- Too many: He has access to tasks that he should not perform.

In Ferraiolo et al. (2007, p. 5), this principle is called "least privilege." Experience shows that in practice, the first problem is rather rare, but the second one is common. One reason is that with the methods that are commonly used in practice to assign permissions, it is often not easy to set the exact amount of permissions needed; we will take a closer look at this shortly. Another reason is that it is sometimes not clearly organizationally defined what exact permissions a user should have.

It makes sense to provide a new user with the necessary permissions in two organizationally separate steps (Föse et al. 2012, Chap. 8):

1. The system administrator creates the user.
2. The permission administrator assigns permissions or a role that includes permissions to this user (see below).

Unlike permissions typically described in books about operating systems, which allow create, read, update, or delete (CRUD) on a resource, permissions in enterprise information systems are usually much more fine-grained. For example, a user

---

[1] I use the terms "ask" and "bid" for explanation, they are not predefined predefined terms of access control.

may be allowed to change a purchase requisition, i.e., change certain attributes such as the quantity or the material, but not release it, i.e., set the "status" attribute accordingly. The latter is also a changing operation but a more specific one.

At first approximation, one could therefore attach a permission to the method that shall be executed on a business object. The method parameters could also be taken into account. For example, a user may be allowed to execute the release method for the purchase requisition 5213. At definition time, the purchase requisition 5213 is of course not known. Instead, attributes of the purchase requisition will be used for permission definition. For example, the release method for purchase requisitions up to a total amount (an attribute of the purchase requisition) of 5000 euros. Since an attribute of a business object A can again be a business object B (see Sect. 3.4), a reference could also be made to attributes of B—and this can be continued transitively. For example, the permission could refer to purchase requisitions for materials of certain material groups, e.g., hazardous goods. The material group is an attribute of the material, and the material is an attribute of the purchase requisition.

Beyond this first approximation, further restrictions of the permissions are possible, for example, if a purchase requisition must be released according to the four-eyes principle. This means that two different people must release a purchase requisition. This procedure could be applied for more sensitive materials. Here, the history of the purchase requisition is important, which could of course be modeled as an attribute of the purchase requisition. The difference to the above example is that when creating the purchase requisition, the later required permission is not yet fully known; it only becomes concrete over time. In enterprise information systems, such dependencies are usually determined less by permissions (in the narrower sense) than by application logic, business process definition, or business rules.

16.2   Roles

One pitfall in assigning permissions is that the administrator needs to know which permissions are required for which function. However, this is not necessarily immediately apparent from the function. Rather permission checks are spread in the program code. The information about which permissions a function requires must therefore be recorded by the software vendor. This information is evaluated in the *role-based* assignment, where only functions are assigned to a role and finally the role is assigned to the user. The corresponding set of permissions can be calculated from the information which function needs which permissions. The role then stores that set of permissions. Example roles for immediate use or as a copy template are often part of standard software (see Sect. 6.3). Roles can also be used in adaptation by configuration (see Sect. 15.4).

16.3   Examples

16.3.1 The Access Control Concept in SAP Software

In SAP software, users are assigned *authorizations* (this term is used instead of *permissions*) (see Fig. 16.1). An authorization refers to a so-called authorization object (not to be understood in the object-oriented sense). An authorization object can be seen as the type of a data structure with several fields. An authorization then is an instance of the authorization object, i.e., a value is set for each field. The user BISBEE, has, among others, an authorization YM_BEST_NB[2] for the authorization object M_BEST_BSA ("Document Type in Purchase Order") with the field values:

- BSART ("Purchasing Document Type") = NB ("Standard PO")
- ACTVT ("Activity") = *

For the first field of the authorization object, the purchasing document type, only the value NB is set for the user. The second field, the activity, on the other hand, contains a wildcard (placeholder), "*" stands for all possible values. An authorization therefore often does not correspond to exactly one instance, in the sense of a data structure corresponding to the type of the authorization object, but to a set of instances. The meaning of the authorization is: The user is allowed to perform all possible activities with normal orders. In fact, many authorization objects in SAP software have a similar structure: first some fields that specify certain customizing data (often organizational objects) or master data (in the terminology of (Ferraiolo et al. 2007, p. 4) specifying the *objects*) and then the field ACTVT, whose value set depends on the authorization object (the *operations* according to (Ferraiolo et al. 2007, p. 4)). It is always a subset of the set of all possible activities, such as "create," "change," or "display prices," or, more precisely, a numerical representation of it.

In the ABAP application program, it is checked with the instruction AUTHORITY-CHECK whether the user has a suitable authorization:

```
...
AUTHORITY-CHECK OBJECT 'M_BEST_BSA'
       ID 'BSART' FIELD lv_bsart
       ID 'ACTVT' FIELD '02'.
IF sy-subrc <> 0.
   MESSAGE ...
ENDIF.
...
```

Let us assume that the value of the variable lv_bsart is NB and the user has the abovementioned authorization YM_BEST_NB. In the above excerpt of an ABAP program, it is checked whether the user has an authorization for the authorization object M_BEST_BSA, which:

---

[2]The "Y" again indicates the company namespace; see Sect. 15.10.4.

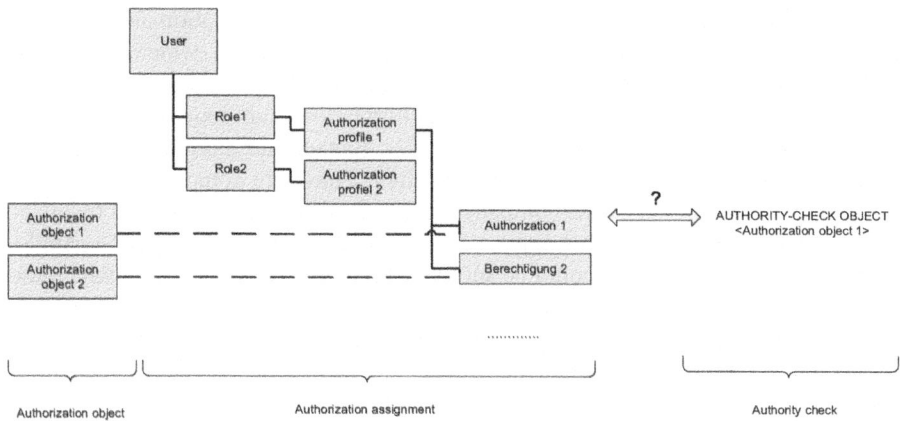

Fig. 16.1 Authorizations in SAP Software

- Matches for the field BSART the value contained in in the variable lv_bsart; "matches" means that in the authorization this value appears as a single value (e.g., NB) or is contained in an interval, which makes more sense with numbers, or a wildcard (e.g., *) is used for a match; the authorization YM_BEST_NB fulfills this requirement.
- Matches the value 02 for the field ACTVT; the authorization YM_BEST_NB also does this.

If this is not the case, an error message is output; otherwise—as with our authorization YM_BEST_NB—the program continues. Usually, the data access follows afterward.

After we have seen how the authorization check technically works, the question arises how to best organize the assignment of authorizations to users. A user needs a variety of authorizations. Assigning all these authorizations to each individual user would require a high administrative effort, and it would also be confusing.

A suitable way is to bundle authorizations into *authorization profiles* and assign one or more authorization profiles to the user. Authorization profiles can be grouped hierarchically, in which case we speak of *composite profiles*. A *simple profile* contains only authorizations. It is not allowed to include both authorizations and other authorization profiles in a composite profile. The assignment of authorization profiles to users is usually done indirectly via roles (see below).

The described authorization concept uses a *positive authorization logic*: This means that the user has exactly those authorizations that are directly or indirectly (through nesting in composite profiles) contained in the assigned authorization profiles. It is not possible to explicitly state that a user does *not* have a certain authorization. It is only implicit, if the authorization does not appear in the authorization profiles. We see in Exercise 16.3 that such assignments can be arduous.

Put simply, a *role* in the SAP system is a set of transactions along with a role-specific menu. For each transaction, the software vendor knows which authorizations with which values are checked. From this information and the set of transactions, an authorization profile is automatically generated, which is assigned to the user from the role. In individual cases, values can be entered manually.

One problem still needs to be solved: authorizations can depend on organizational objects (also called *organizational levels*; Banzer and Sambill 2022, p. 282 f.), e.g., the purchasing organization or the plant. These are company specific and can therefore only be set by the company. Such organizational objects can be imagined as parameters of a role that apply to all contained authorizations. For example, the purchasing organization could be set to 1000 in all authorizations in which the field "purchasing organization" appears. We speak of *master* or *reference roles* (i.e., template roles), in which the organizational objects are open, and *derived roles*, which only differ by the setting the organizational objects (Banzer and Sambill 2022, p. 261).

In addition, it should be noted that in SAP S/4HANA, the technology SAP Fiori is used for user interfaces (see Sect. 3.7.1). A new, native SAP Fiori app calls business logic via REST-based OData services. Therefore, additional authorizations are added for such apps, especially authorizations for calling the OData services (Saueressig et al. 2023, p. 71). Furthermore, new apps use Core Data Services Views (CDS Views) (see Sect. 3.7.1). For these, there are separate, additional access controls (Colle et al. 2024, Chap. 5). We will not go into these aspects further here.

16.3.2 The Access Control Concept in Vtiger CRM

In the access control concept of Vtiger CRM (cf. Sect. 3.7, cf. (Saledif 2014, p. 257 ff.; Piepiorra 2007, Chap. 5; Rossi 2011, p. 47 ff.) for the following), a user can be assigned exactly one *role*, which in turn can be assigned one or more *profiles*. The profile finally contains *privileges*, which corresponds to what we have so far called permissions.

There are several types of privileges, and it is their combination that regulates the access. There are *module privileges* (a "module" corresponds to what is called "business data" in this book); they regulate whether the data of the module can be viewed, created, edited, or deleted. With *field privileges*, it is determined whether a field can be read, written (including read), or should be invisible to the user. And finally, there are *function privileges*, that tell, for example, whether the function "convert lead" is allowed.

An interesting feature of the concept, unlike the permission concept of SAP (see Sect. 16.3.1), is that an added permission can restrict already granted possibilities (so it is not a "positive" access control concept; (Saledif 2014, p. 278)): In a profile, you can generally select "View All" or "Edit All" in a checkbox, which refers to all modules. In addition, however, another profile can be specified using the "Copy privileges from" setting, which, e.g., excludes the viewing of sales potentials. The previous setting "View All" is thus restricted.

The access control concept of Vtiger CRM provides for some other possibilities. We just mention "custom rules" (Saledif 2014, p. 288 f.). This allows to determine how other users can access data owned by someone else. For example, a custom rule for leads could be specified: In "Leads from", the owner of the leads is entered, in "Can be accessed by" a user group that may access the lead is entered, and in another field, it is determined that this group may read and edit.

16.3.3 The Access Control Concept in Pentaho

The analytical system Pentaho was addressed in Sect. 4.2.6.3. Here we look at access control to data cubes. Pentaho users use roles in which access control is designed at different levels. Thus, access to certain data cubes can be granted. However, this does not have to refer to the whole data cube but can be limited to certain dimensions. And within a dimension, it can be limited to certain attributes of a dimension hierarchy. Similar to Vtiger CRM, exceptions can be defined: If you first grant access to an attribute of a hierarchy level and then exclude a specific one at the underlying hierarchy level, all others at the underlying hierarchy level are still accessible (Müller and Keller 2015, p. 212).

16.4 Exercises and Proposed Solutions

(a) Exercises

Exercise 16.1 (Permissions)
How do permissions relate to methods of business objects?

Exercise 16.2 (Authorizations in SAP Software)
In SAP S/4HANA and predecessor systems, cost accounting is carried out in a so-called controlling area. This may include one or more subsidiaries in a group. There is a multitude of cost centers in it. Employees in the companies of the group have more or less restricted access to the master data for cost centers. Thus, some can create and change certain cost centers, while others can only display them.

(a) What would an appropriate authorization object look like in this case?
(b) What authorization would you assign to an employee who is allowed to maintain all cost centers in the controlling area 1000 but only display them in the controlling area 2000?
(c) Can you give an employee the authorization to only display his own cost center?

Exercise 16.3 (Authorization Profiles in SAP Software)
The exercise aims at understanding authorizations. In practice, one would methodologically start with roles.

Assume that the users u1, u2, and u3 have been assigned the composite profile c. c contains, among other things, the simple profile s. s in turn contains an authorization a. Now the situation arises that the composite profile is perfectly suitable for u1 and u2. However, u3 should receive a slightly modified authorization a' instead of the authorization a. How do you make this change?

(b) Proposed Solution for the Exercises

Exercise 16.1 (Permissions)
There will be a permission check to see if a user is allowed to execute a method at all. This is why there are special methods for common use cases, i.e., not only a general method "change" to access (almost) all attributes but also a method "release" to only change the status attribute of the business object. In addition, there will be finer permission checks on which data the user may execute the method. The selection criteria for the data are defined in the permissions.

Exercise 16.2 (Authorizations in SAP software)

(a) The authorization object should have a suitable ID (name) and fields for the controlling area, the cost center, and the activity. The activity has values (IDs) such as "create" (01), "change" (02), and "display" (03). In SAP software, this is the authorization object K_CSKS (Cost Center Master).
(b) Two authorizations for this authorization object with field values:
   1. Controlling area = 1000, cost center = *, activity = *
   2. Controlling area = 2000, cost center = *, activity = 03
(c) With the mentioned authorization object, if the user's cost center in the controlling area 1000 has the ID 1234, the permission would have the following field values: Controlling area = 1000, cost center = 1234, and activity = 03.
   If this is a common use case, the high maintenance effort is disadvantageous, because each user needs a different authorization. An alternative implementation would be another authorization object with the meaning "may display his own cost center" and a corresponding authority check in the software.

Exercise 16.3 (Authorization Profiles in SAP Software)
s is copied to s', in which a is replaced by a'. c is copied to c', in which s is replaced by s'. Possibly, a better modularization can be achieved by restructuring the profiles.

16.5   Self-Assessment

16.1 Permissions, 16.2 Roles

1. Compare the permissions in enterprise information systems with those you know for files. What are the differences, and why?

2. Users often get assigned too many permissions. Why do you think this is the case?
3. How do you know which permission is necessary for calling a function or method of a business object?
4. Compare the direct assignment of permissions to a user (assuming this is possible in an enterprise information system) with the assignment via roles.

16.3 Examples

5. We consider the terms "authorization object" and "authorization" in SAP software. What is used for the definition of the "ask," what for the "bid" (see beginning of this chapter)? And how?
6. What determines which fields are chosen for an authorization object?
7. What is the difference between an authorization object and an authorization?
8. Why is it generally not sensible to use a transaction data ID as an authorization field?
9. Which fields, do you think, are often found in authorization objects?

References

Further Reading

Role-based access control is explained in detail in:
Ferraiolo, D.F., Kuhn, D.R., Chandramouli, R.: Role-Based Access Control, 2nd edn. Artech House, Boston (2007)

Further Cited Literature and Sources

Banzer, A., Sambill, A.: Authorizations in SAP S/4HANA and SAP Fiori. Rheinwerk, Boston (2022)
Colle, R., Dentzer, R., Hrastnik, J.: Core Data Services for ABAP ©, 3rd updated and expanded edn. Rheinwerk, Bonn (2024)
Föse, F., Hagemann, S., Will, L.: SAP NetWeaver AS ABAP—System Administration, 4th edn. Rheinwerk, New York (2012)
Müller, S., Keller, C.: Pentaho und Jedox. Hanser, Munich (2015)
Piepiorra, F.: vtiger CRM v5.x. bomots (2007)
Rossi, I.D.: vtiger CRM. Beginner's Guide. Packt Publishing, Birmingham (2011)
Saledif, T.: vtiger 6.0 kompakt. Brain Media (2014)
Saueressig, T., Stein, T., Boeder, J., Kleis, W.: SAP S/4HANA—Architecture. Rheinwerk, Boston (2023)

System Administration

17

> I love order.
> It's my dream.
> A world where all would be silent and still
> and each thing in its last place,
> under the last dust.
> *Samuel Beckett (Endspiel Fin de partie Endgame,*
> *first edition, Suhrkamp Taschenbuch 171,*
> *Frankfurt a. M., 1974, p. 82)*

Summary

In this chapter, we turn to various tasks of system administration: user management; monitoring of the running system; incident management, in particular software errors, which will occur during operation; and data archiving.

Learning Objective

- To learn about typical tasks of system administration.

17.1 User Management

Users are master data managed by system administration. They are usually employees of the company, but users can also be created for external parties, e.g., for consultants in development systems. In addition to data such as name, office, and email address, the user ID (often simply called "user") and the password must be entered.

Assigning permissions and profiles is an important part; we learned about it in Chap. 16.

If an employee has tasks in multiple systems of a system landscape, he needs a user with the respective permissions in each one. It is cumbersome for him if he has different user IDs and different passwords. Different user IDs can be avoided organizationally: In each system, the employee receives the same user ID, and maintenance can be done (at least partially) at a central location, e.g., in an LDAP directory. At least as annoying are several passwords to be used in parallel. Because an employee could choose different passwords; and even if he always chooses the same one, a policy requiring a change after a certain time could lead to at least temporary inconsistencies: In one system, the employee still has an old password, while in another, he has already chosen a new one. This problem can be solved with the technique of single sign-on, which we learned about in Chap. 9.

17.2 System Monitoring

The ongoing operation of an enterprise information system must be monitored in terms of performance and errors. There are tools for this, which also provide access to the administration data of the system infrastructure. Typical things to look at:

- Current state of system components, e.g., processes, memory usage
- Actions or states in the past, recorded in logs
- Reaction to evaluated system states "critical," "questionable," and "okay" (traffic light mechanism)

17.2.1 Example: System Monitoring in SAP Software

In addition to a server and process view as well as a user view, there are various logs: system log, runtime errors, trace files, and lock entries (Föse et al. 2012, Chap. 9). Let us look at monitoring in more detail (Fig. 17.1).

With *monitoring and alert management* (Föse et al. 2012, Chap. 11), the system administrator sets thresholds for certain system sub-states. The level of deviation is then displayed as a traffic light. Analysis and auto-reaction methods can be defined, e.g., sending an email. In addition to alert monitors delivered by SAP, companies can define their own. Besides exceeding or falling below threshold values, there are

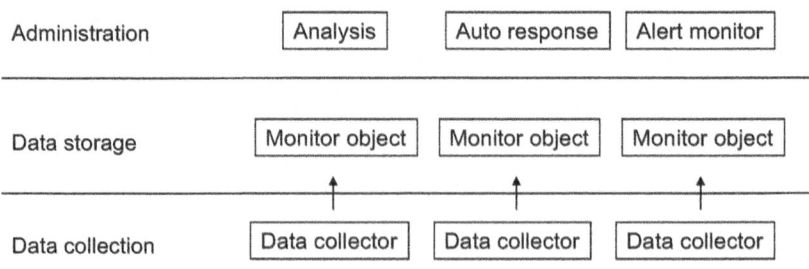

Fig. 17.1 Monitoring

other types of monitor attributes, such as "heartbeat" (alarm in case of failure) or log attribute (searching a log file for a pattern). Monitor attributes are grouped into monitor objects. To get a quick overview, the results of the monitoring are displayed hierarchically in a tree of Monitoring Tree Elements (MTE). On the lowest level, you will find the attributes of monitor objects. The most severe traffic light color of a subordinate MTE determines that of the superior one. The monitoring of a system landscape should take place in its own central system (Föse et al. 2012, Chap. 11).

The tool *System Administration Assistant* (Föse et al. 2012, Chap. 9) shows the most important or frequently recurring tasks. They can be accessed from there, and after execution, they are marked as completed, with the actions and timestamps as well as the executing users being logged.

17.3 Problem Management

During ongoing operation, problems will occur that are due to software errors. They need to be detected, solutions need to be sought, and these need to be implemented. A common organization of problem management (*incident management*) is as follows:

- When employees notice a problem, they usually first turn to the user support ("help desk") in the company. Inexperienced employees might experience problems that are not software errors but user errors. There is no strict boundary to this: When software is difficult to use, an employee can easily run into an error. Is the error due to poor software ergonomics or due to the lack of the user's skill? For pragmatic help, the user support must decide whether the problem can be solved by advice (e.g., different operation or a "work-around") or whether a software error needs to be investigated.
- If it is a software error, the user support or another employee of the company's IT department checks how it can be eliminated. Typically, they look for proposed solutions to already known problems. The software vendor offers information for this.
- If no solution is known, a problem report is recorded for the software vendor. There are special systems for that purpose, which support the bidirectional communication between the company and the software vendor. Among other things, you can see the entire history of the problem report, i.e., the communication between the company and the software vendor, and the updating of the processing status.
- The software vendor searches for a solution in a multi-level process:
    1. Level: Similar to user support, employees of the software vendor look for known solutions to problems.
    2. Level: For complex problems, a second-level employee is involved. This person is often specialized in a functional area and technically adept. In many cases, he can locate the problem and propose a solution.
    3. Level: If the second level does not find a solution, an even more specialized employee, often the developer of the software, can be contacted.

When a new problem is solved, it must be checked whether it also occurs in other software versions. Proposed solutions are then developed for all affected software versions. A proposed solution can be a software correction ("patch"), a description for a manual procedure (e.g., in the software configuration), or a combination of both.

17.4   Archiving

When a system runs for several years, a lot of transaction data accumulates. This results in the problem that performance is worse with a larger database table (the search takes longer), and more storage is required (hard drive, main memory, data backup). Many data are at most still important for later traceability, for example, for legal reasons. Precisely for this reason, business data is usually not deleted but archived, i.e., deleted from the database and written to an external medium. In the past, these were often optical storage systems, mainly because magnetic disks were expensive. With today's cheaper prices for these storage media, they may also be used. Legally, the immutability of data may be required, in which case the data is stored in WORM (Write Once, Read Multiple), DVD, or CD-ROM storage media (Föse et al. 2012, Chap. 12). When archiving, it is important that the data can still be read a long time later. In this sense, permanently usable formats are important.

The process of archiving is basically as follows: Identify data to be archived, extract, compress, store on an external storage medium, and delete from the database after successful storage (i.e., the test whether the data is readable).

Standard software is designed to allow archiving. Different applications handle this differently. It may be that archived data can only be viewed with a special archive viewer. With other archived data, it may be that they can be displayed in the enterprise information system like operational data. Only the slightly larger time delay may make the user realize that it is archived data.

The term "archiving" is also used for a second function: the storage of scanned paper documents in a storage system (archive system, document management system, content management system). The documents are linked to business data via references. The methodology for this type of archiving differs from the archiving of old data.

17.5   Additional Tasks of System Administration

Some additional tasks of system administration are briefly mentioned (Fischer 2024): the installation and configuration of systems (see Sect. 14.2), data backup (including restore and recovery), and developing and testing an emergency plan to be quickly operational again after system failures.

17.6 Exercises and Proposed Solutions

(a) Exercises

Exercise 17.1 (System Monitoring)
During operation, the system administrator notices poor response times on an SAP application server (see Sect. 5.3.2). What could be the reason? And what can he do?

Exercise 17.2 (Data Archiving)
A supplier has gone out of business. Is it sensible to archive the supplier?

(b) Proposed Solution for the Exercises

Exercise 17.1 (System Monitoring)
Maybe not enough dialog work processes are configured. Or programs processed with batch work processes consume a lot of performance. A corresponding reconfiguration of the work processes could help. Possibly, the application server as a whole is reaching its limits. If the load balancing works properly (i.e., there are similar problems on other application servers), it might make sense to permanently set up an additional application server.

Exercise 17.2 (Data Archiving)
Archiving this supplier alone seems less sensible. The amount of master data is rather small compared to transaction data. In addition, the reference in the transaction data, such as purchase orders, to the supplier would be lost. Therefore, the transaction data should be archived together with the supplier.

17.7 Self-Assessment

1. What means could be used to avoid the problem that employees have different users and passwords in different systems? Tip: Chap. 9.
2. How could the system administration of an entire system landscape be designed ergonomically? What requirements would the systems have to meet?
3. What tools could help support employees of the software vendor to quickly recognize problems in a company's system and to find the cause?
4. What could be the advantages if software corrections (patches) were automatically regularly installed in enterprise information systems, as is common with other types of software? What could be the disadvantages?

References

Fischer, O.: Private Communication (October 2024)
Föse, F., Hagemann, S., Will, L.: SAP NetWeaver AS ABAP—System Administration, 4th edn. Rheinwerk, New York (2012)

Summary and Outlook

18

I love the old questions.
With fervour:
Ah the old questions, the old answers,
there's nothing like them!
Samuel Beckett (Endspiel Fin de partie Endgame,
first edition, Suhrkamp Taschenbuch 171,
Frankfurt a. M., 1974, p. 56)

Summary

After a brief summary of the book's content, we compare companies' expectations of business standard software with the current state. Finally, there is a list of abstract concepts that have concrete manifestations in enterprise information systems.

Learning Objective

- To reflect on enterprise information systems as they are today, how they could be, and what we can learn from dealing with them.

18.1   Current State and Expectations

We have seen that a company's business processes rely on business objects in enterprise information systems, primarily for implementing the activities of the business processes. The business objects encapsulate business data. Today, business processes usually span several enterprise information systems, which we can divide into the categories of transactional systems and analytical systems. Together, they form a company's system landscape, and they must be integrated with each other. Also inter-company integration plays a role. Integration is possible at the levels of business processes, objects, and data. It is based on the business interfaces offered by the enterprise information systems. The systems are predominantly standard software that must be adapted to the company's needs after providing them either on-premises or in a cloud. Specific techniques have emerged in all these areas.

Thus, in this book, we have mainly looked at the current state of enterprise information systems. We could now ask ourselves how we would like enterprise information systems to be and compare this with the current state. From my point of view, it looks like this:

(a) *Cost-Effective*

A company would like cost-effective software, which is a good reason for standard software, possibly even a cloud offer. The total costs (total cost of ownership, TCO), especially the implementation costs but also the maintenance costs, which are estimated to be higher for custom software, are decisive. The implementation costs can be high, as can the project risk. Both can be kept as low as possible through a professional implementation project. The costs of switching to another provider (see below) should also be included.

(b) *Consider Changes*

Enterprise information systems should implement current business processes well and allow for improvement if necessary, e.g., when a product needs to be brought to market faster due to economic pressure (see company-specific processes below). Inevitable changes, e.g., due to legal changes, should be integrated automatically, another reason for standard software. Reorganizations, e.g., the merger of companies, should be quickly taken care of in the enterprise information system. This is not so easily possible with today's heterogeneous systems (see possibility of change below).

(c) *Standard Processes Without Effort*

Standard processes, which are the same for many companies, at least in one industry, should be directly usable in the standard software. Adjustment effort should only arise if the company deviates from the standard.

(d) *Company-Specific Processes*

The company should have the opportunity to design company-specific processes individually where there is a differentiation from competitors. However, as much existing functionality as possible should be reused. So custom development should not be necessary but rather individual configuration. The problem does not seem to be well solved today to me. Workflow systems and microservices promise to help here, but at least the effort is still high.

(e) ***Various Enterprise Information Systems and thus Integration***

The fact that the business objects, data, and processes involve various enterprise information systems and thus integration effort arises is primarily not in the interest of the company. The company is interested in the functionality being provided. How the functional distribution takes place can be irrelevant to it. Or less than irrelevant, considering the effort and friction losses due to integration. Similarly, the division into transactional and analytical systems, which is motivated both organizationally (there are currently many data sources) and technically (performance). The purchase of different systems can very well be justified by costs, when two small systems are cheaper than a larger one. The current state is several systems in a system landscape, with corresponding integration effort. Associated with this is that generally conceptual business objects are fragmented, e.g., parts of the customer data are in the ERP system while others in the CRM system. Uniform, cross-system methods would have to be developed with big effort. (Does cloud computing bring an improvement for this? And what impact do other systems have on the enterprise information systems: mobile devices, social media, the Internet of Things?)

(f) ***Easy Migration***

It would be beneficial for a company if it could switch to another product without much effort. Similar to how you can change the telephone provider permanently or even from call to call, which is of course easier with such a standardized service. So it requires standards. The term "standard software" is in contrast to custom software. Only smaller aspects of the functionality are standardized, e.g., certain interface formats. For the migration, at least a standard format for the extraction of business data would be required, and the business objects in the source and target system should not differ at the conceptual level. In addition, implicit and explicit business processes would have to be compatible. We are far from the desired state here ("vendor lock-in"). Cloud software does not solve the problem either—moving between condominiums is comparably expensive as moving between rental apartments.

(g) ***Quality***

Rarely addressed in literature or product brochures, which are mainly about functionality: The software should have good quality. Not the richness of the functionality should be the determinant but its quality. This not only affects the software but also the associated services. With many goods, especially consumer goods, we experience that the quality decreases over time. Software achieves great leaps in technology and functionality, but in my estimation, the quality does not keep up. Better quality would be possible through more careful development, especially more extensive tests, but this means higher effort and thus costs. We observe that the existing price-quality combination prevails in the market. From my point of view, a total cost consideration could give a different picture, both for the software vendor and for the company. For the software vendor, lower quality results in increased service and maintenance effort (see Sect. 17.3). From software engineering, we know that late detected errors are particularly expensive. With standard software, this affects corrections in different software versions. At the company, problem handling effort naturally also arises. A special situation is quality defects in system integration: Two products are supposed to interact. But the integration might not have been tested extensively, as there are many, diverse combination possibilities. Moreover, the responsibility for an integration problem often cannot be clearly assigned to one or the other product. Maybe even a third product is affected by the integration, but this only results from a long analysis. In other words, especially with integration being already sufficiently complex, quality defects are even more aggravating.

(h) *Reliable Relationship with the Software Vendor*
Precisely because a switch to another software vendor is not easy, a reliable relationship is desirable. This includes that the prices, e.g., for maintenance or subsequent versions, are reasonable, that the quality of the software does not deteriorate, and that the software has a long-term existence.

The interests of software vendors and consulting companies, on the other hand, only partially coincide with the company's. Software vendors are interested in a large market share. In large companies, a few big providers mainly share the market, while in medium-sized and smaller companies, there is a much larger number of software vendors. Since growth for the big vendors is limited in large companies, growth opportunities are seen in the SME sector. And as in all industries, there is an interest in retaining customers. (How do you assess these thoughts with cloud software?)

18.2   Concepts

The saying goes that dealing with abstract things trains the mind, regardless of the specific subject of study. In this book, it is rather the opposite approach: It talks about concrete things, and we are interested in abstract concepts derived from them. In computer science, more precisely in software engineering, the term *pattern* is used: design patterns or architecture patterns. My goal is not a formalization of the concepts/patterns. I think it is already helpful to illustrate the patterns by example. In this sense, the concepts addressed in the book are listed, with a reference to which topic and chapter they occurred. We hope that learning a concept by example has a lasting effect.

Concept	Content/purpose	Topic	Chapter
Data aggregation	Focus on the essentials	DWHS	4
Definition vs. runtime	Understanding the impact of definition time settings on runtime; consideration of which steps should take place at which time	Web services, integration using process management systems	11, 12
Factor out	In analogy to the distributive law in mathematics: $(a * b) + (a * c) = a * (b + c)$. To achieve redundancy absence and clarity	Client/server systems, header and line-items	5, 3
Dynamic function call	Provide functions generically	BAdI, Web service	15, 11

Concept	Content/purpose	Topic	Chapter
Indirection	Changeableness	System landscape, abstract agent	8, 3
Hierarchy formation	Structuring, for clarity and easy processing	XML, DWHS	10, 4
Encapsulation	Summarization into one "thing"	Business objects	3
Copying vs. referencing	Change friendliness	ID of a business object	3
Namespace	Making names unique	Namespace in XML, custom development	10, 15
Layering	Mastering complexity	Three-tier client/server architecture	5
Interface	Functional decomposition, flexibility, change friendliness	Business objects, WSDL	3, 11
Standardization	Simplification of the interaction of components	XML, Web service	10, 11
Type vs. instance	Schematic description and syntax checking (error prevention at runtime)	XML Schema, business objects	10, 3
Virtualization	Among other things, easier handling, similar to interface	Client/server systems, business objects, cloud computing, DWHS	5, 3, 6, 4
Data transformation	Mapping from a source to a target format	XML, XSLT, ETL, message broker, legacy data migration	10, 4, 13
Asynchronous vs. synchronous communication	Tighter or looser coupling between communication partners	Message-oriented integration	10, 11
Push vs. pull	Control of information transmission	Workflow management, SCM data exchange	12, 4, 10
Publish and subscribe	Flexible coupling of senders and receivers	Message-oriented integration	10
Data transfer for data reconciliation	Separation into initial transmission and delta transmission to reduce the effort	ETL, planning systems	4
Bottleneck	Performance bottleneck	Client/server systems	5
Parallelization	Performance improvement through shorter runtime	Business processes, DWHS (partitioning), Client/server	5, 4, 3
Scaling	Performance improvement	Client/server systems	5
Storage efficiency vs. runtime efficiency	Store derived information or recalculate each time	DWHS	4
Memory hierarchy	Improve cost and access speed	DWHS, persistent objects, in-memory database, table buffering, archiving	4, 5, 17
Replication	Fail-safe	Client/server systems	5
Single point of failure	Critical point regarding fail-safety	Client/server systems	5

Finished, it's finished,
nearly finished,
it must be nearly finished.
Pause.
Grain upon grain,
one by one,
and one day, suddenly, there's a heap
a little heap,
the impossible heap.
Samuel Beckett (Endspiel Fin de partie Endgame,
first edition, Suhrkamp Taschenbuch 171,
Frankfurt a. M., 1974, p. 10)

Glossary

ACID principle Properties[1] of a database transaction: Atomicity, Consistency, Isolation, Durability.

Advanced Business Application Programming (ABAP) SAP's programming language for standard business software. The majority of SAP's application programs are written in ABAP.

Analytical system Enterprise system for the analysis of data.

API Application Programming Interface, i.e., a programming interface of a software, as opposed to the user interface.

Application Used differently: (1) a related part of an enterprise system ("the purchasing application"), (2) an entire system ("the application SAP S/4HANA"), (3) an application program ("the application 'Create purchase order'"), and (4) as a counterpoint to "technology".

Application platform Underlying application-independent software of an enterprise system, which mediates between the system infrastructure (operating system, database system) and the application programs. An important component: the client/server structure, especially the application servers.

Application server Computer on which business application programs run.

Asynchronous communication The communication partners are not active at the same time. Examples: email, letter.

Authorization Access control mechanism for business data and functions. Authorizations (permissions) are assigned to employees so that they can fulfill their tasks. Example: the authorization to create a purchase order of a certain type.

Background processing Execution of a function without user interface. Example: payroll accounting.

Big Data Processing of extensive, structured to unstructured data volumes, which come from a variety of data sources.

---

[1]The "explanations" of the terms are intended as short descriptions, clarifications, and memory aids, rather than definitions. I think that the full meaning is better derived from the text than from multi-line attempts at definition.

R. Weber, *Enterprise Information Systems*, https://doi.org/10.1007/978-3-662-71718-9

Business data Complex data structure, which summarizes data of a company, stored in a database. Examples: a supplier, a purchase order.

Business object Conceptually object-oriented model for a business data. In addition to the attributes and methods, events may be added. Example: an invoice, with methods such as "create" and "change".

Cache Buffer memory for fast data access.

Cloud Computing Companies rent IT services, such as an enterprise system, which runs at the operator's site and which companies access via the Internet.

Column-oriented database (Columnar database) Relational table data are stored column wise, not as usual row wise. It may be used in analytical systems for a better performance advantages, e.g., when condensing (aggregating) data.

Comma Separated Values (CSV) Data exchange format, in which the data in a file are separated by commas or similar separators.

Content Management System Software system for storing unstructured data, especially documents and images.

Customizing Adaptation of standard software to a company by setting parameters, with impact on all users. Examples: setting up the screen masks for creating a purchase order, defining possible payment terms.

Dialog Processing via a user interface. Opposite: background processing. Example: Creating a purchase order via a screen mask.

Dynamic binding Search for a service and establish connection to it at runtime, as opposed to development time.

Dynamic Link Library (DLL) Software library that is dynamically linked at runtime of the program, not already at development time.

Electronic Data Interchange (EDI) Procedure for inter-company data exchange, where business data is encoded in a data exchange format and flows over a communication channel. Example: EDIFACT.

Enterprise Resource Planning (ERP) Transactional, integrated enterprise system, which largely covers the intra-company data processing. Typical examples: SAP R/3, SAP ERP, and SAP S/4HANA, Microsoft Dynamics 365 Business Central.

Enterprise Information System Business software, usually with its own database. Examples: an ERP system, a data warehouse system, a supply chain management system.

Event Reflects state change of a business object. Examples: Purchase requisition created, purchase requisition changed, purchase requisition released.

Extraction, Transformation, Loading (ETL) Process, according to which data from data sources (extraction) enter an analytical system (loading). For cleaning and standardizing the data, they are transformed.

Historization Storing data with a time reference instead of just saving the current value.

HTTP-POST Method (function) of the HTTP protocol. Data are sent in a request message to a URI and the result is received in a response message. It is a synchronous form of communication.

Implementation project Project for the implementation of standard software in a company; includes all activities after the purchase until the operation of the software begins, especially the adaptation of the software to the company needs.

In-Memory Computing A large amount of data, such as an entire company database, is kept in main memory to achieve short access times compared to persistent memory.

Internet of Things (IOT) "Things" like devices or containers capture their state data via sensors and communicate this over the Internet.

JSON A lightweight notation for the textual representation of structured data; the alternative to XML.

LDAP The Lightweight Directory Access Protocol is used to access a directory. This contains data about users, such as email addresses or public keys for data encryption, and computers (like server addresses).

Machine Learning Parameterized models, especially artificial neural networks, are trained with a selection of existing data to set the parameters and later achieve similar good results with new data as with the training data.

Master data Data that have a long relevance for business transactions and are referenced in transaction data, but do not represent business transactions themselves. Examples: supplier, material.

Microservice Lightweight, self-contained software implementation of a service, with own data storage.

Middleware Application-independent software that provides communication, transformation, and integration services. Not a sharply defined term.

Modification Change of the program code of standard software by a company, without this change being intended by the software vendor.

Persistent date Permanently, usually stored in the database date.

Publish-and-Subscribe Principle Communication principle in which the sender sends data without reference to a specific recipient, it is received by all subscribers.

Remote Procedure Call (RPC) Remote, cross-language and cross-computer procedure or function call.

REST Lightweight Web service; the alternative to SOAP/WSDL-based Web services.

Role Set of functions and permissions that may be assigned to users. Examples: the role "purchaser," the role "employee," the role "manager".

Rollback Resetting a (failed) database transaction, undoing changes.

Service In enterprise software, a set of related functions, provided by a service provider, usable by service consumers.

Service-oriented architecture (SOA) Organizational and software architecture principle, according to which software is designed as a composition of reusable services (services, functions).

Signature In software engineering, the syntactic interface of a function or method, i.e., the names, data types, and parameter types (input, output; transfer mechanism).

Single Sign-on Technical procedure by which a user only needs one login in a system landscape.

Scalability Increase in performance by adding further, similar components. Example: adding another application server in a three-tier client/server architecture.

SQL Structured Query Language, the standard language for data access in relational database systems.

Supply Chain Management (SCM) Methods and techniques to support the supply chain, ideally across several stages (supplier, producer, customer).

Synchronous communication The communication partners are active at the same time. Example: telephone.

System landscape Enterprise systems of a company and their connections to each other.

Thread Lightweight process in operating systems.

Three-tier client/server architecture Technical architecture used in enterprise systems like SAP R/3, consisting of database server, application servers, and presentation servers (clients).

Transaction In database systems: database transaction. In enterprise systems: an application program, usually with user dialogue, for executing a business transaction or for data maintenance. Examples: create supplier, change purchase order.

Transaction data Reflect business transactions. Examples: purchase order, invoice, goods receipt.

Transactional system Enterprise system for day-to-day business. Typical example: an ERP system.

Unified Modeling Language (UML) Graphical notation for software modeling by the OMG, includes, e.g., class diagrams.

Web Service Function without dialogue, which can be called via Web protocols.

Workflow Partially automated business process controlled by a workflow system.

XML eXtensible Markup Language (XML) Language that is popular today for data exchange.

XML Schema Language for describing data types in XML.

Bibliography

Further Reading

Alonso, G., Casati, F., Kuno, H., Machiraju, V.: Web Services. Springer, Berlin (2004)

Bradford, M.: Modern ERP, 3rd edn. North Carolina State Univ, Raleigh, NC (2015)

Burke, B., Monson-Haefel, R.: Enterprise JavaBeans 3.0. O'Reilly Media, Sebastopol (2006)

Chellammal, S., Pethuru Raj, C.: Essentials of Cloud Computing, 2nd edn. Springer Nature, Switzerland (2023)

Coulouris, G., Dollimore, J., Kindberg, T.: Distributed Systems, 4th edn. Addison-Wesley, Harlow (2005)

Ferraiolo, D.F., Kuhn, D.R., Chandramouli, R.: Role-Based Access Control, 2nd edn. Artech House, Boston (2007)

Ferreira, D.R.: Enterprise Systems Integration. Springer, Berlin (2013)

Fowler, M.: UML Distilled: A Brief Guide to the Standard Object Modeling Language. Addison-Wesley, Boston (2004)

Freund, J., Rücker, B.: Real-Life BPMN, 4th edn. Camunda (2019)

Gadatsch, A.: Business Process Management. Springer, Wiesbaden (2023)

Harold, E.R., Means, W.S.: XML in a Nutshell, 3rd edn. O'Reilly, Sebastopol (2005)

Newman, S.: Building Microservices, 2nd edn. O'Reilly, Beijing (2021)

Papazoglou, M.P.: Web Services: Principles and Technology. Prentice-Hall, Upper Saddle River, NJ (2007)

Richardson, L., Ruby, S.: RESTful Web Services. O'Reilly & Associates, Sebastopol (2007)

Silver, B.: BPMN Method and Style, 2nd edn. Cody-Cassidy Press, Aptos, CA (2011)

Silver, B.: BPMN Quick and Easy: With Method and Style. Cody-Cassidy Press, Altadena, CA (2017)

Tanenbaum, A., van Steen, M.: Distributed Systems, 2nd edn, Pearson new international edition. Pearson, Harlow (2014)

Vaisman, A., Zymányi, E.: Data Warehouse Systems: Design and Implementation, 2nd edn. Springer, Berlin (2022)

Varanasi, B., Belida, S.: Spring REST. Apress, Berkeley (2015)

W3C: XML Schema Part 0: Primer, 2nd edn. http://www.w3.org/TR/2004/REC-xmlschema-0-20041028/primer.html (2004). Accessed 10 Oct 2011

Weske, M.: Business Process Management, 4th edn. Springer, Berlin (2024)

Further Cited Literature and Sources

Anane Adusei, D., Rötting, I., Yamada, S.: SAP HANA—Datenmodellierung. Rheinwerk, Bonn (2018)

Baars, H., Kemper, H.-G.: Business Intelligence & Analytics, 4th revised and expanded edn. Springer Vieweg, Wiesbaden (2021)

Balla, J., Layer, F.: Produktionsplanung mit SAP APO, 2nd edn. Galileo Press, Bonn (2010)

Banda, S., Chandra, S., Gooi, C.A.: SAP Business Technology Platform, 2nd edn. Rheinwerk, Boston (2024)

Banzer, A., Sambill, A.: Authorizations in SAP S/4HANA and SAP Fiori. Rheinwerk, Boston (2022)

Bartsch, H., Teufel, T.: Supply Chain Management mit SAP APO. Galileo Press, Bonn (2000)

Bauer, C., Gregory, G.: Java Persistence with Hibernate, 2nd edn. Manning, Greenwich (2016)

Bauer, A., Günzel, H. (eds.): Data-Warehouse-Systeme, 4th revised and expanded edn. dpunkt, Heidelberg (2013)

Baumbusch, L., Jäger, M., Lensch, M.: ABAP RESTful Application Programming Model. The Comprehensive Guide. Rheinwerk, Bonn (2023)

Bavaraju, A.: Data Modeling for SAP HANA 2.0. Rheinwerk, New York (2019)

Bouman, R., van Dongen, J.: Pentaho Solutions. Business Intelligence and Data Warehousing with Pentaho and MySQL. Wiley, Indianapolis (2009)

Braun, M.: Analytics im Online-Handel. In: Haneke, U., Trahasch, S., Zimmer, M., Felden, C. (eds.) Data Science. Grundlagen, Architekturen und Anwendungen, 2nd revised and expanded edn, pp. 239–254. dpunkt, Heidelberg (2021)

Colle, R., Dentzer, R., Hrastnik, J.: Core Data Services for ABAP, 3rd updated and expanded edn. Rheinwerk, Bonn (2023)

Connolly, T., Begg, C.: Database Systems, 6th edn. Pearson, Boston (2015)

Davidenkoff, A., Werner, D.: Global SAP Systems—Design and Architecture. Galileo Press, Bonn (2008)

Demiliani, S., Tacconi, D.: Microsoft Dynamics 365 Business Central Development Quick Start Guide. Packt Publishing, Birmingham (2018)

Dutta, S., Ghosh, N., Goon, K., Jana, S., Mukherjee, A., Rao, S., Rao, Y., Sane, Y., Veshala, N., Viswanathan, S.: Workflow for SAP S/HANA. Rheinwerk, Boston (2024)

Ebert, J., Hauptmann, C.: Microsoft Dynamics 365 Business Central, 2nd updated edn. Hanser, Munich (2023)

Egger, N., Fiechter, J.M., Rohlf, J.: SAP BW Datenmodellierung. Galileo Press, Bonn (2004)

Elsner, M., González, G., Raben, M.: SAP Leonardo. Konzepte, Technologien, Best Practices. Rheinwerk, Bonn (2018)

Fielding, R.T.: Architectural Styles and the Design of Network-based Software Architectures. Dissertation, University of California, Irvine (2000)

Finkbohner, F., Höft, M., Roth, M., Kinold, J., Kuchelmeister, W., Widera, L.: Data Migration for SAP. Rheinwerk, Bonn (2024)

Fischer, O.: Private Communication. 17 Oct 2011 (2011)

Fischer, O.: Private Communication. 12 Sept 2024 (2024)

Föse, F., Hagemann, S., Will, L.: SAP NetWeaver AS ABAP—System Administration, 4th edn. Rheinwerk, New York (2012)

Freiknecht, J., Papp, S.: Big Data in der Praxis, 2nd edn. Hanser, Munich (2018)

Friesen, J.: Java XML and JSON. Apress, Berkeley (2019)

Gamma, E., Helm, R., Johnson, R.: Design Patterns. Elements of Reusable Object-Oriented Software. Pearson, London (1994)

Gronau, N.: ERP-Systeme: Architektur, Management und Funktionen des Enterprise Resource Planning, 4th edn. De Gruyter Oldenbourg, Munich (2021)

Großmann, M., Koschek, H.: Unternehmensportale—Grundlagen, Architekturen. Springer, Berlin (2005)

Gulyássy, F., Hoppe, M.M., Köhler, O., Vithayathil, B.: Materials Planning with SAP, 3rd updated and expanded edn. Galileo Press, New York (2009)

Hammer, M., Champy, J.: Reengineering the Corporation. Addison-Wesley, Reading, MH (1994)

Haneke, U., Trahasch, S., Zimmer, M., Felden, C. (eds.): Data Science. Grundlagen, Architekturen und Anwendungen, 2nd revised and expanded edn. dpunkt, Heidelberg (2021)

Hecker, D., Renner, T., Jacobs, B., Sylla, K.-H., Wohlfrom, A., Kötter, F. (eds.): Marktübersicht In-Memory-Systeme. Fraunhofer-Verlag, Stuttgart (2016)

Heilig, L., Karch, S., Böttcher, O., Hofmann, C.: SAP NetWeaver Master Data Management. Galileo Press, Bonn (2006)

Hengevoss, W., Linke, A.: SAP NetWeaver System Landscape Directory. Galileo Press, Bonn (2009)

Hibernate: https://hibernate.org/. Accessed 1 Nov 2024

Huber, M.: Predictive Maintenance. In: Haneke, U., Trahasch, S., Zimmer, M., Felden, C. (eds.) Data Science. Grundlagen, Architekturen und Anwendungen, pp. 255–274. dpunkt, Heidelberg (2021)

Huvar, M., Falter, T., Fiedler, T., Zubev, A.: Developing Applications with Enterprise SOA. Galileo Press, Bonn (2009)

Inmon, W.H.: Building the Data Warehouse, 1st edn. John Wiley, New York (1993)

Java Community Process: JSR-000168 Portlet Specification. https://www.jcp.org/ja/jsr/detail?id=168 (2003). Accessed 3 Nov 2024

Java Community Process: JSR-000286 Portlet Specification 2.0. https://www.jcp.org/en/jsr/detail?id=286 (2008). Accessed 3 Nov 2024

Java Community Process: JSR-000362 Portlet Specification 3.0. https://www.jcp.org/en/jsr/detail?id=362 (2017). Accessed 11 Oct 2024

JAX-WS: https://www.jcp.org/en/jsr/detail?id=224 (2006). Accessed 13 Mar 2025

jBPM: https://www.jbpm.org/ (2024). Accessed 3 Nov 2024

JSON: http://www.json.org/ (2024). Accessed 15 Oct 2024

JSON Schema: http://json-schema.org (2024). Accessed 15 Oct 2024

Jupyter: jupyter.org/ (2024). Accessed 1 Oct 2024

Kauermann, G.: Data Science—Einige Gedanken aus Sicht eines Statistikers. Informatik Spektrum. **42**(6), 387–393 (2019)

Kayser, V., Zubovic, D.: Data privacy. In: Haneke, U., Trahasch, S., Zimmer, M., Felden, C. (eds.) Data Science. Grundlagen, Architekturen und Anwendungen, 2nd revised and extended edn, pp. 177–190. dpunkt, Heidelberg (2021)

Kees, A., Markowski, D.A.: Open Source Enterprise Software, 2nd edn. Springer Vieweg, Wiesbaden (2019)

Kemper, A., Eickler, A.: Datenbanksysteme, 10th edn. De Gruyter Oldenbourg, Berlin (2015)

Kleppmann, M.: Designing Data-Intensive Applications. O'Reilly, Sebastopol (2017)

Lankhorst, M., et al.: Enterprise Architecture at Work, 4th edn. Springer, Berlin (2017)

Lehmann, S., Buxmann, P.: Pricing Strategies of Software Vendors. Bus. Inf. Syst. Eng. **1**(6), 452–462 (2009)

Lemahieu, W., vanden Broucke, S., Baesens, B.: Principles of Database Management. Cambridge University Press, Cambridge (2018)

Lüdtke, T., Lüdtke, M.: SAP BW/4HANA 2.0. Rheinwerk, New York (2020)

Marx Gomez, J., Rautenstrauch, C., Cissek, P., Grahlher, B.: Einführung in SAP Business Information Warehouse. Springer, Berlin (2006)

Marz, N., Warren, J.: Big Data: Principles and Best Practices of Scalable Realtime Data. Manning Publications, Shelter Island (2015)

Mehrwald, C.: Datawarehousing mit SAP BW 7.5., corrected edn. dpunkt, Heidelberg (2010)

Meier, A., Kaufmann, M.: SQL & NoSQL Databases, 2nd edn. Springer, Cham (2023)

Müller, S., Keller, C.: Pentaho und Jedox. Hanser, Munich (2015)

Nicolescu, V., Klappert, K., Krcmar, H.: SAP NetWeaver Portal. Galileo Press, Bonn (2007)

O'Neill, B., Perfiljeva, J.: ABAP. An Intrduction, 2nd updated and expanded edn. Rheinwerk, Boston (2020)

OASIS: Web Services for Remote Portlets. Specification v2.0. http://docs.oasis-open.org/wsrp/v2/wsrp-2.0-spec-os-01.html (2008). Accessed 3 Nov 2024

Piepiorra, F.: vtiger CRM v5.x. bomots, Saarbrücken (2007)

Plattner, H., Zeier, A.: In-Memory Data Management. Springer, Berlin (2011)

Pradhan, S.: Demand and Supply Planning with SAP APO. Rheinwerk, New York (2016)

PyTorch: https://pytorch.org/ (2024). Accessed 1 Oct 2024

Rechenberg, P.: Was ist Informatik, 4th edn. Hanser, Munich (2006)

Repschläger, J., Pannicke, D., Zarnekow, R.: Cloud Computing: Definitionen, Geschäftsmodelle und Entwicklungspotentiale. HMD Prax. Wirtschaftsinform. 275, 6–15 (2010)

Riedhammer, K.: Private Communication. 22 Dec 2020 (2020)

Rossi, I.D.: vtiger CRM. Beginner's Guide. Packt Publishing, Birmingham (2011)

Saledif, T.: vtiger 6.0 kompakt. Brain Media (2014)

Saueressig, T., Stein, T., Boeder, J., Kleis, W.: SAP S/4HANA—Architecture. Rheinwerk, Boston (2023)

Scheer, A.-W., Thomas, O., Adam, O.: Process modeling using event-driven process chains. In: Dumas, M., van der Aals, W., ter Hofstede, A.H.M. (eds.) Process-Aware Information Systems. Wiley, Hoboken, NJ (2005)

Schneider, T.: SAP Performance Optimization Guide, 8th edn. Rheinwerk, New York (2018)

Schwaninger, J.: ABAP—Development for Materials Management in SAP: User-Exits and BAdIs. Galileo Press, Bonn (2011)

Schwartz, A.: Microservices. Aktuelles Schlagwort. Informatik-Spektrum. **40**(6), 590–594 (2017)

Sebestyen, T.J.: XML. Pearson, Munich (2010)

Seubert, H.: SAP Business Technology Platform, 2nd updated and expanded edn. Rheinwerk, Bonn (2022)

Snapp, S.: Discover SAP SCM. Galileo Press, Bonn (2010)

TensorFlow: tensorflow.org (2024). Accessed 1 Oct 2024

The Open Group: https://pubs.opengroup.org/onlinepubs/9629399/chap4.htm (1997). Accessed 18 Oct 2024

Tilkov, S., Eigenbrodt, M., Schreier, S., Wolf, O.: REST und HTTP, 3rd edn. dpunkt, Heidelberg (2015)

Trahasch, S., Felden, C.: Grundlegende Methoden der Data Science. In: Haneke, U., Trahasch, S., Zimmer, M., Felden, C. (eds.) Data Science. Grundlagen, Architekturen und Anwendungen, 2nd revised and extended edn, pp. 65–100. dpunkt, Heidelberg (2021)

van der Aalst, W.: Process Mining: Data Science in Action, 2nd edn. Springer, Berlin (2016)

van Lessen, T., Lübke, D., Nitzsche, J.: Geschäftsprozesse automatisieren mit BPEL. dpunkt, Heidelberg (2011)

Walmsley, P.: Definitive XML Schema. Prentice Hall PTR, Upper Saddle River, NJ (2002)

Web Services Interoperability Organization: WS-I Basic Profile. http://ws-i.org/profiles/BasicProfile-1.2-2010-11-09.html (2010). Accessed 2 Nov 2024

Willinger, M., Gradl, J.: Datenmigration in SAP, 2nd edn. Galileo Press, Bonn (2007)

Wolf, F.K., Yamada, S.: Datenmodellierung in SAP NetWeaver BW. Galileo Press, Bonn (2010)

workflowpatterns: http://www.workflowpatterns.com/. Accessed 1 Nov 2024

Zitzelsberger, A.: Private Communication. 20 Oct 2011 (2011)

Index

The manufacturer's authorised representative in the EU is Springer
Nature Customer Service Centre GmbH, Europaplatz 3, 69115 Heidelberg,
Germany. If you have any concerns regarding our products, please
contact ProductSafety@springernature.com

Printed and bound by CPI Group (UK) Ltd, Croydon, CR0 4YY

23/04/2026

02095588-0011